AF352516

Worldwide Pre-Raphaelitism

SUNY series, Studies in the Long Nineteenth Century

Pamela K. Gilbert, editor

WORLDWIDE PRE-RAPHAELITISM

Edited by

Thomas J. Tobin

State University of New York Press

Cover illustration: William Holman Hunt, *The Lantern-Maker's Courtship: A Street Scene in Cairo* (1854–61, Manchester City Art Gallery). From W. H. Hunt, *Pre-Raphaelitism and the Pre-Raphaelite Brotherhood*, 2 vols. (New York: Macmillan, 1905), 2:17.

Published by
State University of New York Press, Albany

For information, address State University of New York Press,
194 Washington Avenue, Suite 305, Albany, NY 12210-2365

Production by Judith Block
Marketing by Susan Petrie

Library of Congress Cataloging-in-Publication Data

Worldwide Pre-Raphaelitism / edited by Thomas J. Tobin.
    p. cm. – (SUNY series, studies in the long nineteenth century)
  Includes bibliographical references and index.
  ISBN 0-7914-6265-X (alk. paper)
    1. Pre-Raphaelitism. 2. Arts, Modern–19th century. 3. Arts, Modern–20th century. I. Tobin, Thomas J. II. Series.

NX454.5.P7W67 2004
709'.03'4–dc22   2003070441

10 9 8 7 6 5 4 3 2 1

"The hieroglyphics in question are 'P. R. B.,' and they are the initials of the words 'Præ-Raffaelite Brotherhood.' . . . A glance at some of the minor exhibitions now open will prove what really clever men have been bitten by this extraordinary art-whim, of utterly banishing and disclaiming perspective and everything like rotundity of form. It has been suggested that the globe-shape of the world must be very afflicting to the ingenious gentlemen in question."

A[ngus] B[ethune] R[each], "Town Talk and Table Talk."
Illustrated London News (20 April 1850), 306.

CONTENTS

FIGURES

ACKNOWLEDGMENTS

Introduction

This volume, *Worldwide Pre-Raphaelitism*, is a distinctive collection of fourteen essays by scholars from around the globe who examine for the first time the lasting impact of the Pre-Raphaelite movement on global culture. Previously, scholarship on the movement focused on its place in English (or at most, continental European) art and literature during the nineteenth century. The contributors to this volume chart a new direction for scholarship about Pre-Raphaelitism, arguing for the movement's significance throughout the world, its affinity with various systems of thought, and its enduring effects even today.

Worldwide Pre-Raphaelitism puts to rest the traditional view of Pre-Raphaelitism—a brief, reactionary, and narrowly English artistic movement during eight years of the mid-nineteenth century that was outside the "mainstream" development from Romanticism to Aestheticism. Instead, historians, theorists of art, and literary scholars will discover in these essays a wide-ranging, vibrant, enduring, and globally significant Pre-Raphaelitism, informing and informed by feminism, cultural studies, postcolonialism, deconstruction, socialism, Orientalism, medieval textuality, and legal scholarship.

What is Pre-Raphaelitism? In 1850, this question would have been answered easily enough. Pre-Raphaelitism was a stunt cooked up by three students at the Royal Academy of Art in order to distinguish themselves from their peers and thumb their noses at the establishment. The three students—child genius John Everett Millais, Gabriel Dante Rossetti

1

(son of Italian expatriates) and the poor but talented William Holman Hunt—formed the Pre-Raphaelite Brotherhood (P. R. B.) in 1848 with four other young men: William Michael Rossetti, James Collinson, Thomas Woolner, and Frederic George Stephens. The members of this new secret society drew up several documents attesting to their aims and ideals, among which were the faithful representation of nature in art; the superiority of Italian and Flemish painting before the era of Raphael; the interdependence of the literary, plastic, and painterly arts; and the need for art to instruct its audience. The early paintings of the Brotherhood adhered to these principles, and although their mannered presentation was likely to catch the attention of the critics, the "movement," such as it was, seemed fated to be little more than a footnote in the progress of the arts.

The critical press in the 1850s also had little difficulty in defining "Pre-Raphaelitism": it was an extension of continental European Romanticism. The Pre-Raphaelites took many of their subjects and painting styles from Romantic literature and painting from England, France, Germany, and Italy. There were in their canvases several characteristics of earlier Romantic and Neoclassical paintings: a "hard" finish crammed with minute detail and characterized by scant differentiation of highlights and shadows, a preference for subjects from European literary texts of the medieval and Renaissance eras, and overtly didactic intent in the compositions. The Pre-Raphaelites were connected easily to the paintings of their predecessor and mentor Ford Madox Brown, as well as to the earlier Nazarene movement of the 1830s, whose religiosity, preference for Italian painting before the 1400s, and moral-subject paintings prefigured the Pre-Raphaelite movement.

In the early decades of the nineteenth century, Brown was beginning his painting education on the continent. In his work, we can see the development of some principles that would be fully expressed by the Pre-Raphaelite Brotherhood. As a young man, Brown studied in Bruges and Ghent under Albert Gregorius, who himself had been a pupil of Jacques-Louis David; Brown's early works fit well with the 1830s revival of neoclassical sentiment in European art. Brown moved to the Antwerp Academy in 1837 to study under Baron Wappers, from whom Brown learned the ages-old "wash and varnish" techniques of the Dutch schools, a technique that produced muddy, hazy paintings. Most important to the story of Pre-Raphaelitism, Brown next traveled to Rome and met the Nazarenes, a group of expatriate German painters led by Peter Cornelius and Friedrich Overbeck, who intended to purify German painting by returning to religious and cultural archaism, the result of which was an adherence to Roman Catholicism and to the painting techniques of quattrocento German and

Italian masters. The "clean line" and "simple faith" of the quattrocento were by no means the exclusive province of eccentric German painters. Many English painters on the "Grand Tour" were influenced by the painting techniques and subjects of fifteenth-century paintings. By the late 1840s, there was a general interest in late-medieval design—so much so that the Arundel Society was formed in 1848 to disseminate engravings of important works.

Given this background, why has the Pre-Raphaelite movement come to be seen as an insular and particularly English phenomenon? Part of the answer may lie in the way in which the movement laid claim to a reactionary English identity in several media at the same time as it was mining foreign influences during its early years. Early criticism of the movement often inaccurately dubbed them the "Young England" school,[1] mistaking the Pre-Raphaelite Brotherhood with a group of literary reactionaries whose aims were indeed markedly xenophobic and Anglocentric. Over time, the mislabeling became gospel, especially in light of the early canvases from the Brotherhood and their associates depicting contemporary English scenes, such as Holman Hunt's *Our English Coasts* [*Strayed Sheep*] (1853) and Brown's *The Last of England* (1855).

During the remainder of the nineteenth century, the concept of Pre-Raphaelitism rapidly took on new meanings, new adherents, new detractors, and new theoretical directions. For example, in 1850, the Brotherhood began its own literary magazine, *The Germ*, in adherence to its adoption of the Horatian ideal of *ut pictura poesis*, which holds that painting and poetry are sister arts. *The Germ* lasted only four issues but served to expand the possible media in which one could be thought a Pre-Raphaelite: the literary contributors to *The Germ* were a mix of members of the original Brotherhood—Dante Rossetti, William Michael Rossetti (who was not a painter), Thomas Woolner, and William Holman Hunt—and new voices from outside the original movement. Jerome McGann's ideas about *The Germ* help to support the idea that Pre-Raphaelitism began as a loosely defined movement:

There are strong circumstances to suggest that the magazine was not strictly representative of the aims and ideas of the Pre-Raphaelite Brotherhood, which had been meeting since 1848. For instance, although the Brotherhood itself was rigorously opposed to expanding beyond its original seven members, *The Germ* featured numerous articles by non-members, such as Christina Rossetti, Coventry Patmore, and Ford Madox Brown. None of the poetic works reviewed in the four issues of *The Germ* were produced by Pre-Raphaelite writers, yet the reviews (written by William Rossetti) were, as a matter of policy, highly favorable. All of this points to an ethos of inclusion associated with *The Germ* uncharacteristic of the P. R. B. to that point. In addition, William Rossetti was later to emphasize repeatedly that the various theoretical pieces in *The Germ* were at best incomplete expressions of Pre-Raphaelite ideas. Most significant was the fact that *The Germ* never mentioned, in its contents or on its wrappers, the term "Pre-Raphaelite."[2]

Early on, Pre-Raphaelitism thus came to typify a literary style as well as an artistic one. Thomas Woolner's later sculpture and poetry, along with the literary and art criticism penned by William Michael Rossetti and Frederic George Stephens, expanded the idea of Pre-Raphaelitism even further in terms of media and theoretical stance so that by the end of the nineteenth century, Pre-Raphaelitism encompassed not only a style of painting, but an entire theoretical apparatus supporting many sister arts.

Almost as soon as the Pre-Raphaelite Brotherhood became known to the larger English art-appreciating public, the Pre-Raphaelite movement began to grow beyond the original seven members of the Brotherhood. As noted, the establishment of *The Germ* expanded the number of artists and authors considered to be Pre-Raphaelites. John Ruskin, on learning that the Brotherhood had based many of their precepts on his own *Modern Painters* (1843), offered support to the fledgling movement with letters to the editor of the London *Times*, and, after a while, a pamphlet entitled *Pre-Raphaelitism* (1851), in which he argued that the Pre-Raphaelites and John M. W. Turner were among the vanguard of English painting because both the Pre-Raphaelites and Turner discarded the false progress of English art since the Middle Ages and began afresh, building their art on the last "true" art characterized by particularly English principles: namely, Ruskin's principles.[3]

In the 1860s, after the Brotherhood had effectively disbanded, two students, William Morris and Edward Jones, made contact with Dante Rossetti and initiated the "second wave" of Pre-Raphaelitism, one that differed radically in its aims and methods from those of the first Brotherhood. The members of what is sometimes termed the Early Aesthetic movement focused on the development of English culture as a part of the early origins of pan-European culture during the Middle Ages. Morris translated several Icelandic sagas, and Burne-Jones, as he eventually styled himself, found subject matter in Greek myths and the Grail legends of continental Europe as well as England.

Nineteenth-century writers on Pre-Raphaelitism also minted "new" members of the Pre-Raphaelite movement because of their literary or artistic similarities to the works of the established Pre-Raphaelites. Two examples may serve to illustrate this trend, which was sometimes based on thin evidence. The poet William Bell Scott, although he knew many of the members of the original Brotherhood during its ascendancy, did not identify himself as a Pre-Raphaelite poet until he was retrospectively dubbed one by George W. Thornbury, who, in the *Athenaeum* for 24 February 1855, "revealed" Scott's *Poems* to be a Pre-Raphaelite work.[4] In a similar vein, the French critic Henri Viel-Castel conjured a "new" member of the Pre-Raphaelite movement in June 1855:

> MM. Schaw, Millais et Hunt représentent l'école de réalisme tel que le comprennent nos alliés d'outre-Manche, et comme ces trois artistes forment une exception dans l'exposition anglaise, nous croyons devoir commencer par leurs œuvres l'examen de l'art britannique. [Messrs. Schaw, Millais, and Hunt represent the school of realism such as it is understood by our friends of the outer-Marches, and as these three artists form an exception in the English gallery, we believe it right to begin our examination of British art with their works.][5]

As for the identity of the mysterious Monsieur Schaw, the *Art-Journal* critic clears up the mystery some weeks later:

> All this time many of our readers . . . may be lost in perplexity as to the identity of this new leader of the pre-Raffaelites—this *Monsr. Schaw*: we confess to have ourselves been for some time in the same predicament, until having . . . eliminated the Teutonic c from the name, we found a most estimable artist, Mr. Shaw, known, as we have just intimated, to the literary as well as the artistic world, before Young England had learned to lisp the names of Van Eyck or Perugino, as a most skilful archaeologist—a retrospective reviewer of the old monkish illuminations; some of the choicest of which he gave with a singularly faithful pencil to the public, and who little dreamt that he was becoming the apostle of the new and true school of painting while making facsimiles of those quaint curiosities, wherein the infant struggles of Art are so conspicuous, and in which the suggestions of perspective both of line and tint are so unceremoniously dealt withal. Mr. Shaw will probably be as much surprised as any of us at the paragraph commencing in the Parisian periodical with the words "*MM. Schaw, Millais et Hunt represent l'école de réalisme.*"[6]

During the nineteenth century, Pre-Raphaelitism expanded out of England, as well. Thomas Woolner emigrated to Australia and began to sculpt and write poetry there; the "American Pre-Raphaelites" set up a magazine in emulation of *The Germ*, named the *Crayon*; and French art critics began to proclaim the similarities between the Pre-Raphaelites and the new French Realist school of painting led by Courbet. Criticism and theory about Pre-Raphaelitism appeared in England, Wales, Scotland, Canada, Australia, France, Spain, Italy, Germany, Hungary, and even Japan[7] and Russia,[8] most of which described the Pre-Raphaelite movement in terms of its relation to and influence on the arts in the critics' own countries. Thus, Pre-Raphaelitism was a typically Japanese movement to the Japanese, and the French saw the Pre-Raphaelites as having espoused French ideals.

Later in the nineteenth century, Pre-Raphaelitism even moved beyond being a men-only movement. Critics began reclaiming women painters from the 1850s and 1860s as having been Pre-Raphaelites, and Christina Rossetti's poetry was seen increasingly as equally representative of Pre-Raphaelite poetry along with the poetry of Dante Rossetti, Algernon Swinburne, and William Morris.

Pre-Raphaelitism moved beyond its original didactic aims, as well, beginning with the overt didactic morality of Holman Hunt's *Awakening Conscience* (1853) and finishing with the decorative and aesthetic qualities of Dante Rossetti's *Astarte Syriaca* (1877), for example. The movement came to be defined and redefined throughout the nineteenth century in terms of which artists and authors were "really" Pre-Raphaelites, what qualities of their work made them so, and why the movement's embrace of new figures and theoretical stances was consistent with the original Brotherhood. Often this was difficult, if not impossible, to do, since the original Brotherhood lasted for so short a time (it broke up around 1854) and consisted of such diverse members, each of whom applied the nebulous ideals of the movement in his or her own way. Further muddying the definition of Pre-Raphaelitism is the sheer multivalence of the term by the end of the nineteenth century. One could talk about Pre-Raphaelite painters, sculptors, poets, essayists, and critics: Pre-Raphaelites were men and women from several different countries, some of whom came before and some after the Pre-Raphaelite Brotherhood in England between 1848 and 1854. Pre-Raphaelitism included realistic, didactic genre painting about contemporary social evils; fancifully medieval-looking history painting about the Briar Rose legends; highly mannered and detailed translations of Icelandic sagas; religious paintings of Christ whose backgrounds and models were taken directly from Palestine; essays about the connection between spiritual and physical love; poetry about the need to renounce physical desires in order to obtain a "better resurrection";

hand-crafted wallpaper; and newspaper articles about the need to protect ancient buildings from destruction. By the end of the nineteenth century, the Pre-Raphaelite movement had become broad enough to accommodate many different and sometimes contradictory media, artists, and theories about art. These layers of signifying each expand what the umbrella term "Pre-Raphaelitism" can contain, reaching further and further beyond the movement's supposedly Anglocentric nineteenth-century origins.

Over the course of the twentieth century, the idea of Pre-Raphaelitism in relation to subsequent developments in literature, art, and cultural theory underwent several waves of revision. During the 1900s and 1910s, after the last of the original Brotherhood had died, scholars of the movement returned to a narrower definition of what the Pre-Raphaelite movement was, who its members were, and whether it was properly its own movement or merely a holdover from Romanticism. Scholarship tended to be biographical, enumerative, and historical, rather than theoretical.

For example, several biographical studies[9] appeared before the first World War on individual figures and their relationship with the movement, arguing for their inclusion in or exclusion from Pre-Raphaelitism, depending on individual biographers' opinions about the desirability of belonging to a school at once "uncompromising, assertive, childlike in its naïve charm, [and] childish in its incompetence."[10] After the war, scholarship on the movement dwindled until the mid-1930s, due in part to the ascendancy of Art Nouveau, Expressionism, Dada, and Surrealism, movements that purposely positioned themselves against the traditional aims of Pre-Raphaelitism and other Victorian-era art movements.

The period between the 1930s and the late 1950s saw little scholarship about Pre-Raphaelitism. A few influential reports of Pre-Raphaelitism's effects on world culture did appear, but they tended to be based on older research, such as Lafcadio Hearn's posthumously published lectures on Pre-Raphaelitism from when he was a professor in Japan during the *fin de siècle*.[11] The year 1948 marked the centennial of the founding of the movement: the Tate Museum and the Birmingham City Museum & Art Gallery dutifully put on shows and published catalogues of their Pre-Raphaelite paintings, but relatively little scholarship attended the hundredth anniversary of the P. R. B. Only one dissertation on the Pre-Raphaelites was published between 1942 and 1962.[12] Three representative works from this period demonstrate how narrowly the Pre-Raphaelite movement had become defined. Lelio Luxardo edited a collection of "critical notes" on Pre-Raphaelitism in 1929, which consisted of biographical sketches liberally summarized from nineteenth-century newspaper articles.[13] A second work from this period is a self-published book on *The Influence of British Literature Upon Pre-Raphaelite Painting*,[14] which recapitulates the traditional argument that the Pre-Raphaelites took their subjects from Shakespeare, the Bible, and from favorite Romantic poets. One of the major works to appear in this period is William Gaunt's *The Pre-Raphaelite Tragedy*,[15] an account of the history of the movement's members told through a narrative based on Gaunt's examination of diaries, letters, and other archival materials that were then in private hands. By 1960, however, Pre-Raphaelitism was considered in many scholarly circles to be, at best, an eccentric choice of subject, and the field of Pre-Raphaelite studies languished. However, during the late 1950s and early 1960s, scholarly interest in the movement began to wax again, based on the rediscovery of primary and secondary documents as they became available through auctions, sales, and bequests to academic collections.[16] This era also marked a growing transatlantic critical and academic interest in the Victorian era and in Victorian studies as a discipline, fueled largely by Jerome H. Buckley's *The Victorian Temper* (1951), which refers, against the fashion of the time, to the Pre-Raphaelite movement as a significant element of nineteenth-century art and literary history.

Pre-Raphaelitism as it is studied in the current sense would likely not exist without the bibliographical scholarship of William E. Fredeman. Fredeman's *Pre-Raphaelitism: A Bibliocritical Study* (1965) nearly single-handedly re-energized the field of Pre-Raphaelite studies. His work touched off a revival of Pre-Raphaelite scholarship, and his framework has set the boundaries of the movement, with few exceptions, since 1965. Fredeman's bibliography was notable for several reasons, chief among them his generously inclusive policy about minor figures loosely associated with the movement. The inclusion of minor figures such as Thomas Gordon Hake and Arthur O'Shaughnessy helped boost them into the accepted canon of Pre-Raphaelitism. Also, of several bibliographies on Pre-Raphaelitism written in the early 1960s, Fredeman's was the only one to appear in print.[17] It is instructive to note his bibliography as a founding document of the modern scholarly examination of the Pre-Raphaelite movement, from which much scholarship has since extended.[18] Interestingly, although Fredeman cites in his bibliography several non-English-language pieces of scholarship and criticism from both the nineteenth and twentieth centuries that place Pre-Raphaelitism in a worldwide frame, his introduction perpetuates the narrower, more Anglocentric view of the movement, in keeping with the widely held view of the Pre-Raphaelite movement as an anomaly apart from the progression from Romantic thought at the beginning of the nineteenth century to the Aesthetic movement at its end. Thus, Fredeman's work simultaneously gave new vigor to the field of Pre-Raphaelite studies while strengthening its focus on the English qualities of the movement, a stance that would not be significantly challenged until the late 1990s.

During the 1970s, scholarship about Pre-Raphaelitism concentrated largely on filling out the corpus of primary documents; editions of diaries, journals, and reprints of *The Germ*[19] and nineteenth-century critical works appeared. The *Journal of Pre-Raphaelite Studies* (*JPRS*) was established in 1977 by an interdisciplinary group of editors (including Fredeman), and early articles in *JPRS* largely covered the relationships among the original Pre-Raphaelite Brotherhood and the members of the movement's second flowering. Several primary documents from the movement were reissued, often as part of critical editions,[20] and the original Brotherhood became a renewed source of interdisciplinary scholarly inquiry.[21] The field of Pre-Raphaelite studies was, in a sense, being reinvented whole, especially in light of the new vogue for Marxist, feminist, and deconstructive inquiry.

The 1980s saw scholarship on Pre-Raphaelitism continue in its applications of academic theory but expand away from the original members of the movement to incorporate comparative studies[22] and deeper inquiry into the roles of women (in addition to the consistently-studied Christina Rossetti) in the movement.[23] The appeal of the Pre-Raphaelites was reflected in rising auction-house prices for original works of art and first editions of books, and the Pre-Raphaelite Society was founded in Birmingham in 1988, providing a bridge between the scholarly treatment of the movement and the lay appreciation of Pre-Raphaelite poetry and art. By the end of the 1980s, the definition of Pre-Raphaelitism had broadened to include women artists as well as followers and minor associates of the original members of the Brotherhood. Several academic theories had been applied to the movement with some success, but the one area of Pre-Raphaelitism that had actually narrowed was its perceived geographic scope: Pre-Raphaelitism was considered to be an exclusively English phenomenon. As Quentin Bell reported in 1982,

> The original Brotherhood, although it may have looked abroad for some of its ideas, was essentially an English movement. It had very little commerce with Europe. The second generation gradually attained an international character. The arts and crafts movement became known in Belgium and

Central Europe, the influence of Ruskin was felt, and late in his career Burne-Jones excited the attention of the French Symbolists. Thus the movement as a whole may be regarded as a withdrawal from, and then a gradual *rapprochement* with, the art of the Continent.[24]

After more than 150 years, the question with which this introduction opened, "what is Pre-Raphaelitism?" now takes on a complicated cast.

If the publications of the 1990s and the early years of the twenty-first century are a reliable measure, the scope of Pre-Raphaelitism seems still to be expanding. Recent scholarly works by Elizabeth Prettejohn[25] and the editing team of Alicia Craig Faxon and Susan Casteras[26] evince a willingness to continue to broaden the movement in terms of its members, ideologies, and influences on and from other movements in literature and art. Recent titles on Pre-Raphaelitism demonstrate the desire to add to the canon by many means: since 1990, scholarship on Pre-Raphaelitism has gone "beyond the Pre-Raphaelite Brotherhood";[27] it has been "read,"[28] "re-viewed,"[29] "re-framed,"[30] placed into its larger "European Context,"[31] "collected,"[32] and "haunted."[33] It has been looked at in terms of gender,[34] sexuality,[35] ethics,[36] and has even been implicated in an "Ecclesiastical Crisis."[37] The critical reaction to Pre-Raphaelitism has become a legitimate topic of study in itself, with bibliographies[38] and theoretical studies[39] on the subject appearing recently. It is becoming increasingly important, however, that scholars define the terms under which such expansion takes place.

The essays in this collection set a new direction for Pre-Raphaelite scholarship: they reveal that because of the broad and deep reach of the movement during the lifetimes of its practitioners, Pre-Raphaelitism encompasses several thought systems, scholarly approaches, and avenues of inquiry. Because of the risk of diluting the term's definition to the point of its dissolution, scholarship on Pre-Raphaelitism is obliged to reexamine and redefine both the term itself and the movement to which it is attached. Different theoretical approaches and ideologies permit terminological multivalence and canonical expansion in several directions simultaneously. Instead of a single movement with several practitioners and characteristics, there are now several competing Pre-Raphaelitisms, each informed by a different school of thought, theoretical stance, or disciplinary set of rules. We have passed the point where a widely accepted and well-bounded Pre-Raphaelite movement acts as the ground for the inductions of critics and scholars investigating an unambivalent single history of "what was." Rather, the essays in *Worldwide Pre-Raphaelitism* demonstrate hermeneutical echoes, traces, and affinities between the Pre-Raphaelite Brotherhood and later artists and writers. It is like the difference between finding the charming details in an old house one has inherited and shopping for an old house based on one's idea of what an old house should look like. To carry the metaphor slightly further, when one takes together all of the elements of the House of Idea(l)s—including cultural theory, gender theory, nationalism, deconstruction, and Orientalism—one sees a multifaceted Pre-Raphaelitism. The essays in this volume achieve a necessary historical and theoretical distance from the movement itself, so that it can now be traced in relation to larger movements in global history, literature, and art.

This collection redefines Pre-Raphaelitism in a new way: the movement is diverse in terms of ideology, gender, and geography, and in the act of mapping the extent of Pre-Raphaelitism's influence and reach, this volume tests the boundaries of the movement. These essays also suggest what Pre-Raphaelitism was not and did not, exploring the development of the trope of the term "Pre-Raphaelitism," which became freighted with national, ideological, and gendered ideas as it passed from age to age, country to country, and through different scholarly thought-systems.

The signifier "Pre-Raphaelitism," as it has been passed down, has been diffused into and has incorporated other discourses, creating texts "haunted" by the idea of Pre-Raphaelitism. Pre-Raphaelitism indeed began narrowly, as an extension of the continental Romantic school of thought. It transformed itself throughout the lives of its early practitioners, the better to reflect the literary and artistic currents of an increasingly global perspective, mirroring the increasing rapidity of communications technology and the opening of trade on the world markets during the late nineteenth century.

In the second half of the twentieth century, "Pre-Raphaelitism" became a useful signifier for theorists who put it to use as representing ideas at times reactionary, nationalistic, and theoretical. This collection brings together several different theoretical stances in order to present a wide range of thinking on the subject of what Pre-Raphaelitism currently signifies and where it is headed. Pre-Raphaelitism has come to be a touchstone for artistic and literary thought and discourse, often in places, media, and times far removed from the origins of the movement in 1848 London. The essays in this collection trace the development of Pre-Raphaelitism as a global phenomenon, beginning with its roots in continental European art history and moving away from England in time and geography.

During the first years of the movement, for example, we can trace the influence of the early-Renaissance Italian, Flemish, and German "Primitives" on the new Pre-Raphaelite movement: Béatrice Laurent's essay, "An Inventory of the Pre-Raphaelite Mental Museum, October 1849," explores the continental art tour undertaken by Dante Rossetti and William Holman Hunt before the formation of the Brotherhood; Laurent demonstrates that, rather than rising *ex nihilo* to challenge the established artistic canons of the day, Pre-Raphaelitism had its foundations in the very exhibition halls against which it originally railed.

The early influences on Pre-Raphaelitism were not limited solely to European ones. William Holman Hunt traveled extensively in Palestine during the mid-1850s, and his contact with Islamic and Jewish cultures created reciprocal influences in Hunt's paintings as well as in the communities in which he sought models and suppliers of paint, canvas, and sundries. Francesca Vanke Altman argues in "William Holman Hunt, Race, and Orientalism" that on his return to England, Hunt maintained his ties to the Jewish and Islamic communities, becoming involved with fundraising and charitable events for Middle Eastern groups in London.

Not all of the influences of Pre-Raphaelitism were so deliberate, as can be seen in Christopher M. Keirstead's "Rossetti's 'A Last Confession' and Italian Nationalism," an essay on the manner in which Italian nationalists enlisted an unwilling Dante Gabriel Rossetti to represent their cause, and in Linda Groen's essay, "A Dutch Lady of Shalott," on a Dutch artist whose only (but significant) connection to the Pre-Raphaelite movement was his choice of subject matter. Pre-Raphaelitism served in the late nineteenth and early twentieth centuries as an antithesis against which to set new works, as argued in Tatjana Jukić's essay on the early twentieth-century Croatian writer Miroslav Krleža. Susan Casteras also finds that Pre-Raphaelite tropes appear (and are refashioned) in the Symbolist movement at the turn of the twentieth century.

Academics have long argued about whether the second wave of Pre-Raphaelitism epitomized by Morris, Burne-Jones, and Swinburne comprises the beginning of the Aesthetic movement, the protorumblings of the Arts and Crafts movement, the end of the High Gothic trend, or some other phenomenon entirely. Despite this debate, the influence of this phase of the movement, too, can be seen worldwide. Florence Boos examines "William Morris's Later Writings and the Socialist Modernism of Lewis Grassic Gibbon," while Margaret D. Stetz explores the relationship between later Pre-Raphaelitism and travel monologues by Westerners about "exotic" locations such as colonial India in her "Pre-Raphaelitism's Farewell Tour." Even Hungary seems to have received the Pre-Raphaelite gospel in the late nineteenth century, and Éva Péteri relates in "Pre-Raphaelitism in Hungary" the story of how Walter Crane brought it there.

Pre-Raphaelitism did not always provoke direct reaction, however. In "Pre-Raphaelitism in Colonial Australia," Juliette Peers examines how the impact of Thomas Woolner and Bernhard Smith on Australian art came indirectly, after their own generation had mostly ignored the work of these two English artist emigrants, only to have their cause taken up in the early decades of the twentieth century. Pre-Raphaelitism's second wave reached across the Atlantic, as well; Paul Hardwick's essay on the relation between Morris and the Christian Socialist movement in the United States is balanced by the contribution from David Latham on the aestheticism and socialism of Francis Sherman, the "Canadian Pre-Raphaelite." Sarah Wootton contributes an examination of the Pre-Raphaelite influence on American artists' representations of subjects from Keats's poetry, which brings the volume full circle in a reconsideration of the relationship of the original Pre-Raphaelites to the Romantic movement, now filtered through the viewpoint of early twentieth-century American painters.

Taken together, the essays in this volume demand that Pre-Raphaelitism be viewed in a worldwide frame, a frame which changes our understanding of Pre-Raphaelitism's involvement in and influence on global nineteenth-, twentieth-, and now twenty-first-century art and literary history. This collection is written by art historians, scientists, literary scholars, fashion historians, women's studies professors, and independent scholars. The essays raise issues of commerce, marginality, Orientalism, imperialism, and national culture in relation to Pre-Raphaelitism. Brief essays on individual works or figures have been chosen to complement and challenge those essays that concern broader, more "national" subjects. Although the topics covered in this volume are spread out over many countries, time periods, and disciplines, the common thread is Pre-Raphaelitism, a movement that has to this day lasted as a core set of ideas: truth to nature, minuteness of detail, and sensitivity to the past. Pre-Raphaelitism began by borrowing its ideology from several continental art movements, and has become a literary, artistic, and historical trope from which many cultures and theoretical systems have themselves borrowed. The essays in this volume speak to the multivalence of the Pre-Raphaelite movement and hint at the extent to which the current theoretical *weltanschauung* includes Pre-Raphaelitism as being an inclusively global movement whose traces bridge the concerns of Romantic European ideas and the global aestheticism of the *fin de siècle*, rather than merely an isolated English artistic movement that took place between 1848 and 1854.

These essays uncover a Pre-Raphaelitism which, rather than being a regressive movement working against the flow of developments in world events, is an extension of—an integral part of—the development not only of European thought at the end of the nineteenth century, but of the spread of aestheticism throughout the world, the echoes of which can be discerned in writings and artwork even into the twenty-first century.

Thomas J. Tobin, Ph.D., M.S.L.S.
Southern Illinois University

NOTES

1. See, for example, the following critical articles: [Frank Stone], "Royal Academy: The Eighty-Third Exhibition—1851," *Art-Journal* 13 (1 June 1850): 153–63; Charles Dickens, "Old Lamps for New Ones," *Household Words* 12 (15 June 1850): 12–14; R[alph] N[icolson] Wornum, "Modern Moves in Art. Christian Architecture. Young England," *Art-Journal* (1 Sept. 1850): 270–71; "Fine Arts: Pre-Raphaelitism," *Daily News* [London] 1629 (13 Aug. 1851): 3; and "French Criticism on British Art," *Art-Journal* 17 (1 Sep. 1855): 250–52.

2. [Jerome McGann], "Introduction to *The Germ*." http://www.iath. virginia.edu/courses/ennc986/class/grpintro.html.

3. This is perhaps one source of the notion that Pre-Raphaelitism was an insular English movement.

4. [George Walter Thornbury], *"Poems,"* *Athenaeum* no. 1426 (24 Feb. 1855): 229–30.

5. Henri Viel-Castel, "Exposition Universelle des Beaux-arts: Peinture.—École Anglaise," *L'Athenaeum Français* 4.24 (16 June. 1855): 507–9.

6. "French Criticism on British Art," *Art Journal* 17 (1 Sept. 1855): 250–52.

7. Two examples among many are Kaneko Umaji, "The Poetic Imagination of Rossetti, Distinguished Poet of Romanticism," *Waseda Bungaku* [*Tokyo*

Magazine] 54 (Meiji 26 [Dec. 1893]): 105–8 and Koya Tozawa, "Annotated Review of English Poetry," *Myojo* [*Morning Star*] 6 (Sept. 1900): 20–22.

8. V[ladimir] V[iktorovitch] Chuiko. "Dorafaelisty I Ikh Poslîedovateli eh Anglii," *Vestnik Iziashchnykh Iskustv* 4 (1886): 271–304, 339–74.

9. Examples include Ralph Granger Watkin, *Robert Browning and the English Pre-Raphaelites* (Breslau: Fleischmann, 1905); Gabriel Moury, *Dante Gabriel Rossetti et les Préraphaélites Anglais* (Paris: Laurens, 1909); and A. M. W. Stirling, "A Painter of Dreams: The Life of Roddam Spencer Stanhope, Pre-Raphaelite," in *A Painter of Dreams and Other Biographical Studies* (London: John Lane, 1916): 97–143.

10. Bernhard Sickert, "The Pre-Raphaelite and Impressionist Heresies," *Burlington Magazine* 8 (May 1905): 97–102.

11. Lafcadio Hearn, *Pre-Raphaelite and Other Poets; Lectures* (New York: Dodd, Mead, 1922). Hearn's lectures were reissued in 1968, after the revival of the field of Pre-Raphaelite studies.

12. Elizabeth Mary Cottrell, *The Pre-Raphaelite Movement* (Dissertation, 1952).

13. Lelio Luxardo, *Preraffaelliti e Preraffaellismo in Inghilterra: Note Critiche* (Bologna: N. Zanichelli, 1929).

14. Veola Leona Bohnert, *The Influence of British Literature Upon Pre-Raphaelite Painting* (S. l.: Bohnert, 1933).

15. William Gaunt, *The Pre-Raphaelite Tragedy* (New York: Harcourt, Brace, 1942).

16. For example, *The Pre-Raphaelite Brotherhood: Catalogue No. 73* (Cheltenham: Alan Hancox, 1959) and *Fine Eighteenth and Nineteenth-Century Drawings and Paintings, Including a Group of Victorian and Pre-Raphaelite Works by Madox Brown, Frith, Holman Hunt, Hughes, Burne-Jones, Millais, and Rossetti, the Property of William Alwyn* [Catalogue] (London: Sotheby's, 1962).

17. Two examples of other bibliographies are Rita Wiench, *Bibliographie der Nazarenischen und Präraffaelischen Kunst* (Dissertation, 1963); and Mary Elizabeth Cottrell, *The Pre-Raphaelite Movement* (Dissertation, 1962).

18. My own recent bibliography, *Pre-Raphaelitism in the Nineteenth-Century Press* (Vancouver: English Literary Studies, 2002) began as a reexamination of Fredeman's entries for newspaper and periodical articles.

19. Robert Stahr Hosmon, ed., *The Germ: A Pre-Raphaelite Little Magazine* (1850; repr., Coral Gables: University of Miami Press, 1970).

20. Such as William Rossetti, *The P. R. B. Journal*, William E. Fredeman, ed. (Oxford: Oxford University Press, 1975); and Francis Hueffer, *The Troubadours* (1878; repr., New York: AMS Press, 1977). The AMS Press is famous for its reprint editions of out-of-print works, and many Pre-Raphaelite texts are well known today only because they came out in reissue through AMS in the 1970s.

21. Of several possible examples, some are Raymond Watkinson, *Pre-Raphaelite Art and Design* (London: Studio Vista, 1970); Timothy Hilton, *The Pre-Raphaelites* (London: Thames and Hudson, 1970); James Sambrook, ed., *Pre-Raphaelitism: A Collection of Critical Essays* (Chicago: University of Chicago Press, 1974); Francis Haskell, *Rediscoveries in Art* (Ithaca, NY: Cornell University Press, 1976); Stanley Weintraub, *Four Rossettis* (New York: Weybright and Talley, 1978). There was even a special issue of the *Burlington Magazine* (February 1973) devoted to the Pre-Raphaelite Brotherhood.

22. For example, Maria Angela Cerdà i Surroca, *Els Pre-Rafaelites a Catalunya: Una Literatura i uns Símbols* (Barcelona: Curial, 1981) and Whitney Robert Mundt, *Pre-Raphaelitism in the Early Poetry of Gerard Manley Hopkins* (Dissertation, 1981).

23. Jan Marsh is almost solely responsible for developments in this area of the field. See, for instance, her *The Pre-Raphaelite Sisterhood* (London: Quartet, 1985); *Pre-Raphaelite Women: Images of Femininity* (New York: Harmony Books, 1988); and *Women Artists and the Pre-Raphaelite Movement* (London: Virago, 1989), co-authored with Pamela Gerrish Nunn.

24. Quentin Bell, *A New and Noble School: The Pre-Raphaelites* (London: Macdonald, 1982), 10.

25. Elizabeth Prettejohn, *The Art of the Pre-Raphaelites* (Princeton, NJ: Princeton University Press, 2000).

26. Susan P. Casteras and Alicia Craig Faxon, eds., *Pre-Raphaelite Art in Its European Context* (Madison, NJ: London: Fairleigh Dickinson University Press; Associated University Press, 1995).

27. Debra N. Mancoff, *John Everett Millais: Beyond the Pre-Raphaelite Brotherhood* (New Haven, CT: Yale University Press, 2001).

28. Tim Barringer, *Reading the Pre-Raphaelites* (New Haven, CT: Yale University Press, 1998).

29. Marcia Pointon, *Pre-Raphaelites Re-Viewed* (Manchester: Manchester University Press, 1990).

30. Ellen Harding, ed., *Re-Framing the Pre-Raphaelites* (Burlington, VT: Ashgate, 1996).

31. Casteras and Faxon.

32. Margaretta Frederick Watson, ed., *Collecting the Pre-Raphaelites* (Burlington, VT: Ashgate, 1997).

33. David Latham, ed., *Haunted Texts: Studies in Pre-Raphaelitism* (Toronto: University of Toronto Press, 2003).

34. Jan Marsh and Pamela Nunn, *Pre-Raphaelite Women Artists* (London: Thames and Hudson, 1999) and Christina Elmerfeldt-Böhner, *Das Weibliche in Werk und Leben der Präraffaeliten* (Egelsbach; New York: Fouqué Literaturverlag, 1999).

35. Rickie Burman, *From Prodigy to Outcast: Simeon Solomon—Pre-Raphaelite Artist* (London: Jewish Museum, 2001).

36. Kathryn K. Varness, *From Wickedness to Innovation: Three Victorian Reactions to Early Pre-Raphaelitism* (Dissertation, 2000).

37. Erika Lynne Szendrey, *William Holman Hunt's* Our English Coasts, *1852 (Strayed Sheep): Victorian England's Ecclesiastical Crisis* (Dissertation, 2000).

38. Tobin, *Pre-Raphaelitism in the Nineteenth-Century Press* and Rachael Green, *The Brotherhood of Seven: A Select Bibliography of the Pre-Raphaelite Movement, 1848–1914* (N. p.: n. p., 1995).

39. Examples include Jennifer L. Rinalducci, *The 1857–58 American Exhibition of British Art: Pre-Raphaelite Art and the American Critical Reception* (Dissertation, 2000); Rachel Barnes, *The Pre-Raphaelites and Their World* (London: Tate Gallery, 1998); Steve Rizza, *Criticism as Art: The Reception of Pre-Raphaelitism in Fin de Siècle Vienna* (Frankfurt am Main; New York: P. Lang, 1997); and Thomas J. Tobin, *The Critical Reception of Pre-Raphaelite Painting and Poetry: 1850–1900* (North Manchester, IN: Heckman, 1996).

Chapter 1

AN INVENTORY OF THE PRE-RAPHAELITE MENTAL MUSEUM, OCTOBER 1849

Béatrice Laurent

Mysticism and Primitivism were recurrent aspects of the artistic production in Europe during the first half of the nineteenth century. In England, these trends were observable in literature and architecture before they became in 1848 the founding elements of the Pre-Raphaelite Brotherhood (P.R.B.), an association of artists similar to the ones that had existed in other countries of Europe since 1810: the Brotherhood of S. Luke (also known as the Nazarenes) in Germany, as well as the Brotherhood of S. John the Evangelist and the Brotherhood of the Blessed Angelico of Fiesole in France. The young Pre-Raphaelites had a second-hand knowledge of these movements, thanks to lithographs and to the reports they heard from elder friends such as William Cave Thomas and Ford Madox Brown, as well as from William Dyce and Charles Eastlake, their teachers at the Royal Academy. Brown recorded a vivid memory of his visit to Johann Friedrich Overbeck in 1846:

> He was habited in a black velvet dressing-gown down to the ground and corded around the waist; on his head a velvet cap, furred, which allowed his grey curling locks to stray on his shoulders. He bore exactly the appearance of some figure of the fifteenth century. When he spoke to me it was with the humility of a saint.[1]

The archetype conjured up in this description is that of the artist-saint of the quattrocento, probably inspired by Renaissance self-portraits and Giorgio Vasari's accounts. It reveals the origins of the name the seven chose for themselves: "Pre-Raphaelite" to indicate their affiliation to Renaissance artists, and more particularly to the Italian school, "Brotherhood" to signal their membership in the contemporary European artistico-spiritual revival.

The simple fact that the early Pre-Raphaelite iconography was in major part religious and inspired by Renaissance masterpieces seems to have been understated in the scholarship of the last sixty years. However, if we restrict the scope of Pre-Raphaelitism to the twelve years between 1848 and 1860, and to the members of the original Brotherhood only, then the two characteristics—mysticism and primitivism—appear clearly in Pre-Raphaelite paintings. My purpose in this essay is to help us refocus on the Renaissance models that the Pre-Raphaelites sought to emulate in the early days of the Brotherhood, and to recall the fact that the primordial unity of the Brotherhood consisted in a shared admiration of the Italian and Flemish Old Masters, and a shared belief in the necessary revival of religious art. These two points have been partly forgotten because of the dilution of the concept and the term "Pre-Raphaelite," but also because for a long time the visual culture of the young Pre-Raphaelites was either underestimated or taken for granted but not examined in any great detail.

In the 1940s, William Gaunt asserted that "with the Italian masters of the later Middle Ages, who provided its curious name, [the Brotherhood] had very little to do. . . . They were quite ignorant of the fourteenth century, which was to be their starting point."[2] In the 1960s, the Penguin Dictionary of Art and Artists still held that the Pre-Raphaelites "knew very little about Italian painting earlier than Raphael."[3] These presumptions were supported in part by the account of the genesis of the group delivered by William Holman Hunt—or his wife Edith—in *Pre-Raphaelitism and the Pre-Raphaelite Brotherhood* (1905), who claimed "we knew little of Michelangelo . . . while Tintoretto in his might was not known at all. Della Robia, Donatello, Luini and Angelico were mere names in books."[4] The belief in the Pre-Raphaelites' nearly total ignorance of Renaissance art was further enforced by a chronological misunderstanding.

Indeed, while Victorian observers stated that the Pre-Raphaelites drew their inspiration from the Primitives, a present-day critic of Pre-Raphaelite art would search in vain for influences of trecento artists such as Giotto or Cimabue—whom we now term Primitives—and this is probably what led Gaunt to his conclusion. The explanation for this apparent discrepancy is simply that in the nineteenth century, "Italian Painting before 1500 was generally located in the Middle Ages."[5] In fact, in the minds of many Victorians, "Pre-Raphaelite," "early," and "primitive" were quasi-synonymous adjectives, applied indifferently to the bulk of Western art produced between the end of the Hellenic period and the beginning of the seventeenth century. Consequently, they included what we now call Renaissance art.

The scientific reassessment of Pre-Raphaelite models began in the 1970s thanks to the works of John Christian, Robyn Cooper, and especially George Landow who pinpointed in 1979 some borrowings of William Holman Hunt's from Flemish Renaissance masters. The pioneering research of these scholars enabled Jan Marsh to correct the misunderstanding concerning the P. R. B.s' affiliation, and to state rightly that the Pre-Raphaelites simply "dismissed all post-Renaissance art in the tradition of Raphael."[6] This necessary rectification may clear the Brotherhood of some of its mystery, but it raises fresh questions. How much did the young Pre-Raphaelites know about the art of the past, and especially of the Renaissance? Which artists and which works were in their minds when they were painting?

Following André Malraux's assertion that the destiny of any artist is first nurtured by pastiche, I have tried to compile an inventory of the "mental museum" of the young artists, containing the paintings to which they had access at the moment they founded the Brotherhood in London in 1848.

Prints occupied a large part in the mental museum of nineteenth-century European artists, and of the Pre-Raphaelites in particular. The British Museum, where they spent much of their time, was a bountiful source: by the late 1840s, the Print Collection in the Department of Prints and Drawings would have numbered over 50,000 references, many of which were reproductions of Medieval and early Renaissance works. In addition, the Department of Manuscripts and the Department of Printed Books had colossal collections.[7] Prints permitted a precise knowledge of the German school—indeed, many early German masters had been both painters and engravers—but the technique of engraving at that stage did not allow a fine rendering of Italian colors or Flemish precision. Thus, it seems that the first gallery in the Pre-Raphaelites' mental museum was dedicated to German painter-engravers, among whom Albrecht Dürer was granted special honor. It included many works, almost certainly the complete oeuvre, from the following figures:

Pre-Raphaelite Mental Museum, 1848, German Renaissance Section.[8]

Martin Schongauer (c. 1450–91)

Hans Holbein I (c. 1465–1524)

Albrecht Dürer (1471–1528)

Lucas Cranach I (1472–1553)

Hans Burgkmaier (1473–1531)

Albrecht Altdorfer (c. 1480–1538)

Hans Baldung (c. 1484–1545)

Urs Graf (1485–1527)

Hans Holbein II (c. 1497–1543)

Georges Pencz (c. 1500–c. 1550)

Hans-Sebald Beham (1500–1550)

Aldegrever (1502–1558)

The first Pre-Raphaelite productions consisted mainly of pen-and-ink drawings, remarkable for their sharp and angular lines, their thick outlines, and flat, two-dimensional aspect, all of which evoke the Gothic manner of the early German engravers.[9] However, when the Brethren drew their "List of Immortals," a paper pantheon of fifty-seven names "constituting the whole of (their) Creed,"[10] and despite their shared admiration for the German school, not one German, not even Dürer, was included in the list: the eight "immortal" Renaissance masters are all Italians. We may wonder how and when the young Pre-Raphaelites became knowledgeable about Fra Angelico, Bellini, da Vinci, Michelangelo, Giorgione, Titian, Raphael, and Tintoretto to the point of "immortalizing" them. William Gaunt suggests that Lasinio's book of outline engravings from the frescoes in the Campo Santo at Pisa, which the P. R. B. discovered in August 1848, had a major influence.[11] Yet, not one work reproduced in the book was of the hand of an Immortal.[12] We may indicate several possible criteria according to which the Pre-Raphaelites granted immortality to some artists and not others: popularity could be one—indeed, Raphael, Titian, da Vinci, and Michelangelo were among the most frequently copied artists in Europe between 1815 and 1850[13]—and the admiration of these painters by John Ruskin and Ford Madox Brown, the two mentors of the Brotherhood, could be another. A third criterion could be the Immortals' exemplary biographies, which were in print in 1848. However, the most compelling reason for the P. R. B. to include these artists as Immortals is that the Pre-Raphaelites had first-hand knowledge of their work. Among the twenty-four early Italian paintings at the National Gallery, which, according to Millais' brother William, the Pre-Raphaelites knew by heart,[14] were some of the Immortals' works.

*Pictures in the National Gallery in 1848 by Italian
Renaissance Artists*

Monaco: *Adoring Saints* (attributed in 1848 to Gaddi)

Bellini: *Doge Leonardo Loredano*

Perugino: *Madonna and Child with S. John*

Francia: *Dead Christ Supported by the Virgin*; *Madonna and Child with
Saints*

Luini: *Christ Disputing* (attributed in 1848 to da Vinci)

Titian: *Concert*; *Rape of Ganymede*; *Venus and Adonis*; *Bacchus and
Ariadne*; *Holy Family*

Mazzolino: *S. Francis Adoring the Infant Christ*

Garofalo: *Holy Family with S. John*

Raphael: *Julius II*; *Vision of a Knight*; *S. Catherine of Alexandria*

Piombo: *Raising of Lazarus*

Correggio: *Venus and Cupid "L'Ecole de l'amour"*; *The Madonna of the
Basket*; *Ecce Homo*; *Christ's Agony in the Garden*

Parmigianino: *Vision of S. Jerome*

Tintoretto: *S. George and the Dragon*

A further source of information on the Italian Renaissance was Ford
Madox Brown, who had spent nine months studying in Milan, Florence,
and Rome. His visual memory of the works he had seen there was still
vivid many years later:

What remains strongest printed in my mind are the wall-paintings of
Giotto, . . . the frescoes of Masaccio in the Brancacci Chapel at Florence; . . . the Last Supper and the other works of Leonardo at Milan, and
also some wonderful heads by his pupil Luini. . . . The paintings of Fra Angelico, executed on the walls of his convent in Florence . . . and of course
the great works of Raphael and Michael Angelo in Rome, and lastly, but not
least, all the pictures by Titian that can be seen everywhere.[15]

Whether he communicated to his young friends his enthusiasm by
verbal description or with the help of sketches is uncertain, yet four of his
favorite artists were considered Immortals. This survey of the different

Pre-Raphaelite Mental Museum, 1848, Italian Renaissance Section

	Immortals	Lasinio	National Gallery[a]	F. M. Brown	Royal Academy[b]	Hampton Court
Giotto		x		x		
S. Memmi (Martini)		x				
Laurati (Lorenzetti)		x				
Buffalmacco		x				
Orcagna		x				
A. Gaddi			x			
Spinello		x				
Donatello					x	
Fra Angelico	x			x	x	
Della Robbia					x	
Veneziano		x				
Masaccio				x		
B. Gozzoli		x				
G. Bellini	x		x	x		
A. Mantegna						x
Perugino			x	x		
Francia			x			
L. da Vinci	x		x	x		
Michelangelo	x				x	
Giorgione	x				x	
Titian	x		x	x		
Mazzolino			x			
Garofalo			x			
Raphael	x		x	x	x	x
Piombo			x			
Del Sarto			*			
Correggio			x			
Parmigianino			x			
Luini				x		
Tintoretto	x		x			
Veronese			*			

[a] Asterisks indicate artists mentioned by Fleming (1967, 64n1) but unmentioned in either of the sources used for my compilation (see note 3).

[b] William Holman Hunt, 1:52.

sources accessible to the young Pre-Raphaelites in 1848 shows that the "Italian Renaissance" Gallery in their imaginary museum contained at least thirty names (table 1).

In 1848, the Pre-Raphaelites already knew their illustrious namesakes much better than many biographers, including Hunt himself, later claimed. However, the major encounter with the Renaissance masters occurred in the fall of 1849, during a journey that took Dante Gabriel Rossetti and William Holman Hunt from Paris to Bruges via Brussels, Antwerp, and Ghent. From September 27 until October 31, they traced the works of the then-called Primitives. Because of lack of funds they did not travel to Italy, but at the Louvre they saw the works of major Italian masters. Unfortunately, apart from some poems and a few, sometimes fragmentary, letters, little indication is available to the historian about the effect produced on Hunt and Rossetti by the hundreds of paintings they saw during their trip. Entries referring to the year 1849 in the *P. R. B. Journal* have been severely mutilated, and the sketchbooks that were used during the journey are still unlocated. Yet, Diana Holman-Hunt believes that Rossetti and Hunt took written and graphical notes of what they saw in order to publish a report on their return to England, one that perhaps would have constituted a valuable contribution to *The Germ*.[16] The project of this publication was carried out much later in the form of a private printing so extremely rare that the author has never laid eyes on it. Considering these restrictions, the best possible way to get an idea of what the two Pre-Raphaelite painters saw is to examine contemporary museum and gallery catalogues and to cross these sources with information contained in their letters.

In Paris, they went to the Musée du Louvre at least three times: a first visit on October 3 is mentioned in a letter from Dante Gabriel to William Michael Rossetti, a second visit before October 8 was the occasion for him to write his sonnet about Giorgione's *Rural Concert*,[17] and the "Last Visit to the Louvre" was recorded before the eighteenth.[18] The fact that Rossetti wrote two sonnets, inspired respectively by Mantegna[19] and by Giorgione, confirms that he visited both the Galerie des Primitifs where works by the former artist were presented, and the collection of the Italian School of the sixteenth through the eighteenth centuries where the *Rural Concert* was exhibited. In these two sections, Hunt and Rossetti could see 175 works by seventy-five Italian masters from the thirteenth to the sixteenth centuries (appendix 1). They saw paintings by Simone Memmi (Martini), Filippo Lippi, Sandro Botticelli, Ghirlandaio, Vittore Carpaccio, Andrea Solario, and Lorenzo Lotto. Above all, they feasted their eyes on the works of their Immortals. Dante Gabriel Rossetti wrote to his Pre-Raphaelite Brothers enthusiastically:

> There is a most wonderful copy of a fresco by Angelico . . . some mighty things by that real stunner Lionardo [*sic*], some ineffably poetical Mantegnas, several wonderful early Christians whom nobody ever heard of, some

tremendous portraits by some Venetian whose name I forget, a stunning *Francis I* by Titian. . . . There is a wonderful head by Raphael; another wonderful head by I know not whom; and a pastoral—at least a kind of pastoral—by Giorgione, which is so intensely fine that I condescended to sit down before it and write a sonnet.[20]

All in all, Rossetti estimated that in Paris, he and Hunt had seen "some forty first-rate paintings,—or indeed fifty mayhap"[21] that had enriched the galleries of their minds. Many of these acquisitions were Italian but some were Flemish: in the Louvre, they discovered Rogier van der Weyden's *Annunciation* and Jean Gossart's *Carondelet Diptych*. Jan van Eyck, whose *Arnolfini Marriage Portrait* they already knew from the National Gallery, was also represented by his *Madonna with Chancellor Rolin* (also known as the *Virgin of Autun*). These samples from the Northern school must have stimulated their curiosity, already awakened by Ford Madox Brown who had lived and studied in Belgium, and whose studio Hunt had been sharing since August 1849. Consequently, after they left Paris, the two friends went to Belgium, where they spent two and a half weeks admiring the works of the Flemish masters in museums and galleries.

First, they traveled to Brussels and explored the Royal Museum. On October 18, Rossetti recorded in a letter: "I believe we saw all the town today, except . . . one room at the Museum which we perceived was full of Rubenses, and so held aloof."[22] Thanks to the 1847 and 1984 inventories of the museum, we have a precise idea of what they saw in the other rooms: eighty-seven paintings, the majority representing religious subjects, many of them by unknown artists (appendix 2). They noticed the frequency of three-part compositions—triptychs, standard portable altarpieces, made up over ten percent of the collection—as well as the number of subjects devoted to the cult of the Virgin Mary, especially in the form of "Madonna and Child" and "Adoration" pieces. Hunt and Rossetti believed that they saw many works by van der Weyden—which have since been reattributed to the Master of the Life of Joseph—just as they thought they had discovered Hugo van der Goes, Marten Heemskerk, Jan Mostaert, and Joachim Patinir. Some erroneously attributed or anonymous paintings have since been identified as the works of "Hell" Bruegel and Quentin Massys, and as copies after the Master of Flémalle and Hieronymus Bosch. Unclear or speculative attribution and dating sometimes confused the young visitors. Thus, on October 18, Rossetti declared that he had admired in Brussels "a few very fine early German pictures, among them a wonderful van Eyck."[23] Unfortunately, I have searched in vain for this "wonderful" picture: neither the museum, private collections, nor public sales have registered a van Eyck that would have been in Brussels in October 1849. Rossetti was possibly referring to *The Adoration of the Shepherds*, then attributed to Hugo van der Goes who was thought to have been Jan van Eyck's pupil.[24]

After Brussels, the next destination was Antwerp. Informed by Ford Madox Brown, Hunt and Rossetti expected to find there "no end of these stunning things."[25] We may presume they were not disappointed because, due to the Chevalier van Ertborn bequest in 1841, the Académie Royale des Beaux-Arts in Antwerp had kept 159 paintings from the thirteenth through the sixteenth centuries (appendix 3). Here again, there were many polyptychs and many religious subjects. The collection included four Italian and three German masters, but naturally the Flemish school predominated with thirty-eight artists. In Antwerp, the Pre-Raphaelites could thus become more familiar with Jan van Eyck, Jean Gossart, Jan Mostaert, Joachim Patinir, Hugo van der Goes, and Rogier van der Weyden.

In Ghent, where Hunt and Rossetti stopped next, the Museum of Fine Arts contained no Primitives. However, the church of Saint Bavon housed the famous *Adoration of the Lamb* altarpiece by the van Eycks, which was to have such an enduring influence on William Holman Hunt.

The Pre-Raphaelites then hurried toward Bruges: that town had a special appeal for them, since their friend Madox Brown had studied there between 1835 and 1839. Renaissance paintings were visible mainly at the Academy and the Hospital of Saint John (appendixes 4 and 5). Hunt and Rossetti visited both places and communicated their enthusiasm to the other members of the Brotherhood in a letter dated October 25: "This is the most stunning place, immeasurably the best we have come to. . . . By far the best of all are the miraculous works of Memling and van Eyck. The former is here in a strength that quite stunned us."[26] Paintings by Memling were a revelation to Dante Gabriel Rossetti: he wrote a sonnet titled "A Virgin and Child, by Hans Memling; in the Academy of Bruges," and was struck speechless by the beauty and feeling of the *Mystic Marriage of St. Catherine* triptych:

> [Memling's] greatest production is a large triptych in the Hospital of St. John, representing in its three compartments: firstly the Decollation of S. John Baptist; secondly, the Mystic Marriage of St. Catherine to the Infant Saviour; and thirdly, the Vision of S. John Evangelist in Patmos. I shall not attempt any description; I assure you that the perfection of character and even drawing, the astounding finish, the glory of colour, and above all the pure religious sentiment and ecstatic poetry of these works, is not to be conceived or described.[27]

On their return to England, the two Pre-Raphaelites felt they had found the masters they were looking for: "We came back with richer minds, but without any change of purpose,"[28] Hunt noted in his memoirs. This quote led some biographers, including G. H. Fleming, to infer that the Continental journey of October 1849 had been of little significance to the artistic evolution of the Pre-Raphaelite Brotherhood. However, if we compare their imaginary museum as it may have been, according to our information, in 1848, and as it had become by the end of the tour, we notice that the number of artists represented had swollen from forty-four to 130 (appendix 6). The Italian masters were still predominant, but a sizeable portion of the additions concerned artists of the Flemish Renaissance. This journey was of momentous significance in that it enabled the young Pre-Raphaelites to confirm their initial, yet half-informed, allegiance to the spirit of Renaissance masters, and encouraged them to rely on the treasures of their newly enriched mental museum for shapes, formats, frames, compositions, techniques, chromatic choices, themes, narrative strategies, and even the occasional identifiable detail for use in their own paintings. More than anything, the Continental experience deepened the Pre-Raphaelites' sympathy for the artists whose affiliation they claimed through their chosen name, and it encouraged them as well to bring the spirit of their predecessors alive, as Rossetti confided in his poem *The Carillon*:

> John Memmeling and John van Eyck
> Hold state at Bruges. In sore shame
> I scanned the works that keep their name.
> The Carillon, which then did strike
> Mine ears, was heard of theirs alike:
> It set me closer unto them.

Appendix 1: Italian Renaissance Pictures Acquired by the Musée du Louvre before 1849

Niccolo dell'Abbate	*Chastity of Scipio*
Mariotto Albertinelli	*Madonna and Child with SS. Jerome & Zenobius*
O. Alfani	*Mystic Marriage of S. Catherine; Visitation*

Andrea del Sarto — *Charity; Madonna and Child with S. Elizabeth, Young S. John & Angels; Madonna and Child with S. Elizabeth & Young S. John*

Fra Angelico — *Coronation of the Virgin*

Fra Bartolommeo — *Noli me Tangere* [attributed in 1848 to Albertinelli]

Fra Bartolommeo — *Annunciation; Mystic Marriage of S. Catherine*

Francesco Bassano — *Jesus Christ walking to Calvary* [attributed in 1848 to J. Bassano]

Jacopo Bassano — *Deposition*

Workshop of J. Bassano — *Hitting the Rock*

G. Bedoli — *Adoration of the Shepherds*

Bernardino dei Conti — *Portrait of a Young Lady* [not attributed in 1848]

Biagio d'Antonio — *Bearing of the Cross* [attributed in 1848 to Ghirlandaio]

Giovanni Boltraffio — *Madonna and Child with SS. John Baptist & Sebastian*

Bonifacio de Pitati — *Holy Family*

School of B. de Pitati — *Raising of Lazarus*

Paris Bordone — *Mythological Couple; Portrait of a Young Lady* (H. Crafft)

Sandro Botticelli — *Madonna and Child with Young S. John*

Francesco Botticini — *Madonna and Child in Glory* [attributed in 1848 to C. Rosselli]

Braccesco — *Annunciation*

Agnolo Bronzino — *Noli me Tangere; Portrait of a Sculptor*

J. Cacar — *Portrait of M. von Branweiler*

Cariani — *Madonna and Child with S. Sebastian* [attributed in 1848 to the School of G. Bellini]; *Portrait of Two Men*

Cima da Conegliano — *Madonna and Child with S. John Baptist & S. Magdalene*

Cimabue — *Madonna and Child with Six Angels*

Antonio Correggio — *Mystic Marriage of S. Catherine; Venus, Satyr & Cupid*

Lorenzo Costa — *Allegory of the Court of Isabelle d'Este; Reign of Comus*

Dosso Dossi — *Portrait of a Man* [attributed in 1848 to Piombo]

B. Fasolo	*Madonna and Child Enthroned*
L. Fasolo	*Family of the Virgin Mary*
F. Franciabigio	*Portrait of a Man*
B. Garofalo	*Circumcision; Madonna and Child with SS. Joseph & Elizabeth; Sleeping Infant Jesus*
B. Gatti "Sojaro"	*Deploration*
Gentile da Fabriano	*Presentation in the Temple*
Ghirlandaio	*Visitation*
Giannicola di Paolo	*Madonna and Child with Four Saints*
Giotto di Bondone	*S. Francis Receiving the Stigmata*
Giolio Romano	*Nativity; Madonna and Child with Young S. John; Triumph of Titus & Vespasian*
Workshop of G. Romano	*Venus & Vulcan*
Benozzo Gozzoli	*Triumph of S. Thomas Aquinas*
Leonardo da Vinci	*S. John Baptist; Madonna and Child with S. Anne; Virgin of the Rocks; Portrait of a Lady; Mona Lisa; Bacchus*
Filippo Lippi	*Coronation of the Virgin* [attributed in 1848 to Piero di Cosimo]
Lorenzo di Credi	*Madonna and Child with SS. Julian & Nicholas*
Lorenzo Monaco	*Herod's Banquet/Crucifixion/S. James* [attributed in 1848 to Gaddi]
Lorenzo Lotto	*Christ and the Adulterous Woman; Adoration of the Infant Christ*
Bernardino Luini	*Holy Family; Sleeping Infant Jesus; Salome with the Head of S. John Baptist*
Andrea Mantegna	*Calvary; Madonna and Child with Six Saints; Mars & Venus; Minerve Chasing Vice from the Garden of Virtue*
Marco da Oggiono	*Holy Family with SS. Elizabeth, Joachim & John Baptist*
Francesco Marmitta	*Madonna and Child with SS. Benedict & Quentin* [attributed in 1848 to F. Bianchi]
Simone Martini	*Bearing of the Cross*
Ludovico Mazzolino	*Holy Family with Holy Trinity*
Alessandro Moretto	*SS. Bernardin of Sienna & Louis of Toulouse; SS. Bonaventure & Anthony of Padua*
Niccolo da Foligno	*Two Angels Bearing a Scroll/Christ on the Mount of Olives/Bearing of the Cross/ Crucifixion/Joseph of Arimathea with Nicodeme*

Antonio Palma	*Madonna and Child with SS. Catherine, Agnes & Young S. John* [attributed in 1848 to B. de Pitati]
Palma Vecchio	*Adoration of the Shepherds*
Francesco Parmigianino	*Portrait of a Young Man* [attributed in 1848 to Raphael]
Parmigianino (copy)	*Madonna and Child with SS. Margaret, Benedict & Jerome*
Perugino	*Madonna and Child with SS. John Baptist & Catherine; A Saint; Fight of Love against Chastity*
Pesellino	*S. Francis Receiving the Stigmata; SS. Cosme & Damian Curing an Invalid*
Polidoro da Caravaggio	*Psyche Received in Olympus*
Polidoro Lanzani	*Holy Family with Young S. John Baptist* [attributed in 1848 to Titian]
Jacopo Pontormo	*Madonna and Child with S. Anne & Four Saints; Portrait of a Jeweller*
Francesco Primaticcio (copy)	*Concert*
Raphael	*Madonna and Child with Young S. John; Madonna of the Veil; Holy Family; S. John Baptist; S. Michael; S. George & the Dragon; S. Michael & the Devil; Balthazar Castiglione; Jeanne d'Aragon; Portrait of the Artist with a Friend*
Workshop of Raphael	*Holy Family; S. Margaret*
Rosso Fiorentino	*Pietà; Challenge of the Pierides*
Lorenzo Sabatini	*Madonna and Child with Young S. John Baptist*
Pier Francesco Sacchi	*The Four Doctors of the Church*
Francesco Salviati	*Incredulity of S. Thomas*
Giovanni Savoldo	*Self-portrait; Bernardo di Salla* [attributed in 1848 only as 16th-century Italian]
Sebastiano del Piombo	*Holy Conversation* [attributed in 1848 to Giorgione]; *Visitation*
Cesare da Sesto	*Madonna and Child with SS. Elizabeth, John & Michael*
Luca Signorelli	*Birth of S. John Baptist*
Andrea Solario	*Crucifixion; Madonna of the Green Cushion; Charles d'Amboise*
Tintoretto	*Susan Bathing*
Titian	*Rural Concert* [attributed in 1848 to Giorgione]; *Madonna & Child with*

	SS. Steven, Jerome & Maurice; Madonna of the Rabbit; Supper at Emmaus; Christ Crowned with Thorns; Entombment; S. Jerome; Venus of the Pardo "Jupiter & Antiope"; François I; Allegory of Alphonse d'Avalos; Portrait of Woman Combing her Hair; Portrait of a Man; Man with a Glove
Workshop of Titian	*Ecce Homo* [attributed in 1848 to Titian]
Turino Vanni	*Madonna and Child with Angels*
Giorgio Vasari	*Annunciation*
Paolo Veronese	*Susannah and the Elders; Swooning Esther; Madonna and Child with SS. Justine & George; Resurrection of Jaire's Daughter; Marriage at Cana; Calvary; Pilgrims at Emmaus; Jupiter Striking Vice; S. Mark Crowning Virtues; Woman with a Child and a Dog*
Workshop of Veronese	*Christ Falling under the Cross; Lot's Family Fleeing Sodom; Holy Family with SS. Elizabeth & Magdalene*
Tommaso Vincidor	*Circumcision* [attributed in 1848 to Bagnacavallo]

APPENDIX 2: RENAISSANCE PICTURES ACQUIRED BY THE MUSÉE ROYAL DE BELGIQUE, BRUSSELS BEFORE 1849[29]

H. Bosch (copy)	*Adoration of the Shepherds* [not attributed in 1848]
A. Bouts	*Assumption of the Virgin; Portrait of a Man, Protected by S. Jacob; Portrait of a Lady, Protected by S. Catherine* [not attributed in 1848]
A. Bouts (copy)	*Head of Christ* [not attributed in 1848]
P. Brueghel II	*Massacre of the Innocents* [not attributed in 1848]
J. van Cleve	*Madonna and Child* [not attributed in 1848]
Workshop of J.van Cleve	*Madonna and Child with S. Bernard* [not attributed in 1848]
P. Coeck	*Adoration of the Kings* [not attributed in 1848]
Workshop of P. Coeck	*Portrait of a Lady with a Carnation* [not attributed in 1848]

J. van Coninxloo	*Holy Family; Marriage Feast at Cana; Christ among the Doctors*
J. van Coninxloo II	*The Broken Sieve* [attributed in 1848 to Jan Mostaert]
Workshop of J. Coninxloo II	*S. Benedict* [not attributed in 1848]
C. de Coter	*Deposition* [attributed in 1848 to J. van Hemmisten]
French School, 16th c.	*Creation of Eve; Sacrifice of Abraham; Adoration of the Kings; Noah and his Family before the Arch; Meeting of Esaü and Jacob; Esaü before his Father* [none attributed in 1848]
German School, 16th c.	*Portrait of Edward, King of England* [not attributed in 1848]
J. van Hillegom	*Two Monks* [not attributed in 1848]
W. Key	*Portrait of a Man; Portrait of a Lady* [not attributed in 1848]
Workshop of W. Key	*Portrait of a Man* [not attributed in 1848]
Q. Massys	*Madonna and Child* [not attributed in 1848]
Workshop of Q. Massys	*Madonna of the Seven Sorrows* [attributed in 1848 to J. Patinir]
M. of the Antwerp Epiphany	*Adoration of the Kings* [attributed in 1848 to J. van Scorel]
M. of the Brussels Epiphany	*Adoration of the Kings* [not attributed in 1848]
M. of Flémalle (copy)	*The Eternal Father; Portrait of Jean Barat; Portrait of his Wife, Jehanne Cambri* [none attributed in 1848]
M. of the Legend of S. Ursula	*Madonna and Child* [attributed in 1848 to J. Gossart]
M. of the Life of Joseph	*Carrying of the Cross; Crucifixion; The Child Virgin Received at the Temple; Christ among the Doctors; Annunciation; Nativity; Adoration of the Kings; Circumcision; Christ entombed; Disciples and Holy Women Departing from the Sepulchre* [all attributed in 1848 to R. van der Weyden]
M. of the Orsoy Altarpiece	*Circumcision* [not attributed in 1848]
Master of 1518	*Christ at the House of Simon the Pharisee* [attributed in 1848 to J. Gossart]
Netherlandish School, 15th c.	*Annunciation* [not attributed in 1848]
Netherlandish School, 16th c.	*Madonna and Child; Madonna and Child; Consecration of S. Gregory; Madonna in*

	Glory; Madonna and Child; Mass at Elevation Time; The Last Supper; Woman Praying; Portrait of Guillaume de Croy [none attrib uted in 1848]; *Life of S. Hubert* [attributed in 1848 to J. Grimner]; *The Saviour Falling under the Weight of the Cross* [attributed in 1848 to M. Heemskerk]
Northern French School	*Christ of the Column/Resurrection* [not attributed in 1848]
A. van Noort	*Christ Calling the Little Children* [not attributed in 1848]
L. van Noort	*Adoration of the Shepherds*
B. van Orley	*Dead Christ with Saints*
B. van Orley (copy)	*Adoration of the Kings* [attributed in 1848 to J. Swart]; *Deposition* [attributed in 1848 to L. van Noort]
Workshop of B. van Orley	*Adoration of the Shepherds* [attributed in 1848 to H. van der Goes]; *Holy Family* [attributed in 1848 to B. van Orley]; *Christ Taken Down from the Cross* [attributed in 1848 to Pieter Cock]
J. Rillaert II	*Birth of S. John Baptist; Death of a Holy Priest* [both attributed in 1848 to J. van Coninxloo]; *Consecration of S. Gregory* [not attributed in 1848]
Spanish School, 16th c.	*Portrait of Mary, Queen of England* [not attributed in 1848]
J. C. Vermeyen	*Warrior and his Family* [not attributed in 1848]
W. W. van der Vliet	*Portrait of a Man* [not attributed in 1848]
G. van der Weyden	*Two Portraits* [not attributed in 1848]
R. van der Weyden (copy)	*Head of Woman in Tears* [attributed in 1848 to R. van der Weyden]
Unknown	*Knight; Head of Christ; Head of the Virgin* [not attributed in 1848]

APPENDIX 3: RENAISSANCE PICTURES ACQUIRED BY THE MUSÉE ROYAL DES BEAUX-ARTS, ANTWERP BEFORE 1849[30]

Jan van Amstel	*Calvary*
A. da Messina	*Virgin and S. John at the Foot of the Cross*

Derick Baegert	*S. Anne and her Descendants*
Joos van der Beke	*Child Jesus* (copy of a Vinci, whereabouts unknown); *Adoration of the Kings* (copy)
Hugo van der Goes	*"Deipara Virgo" Announced by Prophets and Sibyls*
Ambrosius Benson	*Noble Lady*
Bicci di Lorenzo	*S. Paul/S. Nicholas* (pair)
Albrecht Bouts	*Adoration of the Shepherds; Holy Face; Portrait of a Canon; Holy Family of the Seraph*
Dierick Bouts	*Madonna and Child*
Dierick Bouts (copy)	*S. Leonard Freeing the Prisoners; Translation of the Body of S. Hubert*
Ch.van den Broeck	*Last Judgement*
Barthel Bruyn	*Portrait of a Gentleman; Portrait of a Young Man; Resurrection; Portrait of a Man/Portrait of a Lady* (diptych)
J. Clouet (the Young)	*Dauphin François*
Hieronymus Cock	*Passion of the Saviour*
M. Coffermans	*Baptism of Christ*
Albrecht Cornelis	*Patrician*
J. Cornelisz	*Madonna and Child with Donors* (triptych); *Portrait of an Old Gentleman*
Corneille de Lyon	*Portrait of a Young Gentleman; Portrait of a Young Man*
M. van Coxcyen	*Martyr of S. Sebastian/Triumph of Christ* (triptych)
Lucas Cranach	*Adam and Eve; Caritas*
Gerard David	*Crucifixion* (side panels of the triptych); *Repose during the Flight into Egypt*
A. Dürer (copy)	*Frederic III*
C. Engebrechtsz	*Before the Crucifixion*
Jan van Eyck	*S. Barbara; Madonna of the Fountain*
Jan van Eyck (copy)	*Madonna with SS. George and Donatian*
C. F. von Creuznach	*Portrait of a Lady*
F. Floris de Vriendt	*The Fall of the Angels* (central panel of a triptych); *Adoration of the Shepherds; S. Luke; Judgement of Salomon*
Jean Fouquet	*Madonna and Child* (central panel of a triptych)
Jan Gossart	*Ecce Homo; Portrait of a Gentleman; Afflicta Virgo*
C. van Hemessen	*Portrait of a Young Lady*

Hans Holbein II   *Portrait of a Man*
Pieter Huys   *Temptation of S. Anthony* (copy after H.
                                       Bosch)
Lucas van Leyden   *The Betrothal; David and Saul; Holy Family*
                                       (triptych); *SS. Mark, Matthew, Luke* (series
                                       of three paintings)
Master of Flemalle?   *Glorification of the Virgin*
Geertjen tot S. Jans (copy)   *Madonna and Child/S. Christopher/*
                                       S. George (diptych)
Master of Frankfurt   *Carrying of the Cross; Adoration of the*
                                       Shepherds (triptych; copy after H. van der
                                       Goes)
Simone Memmi   *Angel of the Annunciation/Virgin of the*
                                       Annunciation; Crucifixion with Spear;
                                       Deposition
Hans Memling   *Portrait of J. de Candida; Portrait of a*
                                       Canon from the Order of S. Norbert
Jan Massys   *Hospitality Refused to the Virgin and*
                                       S. Joseph; Cure of Tobias; Young Courtesan
Quentin Massys   *S. Christopher; Salvator Mundi/Adoring*
                                       Madonna (diptych); *Magdalene;*
                                       Entombment of Christ/Decollation of S. John
                                       Baptist/S. John Evangelist in Boiling Oil
                                       (triptych); *Pietà*
Jan Mostart   *Sibyl predicting the Birth of Christ to*
                                       Emperor Augustus
Lambert van Noort   *Sibyl with the Church of Christ; Sibyl*
                                       Agrippine; Sibyl of Hellespont; Sibyl of
                                       Delphes; Sibyl of the Spear and Sponge;
                                       Sibyl of the Column; Sibyl of the Chalice;
                                       Nativity; Christ washing Peter's Feet; Last
                                       Supper; Christ of the Mount of Olives; Christ
                                       of the Crown of Thorns; Carrying of the
                                       Cross; Calvary; Entombment; Resurrection
Bernard van Orley   *Margaret of Austria; Seven Sorrows of the*
                                       Virgin (part of a triptych); *Carrying of the*
                                       Cross (panel of a lost triptych); *Last*
                                       Judgement/Seven Works of Pity (triptych)
Joachim Patinir   *Landscape: Flight into Egypt*
Pierre Pourbus van Reymerswael   *Portrait of Gabriel Cambry*
                                       The Accountants; Conversion of S. Matthew
                                       (copy); *Portrait of a Banker and his Wife*
Jan Swart   *Adoration of the Kings*
Titian   *Bishop Jacob Pesaro Presented to S. Peter*

Marten de Vos	*Crucifixion; Triumph of Christ/Baptism of Constantine/Emperor Constantine Ordering the Building of a Church* (triptych "Serment de l'Arbalète"); *Incredulity of S. Thomas/ Baptism of Christ/Decollation of S. John Baptist* (triptych "des pelletiers"); *Nativity; Cesar's Pence/The Tribute/The Widow's Mite* (triptych "des Monnayeurs"); *S. Luke Painting the Virgin; Apparition of S. Luke in the Church of Our Lady of Tripoli in Antioch; Old Man Giving Alms to Three Pilgrims; Temptation of S. Anthony* (central panel of a triptych)
R.van der Weyden	*Philip of Croy; The Seven Sacraments* (triptych); *Annunciation; Portrait of Lefebvre de Saint-Remy* (copy)
Workshop of van der Weyden	*Philip the Good*
Unknown	*Calvary of Hendrik van Rijn; Coronation of the Virgin; S. Leonard; Madonna; Portrait of Jean sans Peur; Donor with his Patron, S. Simon of Cana; Donor with his Patron, S. Jerome; Madonna and Child/Donors* (diptych); *double diptych: recto Madonna/Donor, verso Salvator Mundi; Benediction; Ecce Homo; Portrait of a Young Man; Portraits of Abbot Robert le Clerc; Calvary; Madonna; Legend of S. Christopher; Ecce Homo; Seven Sorrows of the Virgin* (series); *Portrait of a Man; Madonna and Child: Holy Woman Praying; Mater Dolorosa; Madonna and Child; Crucifixion with Donors; Holy Family; William of Orange*

APPENDIX 4: RENAISSANCE PICTURES ACQUIRED BY THE ACADÉMIE DES BEAUX-ARTS, BRUGES BEFORE 1849[31]

Lancelot Blondeel	*S. Luke Painting the Madonna & Child; Legend of S. George*
Anthony Claeissins	*Banquet at the House of Esther*
P. Claeissins the Younger	*Tournai Convention*

Gerard David	*Baptism of Christ* (triptych). *Judgement of Cambyse/Flaying of the Judge* (pair)
Workshop of G. David	*Prophet Elie/Widow of Sarepta* (pair)
Hans Memling	*SS. Christopher, Maur and Gilles* (triptych)
Pieter Pourbus	*Portraits of Jean Fernaguut/Adrienne de Buc* (pair); *Last Judgement; Crucifixion* (triptych); *Resurrection; Adoration of the Shepherds; Annunciation; Circumcision*
Jean Provoost	*Last Judgement*
Workshop of Provoost	*Donors with SS. Nicholas and Godelieve* (panels of a triptych)
J. Provoost/Q. Massys	*Miser and the Death* (diptych)
Jan van Eyck	*Madonna and Donor; Portrait of the Artist's Wife*
Hugo van der Goes	*Death of the Virgin* [attributed in 1848 to Jan van Scorel]
Workshop of H. van der Goes	*S. John Writing the Apocalypse*
Unknown	*Legend of S. George* (polyptych); *Christ as Judge; Adoration of the Kings; Vocation of S. Peter/Bleeding Woman; Life of S. Roch; Madonna & Child; Madonna & Child with S. John Baptist; Adoration of the Shepherds/Adoration of the Kings* (diptych; verso: Prophet/Widow)

APPENDIX 5: RENAISSANCE PICTURES ACQUIRED BY THE HOSPITAL OF SAINT JOHN IN BRUGES BEFORE 1849

D. Bouts (copy)	*Christ at the House of Simon*
H. van der Goes (copy)	*Deposition*
Hans Memling	*Madonna/M. van Nieuwenhove* (diptych); *Mystic Marriage of S. Catherine* (polyptych); *Deploration* (triptych); *Adoration of the Kings; Shrine of S. Ursula; Portrait of a Lady: Sibyl Sambeth*
J. Provoost	*Bearing the Cross/Portrait of a Friar*
R. van der Weyden (copy)	*Deposition*
Unknown	*Trinity* (triptych)

APPENDIX 6: HUNT AND ROSSETTI'S MENTAL MUSEUM, NOVEMBER 1849, OLD MASTERS SECTION.

German	*Italian*	*Flemish*
	Cimabue (1240–1302)	
	Giotto (1266–1336)	
	Laurati (Lorenzetti) (1280?–1348)	
	S. Memmi (Martini) (1285–1344)	
	Buffalmacco (act. c. 1340–51)	
	Orcagna (act. 1343–68)	
	A. Gaddi (1346–96)	
	Spinello (act. 1373–1410)	
	Gentile da Fabriano (1370–1427)	
	Bicci di Lorenzo (c. 1373–1452)	
	T. Vanni (1380–1416)	
	Donatello (1386–1466)	
	Fra Angelico (1387–1455)	
	Paolo Ucello (1397–1475)	
	Domenico Veneziano (1400?–61)	R. van der Weyden (1400?–64)
	Masaccio (1401–28)	
	Fra Filippo Lippi (1406?–69)	
	B. Gozzoli (1420–97)	D. Bouts (c. 1415–75)
	F. Pesello (1422–57)	J. Fouquet (c. 1415–c. 80)
	G. Bellini (1426–1516)	J. van Eyck (?–1441)
	A. da Messina (c. 1430–c. 79)	H. Memling (c. 1433–94)
	A. Mantegna (1431–1506)	
	Signorelli (1441–1523)	
	Perugino (1445–1523)	
	Botticelli (1447–1510)	
	Ghirlandaio (1449–94)	
	G. Rizzi (c. 1520)	
M. Schongauer (c. 1450–91)	Francia (1450–1518)	
Hans Holbein I (c. 1465–1524)	Leonardo da Vinci (1452–1519)	H. van der Goes (c. 1450–82)

APPENDIX 6: *Continued*

German	Italian	Flemish
A. Dürer (1471–1528) (c. 1455–1549)	Carpaccio (1455–1525)	A. Bouts
Lucas Cranach I (1472–1553)	L. di Credi (1458–1537)	D. Baegert (act. 1476–1515)
Hans Burgkmaier (1473–1531)	Braccesco (act. 1478–1501) N. da Fologno (?–1502) Solario (1460–1520)	Geertgen (c. 1460–90) G. David (c. 1460–1523)
A. Altdorfer (c. 1480–1538)	Cima da Conegliano (1460–1517?) Lorenzo Costa (1460?–1535) G. A. Boltraffio (1467–1516) M. da Oggiono (1470–c. 1540) Albertinelli (1474–1515) Fra Bartolommeo (1475–1517) Michelangelo (1475–1564) Giorgione (1477?–1510)	Q. Massys (c. 1460–1530) J. van der Beke (c. 1464–1540) J. Provoost (c. 1465–1528) C. Engebrechtsz (1468–1553) J. Cornelisz (c. 1470–c. 1533) J. Patinir (c. 1475–1524) J. Clouet II (c. 1475–c. 1540)
	Titian (1477–1576)	J. Mostart (c. 1475–c. 1555)
	L.Mazzolino (c. 1480–1528) Lorenzo Lotto (1480?–1556) Palma Vecchio (1480–1528) B. Garofalo (1481–1559) Lo Spagna (?–1532?) Raphael (1483–1520)	J. Gossart (c. 1480–c. 1535)
Hans Baldung (c. 1484–1545)	G. di Paolo (1484–1544)	
Urs Graf (1485–1527)	P.F. Sacchi (1485–1528) Piombo (1485–1547) Cariani (1485?–1547?) A. del Sarto (1486–1531) B. de Pitati (1487–1553) Luini (act. 1507–47) Correggio (1489–1534)	

Appendix 6: *Continued*

German	Italian	Flemish
	Fasolo B. (1489–1526?)	B. van Orley (c. 1492–1542)
	Polidoro da Caravaggio (c. 1490–1543)	B. Bruyn (1493–c. 1555)
	G. Savoldo (act. 1508–48)	
	J. Pontormo (1494–1556)	L. van Leyden (1494–1533)
	B. Gatti (1495–1576)	J. van Scorel (1495–1562)
	Rosso Fiorentino (1496–1540)	L. Blondeel (1496–1561)
Hans Holbein II (c. 1497–1543)	Moretto (Bonvicino) (1498–1555)	M. van Coxcyen (1499–1592)
	Giulio Romano (1499?–1546)	
	Cacar (1499–1546)	
	Bronzino (1503–72)	M. van Reymerswael (c. 1500–?)
	G. Bedoli (c. 1500–c. 1569)	J. van Amstel (c. 1500–c. 1540)
G. Pencz (c. 1500–c. 1550)	P. Bordone (1500–1571)	A. Cornelis (c. 1500–1532)
H.-S. Beham (1500–1550)	Parmigianino (1503–40)	Von Creuznach (c. 1500–c. 1553)
Aldegrever (1502–58)	N. Abate (1509?–71)	J. van Hemessen (c. 1500–c. 1567)
	J. Bassano (c. 1510–92)	J. Massys (c. 1509–75)
	O. Alfani (1510?–83)	H. Cock (c. 1510–70)
	Salviati (1510–63)	P. Pourbus (c. 1510–84)
	G. Vasari (1512–74)	F. de Vriendt (c. 1516–70)
	Tintoretto (1519–94)	A. Benson (1519–c. 50)
	Campi (1522–90?)	A. Mor (1519–75)
	Veronese (1528–88)	P. Huys (c. 1519–c. 81)
		L. van Noort (1520–71)
		Ch. van den Broeck (1524–91)
		C. van Hemessen (c. 1527–?)

NOTES

1. Brown, quoted in Teresa Newman and Ray Watkinson, *Ford Madox Brown and the Pre-Raphaelite Circle* (London: Chatto & Windus, 1991), 25.

2. William Gaunt, *The Pre-Raphaelite Dream* (London: Butler & Tanner Ltd, The Reprint Society Ltd, 1943), 40.

3. Peter and Linda Murray, *Dictionary of Art and Artists* (Harmondsworth: Penguin, 1969), 330.

4. William Holman Hunt, *Pre-Raphaelitism and the Pre-Raphaelite Brotherhood* (London: Macmillan, 1905), 1:52.

5. Robyn Cooper, "The Popularization of Renaissance Art in Victorian England, The Arundel Society," *Art History* 1.3 (1978): 265.

6. Jan Marsh, *The Pre-Raphaelites: Their Lives in Letters and Diaries* (London: Collins & Brown, 1996), 15.

7. Information graciously provided by A. V. Griffiths, Keeper of the Department of Prints and Drawings at the British Museum.

8. Information checked with A. V. Griffiths. Unfortunately the print collection, not being computerized yet, makes it difficult to provide an exhaustive list.

9. For example, J. E. Millais, *Lovers by a Rose Bush* (1848), Birmingham Museum and Art Gallery; W. H. Hunt, *Study for "A Converted British Family Sheltering a Christian Priest from the Persecution of the Druids"* (1849), Johannesburg Art Gallery; and D. G. Rossetti, *Dante Drawing an Angel on the First Anniversary of the Death of Beatrice* (1849), Birmingham Museum and Art Gallery.

10. G. H. Fleming, *Rossetti and the Pre-Raphaelite Brotherhood* (London: Rupert Hart-Davis, 1967), 78–79.

11. Gaunt, 39.

12. The Campo Santo wall paintings reproduced in the book were attributed by Lasinio to Benozzo Gozzoli, Giotto, Spinello Aretino, Simone Memmi, Domenico Veneziano, Pietro Laurati, Buffalmacco and Andrea Orcagna (Fleming, 64n1).

13. For an interesting analysis of fashionable and extensively copied Renaissance masters in the nineteenth century, see Bruno Foucart, *Le Renouveau de la peinture religieuse en France, 1800–1860* (Paris: Arthena, 1987), 95.

14. John Guille Millais, *The Life and Letters of Sir John Everett Millais* (London: Methuen & Co., 1899), 18.

15. Fleming, 34.

16. Diana Holman-Hunt, *My Grandfather, His Wives and Loves* (London: Columbus Books, 1987), 57–58.

17. Many modern art critics attribute this painting to Titian.

18. Oswald Doughty and John Robert Wahl (eds.), *Letters of Dante Gabriel Rossetti* (Oxford: Clarendon Press, 1965), 1:65, 73.

19. "A Dance of Nymphs, by Andrea Mantegna; in the Louvre," *The Germ* 1.4 (May 1850), 181.

20. Doughty and Wahl, 1:65-66, 71.

21. Ibid., 1:75.

22. Ibid., 1:81.

23. Ibid., 1:82.

24. The 1847 catalogue holds that "van der Goes (1366–1427) was born in Bruges, and that he was the pupil of van Eyck." We know now that he was born in Ghent in about 1440, and could not possibly have studied under van Eyck, who died in 1441.

25. Doughty and Wahl, 1:82.

26. Ibid., 1:84.

27. Ibid., 1:84.

28. Fleming, 113.

29. List compiled after the catalogue *Musée Royal de Peinture et de Sculpture de Belgique* (Commission administrative, Bruxelles: Imprimerie de J. Stienon, 1847) and the *Catalogue Inventaire de la Peinture Ancienne* (Musées Royaux des Beaux-Arts de Belgique, Bruxelles: Presses de van Muysewinkel, 1984). I wish to thank Sabine van Sprang, Attachée du Département d'Art Ancien, for her kind assistance.

30. List compiled after the *Catalogue Descriptif, Maîtres Anciens*, A. J. J. Delen, trans. (E. Buschmann-van Rijswijck & G. Gepts-Buysaert, Antwerp: Musée Royal des Beaux-Arts d'Anvers, 1948). Unfortunately, I have been unable to consult archive material that would indicate 1849 attributions.

31. List compiled after E. Hostein and E. I. Strubbe, *Catalogue Illustré du Musée Communal des Beaux-Arts de Bruges*, 2nd ed., trans. F. S. (Bruges: Desclée de Brouwer et Cie, 1935).

Chapter 2

William Holman Hunt, Race, and Orientalism

Francesca Vanke Altman

The word "Orientalism" has acquired two kinds of meanings. As an art historical term it refers to the work of the hybrid group of nineteenth-century European artists who painted on Oriental or exotic themes as a result of their travels and/or aesthetic interests in the Middle East and North Africa. Alternatively, in the last twenty years, "Orientalism" has acquired another meaning, which adds layers of complexity to the use of the word in any context. Edward Said's *Orientalism* uses the term to sum up the way he perceived the relationship between the Western world and the Islamic East to have been structured during the so-called imperial period from the mid-nineteenth century onwards. The West, he considered, reduces this part of the world to a type of discourse, a set of constructs, defining, limiting, and denigrating the Orient as a justification for imperial control and conquest. The Islamic East is seen as the West's ultimate Other, used to contain all the qualities the conquering West did not want to acknowledge in itself. Said uses only written texts to support his theories, although other writers, such as Linda Nochlin in *The Politics of Vision* (1991), have since discussed Saidian Orientalism with reference to Orientalist painters arguing, in agreement with Said, that portrayals of exoticism, barbarism, and sexuality from the point of view of a perceived unassailable superiority formed the primary motives for these artists' work.[1]

The artistic aims and ideals of Pre-Raphaelitism have been well documented and analyzed by many authors, including Leslie Parris, Tim Barringer, and Elizabeth Prettejohn[2] and will therefore not be discussed here, but the Pre-Raphaelites are not usually associated with a special interest in the East as a subject. Influences from the Eastern world impinged on many aspects of Victorian fine and applied arts however, and what Pre-Raphaelite interest there was in the Orient was consistent with the concerns of their times and their movement. Englishness and identity were of abiding importance. They sought to revitalize English art and to find a new, appropriate idiom for religious and historical subjects. The ideas of John Ruskin, one of the movement's earliest high-profile supporters,[3] concerning honesty in art and the absolute necessity for a detailed study of nature were highly influential. As Elizabeth Prettejohn has observed,[4] this passion for "truth-to-nature" realism coexisted with an interest in "primitivism" in terms of the Pre-Raphaelites' admiration for early Italian art.

In fine art, depictions of the Oriental world were confined to subject matter, since during the nineteenth century the canons of Western style and technique, with their emphasis on the figurative and on the naturalistic depiction of form, were not challenged in the same way as the decorative arts by non-European art forms and techniques.[5] There is a suggestion of the occasional influence from Persian miniature painting in some of the works of the genre painter John Frederick Lewis (1805–76)[6] but he, although an older contemporary of the Pre-Raphaelites and discussed by Ruskin in *Pre-Raphaelitism*[7] was not part of the movement, and serious questioning of the supremacy of Western perspective and modes of representation by European painters did not begin to occur until the early twentieth century.[8]

The most common subject associated with traditional European Orientalist painting is that of the voluptuous nude in an interior sumptuously decorated with Oriental fabrics and furniture. This, however, was not a feature of Pre-Raphaelite art. There are no Pre-Raphaelite harem scenes comparable to those of John Frederick Lewis or exotic odalisques like those of contemporary French painters Jean-Auguste-Dominique Ingres (1780–1867) or Jean-Leon Gerome (1824–1904). Of all the Pre-Raphaelites, it was Dante Gabriel Rossetti (1828–82) who painted the most sensual images of women, but his predilection lay more in portraying particular women and not in portraying their surroundings in detail. Apart from his depiction of Jane Morris as the Syrian goddess *Astarte Syriaca* (1875–77, Manchester City Art Galleries) and an occasional incidental use of Japanese pattern,[9] he had no real interest in adopting Orientalist settings and accessories in order to increase the visual appeal or sexuality of his subjects. Especially in the case of the ubiquitous Jane, as Prettejohn has observed,[10] there is always the underlying sense that the image is intended to portray Jane herself, no matter what the title of the picture. Rossetti was simply commenting on what he saw as Jane's divine and mysterious beauty, whether he visualized her as Astarte or as a goddess from any other religious tradition.

However, aspects of other perennial themes of Orientalist painting do appear in Pre-Raphaelite works. The portrayal of ancient monuments and desert landscapes by European artists who had traveled in the East could be potent symbols both of romantic timelessness and the origins of civilization. Within the Pre-Raphaelite movement, it is William Holman Hunt (1827–1910) whose attitudes and works display the most extensive, important, and complex interest in these and other aspects of Orientalism. Hunt made several extended trips to the Middle East and was highly unusual[11] among the Pre-Raphaelites both in his choice to journey to this part of the world, and in his reasons for doing so, although there had been a steady trickle of earlier European artists traveling in the Middle East and North Africa during the first half of the nineteenth century.

A major concern of the mid-nineteenth century was to discover the historical roots of the Bible, in order to counteract the scientific and evolutionary upheavals that were shaking the roots of faith and, as many people thought, undermining the primacy of Christianity. It was in a spirit of truth-seeking that Hunt went to the Holy Land and to Egypt, his idea being to paint directly from nature religious scenes located in the actual places where the original events had occurred: to gain, as he said later,

> a larger idea of the principles of design in creation which should affect all art. I was . . . pursuing in my chosen region the principles which my fellows and I had agreed upon, and which they were to follow in their own way at home.[12]

His approach took Ruskin's exhortation to artists to "go directly to nature" to its extreme.[13] Hunt famously summed up his Pre-Raphaelite aims in his account of the Brotherhood: "It is simply fuller Nature we want. Revivalism, whether it be of classicism or mediaevalism, is a seeking after dry bones."[14]

For Holman Hunt, the East represented this fullness of nature. Leslie Parris has described Hunt's artistic style as a kind of "symbolic realism" inspired by Ruskin,[15] implying that every detail in a painting had a meaning. The Middle East epitomized both symbolism and reality as no other part of the world could. It combined the aims of newness, realism, tradition, and historical verisimilitude.

Despite the perception in Britain during the nineteenth century of the Oriental world as racially inferior, other, more contradictory ideas were in operation at the same time. The Islamic East was seen in some contexts as a site of primitive barbarism but in others as an original fount of inspiration and authenticity, particularly in the context of the arts. It was seen as a world in which beautiful objects were made by craftsmen who possessed more skill than most Western artists saw themselves as able to equal. This contradicts the idea that a consciousness of racial superiority was the West's standard or only response to the Eastern world, or that the concept of the Eastern world as the West's "Other" was necessarily clear-cut. As the nineteenth century continued and Britain became increasingly imperialistic in its outlook, there was considerable ambivalence among those involved with the arts over the advantages of "progress."[16]

Similarly, during the nineteenth century, it was widely held as fact by many in Britain and Europe that the Oriental world was in some inexplicable way a living embodiment of the past in the present. This view is seen in various theories of civilization put forward by Georg Friedrich Hegel (1770–1831) in *The Philosophy of History*,[17] in the ideas of pre-Darwinian ethnologists such as Scotsman Robert Knox (1792–1862),[18] and in the later developments of "social Darwinist" thinkers like Henry Maine (1822–88).[19] Thinkers like these considered the Eastern world either to dislike "progress," as the West defined the term, to be racially incapable of achieving it and to live entirely according to ancient tradition, or, as Hegel expressed it, to believe that the "moment" of Oriental civilization had occurred in the distant past and so had handed on the torch of civilization and knowledge to Europe and "vanished from the stage of history at large."[20] These views, although inclining Western peoples toward racial prejudice, conversely also meant that, for those who, like Hunt, sought to get as near to historical truth as possible, studying the Eastern world was considered the best possible means of achieving this aim.

Hunt's letters and diaries from his journeys provide the greatest insights into his views on the Eastern world, although the historians who have analyzed these have been sharply polarized in their interpretations of the meanings and motives behind Hunt's travels and opinions on the East. Marcia Pointon's essay "The Artist as Ethnographer: Holman Hunt and the Holy Land" in *Pre-Raphaelites Re-viewed* (1989)[21] treats Hunt's Eastern journeys in the greatest detail. Taking a Saidian line, she concludes that the artist was "profoundly racist"[22] in his attitudes, noting Hunt's lack of understanding and empathy with the Arabs and Jews he encountered in Palestine and Egypt. She notes his many angry tirades against the native inhabitants, particularly the Arabs whom he encountered on his first visit in 1854–56, with whom, he said, it was "impossible

to have dealings without losing one's temper."[23] She views these comments
as purely racially motivated, a result of his consciousness of superiority
as an Englishman and a potential colonizer among savages. Another contemporary art historian, Julie Codell, in *Re-Forming the Pre-Raphaelites*,
espouses a similar view, considering Hunt obsessed with racial difference.[24]
Tim Barringer, who also discusses Hunt's Eastern journeys in *Reading the
Pre-Raphaelites*,[25] suggests that Hunt's aggressive Englishness could be
allied to his attempts in his religious paintings to reject decadent traditions, whether these were of Judaism, Islam, or Catholicism, and formulate an art of pure Protestantism.

The truth of Hunt's intense interest in the Middle East lies in viewing it neither as purely apolitically Romantic and historical, nor in seeing
his motives as blatantly and simplistically Orientalist in the Saidian
sense of the word. Barringer is correct to argue that religious identity and
truth were of the profoundest importance to Hunt, although his beliefs
were far less fixed, and more complex and personal, than Barringer allows
for. His diaries and letters suggest that his cast of mind was very literal in
many ways, not only in his youth but throughout his life: he wanted to
paint nothing but what could be proved as scientific or historical fact. In
a fragmentary letter to an anonymous recipient in 1872,[26] Hunt discusses
his ambitious canvas *The Finding of the Saviour in the Temple* (1854–60,
Birmingham Museum and Art Gallery: Figure 2.1), a scene from Luke's
gospel depicting the young Christ being found by Mary and Joseph disputing with the Rabbis in the temple in Jerusalem, and a later picture *The
Shadow of Death* (1870–73, Manchester City Art Galleries), which portrays Jesus and Mary in the carpenter's shop, symbolically prefiguring the
Crucifixion. He considers them

> strictly . . . *historic* with not a single fact of any kind . . . of a supernatural
> nature, and in this I contend it is different from all previous work in reli-
> gious art . . . I have painted nothing . . . . that belongs to a region of fact I
> cannot be sure of. My faith goes far beyond this but so far I have not felt
> justified in teaching more than I know.[27]

This level of literalism was not shared by all the Pre-Raphaelites, despite
their attention to the realistic depiction of natural detail, but such obsessive searching for precise fact was a pronounced and abiding feature of
Hunt's personality. He saw visiting the East both as a means of getting as
close as possible to this truth and as reassuring himself that he had succeeded in doing so. Many of his fellows chose to depict biblical scenes,

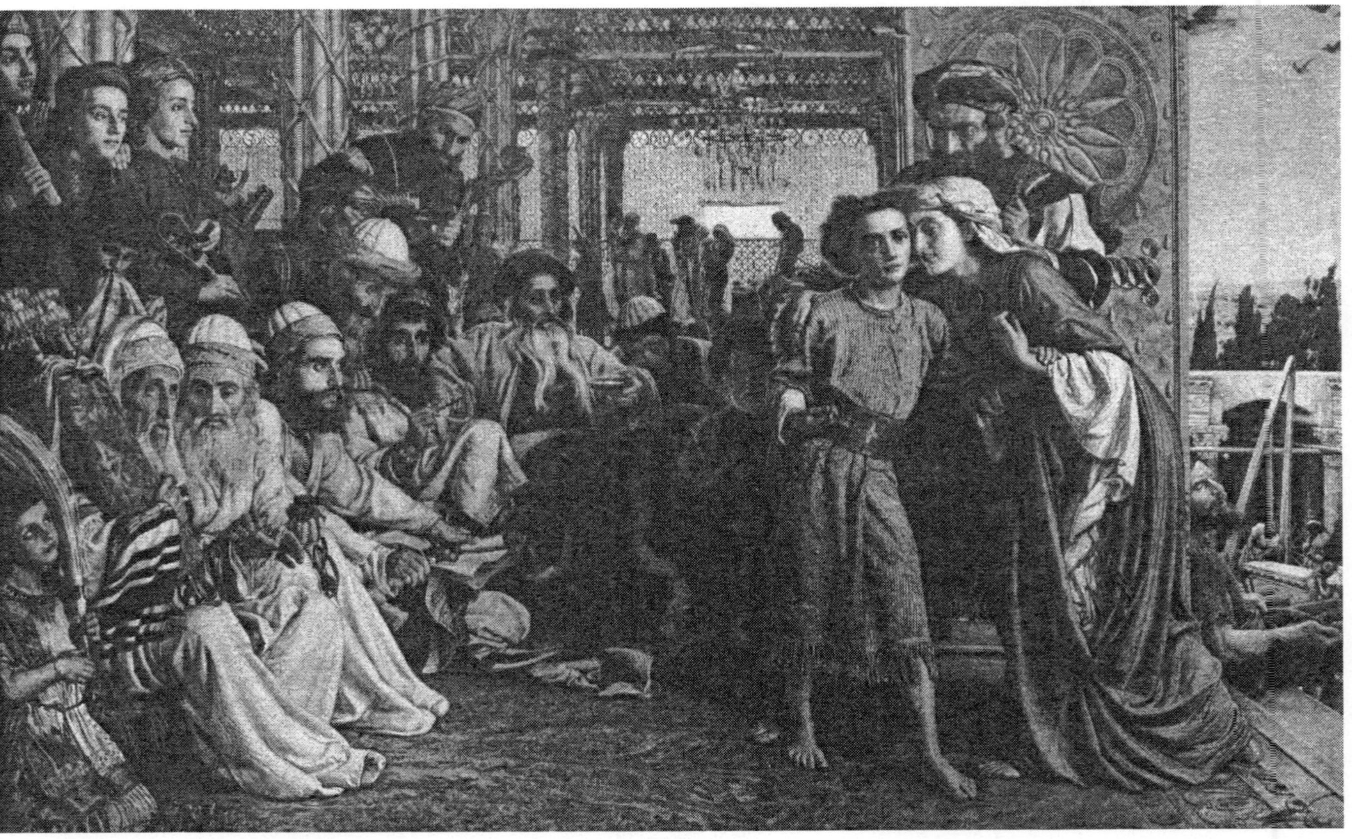

Figure 2.1. William Holman Hunt, *The Finding of the Saviour in the Temple* (1854–60). From W. H. Hunt, *Pre-Raphaelitism and the Pre-Raphaelite Brotherhood*, 2 vols. (New York: Macmillan, 1905), 2:176.

such as Rossetti's *The Beloved* (1865–66, Tate Gallery, London)[28] and Ford Madox Brown's *The Coat of Many Colours* (1864–66, Walker Art Gallery, Liverpool), but only Hunt felt the need to go to the East in person in order to do this. A more typical attitude was that of Brown, who, as Parris has noted,[29] was concerned to get all the correct contextual details when painting *The Coat of Many Colours*, but took the approach of the more traditional history painter and was content to copy accessories and background landscapes secondhand from books and watercolors. Edward Burne-Jones, much later, commented in his memoirs that he did not think that accuracy of accessories should be overemphasized. Concerning another artist's portrayal of the Virgin Mary in authentic costume, he said:

> I am not to be put off with turban and burnous . . . it is not enough . . . I've no dislike of Arab dress in itself, and it is probably not unlike what was worn at the time . . . but it's no use trying to put me off with it in place of the subject.[30]

For Hunt, however, all these details were intrinsic parts of the subject, and part of the absolute truth he sought, and he went to the utmost painstaking lengths to ensure accuracy in every possible aspect. He asked Thomas Seddon to obtain textiles for him in Cairo,[31] elicited the help of Jewish acquaintances in Britain to supply him with details of Rabbinic dress[32] and read the Talmud to find the correct kind of wool to paint around the temples of the goat in *The Scapegoat* (1854–55, Lady Lever Art Gallery, Port Sunlight).[33] The long and involved explanation he published to accompany *The Finding of the Saviour in the Temple* (now in the Birmingham City Museum and Art Gallery, hanging with the painting itself) includes a key to all the items in the picture, noting where he had copied ornamentation from the synagogue in Jerusalem, a sistrum from the British Museum, or a harp from an Assyrian sculpture.

Hunt overcame extreme practical difficulties in painting both *The Scapegoat* and *The Finding of the Saviour in the Temple* during his first visit to the East. He took considerable risks to carry a goat to the Dead Sea through land inhabited by hostile tribes in order to paint in the most authentic location possible. His determination to use only Jewish models for *The Finding* meant that in Jerusalem he had a great deal of trouble obtaining sitters. This was partly because, at the time, the Jews and Christian missionaries were engaged in serious disputes in Jerusalem and partly because, not surprisingly, there was good deal of local suspicion concerning the motives of a Christian artist. Hunt showed no cultural understanding or tolerance of the norms of the society he was working in, only annoyance at not getting exactly what he wanted and anger at (as he saw it) the slowness and stupidity of his Arab servants to carry out his wishes.[34] Pointon has seen this as part of his all-inclusive sense of racial superiority,[35] but although he clearly had the undoubted cultural arrogance and ethnocentricity of the typical traveling Englishman of his time, one could also argue that the issue is more complex. There were two distinct sides to Hunt's personality, outspoken arrogance and spiritual insecurity, and his determination to visit the East, and his behavior when he got there, encapsulated both sides.

It is clear that Hunt was impatient and driven, and his potential for high-handed rudeness and tactlessness when expressing his opinions differed little, no matter what the subject of his annoyance or to whom his pronouncements were addressed. An apposite passage from Ford Madox Brown's diary illustrates this point. Thomas Seddon had spoken to Brown of Hunt's behavior while they were traveling together in the East:

> Hunt used to . . . lecture him [Seddon] and get mighty sulky if things did not go right—and tell him secrets of great worth for his getting on in the world, and expect him to do all the housekeeping . . . and indulge in many whims incompatible with the locality and circumstances.[36]

This indicates that Hunt was not above laying down the law in just as arrogant a manner to his English companions as to the Arabs and Jews he encountered. In other words, race was not the trigger for this particular feature of his character. At the same time, the less unattractive side of this trait was that he was fearlessly outspoken concerning what he saw as injustice or immorality, wherever he encountered it. Neither Pointon, Barringer, nor Codell emphasize sufficiently the implications of his many disputes with the Christian community in Jerusalem. He soon made himself highly unpopular with the missionaries because he felt that they were complacent and gave themselves airs. "I think," he noted in his diary, "that they might do their work with less chance of being misunderstood were they to imitate the poor apostles more [closely.] . . . Assuredly, Christianity can be but little served by such [behavior.]"[37]

More distasteful still to Hunt was the corruption, hypocrisy, and moral laxity he saw among some of the missionary community, particularly a certain Bishop Gobat. A full account of the artist's dealings with this individual is given in Anne Clark Amor's *William Holman Hunt: The True Pre-Raphaelite* (1989),[38] but it is wholly in keeping with Hunt's character that when he wanted to take the Bishop to task about an especially reprehensible aspect of his behavior, he followed him after a church service and confronted him in the vestry. His bludgeon-like approach when he considered himself in the right over any issue was undeniably arrogant in the extreme, but also fearless, even when, as with his dealings with the Bishop, he made life difficult for himself in consequence. He would also make an effort on behalf of his native servants, on occasion. Despite his frequent outbursts of rudeness about their shortcomings, when he reencountered on board ship a Syrian who had worked for him earlier on his journey, Hunt interceded for one of this servant's friends who felt he had been unjustly treated by the ship's captain.[39]

Equally, it is clear that his annoyance with unreliable models was not by any means racially specific, despite his bad-tempered intolerance of his Jewish models in Jerusalem and rage at what he saw as their laziness and unreliability. In a letter to Millais in 1887 concerning painting in Florence, he complains about his Italian models in just as vicious terms as he ever used about Arab or Jewish ones. He considered them "bad dirty idle and lying like all the other people . . . when they do condescend to come to sit they've been so spoilt by the stupid natives or by still more mischievous English amateurs that they'll never sit still a minute."[40] This comment, and especially his use of the phrase "stupid natives" in this context, suggests that he may be applying the phrase as an indiscriminate insult, using it, if anything, more in a "classist" than a racist manner and being more imperious than imperial in his approach, since here he is not in a potentially colonizing situation, but simply frustrated at not achieving what he wanted.

The other side of Hunt's personality and his obsessive search for facts could be viewed as a symptom of considerable insecurity. George P. Landow discusses the varying stages of Hunt's disillusionment with the Christian religious establishment, despite his managing to retain a personal religious faith.[41] The strongest early manifestation of this phenomenon is most revealingly given in a passage in Hunt's Eastern diary of 1855:

I am in a most disturbed state as to religious conviction. I have no faith in any idea approaching to the infallibility of any establishment. I see too much danger in views of this tendency yet I am afraid of trusting to my own most fallible most self-deceiving judgment almost as much so as of white-neckcloth self-complacent logic. I see no way to turn. I pray to God for the truth but all have done so and each become or remained Catholic, Roman, Greek, Protestant, Jew or Moslem and perfectly satisfied in looking on

their neighbours as damned. Are all to teach themselves religion? If I felt
myself strong I would begin a complete study of scriptures resolutely, and
reject any idea that I did not find therein but unfortunately I have no hope
of seeing one system in such a world of matter to be firmer and less assail-
able than any other that might be brought against it by a positive person of
better-ordered memory for his authority than myself.[42]

Writing prior to Pointon, Codell, or Barringer, Landow has seen Hunt as
possessing a more liberal turn of mind than the later historians allow him,
and has commented both on Hunt's "disillusionment" with the Evangeli-
cals after his experiences of missionary life in the East and the fact that
he was in many ways religiously radical.[43] The majority of Landow's articles on Hunt were published before the impact of Said's *Orientalism* was
felt in art history, which may partially account for his taking a less politically led approach. In the *Pre-Raphaelite Review*, Landow plots the
course of Hunt's increasingly unorthodox views on religion, noting that by
1872 he was reaching the conclusion, expressed in a letter to his friend
Jack Tupper, that "I see so many signs that the Church and even Christianity must go to the ground unless some radical changes be made in
it."[44] However, Landow's lack of emphasis on Hunt and race has also
meant that he does not comment on the contradictions in Hunt's attitudes
toward the East, the lack of consistency between his racial tirades and his
free-thinking attitudes toward religion.

This contradiction between religious liberalism and relativism,
combined with the use of such vehement racial insults, is something previous historians have not discussed in detail. Hunt appears on the one
hand to consider himself, as an Englishman, superior to the foreigners he
encounters, while at the same time prepared to acknowledge that the re-
ligions of other races may be as valid as Christianity, and not apparently
to realize any contradiction in holding these two beliefs. However, it is
possible that there is a certain amount of doubt over how seriously he took
his role as an Englishman in the East. On the majority of occasions, he
appears sincerely to believe in his own superiority and his inalienable
right to preferential treatment, as exemplified by his highly unpleasant
manner toward the sheik he met on his first trip.[45] On the other hand,
there are times when there is some suggestion that he might have been
consciously adopting the role of the imperial Englishman in order to get
what he wanted. His remark, for instance, that "I find it is very necessary
to play the 'superior' with Moslems,"[46] may be an expression of contempt
for them, or simply a realization of what he saw as the most efficient way

to achieve what he wanted from them. In another comment, he mentions Arabs "cringing in obedience,"[47] which seems most of all to express sheer amazement over what an Englishman is able to get away with.

Other evidence also suggest that Hunt's ideas on race were neither simple nor static. Despite his assumptions of superiority as an Englishman in the Holy Land, he does not discuss the technical racial terminology being formulated during the 1850s, and, although the Pre-Raphaelites as a whole clearly had an interest in the contemporary concerns of phrenology and physiognomy,[48] Hunt is silent on the subject of Arabs and Jews being of the same Semitic race. It may be that his theories on race and nationality were not clearly defined, despite his readiness to direct racial insults at assorted models, servants, and any foreigners who did not do what he wanted. It may also be that class was an important factor dictating the way he treated any non-Aryans he encountered.

The question of the common ground and/or differences between the ways Arabs and Jews were viewed as Semites in nineteenth-century Britain has been little discussed by contemporary commentators in the context of Orientalism and "Otherness." On his first journey, Hunt discusses both the Arabs and Jews he encounters in similar ways, suggesting that he is eliding the two as Orientals, with little distinction made between them. However, what can be pieced together of Hunt's relations with British Jews after he returned from the Holy Land suggests that he was not anti-Semitic per se and that his attitudes toward race later developed in a similar, unorthodox way to his thoughts on religion.

Hunt's encounters with the Jewish community in London have not yet been fully investigated and are worth exploring, particularly as they add an extra, important dimension to his views on race. Having, not unpredictably, never succeeded in locating either a Jewish or an Arab woman to sit for the Virgin Mary for *The Finding of the Saviour* in the Holy Land, he found a Jewish woman in London to model for the figure: Mary Ada Mocatta (1836–1905), the wife of Frederic Mocatta (1828–1905), a banker, philanthropist, and art patron. This suggests that Hunt's relations with this family must have been at least moderately friendly from an early date. The first mention of his dealings with them occurs in Jerusalem in 1854 when, as he reports in his memoirs, he asked Frederic Mocatta and another prominent British Jew, Sir Moses Montefiore, to intercede for him with the native Jewish community in Jerusalem over the matter of models. He called them his "friendly Hebrew advocates"[49] and commented that Frederic Mocatta's "knowledge of art and artists enabled him to understand my difficulties the better."

It must have been this support for his work in Jerusalem that prompted Hunt to ask Mary Ada Mocatta to model for the Virgin Mary. The family must have been well aware of the nature of the picture, and had clearly allowed themselves to be at some level associated with it afterwards, as Frederic Stephens' *William Holman Hunt and His Works: A Memoir of the Artist's Life* commented on the "lady of the ancient race, distinguished alike for her amiability and beauty"[50] who had modeled for the Virgin.[51] This same memoir also mentions that "this lady's husband" had "friendlily furnished an introduction" to pupils from one of the Jewish schools in London for further potential models. The Mocattas were successful and wealthy, members of the old-established Sephardic family who had founded the major banking house of Mocatta and Goldsmid in England in the late seventeenth century.[52] Financial success in itself would not necessarily have conferred social status in gentile society on Jews at this time, since they were still subject to considerable restrictions and prejudice both officially and unofficially,[53] but Frederic Mocatta was an exceptional individual whose philanthropic and intellectual achievements attained widespread acknowledgment. In 1889, he was commended in an article on "Leading London Jews" in *The Graphic*[54] for his "proverbial . . . generosity and amiability," his "strong literary and artistic tastes," and his "deep and extensive interest in the welfare of the community as a whole." A memoir, edited by his niece Ada Mocatta, published to commemorate his death,[55] details his support for a vast number of both Jewish and gentile charities and educational projects, noting that he was also a Fellow of the Society of Arts, the Royal Geographical Society, and the Palestine Exploration Fund, and that he was the vice-president of the Society of Biblical Archaeology.[56]

These achievements were mostly in the future when Mary Ada Mocatta modeled for Hunt, but there is no reason to believe that any particular social advantage would have been gained or needed by her sitting for an artist who, although well known, was something of an outsider and maverick in the artistic establishment of the 1850s. At the same time, unlike the poorer Jews who had modeled for Hunt in Jerusalem, she would have had no financial need to do so, so that the only remaining reason for her having done Hunt this favor can have been that the family was well disposed toward him. Unfortunately, evidence examined so far has not uncovered any extant direct correspondence between Hunt and the Mocattas. There is none in the Mocatta Collection at the Jewish Studies Library at the University of London, for example, although a reference to *The Finding of the Saviour* may be found in Frederic Mocatta's copy of Francis

Palgrave's *Essays on Art* (1866), which includes an essay on Hunt's painting.[57] This book appears in the catalogue of Mocatta's library published the year before his death.[58]

It may have been this link with one of the most well-known families in British Jewry that prompted the *Jewish Chronicle* to mention *The Finding of the Saviour in the Temple* when the picture first went on show in Bond Street in 1860. The interest expressed by the paper was historical, the anonymous article commenting that "it would be interesting to see how far [Mr. Hunt] has been successful in representing both the habits, usages and garments" of ancient Judaea.[59]

However, Hunt's link with the Mocattas was not confined to Mary Ada's modeling. It is not known how frequent or cordial their association was initially, but thirty years later, in 1887, Hunt's name appears on the committee of the Anglo-Jewish Historical Exhibition, of which Frederic Mocatta was the chairman. Originally conceived by Sir Isidore Spielmann (c. 1854–1905), the purpose of this exhibition (held in the Albert Hall, with subsidiary displays at the British Museum, South Kensington, and the Public Record Office) was given in the catalogue as "to promote knowledge of Anglo-Jewish history, to create deeper interest in its records and relics and to aid in their preservation."[60] Hunt lent two items, listed as a "Hanuca [*sic*] lamp" and a "Tephillin for head."[61] From the *Jewish Chronicle*, which published a special supplement on the exhibition, it is known that Hunt's name is included on the guest list for the "opening soireé, given by Mr Frederic Mocatta," which was attended, among many Jewish guests, "by a number of distinguished Christian visitors."[62]

It is interesting to contemplate how Hunt's membership in this organization fitted with his views on race and religion in general. It is well known that he collected Islamic art, since his name appears on a list of lenders to the Burlington Fine Arts Club Persian and Arab Art Exhibition in 1885.[63] By the 1880s, this was a common pastime among the most aesthetically advanced artists, designers, and patrons of London (the names of Frederic Leighton, William Morris, Alexander Ionides, and Burne-Jones also appear as lenders in this same catalogue), and this fashion is unsurprising given the important role Islamic-influenced design was by that time playing within Aesthetic and Arts and Crafts interiors, and the increasing numbers of Islamic artefacts reaching the major museum collections. However, Hunt is the only member of this circle whose name is also connected with an interest in Jewish historical art, although, if his racial prejudices were as fixed as they might seem, he is the last person one would expect to cultivate an interest in this kind of material. There is

no indication of exactly where, when, and how Hunt acquired his *tephillin*
and Chanukah lamp, although they must have been acquired during one
of his journeys to the East, and it is possible that the *tephillin* is the same
as that which appears in the hand or bound around the head of two of the
seated rabbis in the group in *The Finding of the Saviour in the Temple*.

However arrogant and indiscriminately ethnocentric Hunt's behavior while in the Middle East, he was clearly not viewed as anti-Semitic or
racially prejudiced among London's Jews; had he been so, he would have
been unlikely to have been asked to take part in this exhibition both organized by and primarily aimed at the Jewish community. This was fundamentally different in character from the aforementioned 1885 Persian
and Arab Art Exhibition. This exhibition, though displaying Islamic artefacts and discussing them in an intelligent and scholarly manner with little resort to racial prejudice, was organized by and for the British artistic
elite, with no contact with, nor input from, any individuals from the Islamic world.

There were other Jews besides the Mocattas within the Pre-Raphaelite
circle of acquaintances who were also known to Hunt. Apart from the artist
Simeon Solomon (1840–1905) and his family, there was the art dealer
Murray Marks, whose biography describes him as having been friends with
Millais, Burne-Jones, and Dante Gabriel Rossetti.[64] There was also the international exhibition organizer Isidore Spielmann, to whom a letter from
Hunt's second wife Edith still exists.[65] Though evidence reviewed so far has
not uncovered correspondence between Hunt and the only Jewish painter
among the Pre-Raphaelites, Simeon Solomon, a letter from Hunt to someone
he addresses as "My Dear Solomon" in the early 1850s is most likely to
Abraham (1824–62), Simeon's elder brother and a fellow artist.[66] The tone of
this letter is cordial, admitting "I am ashamed of being ignorant of what
should be a matter of general information," and politely asking to be enlightened over details of various aspects of Jewish religious observance and
dress for a picture he is working on. Although this is unnamed, it must refer
to the *Finding of the Saviour in the Temple*.

It is arguable that, in the 1850s, Hunt might simply have cultivated
the acquaintance of Jews through expediency, in order to gain information
for his pictures. However, by the time of the Anglo-Jewish Historical Exhibition, Hunt was a well-established artist whose name would have been
a prestigious addition to any committee. The organizers of this exhibition
may have been keen to include him for this reason alone, but if Hunt had
had underlying anti-Semitic racial views, he would have had no need to
become involved in an exhibition of this kind.

The most cogent evidence that, in old age, Hunt's ideas had shifted considerably, becoming both more sophisticated and more thoughtful, is provided by his espousal of the cause of the newly developing Zionist movement in the 1890s. The complex issues involved were much debated in the *Jewish Chronicle*,[67] and in 1896, a long letter from "Mr Holman Hunt, the distinguished painter" appeared in this newspaper.[68] Originally a private letter to an "eminent Jew" but sent to the *Jewish Chronicle* for publication a month later,[69] Hunt's letter expressed the strongest possible ideological support for the return of the "sons of Abraham" to the "Patriarchs' chosen home." He suggested that his correspondent, (unnamed in the newspaper but possibly Frederic Mocatta) as a man of "untiring benevolence towards . . . poor Jews" should raise funds for this cause, to which he, Hunt, would also contribute. He was not, he said, merely "pointing out that the work would be in accordance with the promises made by the ancient prophets," but also suggesting resettlement in Palestine for the Jews for practical reasons. Anti-Semitic persecution was active in Europe: the "cruelly-used people" needed a "proper national metropolis and a representative spokesman" and Palestine, at present under the control of the Turks, could easily become a source of contention to be fought over by other European powers, since the Ottoman Empire was politically weak. Hunt suggested negotiating peacefully with the Ottomans for Palestine, and that the Arabs in the Empire would be unlikely to object, because "all Arabs would rejoice at escape from the iniquitous rule of the Turk."

The full text of this letter shows more than a superficial knowledge of the issues of the Zionist debate, and the date of its writing suggests that it was conceived partly in response to the visit to Britain in late 1895 of Theodor Herzl (1860–1904), an Austro-Hungarian journalist, one of the founding fathers of Zionism, and author of a seminal text.[70] Herzl had given talks on his ideas in London, and whether or not Hunt had attended any of these himself, his opinions show a similarity to many of Herzl's own.[71] Hunt's letter provides a great many clues to the more sympathetic side of his character with regard to racial politics. His support for a cause he considered just and noble was forthright, sincere, and idealistically, if romantically, expressed. He emphasizes his own many years' residence in the Middle East and stated he had many intimate friends among "people of your race," both there and in England. He was clearly still aware of what he saw as his duty as an Englishman to speak out against injustice, but expressed this in terms of his country's shortcomings and "sins of omission" in not doing sufficiently to help weaker nations. "I have a sense," he said, "that every Englishman is bound to do his boldest to remedy such evils." Although this still expresses a certain level of cultural arrogance, it is important to note that Hunt does not, as a result, claim special authority or imagine an exalted role for either England or himself in the Zionist cause. He offers to make a financial contribution to any fund that the "leading Jews" in England were to set up, but otherwise opines that there would quite sufficient "enlightened and wide-minded intellect" among the Jews in any new state to "train a second generation in its full number to take possession of the promised land as it was with the due discipline under Moses."

Hunt's views on education as expressed in this letter also provide evidence for the possibility, discussed earlier, that his attitudes to race were greatly affected or modified by his ideas concerning class. He was clearly not a socialist, and one thing he may have had in common with the British Jews he counted among his friends was a belief in the need for the educated elite to improve the working classes. "Jews of refined class in England," he commented, "tell me that their poor brethren are quite unfit to be entrusted with independence; that their ignorance, their bigotry and their habits, contracted under oppression, would make the boon of freedom an evil." He did not cite any racial barriers to educational progress however, but considered this ignorance a merely temporary state of affairs. In "a country in the hands of their own native Princes and appointed teachers" the present condition of the "lower class" would soon be ameliorated. The foundation of such a state would provide an ideal opportunity to create a nation where "the principles of morals and religion should be so perfected that previous systems should seem but the scattered pieces of a puzzle." The editorial comment of the *Jewish Chronicle* on Hunt's letter was that though his vision might be somewhat utopian, his views should provide "abundant food for serious thought" and be read with "respect and sympathy" for his "disinterested and spirited championship" of Israel's cause.[72]

Hunt's attitudes toward race as they appear in his comments on his Oriental journeys must be weighed against his, for his time, enlightened and progressive views on Judaism later in life. It is tempting for contemporary historians who follow Said's ideas of Orientalism to see a metanarrative in all Western dealings with Eastern Others. However, if one looks at empirical evidence, it is more common to find opinions that are neither clear-cut nor straightforward but idiosyncratic in the extreme, although few individuals encompassed views comparable to those of Hunt in both their breadth and contradictory qualities.

It is undeniable that in his major religious work concerning the Holy Land, *The Finding of the Saviour in the Temple*, Hunt was setting up a very definite dichotomy between Christianity and Judaism as the old and new dispensations, and showing the rabbis as belonging to the "old," backward world that refused to accept the truth of Christianity, as Barringer has discussed.[73] Despite his painstaking attempts to aim for absolute accuracy in his depictions of the rabbis in their historical and religious context, there are many inaccuracies and anomalies, from his references in his published notes on the painting to Egyptian and Assyrian artefacts, such as the sistrum held by the standing youth, which do not belong historically in this setting, to elementary errors in Jewish religious observance.[74] The *tephillin*, for example, are worn one on the head, the other on the left arm, during prayer, never during conversation, and in the picture two rabbis are seen wearing, or to be about to put on, what appears to be half a set each, still talking to their companions, while the others do not wear any at all. This would not have happened in reality, neither in biblical times nor at any time subsequently. The other most obvious error is in the appearance of the Torah scroll on the shoulder of the old rabbi in the foreground. Again, this is carried and read only in specific ways, in specific sacred contexts. For comparison, one could contrast Hunt's picture with Simeon Solomon's *Carrying the Scrolls of the Law* (1867, The Whitworth Art Gallery, University of Manchester: Figure 2.2). Seminars to discuss religious texts are an important part of Jewish rabbinical practice, and it is probable that this is what the overall scene is portraying, although if this is the case, the passage being debated is most likely to be that inscribed on the small scroll held by the younger man in the center of the group. A Torah scroll is never, any more than an illuminated Christian Gospel would be, held casually like an ordinary book during discussion, religious or otherwise. In this picture, Hunt, for all his efforts to attain historical truth, produced a hybrid assemblage.

However tempting it is to dismiss Hunt's failures in this context as blatant tokenism, the polarized and simplistic racial and religious approach taken in *The Finding* is undercut and complicated by his later theoretical, religious, and political position. The boundaries between selfhood and Otherness were not uncrossable and rigid. His ideas also belie the notion of the existence of a single Other, suggesting that, for him, there were many, and that he saw himself as holding several sets of ideological allegiances simultaneously. His chief consistent source of cultural arrogance was that he was an Englishman and, as such, held self-

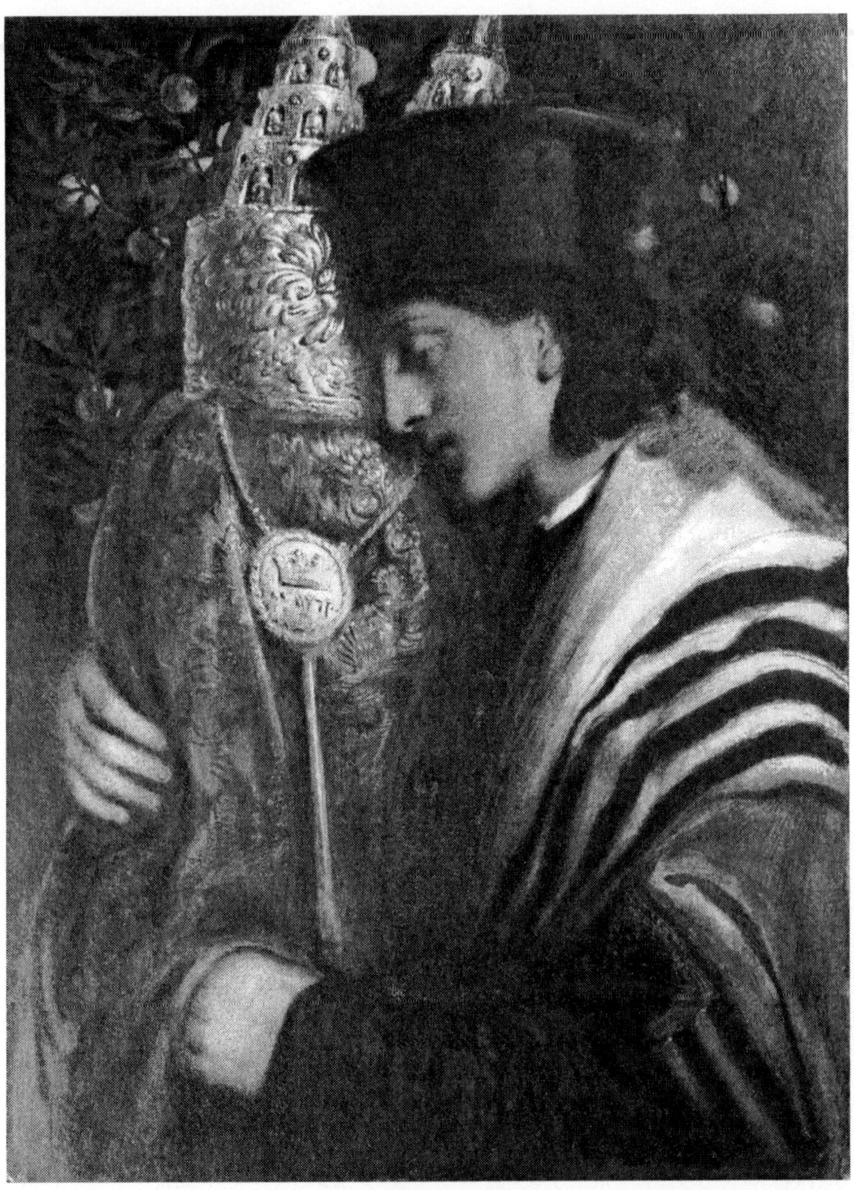

Figure 2.2. Simeon Solomon, *Carrying the Scrolls of the Law* (1867). Used by kind permission of the Whitworth Art Gallery, University of Manchester.

important beliefs about his own role and duties. On the other hand, he did not follow all the stereotypical qualities of Englishness without question. Within the Christian establishment, he was himself an Other, by choice and through possession of a personality that was unable not to impose certain conclusions on himself, as well as on other people, once he had thought them through. He saw the peasant "natives" he encountered in the Holy Land, and elsewhere, as Others, but not the British Jews with whom he clearly sustained some level of friendly relationship for much of his life. In his belief in the absolute justice of a Jewish homeland, and for the education of the lower classes before they could achieve this, he allied himself with the Jewish intellectual elite, who themselves were seen as Others in much mainstream gentile British society. At the same time, by supporting Zionism at all, he was allying himself to a cause considered controversial and radical in the extreme, by Jews and non-Jews alike and so in this way was embracing a different Otherness. The most likely conclusion is that, highly aware of racial differences though he was, Hunt's attitudes were far more dependent on the situation he was in, the individuals he encountered, and the personal relations he formed with these individuals than on any consistent or clearly thought-out racial policy.

It is ironic that Hunt's interpretation of the Pre-Raphaelite principles of truth to nature sincerely attempted to achieve the opposite of what Said accused the Western Orientalists of trying to do: to rely on "representations" of the East, rather than on "truth."[75] Hunt, rather than relying on texts, wanted to go and see it all for himself and record only fact in order to get past opinion and into real, absolute truth. On one level this shows the artist's naïveté and arrogance, though it may also demonstrate the emptiness and ahistoricity of Said's accusation in this context, in applying phenomenological uncertainty to a time when such a concept had yet to be adopted as a cultural construct.

For Holman Hunt, his visits to the Middle East fulfilled vital emotional and artistic needs to search for religious and historical truth and to put this truth to the service of fulfilling the principles of Pre-Raphaelitism as he saw them, which involved, among other aims, creating a British identity for religious and historical art. Despite his arrogance and ethnocentricity and the insecurities in his personality, his genuine belief in religious relativism, Zionism, and his friendly relations with British Jews belie any kind of blanket dismissal of his character as simply "racist." A more constructive view of this artist's attitude toward race is not to attempt to make him fit any preconceived theory, but to allow his many idiosyncrasies their inconsistent complexity.

NOTES

1. Linda Nochlin, *The Politics of Vision* (London: Thames and Hudson, 1991), 33–59.

2. Leslie Parris, ed., *The Pre-Raphaelites* (London: Tate Gallery, 1984); Tim Barringer, *Reading the Pre-Raphaelites* (London: Weidenfeld and Nicolson, 1998); and Elizabeth Prettejohn, *The Art of the Pre-Raphaelites* (London: Tate Gallery, 2000).

3. Expressed in Ruskin's letters to the *London Times* in May 1851, and in his publication *Pre-Raphaelitism* (London: 1851).

4. Prettejohn, 59–60.

5. The lack of identity in English machine-manufactured goods became clear at the Great Exhibition of 1851. On this occasion, unfavorable comparisons were made by the exhibition's organizers and the foremost arbiters of contemporary taste between British goods and those from the Eastern world: from India, Persia, and North Africa. There was a move toward detailed study and imitation of Oriental art objects like those seen at the Exhibition in the hope of improving the design and decoration of British manufactures. In the decorative arts of the later manifestations of Pre-Raphaelitism and the Arts and Crafts movement, there was an extensive and varied Oriental influence, particularly from the Islamic world, discernible in the works of such designers as William Morris (1834–1904) William De Morgan (1839–1917) Lewis F. Day (1845–1910) and Walter Crane (1845–1915).

6. John Sweetman, *The Oriental Obsession* (Cambridge: Cambridge University Press, 1982), 135–36.

7. John Ruskin, *Pre-Raphaelitism* (London: 1851), 29–30. Ruskin's description of the works of Lewis, who lived for ten years in Cairo, suggests that he considered the painter allied to the Pre-Raphaelites through his close observation of the natural world. Ruskin admires Lewis's "perception and refinement" in this area, although he emphasizes that Lewis chose "the comparatively animal life of the Southern and Eastern families of mankind" for his subjects, a practice of which Ruskin later came to disapprove for English artists.

8. See, for example, Fereshteh Daftari, *The Influence of Persian Art on Gauguin, Matisse and Kandinsky* (New York: Garland, 1991).

9. For example, in the background to *The Blue Bower* (1865, Barber Institute of Fine Arts, University of Birmingham) and on the bride's dress in *The Beloved* (1865–66, Tate Gallery).

10. Prettejohn, 205.

11. One of the lesser-known Pre-Raphaelite artists, Thomas Seddon (1821–56), accompanied Hunt to the Middle East on his first journey.

12. William Holman Hunt, *Pre-Raphaelitism and the Pre-Raphaelite Brotherhood*. 2 vols. (London: Macmillan, 1905), 2:75.

13. Ruskin, however, claimed not to understand the motives for Hunt's Eastern travels, doing his best to dissuade him from his first journey, and later disapproving of English artists who painted foreign instead of English scenes. See, for example, Ruskin's *Notes on the Principal Pictures Exhibited in the Rooms of the Royal Academy* (London: George Allen, 1875), 35–36.

14. Hunt, *Pre-Raphaelitism and the Pre-Raphaelite Brotherhood*, 1:87.

15. Parris, 12.

16. These issues are discussed in detail by John MacKenzie in *Orientalism, History, Theory and the Arts* (Manchester: Manchester University Press, 1995) and in my doctoral thesis, *British Cultural and Aesthetic Relationships with Decorative Arts of the Islamic Orient, with Special Reference to Ceramics, 1851–1914* (Open University, 1999).

17. Georg Friedrich Hegel, *The Philosophy of History* (Mainz: 1830). Trans. J Sibree (New York: Dover, 1956), 221.

18. Robert Knox, *The Races of Men* (London: 1850), 599.

19. Henry Maine, *Village Communities in the East and West* (London: John Murray, 1871), 25–28.

20. Hegel, 360.

21. Marcia Pointon, ed., *Pre-Raphaelites Re-viewed* (Manchester: Manchester University Press, 1989), 22–44.

22. Ibid., 30.

23. William Holman Hunt, diary, John Rylands University Library, Manchester (Eng. Ms 1210, 1855), 3.

24. Julie Codell, "The Artist Colonized: Holman Hunt's Bio-History, Masculinity, Nationality and the English School," in *Re-Framing the Pre-Raphaelites: Historical and Theoretical Essays,* ed. Ellen Harding (Aldershot: Scolar, 1996), 211–30.

25. Barringer, 118–33.

26. Letter, William Holman Hunt to unknown recipient, Bodleian Library, Oxford University (Ms. Eng. Lett. C296.195).

27. Ibid.

28. For date and institution see note 10.

29. Parris, 206–7.

30. Edward Burne-Jones, quoted in Georgiana Burne-Jones, ed., *Memorials of Edward Burne-Jones*, 2 vols. (London: Macmillan, 1904), 2:281.

31. John Pollard Seddon, *Memoir and Letters of the Late Thomas Seddon, Artist, by His Brother* (London, 1858), 164.

32. See, for example, Hunt's letter in the National Art Library (MSL.1977/539) ca. 1851, to be discussed below.

33. William Holman Hunt, diary, 1855, 1.

34. Ibid., 3.

35. Pointon, 24.

36. Virginia Surtees, ed. *The Diaries of Ford Madox Brown*, 2 vols. (New Haven, CT: Yale University Press, 1981), 2:117.

37. William Holman Hunt, diary, 1855, 3.

38. Anne Clark Amor, *William Holman Hunt: The True Pre-Raphaelite* (London: Constable, 1989), 134–37.

39. Ibid., 140.

40. Letter, William Holman Hunt to John Everett Millais, April 26, 1887 (JRL, Eng. Ms. 1216.5).

41. For example, in George P. Landow, "William Holman Hunt and the Missionaries," *Pre-Raphaelite Review* 1 (Nov. 1977): 27–33.

42. William Holman Hunt, diary, 1855, 10.

43. Landow, 30.

44. Ibid., 32 (Landow cites the letter from the Huntington Library Ms., Uncat. LF).

45. Hunt, *Pre-Raphaelitism and the Pre-Raphaelite Brotherhood*, 1:466–67.

46. Letter, William Holman Hunt to unknown recipient, undated (JRL, Eng. Ms. 1213, 35).

47. Hunt, *Pre-Raphaelitism and the Pre-Raphaelite Brotherhood*, 1:381.

48. See the cogent article by Stephanie Grilli on "Pre-Raphaelitism and Phrenology" in *Pre-Raphaelite Papers*, ed. Leslie Parris (London: Tate Gallery 1984), 44–60.

49. Hunt, *Pre-Raphaelitism and the Pre-Raphaelite Brotherhood*, 2:16.

50. Frederic Stephens, *William Holman Hunt and His Works: A Memoir of the Artist's Life with Description of His Pictures* (London: 1860), 51.

51. The most likely date for Mary Ada having sat for the picture is 1857, since a finished sketch of the Virgin with Jesus from *The Finding of the Saviour in the Temple*, now in the Walker Art Gallery, Liverpool, was completed in 1858.

52. The majority of the Sephardim in London had migrated from Spain and Portugal via Holland after being readmitted into Britain by Oliver Cromwell from 1656 onwards and formed something of an elite among the Jewish community, compared with the poorer, more recent Ashkenazi immigrants from Eastern Europe. For the foundation of the Mocatta and Goldsmid bank, see Harold Pollins, *Economic History of the Jews in England* (London: Associated University Press, 1982), 56–57.

53. See Israel Finestein, *Jewish Society in Victorian England* (London: Vallentine Mitchell, 1993); and Anne Cowen and Roger Cowen, *Victorian Jews Through British Eyes* (Oxford: Oxford University Press, 1986).

54. "Leading London Jews," *The Graphic* (16 Nov. 1889). Quoted in Anne Cowen and Roger Cowen, 99.

55. Ada Mocatta, ed. *F. D. Mocatta: A Brief Memoir, Lectures and Extracts From Letters* (London: Baines and Scarsbrook, 1911).

56. Ibid., 15–24.

57. Francis Palgrave, "Recent Works by Mr Holman Hunt," in *Essays on Art* (London: 1866), 160–68.

58. Reginald Rye, *Catalogue of the Printed Books and Manuscripts Forming the Library of Frederic David Mocatta, Esq.* (London: Harrison and Sons, 1904).

59. Untitled, unsigned article, *Jewish Chronicle (and Hebrew Observer)* (18 May 1860): 2.

60. *Catalogue of the Anglo-Jewish Historical Exhibition, Royal Albert Hall, 1887* (London, 1887), vii.

61. Ibid., 111, 117. Tephillin, or phylacteries, are two small boxes containing biblical passages written on strips of parchment. Attached to leather straps, they are bound around the head and left arm of the Jewish man during prayer, as a physical reminder of the word of God, and of the wearer's religious duties.

62. Untitled, unsigned article, *Jewish Chronicle (and Hebrew Observer)* (8 April 1887): 1.

63. The first exhibition devoted exclusively to Islamic art in Britain, this was an impressive and important show consisting wholly of loans from the personal

collections of Burlington Fine Arts Club members. The accompanying catalogue included lavish lithographs and a thoughtful historical survey of the state of knowledge of Islamic art at the time. See *An Exhibition of Persian and Arab Art* (London: Burlington Fine Arts Club, 1885).

64. G. C. Williamson, *Murray Marks and His Friends* (London: John Lane, 1919), 164.

65. Letter, Edith Hunt to Isidore Spielmann, dated "Oct. 25," Victoria & Albert Museum, National Art Library (Ms. L 1999/2/1264).

66. NAL Manuscript Collection. For reference see note 29.

67. For discussion of the response of Britain's Jews to early Zionism, see David Cesarani, *The Jewish Chronicle and Anglo-Jewry, 1841–1991* (Cambridge: Cambridge University Press, 1994), 85–88.

68. "Mr Holman Hunt on the Resettlement of Jews in Palestine," *The Jewish Chronicle* (21 Feb. 1896): 8.

69. The letter is dated January 6, 1896. It is unspecified as to whether Hunt himself or the letter's recipient sent it for publication.

70. Theodor Herzl, *Der Judenstaat* (Vienna, 1896).

71. Following Herzl's visit to London, a first draft of *Der Judenstaat* was published as "A Solution of the Jewish Question," *Jewish Chronicle* (17 Jan. 1896): 12–13. Since this was after Hunt's original letter was written, the artist cannot have used this article as the source of his own views, making it more probable that he had attended Herzl's lectures. Although Palestine was not the only land under discussion for a potential Jewish settlement, one of Herzl's ideas was that wealthy Jews should raise funds for bargaining with the Ottomans in order to purchase Palestine. Hunt's comment on fundraising may refer to this point.

72. *Jewish Chronicle* (21 Feb. 1896): 5–6.

73. Barringer, 125–27.

74. I owe thanks to Colin Altman for the detailed information in this section.

75. Edward Said, *Orientalism* (New York: Pantheon, 1978), 21.

Chapter 3

Rossetti's "A Last Confession" and Italian Nationalism

Christopher M. Keirstead

When it was suggested to Dante Gabriel Rossetti that his Risorgimento-inspired "A Last Confession" (1870) bore a strong debt to the dramatic monologues of Robert Browning, he responded, somewhat indignantly, "Browning by travel and cultivation, imported the same sort of thing into English poetry on a much larger scale; but this subject, if any, was my absolute birth-right."[1] Cosmopolitan, multilingual, with an Italian father exiled for politically subversive poetry of his own, Rossetti could indeed assert a unique authority to address an English audience on the subject of Italian politics. Yet Rossetti wrote on it rarely. Further, in his writings on the Risorgimento, the Italian political movement seems less a subject in its own right than a backdrop for more typically Rossettian kinds of concerns, such as the "fallen woman." Indeed, had "A Last Confession" been written by someone without the kind of cultural capital and familial reputation Rossetti cites above, the poem could even be interpreted as a reactionary assault against the Risorgimento, since it features a somewhat stereotypical, mentally unstable revolutionary driven to murder by a combination of patriotic zeal and jealous rage. The poem appears hostile—or at least indifferent—to the politics that form its subject. The fact that most critical commentary on the poem has largely ignored its political dimensions reinforces this impression.[2]

By returning "A Last Confession" to its historical roots and examining it as a political and cultural allegory, I hope to show that to regard the poem as politically indifferent or inept is to miss the unique contribution that Rossetti made to Risorgimento poetry, a subgenre of Victorian verse with which he and the Pre-Raphaelite movement are not readily associated. The poem, in fact, reveals why they are not, for it ruthlessly exploits and ultimately undermines the symbolic capital of mid-century nationalist poetry about Italy. Begun in 1848 amid a surge of British poetic activity on behalf of Italian independence, and later significantly revised in 1869, one year before Italy finally achieved complete unification, the poem occupies two important historical moments, serving first as a critical intervention at mid-century and later as a reflection on the struggle that was then coming to a close. "A Last Confession" questions the prevailing English understanding of Italy, which, despite widespread support for Italy's independence, tended to idealize the country as an apolitical repository of culture—a perpetual tourist destination—rather than as a nation-state in the making. In this way, the poem is Rossetti's own "last confession," his apology for not embracing the politics of nationalism as enthusiastically as other poets had done.

To appreciate Rossetti's motives fully, one must first understand the myth of Italy as it existed in Victorian poetry around 1848. The phrase "myth of Italy" does not imply a one-dimensional set of beliefs to which all Victorian poets adhered. On the contrary, the Risorgimento is remarkable for the variety of artists and the diverse points of view it inspired, from the pained irony of Arthur Hugh Clough in *Amours de Voyage* (1858) to the alternately desperate and millennial faith placed in Italy by Elizabeth Barrett Browning in works such as *Casa Guidi Windows* (1851) and *Poems before Congress* (1860).[3] For most poets, however, and the culture at large, the myth of Italy clustered around a series of recurring tropes and symbols identified by Maura O'Connor in *The Romance of Italy and the English Political Imagination* (1998). In O'Connor's words, to understand what prompted Victorians liberals to invest so heavily in Italy, "[w]e must not separate out the fancy . . . from the facts, because in the minds of English men and women there was no separating the two."[4] The "fancy" she identifies emerged out of the vast body of travel writing, poetry, and fiction focused on Italy. Influential works such as Byron's *Childe Harold's Pilgrimage* (1812–18) and Madame de Staël's *Corinne* (1807) helped to produce the most enduring metaphor of Italy: the image of a feminized realm of the imagination that, according to O'Connor, "possess[ed] a cultural and a spiritual power but lack[ed] the necessary prerequisites to become a modern nation."[5] If Italy had been gendered female—fluctuating between the roles of grieving mother and wronged maiden—then the political movement that would redeem her was invested with the role of the male revolutionary, filled initially by Giuseppe Mazzini and, later, by Giuseppe

Garibaldi. Their popularity in Britain, as O'Connor shows, was thus in part fueled by a combination of middle-class gender ideology and cultural myth-making about Italy.

One of the more illustrative poetic renderings of this myth produced by Rossetti's contemporaries is *The Roman*, a verse-drama published in 1850 by Sydney Dobell of the ill-fated Spasmodic School.[6] *The Roman* tells the story of Vittorio Santo, a clandestine revolutionary who wanders the Roman countryside, in Dobell's words, "to preach the Unity of Italy, the Overthrow of Austrian Domination, and the Restoration of a great Roman Republic."[7] Near the close of the poem, he is charged with treason, but at his trial a riot ensues, led by a band of peasants he has inspired, including a young girl named Francesca. The poem ends with their cries of "Down with the Austrians! Arms! Blood! Charge! Death—death to tyrants. Victory! Freedom!"[8] Ultimately, the poet does not claim for himself the role of leader but instead, the role of instigator—one who senses the greatness of the cause and acts with an almost mystical force in bringing political events to fruition. Indeed, Mazzini, who may have recognized something of himself in Dobell's Santo, or at least his well-worn celebrity image, praised the poet for writing "about Rome as I would, had I been a poet. And what you did write flows from the soul, the all-loving, the all-embracing, the prophet-soul."[9] As Mazzini's remarks imply, *The Roman* was a politically useful means of vindicating the Italian cause in the minds of the British public at a time when it needed reassurance after the downfall of Mazzini's short-lived Roman Republic in 1849. To other contemporary poets, many of whom clung to the belief that poetry could and must have active consequences in the realm of politics, Dobell's success reinforced the impression that versifying the Risorgimento was a dutiful and potentially quite popular undertaking. Indeed, for a poet with Italian ancestry, such as Rossetti, it must have seemed positively odd not to take up the "Italian Question" in one's work.

Against these expectations, Rossetti composes his own ambiguous foray into the arena of Anglo-Italian cultural politics. "A Last Confession" is the death-bed confession of an Italian patriot wounded in an 1848 uprising in Lombardy. The speaker of the poem seeks forgiveness for an earlier crime, the killing of a young woman he suspected of political and sexual betrayal—the truth of either, however, is never made certain. The girl has been the focal point of his life ever since he had saved her from abandonment as a small child, but as she ages and matures, the speaker comes to see her as a potential mate. From this point onward, the poem abounds in confusion over the girl's identity and the motives behind

the speaker's obsession with her; significantly, the girl is never named.
From the opening lines of the poem, Rossetti draws attention to this confusion and to the speaker's tendency to define the girl in terms that match
his sense of what Italy and an Italian should be:

> Our Lombard country-girls along the coast
> Wear daggers in their garters; for they know
> That they might hate another girl to death
> Or meet a German lover. Such a knife
> I bought her, with a hilt of horn and pearl. (1–5)[10]

Rossetti here reveals the ease with which the speaker's subjective desires
are projected onto the girl and onto the larger political cause that con-
sumes him. His phallic choice of a gift for the girl is an attempt to possess
her and to proscribe her behavior. The opening also introduces the contradictions that arise out of the merger of regional, national, and feminine
identity in the speaker's mind: like a woman, Italy must protect her virtue
from outside lovers, but to do so, she must adopt an aggressive, assertive
posture that seems at odds with how the speaker wishes to construct her
later. Ironically, he eventually kills her with the same knife he had bought
for her defense, revealing the contradictory and self-destructive nature of
his nationalist desire.

The speaker equates preserving the girl's identity with recreating an
idealized past, another way that her allegorical connection to Italy, "the
land of all men's past," to quote Barrett Browning's *Aurora Leigh* (1856),
is made evident.[11] He says that

> At places we both knew along the road,
> Some fresh shape of herself as once she was
> Grew present at my side; until it seemed—
> So close they gathered round me—they would all
> Be with me when I reached the spot at last,
> To plead my cause with her against herself
> So changed. (11–17)

His memories of the girl come alive and almost overtake her present self.
The girl, like the nation, becomes a glorified, largely invented construct,
a merger of myth and history. Paradoxically, Italy must be preserved from
change even as it seeks the new identity of statehood—a contradiction
that the French historian Ernest Renan recognized as characteristic of

the nationalist movements that dominated his century: "getting history wrong . . . is an essential factor in the formation of a nation, which is why the progress of historical studies is often dangerous to a nationality."[12] Later, the speaker reveals how his life has always been defined by this illusory backward-looking glance: "Life all past / Is like the sky when the sun sets in it, / Clearest where furthest off" (108–10). Ultimately, he becomes obsessed with returning the girl to childhood and returning Italy to the blessed past of Romantic nationalism.

Making this return difficult, however, is the girl's evolution from child to object of sexual desire in the mind of the speaker. To have one, he must destroy the other, an act from which he never recovers. While she was "still a merry loving child" (143), he makes her a gift of a glass Cupid, but as he assists her in hanging up the figure, it falls and breaks, cutting her hand. Horrified by what he has done, the speaker proclaims, "'That I should be the first to make you bleed, / Who love and love and love you!'" (174–75). This not-so-subtle scene takes on the air of a clumsy, botched first sexual encounter, drawing attention to the confused mixture of desires he has toward the girl. Eventually, he claims, "being always with her, the first love / I had—the father's, brother's love—was changed, / I think, in somewise; like a holy thought / Which is a prayer before one knows of it" (201–4). The last two lines, of course, seem more of an afterthought than a holy thought, as if he suddenly recalls the need to purify his desire with more idealistic terms. Nonetheless, following this scene, the speaker reverts to a highly sexualized description of the girl, and as his love for her assumes physical overtones, so too, it seems, do his politics. He recalls,

> I was a moody comrade to her then,
> For all the love I bore her. Italy,
> The weeping desolate mother, long has claimed
> Her son's strong arms to lean on, and their hands
> To lop the poisonous thicket from her path,
> Cleaving her way to light. And from her need
> Had grown the fashion of my whole poor life
> Which I was proud to yield her, as my father
> Had yielded his. And this had come to be
> A game to play, a love to clasp, a hate
> To wreak, all things together that a man
> Needs for his blood to ripen: till at times
> All else seemed shadows. (252–64)

Rather than preserve the chaste domestic ideology typically projected onto the Italian cause, Rossetti here portrays a dysfunctional family. The speaker's nationalism emerges out of a confused assortment of gender roles, encompassing both a sense of filial duty toward the mother Italy as well as a lover's longing, lending an Oedipal overtone to a desire that already seemed incestuous. With so much invested in the nationalist cause and in the girl, any betrayal is like a loss of identity and being—abandonment by the mother and the lover. The move from nation-as-memory to present-day nation-state is thus allegorically portrayed in the poem as the interference and disruption caused by sexual desire, a fall from the ideal to the real. This transformation foreshadows a later scene that makes the poem's allegorical connection unmistakable.

As part of his 1869 revisions to the poem, Rossetti attempted to clarify when, in the speaker's mind, the "first glimpses came / Of some impenetrable restlessness / Growing in her to make her changed and cold" (369–71). He happens upon the girl in church as she prays to a statue of Mary "wrought / In marble by some great Italian hand / In the great days when she and Italy / Sat on one throne together" (356–59). Such a sight, of course, pleases the speaker, for at this moment the girl is imbued with the kind of timeless perfection he has sought to preserve all along. The girl, the Virgin Mother, and Italy assimilate into one ideal: "They seemed two kindred forms whereby our land / (Whose work still serves the world for miracle) / Made manifest herself in womanhood" (363–65). The scene reveals the kinship of nationalism to the iconographic worship of religion. More specifically, Rossetti links nationalism with the cult of Mary—a somewhat hazy object of male desire that assumes the form of filial devotion but, in the speaker's mind, also becomes vaguely sexual. This ideal image, however, is soon shattered. Returning later to the same church, he finds that the girl has committed an important act of betrayal: "Before some new Madonna gaily decked, / Tinselled and gewgawed, a slight German toy, / I saw her kneel, still praying" (384–86). Two changes have occurred with this transference of devotion: no longer worshipping the Italian Virgin Mother, she now worships an Austrian statue with the overwrought appearance of a prostitute. The Austrian Madonna also seems peculiarly modern—mass-produced and aesthetically inferior to the Italian statue. When asked to explain her action, the girl says, " 'The old Madonna? Aye indeed, / She had my old thoughts,—this one has my new' " (391–92). The scene thus represents not just a personal betrayal, but the move from old to new and, politically, from the nation as myth to the nation as modern reality. Her crime is as much looking toward the future, seeking change and a new identity, as it is treason. The speaker, in fact, never accuses her of a specific sexual betrayal. Rather, her rejection of the old Madonna commences a chain of associations and coincidences that end up driving him to murder: he finally kills the girl when her laugh recalls for him the scornful laughter of a prostitute in the arms of a German lover. Ultimately, he can no longer shape and define her, as her "impenetrable restlessness" at last asserts itself.

The speaker's actions suggest an immediate parallel to one of the most well-known poems of the Victorian period, Browning's "Porphyria's Lover" (1836; revised 1842), where another exacting lover commits murder so that he might preserve that moment when "she was mine, mine, fair, / Perfectly pure and good" (36–37).[13] As Rossetti himself acknowledged, "A Last Confession" begs to be understood in juxtaposition with Browning—not just as a poem about Italy—but as a dramatic monologue, a form obsessed with the question of female subjectivity.[14] Rossetti's reading of Browning may have steered him toward the dramatic monologue for his subject, given that Browning had already probed intersections of nationalism and male sexual desire in "The Italian in England" and "The Englishman in Italy," two companion monologues published in 1845. Of the two, "The Italian in England," spoken by an exiled Italian revolutionary, most resembles "A Last Confession" in theme and subject matter, although Browning's poem seems remarkably optimistic in comparison to Rossetti's. The speaker of "The Italian in England" fondly recalls the assistance he once received from a poor peasant girl, and the memory continues to inspire his political goals: "I think then, I should wish to stand / This evening in that dear, lost land, / Over the sea the thousand miles, / And know if yet that woman smiles / With the calm smile" (145–49). In its idealized form, Browning's Italy often seems to take the shape of an innocent, victimized young girl: notable examples include the street urchin who claims his attention in *Sordello* (1840), the eponymous heroine of *Pippa Passes* (1841), and Pompilia of *The Ring and the Book* (1868–69).[15]

In Rossetti, however, Italy-as-woman is transformed in a way that distinguishes him not only from Browning but from the prevailing tenor of almost all Victorian poetry on Italy: the nation becomes a whore, shorn of purity and innocence. Thus, it is doubtful that Mazzini, had the poem been available to him, would have read "A Last Confession" to inspire his followers, as he claimed to have done with "The Italian in England." But the nation-as-whore refuses to remain passive. As was clear by 1869, when "A Last Confession" took its final shape, Italy had reached a new stage of its struggle. Mazzini had long since been eclipsed by Garibaldi, whose fame was in large part sustained by his willingness to work with the political establishment of northern Italy and sympathetic European countries. The success of Italian unification had clearly depended as much on the shrewd dealmaking practiced by Cavour and Napoleon III as on individual heroics. Nationalism, by 1869 a diplomatic process as much as a military one, was tarnished and—like the German Madonna—increasingly less likely to inspire religious devotion.[16]

Given his aesthete's reputation for tuning out political matters, one might ask how Rossetti developed such a seasoned response to an issue that supposedly did not greatly concern him. The answer may lie in another comment Rossetti made in his efforts to establish the originality of his poem against Browning's. As noted above, he claimed the subject of "A Last Confession" as his "birth-right," adding that the poem was "the simple and genuine result of my having passed my whole boyhood among people just like the speaker in the poem" (*Letters* 3:1233). Similarly, he had described the poem earlier to A. C. Swinburne as "the outcome of the Italian part of me" (*Letters* 2:763). Both comments suggest that "A Last Confession" was Rossetti's attempt to reclaim something that was authentically Italian in him—to recover that part of his identity shaped in boyhood by the dreams and frustrations of the exiled Italian patriots who visited his father on an almost daily basis. Such a quest, however, would be problematic and fraught with anxiety. One the one hand, Rossetti was, by all accounts, committed to the idea of a unified Italian nation as well as to promoting the legacy of Italian culture, even if, on balance, he was not as fervent a patriot as his father. On the other hand, the experience of living with his father may have been what made it difficult for him to participate wholeheartedly in the myth of Italy and to write the kind of Risorgimento poetry that would have been expected of someone with his background and family connections. From his youth, Rossetti seems to have inherited a profound skepticism of political enthusiasm, an awareness that the idealistic rhetoric of nationalism never satisfies and actually can prove quite destructive.[17] William Michael Rossetti suggested as much when he recalled the politically charged household of their youth: "I regard it is more than probable that the perpetual excited and of course one-sided talk about . . . political matters had something to do with the marked alienation from current politics which characterized my brother in his adolescence and adult years."[18] Read closely, William Michael's remarks do not imply that his brother was indifferent to politics but, more precisely, that he could not find a place for himself in its extremes. "A Last Confession," according to its author, was the story of a "savage penalty exacted for a lost ideal."[19] Rossetti could just as easily have made the same remark about the lost Italy of his childhood.

In arriving at a final assessment of Rossetti's attitude toward Italian nationalism, it may be helpful to recall Jerome McGann's comment on the prevalence of religious themes and symbols in his paintings and poetry: "the vision conveyed through Rossetti's work . . . is religious in tone but skeptical in its understanding."[20] As much can be said of "A Last Confession." It is imbued with the symbols and tropes of nationalism, but it subjects those symbols to exacting scrutiny, pursuing them to their logical and melodramatic extremes and, in the process, revealing that nationalism contains the seeds of its own contradictions. Like the daughter-lover figure of "A Last Confession," Italy was growing up, making the transition from hopeful dream to European nation-state. "A Last Confession" thus calls attention to an oversight to which a good deal of political verse was prone, in which the nation ceases to be a self-interested political entity and becomes instead an artistic canvas upon which images and myths can be rendered. Published in 1870, the year Italy finally achieved complete unification, Rossetti's poem sought to bury one Italy and invite the possibility of a new one—a nation that, for better or worse, would have to be recognized as a new partner in a rapidly changing and realigning Europe.

NOTES

1. Oswald Doughty and John Robert Wahl, eds., *Letters of Dante Gabriel Rossetti*, 4 vols. (Oxford: Clarendon, 1965): 3.1233. Rossetti's comments were in reply to Franz Hüffer, who was preparing a study of the poet's work in 1873. Subsequent references to Doughty and Wahl's edition of Rossetti's letters will be made in the text.

2. In some sense, critical discussion of "A Last Confession" has yet to catch up with new trends in the study of the dramatic monologue form. Isobel Armstrong's groundbreaking *Victorian Poetry: Poetry, Poetics, Politics* (New York: Routledge 1993), for instance, stresses the importance of reading dramatic monologues with a deeper awareness of the cultural contexts that produced them, thereby resisting the temptation to dehistoricize individual poems as case studies of moral or psychological deviance. Without this historical attention, the political matter in the poem becomes tangential, merely a contributing factor to the speaker's mental state rather than a subject in itself. Ronnalie Roper Howard, for

instance, calls the speaker a "victim of his times," an example of "the instability and desolation of human existence in a time of war" (*The Dark Glass: Vision and Technique in the Poetry of Dante Gabriel Rossetti* [Athens: Ohio University Press, 1972], 100). More recently, Christopher S. Nassaar has argued that once the speaker "commits himself to the outside world and becomes an Italian patriot," he violates the Catholic religious ethic of the poem ("The Silent Priest: Rossetti's 'A Last Confession' Revisited," *Journal of Pre-Raphaelite Studies* 6 [1997]: 35). These readings do not misinterpret the poem, but they do overlook the extent and complexity of Rossetti's engagement with contemporary Anglo-Italian politics. Such readings remove the poem from its specific historical context, Roper by stressing a universal antiwar theme and Nassaar by turning the poem's dominant political issue into a religious one.

3. Harry W. Rudman's *Italian Nationalism and English Letters: Figures of the Risorgimento and Victorian Men of Letters* (1940; repr., New York: AMS Press, 1966) remains the best overall survey of the English literary response to the Risorgimento. While Rossetti does not figure prominently in his analysis, Rudman does offer an extended portrait of Dante Gabriel's father, Gabriele Rossetti (186–98).

4. Maura O'Connor, *The Romance of Italy and the English Political Imagination* (New York: St. Martin's, 1998), 9.

5. O'Connor, 31.

6. See Martha Westwater, *The Spasmodic Career of Sydney Dobell* (Lanham, MD: University Press of America, 1992), for an extended analysis of *The Roman* and its contemporary reception.

7. Sydney Dobell, *The Poetical Works of Sydney Dobell*, 2 vols., ed. John Nichol (London: Smith, Elder, 1875), 1:3.

8. Dobell, *Poetical Works*, 1:185.

9. Emily Jolly, ed., *Life and Letters of Sydney Dobell*, 2 vols. (London: Smith, Elder, 1878), 1:200.

10. References to Rossetti's poetry are to Jan Marsh, ed., *Dante Gabriel Rossetti: Collected Writings* (Chicago: New Amsterdam Books, 2000).

11. Elizabeth Barrett Browning, *Aurora Leigh*, ed. Margaret Reynolds (Athens: Ohio University Press, 1992), 7:1158.

12. From Renan's lecture "What is a Nation?" (1882), quoted in Eric J. Hobsbawm, "Ethnicity and Nationalism in Europe Today," *Mapping the Nation*, ed. Gopal Balakrishnan (London: Verso, 1996), 255. The translation is Hobsbawm's.

13. References to Browning's poetry are to John Pettigrew and Thomas J. Collins, eds., *The Poems: Volume One* (New Haven, CT: Yale University Press, 1981).

14. On the portrayal of women in the Victorian dramatic monologue, see Cornelia D. J. Pearsall, "The Dramatic Monologue," *The Cambridge Companion to Victorian Poetry*, ed. Joseph Bristow (Cambridge: Cambridge University Press, 2000): 67–88, particularly her discussion of "Porphyria's Lover" and "My Last Duchess" (78–79). A more extended treatment of the subject can be found in Melissa Valiska Gregory, "Robert Browning and the Lure of the Violent Lyric Voice: Domestic Violence and the Dramatic Monologue," *Victorian Poetry* 38 (2000): 491–510.

15. The image of Italy presented in "The Italian in England" is, in my opinion, not meant to be taken ironically. While Browning always seems to invite skepticism toward the claims of his speakers, "The Italian in England" provides little evidence with which to doubt the sincerity of the speaker, or the author's sympathy with him. The perpetuation of the Italy/young girl metaphor in later Browning poems also lends support to this view.

16. Rossetti's 1849 poem "On Refusal of Aid Between Nations" illustrates this skepticism further. Even as it chastises England and France for not supporting the Italian cause more vigorously, the poem accepts that such cooperation is rendered difficult by the concept of the nation-state itself: "But because Man is parcelled out in men," no nation disinterestedly pursues the course of justice, proclaiming instead, " 'He is he, I am I' " (9, 13). By the time he finished "A Last Confession," Rossetti, like many in Europe, seems to have become even more aware that nationalism is fundamentally about self-promotion and might have dangerous consequences for the future.

17. William Holman Hunt's recollection of a dinner at the Rossetti household gives the sense that the children generally chose to dissociate themselves from their father's political activities. As Hunt, the Rossetti children, and their mother ate dinner in one room, the father and a group of Italian exiles noisily discussed Italy in another, until, according to Hunt, "[w]hen it was impossible for me to ignore the distress of the alien company, [Dante] Gabriel and William shrugged their shoulders, the latter with a languid sign of commiseration, saying it was generally so" (*Pre-Raphaelitism and the Pre-Raphaelite Brotherhood*, 2 vols. [New York: Macmillan, 1905], 1:154).

18. William Michael Rossetti, *Family Letters and a Memoir of Dante Gabriel Rossetti*, 2 vols. (1895; repr., New York: AMS Press, 1970), 1:55. In fact, of all the Rossetti children, William Michael was the only one to show a sustained interest in the kind of patriotic verse that preoccupied his father. His *Democratic Sonnets* (1907), for instance, include numerous poems in support of

Italy. The limits of the present study, however, prevent me from affording his work the critical attention it deserves in its own right.

19. "The Stealthy School of Criticism," *Athenaeum* (16 Dec. 1871): 793.

20. Jerome J. McGann, *Dante Gabriel Rossetti and the Game that must be Lost* (New Haven, CT: Yale University Press, 2000), 43.

Chapter 4

A DUTCH LADY OF SHALOTT

Linda A. Groen

e owe it to the Pre-Raphaelites and their followers that in the nineteenth century, Alfred Lord Tennyson's "The Lady of Shalott" appeared frequently in the visual arts. The illustrations by Rossetti and Hunt for the Moxon edition of Tennyson's poetry published in 1857 are well known, as are Hunt's refined compositions of the Lady in two large oil paintings. The three *Ladies of Shalott* by John William Waterhouse are also popular, and furthermore those by Elizabeth Siddal, Sidney Meteyard, Arthur Hughes, and many other artists' Ladies are brought together in the catalogue that was published along with the exhibition *Ladies of Shalott: A Victorian Masterpiece and Its Contexts* in 1985.[1] From this catalogue, it appears that the choice of representing the Lady of Shalott seems to be confined to Anglo-Saxon artists. It is thus surprising to see that a Dutch artist, too, has represented the Lady of Shalott, and not merely as an illustration, but as a substantial work of art. This artist is Matthijs (also called Matthew) Maris (1839–1917).

> On either side the river lie
> Long fields of barley and of rye,
> That clothe the wold and meet the sky;
> And thro' the field the roads runs by
>   To many-towered Camelot;
> And up and down the people go,
> Gazing where the lilies blow
> Round an island there below,
>   The island of Shalott.[2]

In a tower chamber of a castle on the island of Shalott, there lives a mysterious Lady. She is never seen outside her castle, but from time to time she is heard chanting. The Lady of Shalott does not take part in the world outside her chamber; in complete solitude, she dedicates herself to her art. "And little other care hath she, The Lady of Shalott."

In 1869, in another secluded chamber, high up in a building in the Parisian Montmartre, Matthijs Maris tried to make a living of his art. The Dutch artist lived and worked in solitude, interrupted only by the visits of his brother Jakob, another would-be painter. The brothers came from a family of five children; their brother Willem was an aspiring painter as well. The father of the Maris family was a printer, and when the boys were little he often brought home prints from his work for the children to copy. Matthijs and Jakob proved to be so talented that they were allowed to take art lessons, first at the Academy in The Hague and afterwards at the Academy of Antwerp. In 1856, Jakob tried his luck in Paris, and ten years later he invited his brother Matthijs to join him there. But after the French-German War, Jakob returned to the Netherlands, while Matthijs stayed behind.

Living as an artist was far from easy for Matthijs Maris; his poverty was so grave that it made him advise the young Vincent van Gogh: "Go take a rope and hang yourself."[3] The necessity of an income forced Maris to depict topics and to adopt a manner of painting that he would not have chosen had he been free to follow his own tastes. After his brother Jakob had introduced him at the Maison Goupil gallery, Matthijs painted realistic pictures for Adolphe Goupil in the style of the Old Dutch Masters, representing Dutch interiors, which were very well sought after. Maison Goupil was a statement in the Parisian art scene, "La plus grande maison du monde,"[4] as Maris named it. Goupil was one of the biggest French buyers of Pre-Raphaelite art in the 1850s and 1860s, and Goupil's London gallery held a huge exhibition of Pre-Raphaelite art in 1870. One of the customers at Maison Goupil was the Scottish art dealer Daniel Cottier (1838–91), who at first bought some of Maris's paintings, then visited the artist several times in his Montmartre room, and eventually persuaded him to come to London. Cottier saw the value of the artist and his paintings. Maris described in a strange mixture of Dutch and English his encounter with the Scotsman as follows:

> It happened in these days, when I was working hard for creditors "en huren en belastingkantoren" [and rents and tax offices], that a man came to me from over the water. . . . He bought from Goupil every bit there was left of

> my things. I felt ashamed . . . he was showing himself so friendly and gen-
> erous [*sic*] disposed towards me, that after a year or two, talking and talk-
> ing, and trying his best to get me to come over to England, I did. I should
> be so nice, be amongst friends, and have a little home for myself and try to
> work out quietly my own capacities. These [*sic*] was a temptation for me to
> jump at.[5]

At the arrival of Maris in London in 1877, Cottier offered him a "little home" in exchange for art, and at first Maris felt sure he had met with a kind of patron who protected the arts for beauty's sake. But soon he found out that the "little home" was just a small room in Cottier's attic, and Cottier himself turned out to be a thorough businessman who required Maris to paint as many sure-to-sell genre paintings as possible. "The art deal-ers," Maris later complained, "desired no art of me, only paint."[6] Maris wanted to paint his own fantasies of medieval damsels and fairy tale princesses, in his own painstaking way and in as much time he thought necessary—not to produce two pictures a week, but to create one piece of true art during several months. In the many letters Maris wrote to his friends and relatives in the Netherlands, he expressed his disappoint-ment and bitterness:

> Once upon a time, when hard at the potboiler's job, a millionaire came
> from over the sea with castles and parks, making me believe if ever I s^d
> come to London, I s^d be more comfortable, a nice house and the rest, and
> not obliged to work for the market, but work out my own notions after my
> own fashion. . . . So when I arrived at the world's city, parks and castles
> and millions were "verschwunden" [vanished].[7]

Now that he had succeeded in bringing Maris to his house in London, Cottier commissioned him to do all sort of jobs in order to profit from the reluctant Dutchman. Besides painting pictures in the style of "Peter de Hook" (Pieter de Hoogh), the artist was ordered to copy the work of oth-ers and to make minor restorations. This was such a disappointment to Maris that he fixed all his feelings of vexation on Cottier and started to hate the art dealer. The artist's distaste for the necessity of money and commerce made the relation between the two men grow worse and worse. Maris became a bashful introvert and went outdoors rarely. He dedi-cated every free moment to the art of etching: a small, intimate way of creating art, suitable for Maris's escapism. As soon as Cottier found out Maris was qualifying himself in a new medium, he immediately bought Maris a Cadart press, copper plates, and the proper etching tools. It was well-known that etchings like those of Jean-François Millet were good merchandise, and Cottier pressed Maris to produce etchings in a similar style. However, Maris's etchings from that period, like *The Enchanted Castle, The Outskirts of a Wood,* and *The Lady of Shalott* were no pot-boilers. Maris took his time, and occasionally dedicated three months to one etching; to him the dreamy visions never seemed to be finished. Maris recollected later that

> I had to try at night, what I wanted myself, and in the daytime I had to do what the swindler wanted me to do, but now neither the one nor the other would succeed. . . . The stupid fellow, if he had only given me a little place, where I would be able to work by myself, it would have been for his own profit.[8]

When it became clear to Cottier that the shadowy etchings—the "pro-beerseltjes," or "little experiments" as the artist called them—were without any commercial value, he sold the Cadart press.

In 1882, Maris created an etching showing a woman in medieval dress and with Pre-Raphaelite abundant long hair. She wanders through the woods and seems to be singing. On the horizon, the vague surroundings of a castle are to be detected. The woman's pose is reminiscent of Jean-François Millet's *Sower*: an artist whose work Maris highly admired and often copied. Maris titled his etching *The Lady of Shalott* (Figure 4.1).[9] It illustrates the moment in Tennyson's poem when the Lady is driven from her paradise: "Down she came." The Lady risked the safety of the existence in her tower chamber when she surrendered to the world outside the four walls of her room.

The castle in the etching must be Camelot, symbolizing a world out of reach for a living Lady of Shalott. Maris depicts the castle as almost im-material, a castle in the air, in the full bright light that the Lady (and Maris) tried to avoid. The window next to where Maris used to work was painted over in its lower two thirds so that there was just enough light in the room to work by. The artist did not want to be confronted with the world outside his chamber. The uncovered part of the window provided a view of some chimneys and tree tops. "I used to work at evening," he writes: "I dislike daylight, blue skies and white clouds . . . I rather work with the light of a lamp."[10] Maris hated cities, for they reminded him of corruption and commerce. At the times when he did leave his safe little room, he made sure it was in the evening or at night, when the light was dimmed and he could imagine that the gloomy city buildings were castles.

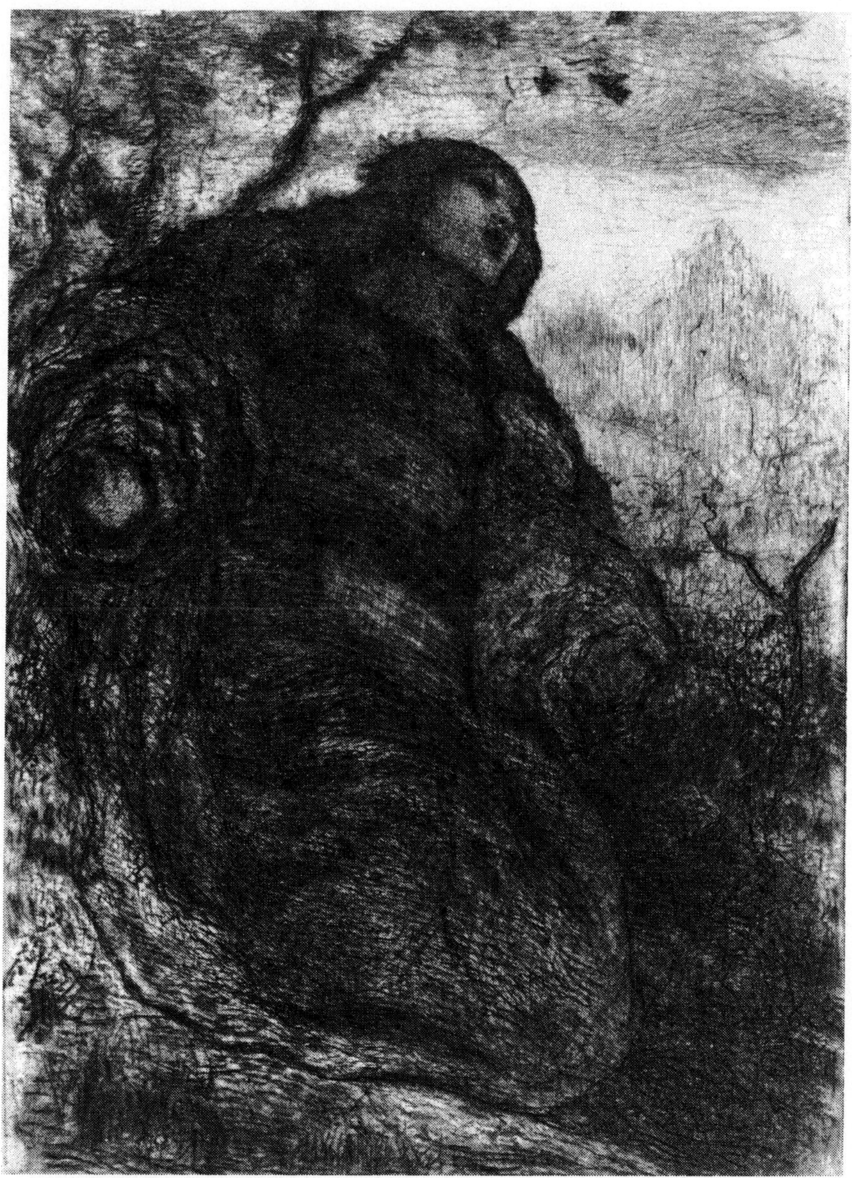

Figure 4.1. Matthijs Maris, *The Lady of Shalott* (1882). Reproduced by kind permission of the Haags Gemeentemuseum, The Hague, The Netherlands.

Maris had yielded to the distractions of the world, but, different from that of the Lady of Shalott, his situation was not hopeless and not unchangeable. His biographer Arondeus writes about this: "somewhere the man of realities has captured the dreamer, and somewhere the dreamer has wanted this captivity; somewhere the shy refugee has admired the boasting victor."[11] The artist chose safety instead of freedom, for it was impossible to gain safety without an artistic imprisonment and sacrifice. So Maris stayed on with Cottier, year after year, for this stay guaranteed— if only for a couple of hours a day—a certain freedom to dream. His basic needs were met, and he did not have to try to sell his own work. Despite all his complaints about the man, Matthijs Maris worked more than ten years for Cottier.

After Maris left Cottier in 1888, he was financially supported by Elbert Jan van Wisselingh, a Dutch art dealer he had become acquainted with during the time both had worked for Maison Goupil in Paris. Van Wisselingh donated a monthly amount of money to Maris over a period of twenty years, even in times—for instance, during the crisis after the Boer War— when it was hard for Van Wisselingh to share his income. However, Maris's gratitude was huge. "Everything I have I owe to Van Wisselingh."[12] He made Van Wisselingh's widow, Isabella Angus, the sole heiress of his artistic inheritance. But Van Wisselingh was not Maris's only patron, for until Maris's death in 1917, P. F. Thomsen, a shipowner from Rotterdam, supplied the artist with an annual allowance of twenty pounds.

During the forty years Maris spent in London, he inhabited several rooms. The removals were never voluntary, and the artist thought them dreadful; he disliked all changes. But Maris had not always been such a hermit. As young men, he and his brother Jakob once made a long journey through Germany, Switzerland, and France, visiting places were they could marvel at the architecture of the Middle Ages.[13] Cottier also occasionally took Maris with him on business trips, a sign that the relationship between the two of them was not as bad as it seems from Maris's letters. In the company of the Scotsman, Maris traveled to Ireland, Norway, and Brittany.

As far as his manner and style of painting are concerned, Maris did not identify with the basic principles of the Pre-Raphaelites. His pallete contained not bright colors, but brown and grey hues, and his paintings were lusterless and of a granular texture, for he extracted oil from the paint. When Maris was painting, there were little heaps of oil paint on brown paper all over in his room. The oil was absorbed by the paper, making the paint rather dry, which created a rough surface on the canvas. Moreover, by this treatment, the oil paint became less shiny. Quite an advantage, thought the artist, since luster only troubled the eye while looking at a picture. Maris avoided sharp lines and seemed to prefer dreamy apparitions. Both in his work and his life, he strove to escape from the material world. In his work, at least, he succeeded by creating blurred images. The slow process of abstraction in his art can be regarded as an escape from reality.

From a technical point of view, there is hardly any affinity between Maris and the Pre-Raphaelites, unless it is with Rossetti, whose brush-strokes could be more loose than those of, for example, Hunt or Millais, or with Burne-Jones whose thick layers of scraped paint resemble those on Maris's paintings. The Old Masters highly admired by Maris did not have a place within the pantheon of the Pre-Raphaelites. On the chamber walls of the Dutchman hung reproductions of a landscape by Claude Lorrain, Da Vinci's *Mona Lisa*, and *The Plague* by Raphael. In his youth, he had been an ardent admirer of the Nazarenes, but later in life he no longer aimed at clear contours and he started to appreciate the work of Rembrandt. Maris loved Whistler and detested Ruskin.

Nevertheless, the Pre-Raphaelites and Maris are related in their choice of subject matter. The gruff, uncommunicative Dutchman was a romanticist to the bone. He enjoyed the mood of the Middle Ages, which the works of Goethe and Schiller aroused in him; he dreamed of Grimm's fairy tales, and cited Shakespeare, Shelley, Burns, and Blake for the select company of initiates whom he granted entrance to his chamber. In his paintings and etchings, Maris showed himself a true poet, Arondeus writes: "For in his time there has been none so great as Matthijs Maris in what is to be considered pictorial poetry."[14]

The link between Maris and the Pre-Raphaelites was based on their mutual interest in romanticism and literature, for although he socialized with John Swan and James Whistler, Maris did not feel attracted to any particular school of painting. He was of the opinion that the finest work of his contemporaries appeared as book illustrations and not on the walls of the Royal Academy or the Grosvenor Gallery. For this reason, it is very likely that Maris first met the Lady of Shalott as a book illustration for Tennyson's poem, perhaps in the Moxon edition illustrated by the Pre-Raphaelites. Apart from the National Gallery in London, Maris did not visit art galleries, although his little room was stuffed with volumes of *The Studio*, which means that he must have been well-informed about contemporary art in England. And there was his extensive correspondence with relatives and friends in the Netherlands who discussed Pre-Raphaelitism with him.

The increased ease of travel in the 1880s and 1890s strengthened international contacts between artists, who could inform each other about their ideas and see each other's work. There was a vast extent of art journals and magazines, and reproductions and prints—most containing Pre-Raphaelite paintings—going overseas. At the end of the nineteenth century, the influence of Pre-Raphaelite art and poetry had reached the Netherlands. Jan Toroop visited London several times and was impressed by the art of the Pre-Raphaelites and their followers, as did Richard Roland Holst, who visited London in 1894, where he especially admired the art of Rossetti, the painter and poet about whom he would write a biographical chapter.[15] Roland Holst is known to have owned a copy of the Moxon Tennyson, as well as a reproduction of Hunt's 1857 *The Lady of Shalott*, although it is not clear whether he had contact with Maris about them. An influence of Pre-Raphaelite subject matter and style is obvious in the work of Roland Holst, for example, in his *Helga*, which he created after a poem by William Morris. And there are more traces of Pre-Raphaelitism to be found in the Netherlands. For instance, Johan Thorn Prikker made a drawing titled *The Blessed Damozel*, and the writer Henri Borel referred to Rossetti's damozel in his novel *Een Droom*. Hermanus Daalhoff, S. Moulijn, Bernard Essers, and Antoon van Welie all chose to depict Ophelia, and the pose of Rossetti's *Beata Beatrix* is copied in many of Toroop's ladies.

The Lady of Shalott is a subject that especially appealed to Maris. It is a romantic tale about a lady in the Middle Ages whose existence has some elements in common with that of Maris. The Lady, too, was an artist and a loner who did not mingle with society and with whom everything went wrong at the moment she did approach the world outside. Lonely and lofty, both Maris and Lady dedicated themselves to their art, and both made a fall. In 1916, Maris wrote that "there is no crime worse than to take from the Tree of Knowledge; damnation and excommunication will be the result."[16] The idea even haunted him in his dreams:

> one night he dreamed he saw a multitude of vigorous young men marching all forward towards a sun-like light—and as they came within a certain distance of it they fell down one by one and died. This he would say was symbolic of his life—always as it were "lured on towards destruction."[17]

Maris elaborately visualized the theme of the Fall in his paintings and etchings of Gretchen from *Faust*. "It is my own misery in it,"[18] he wrote about one of his Gretchen-paintings, for just like her (and the Lady of

Shalott), he felt "the curse" had come on him. Maris's paradise lost was not Paris, for he was unsatisfied with Goupil's business as well. The ultimate paradise Maris referred to must have been the attic room he inhabited as a boy at his parents' house. "If it was up to me I would still be in my little garret,"[19] he claimed at the end of his life. So the paradise lost is the loss of childhood, of innocence, of a world passed by never to be gained again. In this respect, it is clear Maris had etched his *Lady of Shalott* purely for himself, in order to express his feelings, and not as an illustration or a Pre-Raphaelite riddle full of iconographic details. For him it was unnecessary to make his Lady known as the one from Shalott by putting her crashed mirror in the picture or her boat. His *Lady of Shalott* was not a tale to tell the world, but a personal meditation on his own fall. This lifelong obsession with the expulsion from paradise accounts for his representation of *The Lady of Shalott* and for the particular part of the poem he chose to illustrate. Instead of representing the Lady at the moment she sets eyes on Lancelot, or the dead Lady floating downstream, which occur most frequently in visual art, Maris chose to depict the direct consequence of the Lady's fall: the expulsion from the safe enclosure of her castle walls. She seems to be singing; she will continue doing so all the way downstream to Camelot, until "singing in her song," she dies.

Maris's *Lady of Shalott* is not a portrait of a lady admired by Maris in life, although the figure shows similarities with that in the *Siska*-etchings and *De Vreugdevolle Wandeling* ["The Joyful Walk"], all depict a flower in the central figure's abundant hair. However, there is not a trace of romantic love to be detected in Maris's life. In his opinion, a love relationship formed an obstacle for artistry. He could not understand how one could work as an artist and be married at the same time. A confirmed bachelor, he was not able to divide his life between love and art. To him it was clear that either one dedicated oneself to a life for art, or to a family life. As were many in the nineteenth century, Maris was convinced that all things concerning the soul and the spiritual life were of a higher order than the world of the senses and the animal instincts, the physical and material. Therefore, the ideal love was an unearthly love, pure and spiritual, like Dante's love for Beatrice or the idolization of the Blessed Damozel.

The lady in the etching has most likely arisen from Maris's imagination; he did not work from models. Even though his brother Jakob recommended it from time to time, Maris refused flatly, saying the ideal shapes he desired to paint were to be found only in his imagination. His biographer, Fridlander, remembers once showing a drawing to the Dutchman:

> he exclaimed before looking at it, and almost fiercely, that he hoped there
> were no "bones" in it. . . . On my saying to him once, à propos of what I do
> not now recall, words to the effect that an artist must study Nature, he said
> with deepest emphasis: "You must *feel* Nature."[20]

Maris did not want to work after nature, not any longer. He had done it for
so long when he was producing potboilers in Paris. Nature had to be re-
leased from reality, and that process took place in Maris's head. "What is
material is no art to me,"[21] he proclaimed. This was a fundamental contrast between the material, the reality as it was to be seen, and the mental, the higher reality: in short, between Nature and the Ideal. That is why
according to Maris art and earthly goods were an impossible combination.
Hence, the Lady of Shalott was unable to maintain herself in reality.

However, slowly Maris's art and earthly goods did became entangled.
His romantic paintings and the "little experiments" in copper were appreciated in the 1890s, and Maris's name became well known in the Dutch
and English art scenes at the end of the nineteenth century. The menace of
the potboilers had disappeared, although that of commerce had not.

> Not so long ago a "hollandsche centjes-man" [wealthy Dutchman] came to
> visit me and made remarks that I surely would be able to find myself a bet-
> ter place to work: "you can make such pretty pictures, for you are so very
> smart; you can do it with such a speed, so why don't you do it; then you can
> make enough money to buy a better place." That has been my curse, that I
> had the reputation to be smart.[22]

Since that event, Maris kept his door locked to everything that smelled of
commerce. Still, occasionally it happened that commerce paid him a
visit. One day, a lady from The Hague appeared on his doorstep. She had
heard rumors of the hidden masterpieces in the artist's room and of the
good prices they could make. She surprised the old eccentric at his work,
and Maris—overwhelmed and panicstricken by the violently broken silence ("I thought she was going to kill me")[23]—quickly gave the lady
what she wanted: a couple of sketches and an autograph on a document
she had brought with her. Fortunately, after hearing of the event, the
Dutch consul in London and the police in The Hague interfered, and the
lady had to return the sketches and the contract—in which she had
obliged Maris to hand over his next oil painting to her. Now that greed had
actually entered his little domain, Maris became even more suspicious toward people. Yet, the interest for the artist and his work continued to

grow. With Maris's fame, there began a kind of international conflict between the Dutch and English art scenes about who was allowed to claim the artist for their country. Matthijs Maris cared little. In August of 1894, Maris was appointed a Knight of the Order of the Dutch Lion. His brothers in the Netherlands hesitated to send him the news of the honor, fearing a refusal. Therefore, the medal and proclamation were brought to him, along with a Dutch liver sausage, by Jakob's daughter when she went to visit her uncle in London. The knight put the box with the honors aside without opening it and did not mention it once, but with the liver sausage he was reported to have been very well pleased.[24]

Maris led a life like that of the Lady of Shalott. In his tower chamber, he dedicated himself in complete solitude to the creation of his art and seemed to be content with it. But deep inside, there was a desire to a grander way of life outside the walls of his room. And when Cottier made him an offer, the artist yielded to him like the Lady of Shalott had done to Lancelot. From then on, the Lady went down while singing a song to end her life, unknown to the world. In contrast, Maris went from tower chamber to tower chamber, stubbornly creating his dreams on canvas and in copper until his name finally reached the court during his own life. Although Maris was not influenced by the Pre-Raphaelite artists, he lived as though he himself had been fashioned by them: "Who is this, and what is here?" Matthijs Maris, a Dutch Lady of Shalott.

Notes

1. *Ladies of Shalott: A Victorian Masterpiece and Its Contexts* (Providence, RI: Brown University Press, 1985).

2. From the 1842 version of the poem in Christopher Ricks, *Tennyson: A Selected Edition* (Harlow: Essex, 1989), 20.

3. Ernest D. Fridlander, *Matthew Maris* (London, 1921), 27.

4. W. Arondeus, *Matthijs Maris: De Tragiek van den Droom* (Amsterdam, 1939), 72. All translations of Arondeus's text are my own.

5. Ibid., 108, 109.

6. Ibid., 121.

7. Ibid., 109.

8. Anna Wagner, *Matthijs Maris* (Vloardigen: Den Haag, 1974), 21.

9. Matthijs Maris, *The Lady of Shalott* (1882, 15.7 × 11.7 cm, Haags

Gemeentemuseum). With many thanks to Peter Couvee of the Haags Gemeentemuseum, The Hague, The Netherlands.

10. Arondeus, 153.

11. Ibid., 108.

12. Ibid., 143.

13. See also the essay by Beátrice Laurent in this collection about a similar pilgrimage made by Dante Gabriel Rossetti and William Holman Hunt.

14. Arondeus, 16.

15. Richard Roland Holst, "Dante Gabriel Rossetti," *Mannen en Vrouwen
van Beteekenis in Onze Dagen: Levensschetsen en Portretten* (Haarlem: Tjeenk
Willink, 1898).

16. H. E. M. Braakhuis and J. van der Vliet, "Bruiden, Gretchens, Prins-
essen en Kastelen," *Kunstlicht* [Maris special issue] (1990): 10.

17. Fridlander, 20.

18. Braakhuis and van der Vliet, 12.

19. Wagner, 6.

20. Fridlander, 47, 48.

21. Braakhuis and van der Vliet, 9.

22. Arondeus, 156.

23. Ibid., 164.

24. Ibid., 150.

Chapter 5

"Pre-Raphaelite Ornaments in the European Slaughterhouse": Pre-Raphaelitism and Croatian Culture

Tatjana Jukić

In the context of Croatian culture, the legacy of Pre-Raphaelitism seems a nonpresence: there are no marked traces, no major studies, no acolyte's discourse, pictorial or verbal. However, the concept of Pre-Raphaelitism does surface in Croatian culture, seemingly uninvited by the dominant thrust of discourse. Contrary to their apparent insignificance, the occurrences of Pre-Raphaelitism in Croatian culture operate as markers of the mappings in which they take part, helping to organize symbolic spaces of contact zones with other discourses and negotiate unstable cultural boundaries.

Early twentieth-century Croatian art and literature use the trope of Pre-Raphaelitism to signal that the new cultural context persists in recognizing the imported discourse as foreign, eccentric, and alien. Thus references to Pre-Raphaelitism in the works of Miroslav Krleža (1893–1981)—a severe critic of Croatian culture and by far the most influential writer of the Croatian twentieth century—perform as the traces of boundary itself, charting the contact zones between the Croatian and the Other.

Further, the references to Pre-Raphaelitism in Krleža's work illuminate blindspots enveloping more overt cultural imports, indirectly reflecting instance of cultural otherness that have been successfully assimilated and made invisible. In other words, by their conspicuous "out-of-placeness," references to Pre-Raphaelitism in Krleža's writings reveal a central principle of culture construction to be the semiotic taming of hybridity.

As such, Krleža's references to Pre-Raphaelitism chart both the scope of its figural performativity and the relation of the movement to different cultures that Pre-Raphaelitism charges and is charged by. As Alicia Craig Faxon remarked in 1995, "[t]he influence of Pre-Raphaelitism as a movement has yet to be definitely charted,"[1] especially in view of her argument that "the separation of Pre-Raphaelite art from European art is an arbitrary one created by modern art historians."[2]

An understanding of Krleža's use of Pre-Raphaelitism, however, necessitates an inquiry into two other Croatian writers who made use of Pre-Raphaelitism in their own different ways and whose texts often serve as groundwork for Krleža's handling of Croatian culture: Antun Gustav Matoš (1873–1914) and Milan Begović (1876–1948).

Matoš and Begović anticipate the cultural framework and the principal concerns of Krleža's handling of Pre-Raphaelitism. Matoš was the leading Croatian turn-of-the-century writer and critic. His views on symbolism and aestheticism, in visual arts and in literature, reflect his intense experience of Paris at the time, where he lived from 1899 to 1904. As a result, Matoš's references to Pre-Raphaelitism convey the contemporary French reception of Pre-Raphaelite works. Yet, though capitalizing on the French connection, Matoš's art criticism is as influenced by his long history of political exile from Croatia first to Belgrade, then to Munich and Geneva, and finally to Paris.[3] Begović's plays and poetry, however, originate on an unstable boundary between the turn-of-the-century Italian language and culture, and Croatian culture, especially in Dalmatia. Through his evident copying of Gabriele D'Annunzio, Begović imported the elements of Pre-Raphaelitism as used and reorganized by his Italian model. This interaction of various imports in the case of Begović is all the more dynamic in view of the fact that Croatian critics at the time saw D'Annunzio as an imitator of Pre-Raphaelitism. Matoš, for instance, writes in 1905 that "Gabriele D'Annunzio represents virtuosity rather than truly great, original art, and his chasing after all the new literary fashions, from Wagner to Nietzsche, from the English Pre-Raphaelites to French naturalists and psychologists, testifies vividly to the lack of independence of Italian art and literature."[4]

A recent revival in Croatia of academic interest in Milan Begović has produced readings that attempted to detect traces of Pre-Raphaelitism in Begović's writing. These readings managed to locate, however, only the places of indeterminacy, because traces of Pre-Raphaelitism in Begović are obscured by the several layers of translation and reorganization of the foreign discourse. According to Morana Čale,

Bloody Lilies (*Krvavi ljiljani*)—the title of an imaginary theatrical piece in Begović's play *Sweet Jeopardy* (*Slatka opasnost*, 1906)—is a possible working out of the interrupted "lilies" novel series by D'Annunzio, whose unfinished narrative lilies are in turn a result of D'Annunzio's own refashioning of Dante Gabriel Rossetti's handling of the lily symbol. Čale corroborates her hesitant detection of D'Annunzio's Rossetti in Begović by quoting from Gianni Turchetta, who recognizes D'Annunzio's lilies as a "symbol of purity, *possibly* a memento to Rossetti's painting" [emphasis mine].[5] Zoran Kravar describes Begović's lyrical cycle *The Boccadoro Book* (*Knjiga Boccadoro*, 1900) as another reworking of D'Annunzio's views on the historicized, the erotic, and the literary, which capitalized on nineteenth-century lyrical cycles, such as Dante Gabriel Rossetti's *The House of Life* or Christina Rossetti's *Monna Innominata*. Kravar traces the elements of Pre-Raphaelitism in Begović to his interest in the very form of the early modern lyrical cycle, which narrates a love story (as in *Monna Innominata*), but also to the pressure to hide behind a pseudo-historical mask. Kravar is explicit in his comparison of Christina Rossetti's persona as Petrarch's Laura and Begović's mask as an imaginary Spanish aristocrat "Xeres de la Maraja" in love with "countess Boccadoro," especially because both Christina Rossetti's and Begović's cycles explore the poetic construction of the boundary between the strict formal requirements of style and the repression of the sensual.[6]

The case of Begović facilitates the discussion of Krleža's handling of Pre-Raphaelitism. First, the wavering and uncertain presence of Pre-Raphaelitism in Begović pushes to the limit our ability to detect the intertextual trail from Rossetti to D'Annunzio to Begović. A progressive withdrawal of Rossettian discourse in D'Annunzio, and its transposition in Begović, seems to manifest an unsettled gap in contemporary literary theory; rather than describing this progression as intertextual, a better term might be interdiscursive, or even the—much disputed—"influence." On the one hand, "influence" allows for the deeply contingent, critical uncertainty of detection; on the other, it highlights not so much the positive knowledge as the very performance of discourse as impact, work, and effect, thus paving the way for a reading based on interdiscursive acts rather than intertextuality.

Second, the impact of Pre-Raphaelitism in the case of Begović, Matoš, and Krleža involves a difficult dialogue of different languages and different cultures. The progressive loss of the discursive trace from Rossetti to the Croatian writers means here a translation from the English language and the specificities of Victorian culture first into the Italian of

D'Annunzio and then into Croatian of Begović, only to be cancelled as "too foreign" in the works of both Matoš and Krleža (not to mention the original linguistic fissure that so often operated as the very birthsite of Rossetti's own Anglo-Italian discourse).

Though this may be true of most discursive transactions, the dialogue of different languages and cultures in the case of Begović's, Matoš's, and Krleža's handling of Pre-Raphaelitism entails the general predicament of translation, but above all posits these languages and cultures as stakes in the politics of cultural construction, naming, and identity. This disturbing hyperactivity of politics in Begović, Matoš and Krleža is a constituent part of these authors' cultural and historical legacy. The construction of Croatian national and cultural identity in the nineteenth and twentieth centuries involved an unstable notion of territoriality and language (most nineteenth-century Croatian intellectuals spoke German or Hungarian better than they did Croatian). Foreign cultural influence was perceived as a political affair, not least because the very notion of foreignness—and hence any construction of cultural identity—eluded demarcation.

At the time of the formation of the Pre-Raphaelite Brotherhood in 1848, Croatia was part of the Hapsburg Empire, a kind of geographic and symbolic *cordon sanitaire* between Vienna and the Ottoman Empire. Croatia remained part of Austria-Hungary until 1918. Between the two World Wars, it was part of the Kingdom of Yugoslavia, and part of its Adriatic coast was held by Italy. After 1945, Croatia was part of the socialist republic of Yugoslavia, and it was not until 1991 and 1992 that it was internationally recognized as a sovereign country. Thus, although Begović, Matoš, and Krleža all wrote in Croatian at roughly the same time and in the same place, their texts are products of fundamentally different cultural, historical, and political mappings.

However different, these mappings all depend on an experience of the instability of borders. While the experience of volatile boundaries makes the mapping of Croatian culture and territoriality open to present-day cultural theory, it also calls to mind the history of Pre-Raphaelitism itself, with its own legacy of difficult border crossings. Pre-Raphaelitism relies on histories of exile or on some more contractual forms of cultural exchange. Rossetti's father came to England as a political émigré, using the writing of Dante Alighieri as a political metaphor of exile and committing this metaphor to the name and the cultural memory of his son. Ford Madox Brown developed the original Pre-Raphaelite dogma while working with German painters in Rome. William Holman Hunt was an obsessive traveler to the Holy Land and its Jewish and Arab communities. William

Morris was quite as obsessed with Iceland and its past. Furthermore, it might be possible to argue that the heightened visibility of Pre-Raphaelitism in recent revisions of Victorian culture might be due precisely to its adherence to the protocols of discourse production highly valued by present-day theory, since all these protocols eventually boil down to the discursive work of the borderline, be it the borderline between cultures, histories, media, languages, scientific disciplines, or psychic structures. It is equally possible to argue that the recent heightened visibility of the European East in cultural theory has to do with this same view of geography as a cultural, symbolic, and political borderline, because the post-communist territories of the New Europe have come to constitute an uneasy portal between the theorizing Occident and the still phantasmatic Orient.

Miroslav Krleža uses such a framework to transform Pre-Raphaelitism into a trope in his political and politicizing literary discourse. Krleža's work focuses on the unsettled definition of Croatian culture and its borderliness, as it were, when compared to the cultural histories of other European nations. Because this interest of Krleža's writing has hitherto been largely ignored in academic discussions of his eccentric leftism, the Pre-Raphaelite traces in his texts are a blind spot, awaiting the keen gaze of cultural theory.

Though Pre-Raphaelitism surfaces only sporadically in Krleža's work, it takes shape in his most influential essay of the 1930s: "The Foreword to the 'Podravina Motives' by Krsto Hegedušić" ("Predgovor 'Podravskim motivima' Krste Hegedušića"), first published in 1933 as part of the map containing thirty-four drawings by Hegedušić. This essay is important for the cultural history of Croatia, since it is the manifesto of a unique local variant of modern art, which has not been seriously disputed ever since the moment of its publication.

The importance of this essay derives from Krleža's argument that art cannot and should not sustain the political opposition between the symbolic right and the symbolic left. Instead, it should overrule both disinterested aestheticism and social realism, and constitute its own intrinsic responsibility toward practices of representation. Both aestheticism and social realism are positions that need to be deconstructed in order to make room for a locally valid definition of art. In Krleža's words, "the meaning of beauty is not—exclusively—in its being left or right (because even the most leftist social tendencies aim towards a situation in which there will be no left or right, and in which beauty will be recognized as the effected intensity of life)."[7] Hegedušić's idiosyncratic works manage to effect precisely such an intensity: "this visual representation of our reality has its own groundwork, its own powerful logic and its own wild, unrestrained eloquence."[8]

While Krleža constructs his view of social realism around the politicization of art as required by the official Soviet cultural programs at the time (the programs that Krleža usually refers to as "the Kharkov line"), he sees aestheticism as representation deliberately void of politics and of responsibility towards its subjects and its consumption. According to Krleža, the concept of beauty, especially in its aestheticist rendering, failed to sustain the new cultural politics generated by the violence of World War I and its victims:

> [t]hat degenerate carcass of the aesthetic doll, that fake mannequin of *l'art-pour-l'artiste* Beauty, was raped by Dada in the fire-squad ditch, while Surrealism aimed carefully and shot this academic phantom from its Parabellum. It was the international artillery rather than international art that caused all the aesthetic anarchy of our times.[9]

Krleža is equally critical of social realism in Soviet art: "[Alexander] Voronsky says that contemporary Russian fiction resembles the endeavors of the fourteenth-century Russian monks, the iconographers of the Kiev— or the Pskov schools—it gilds the halos around the literary schemes on revolutionary subjects."[10]

The problem of both these positions, however, is not merely one of overcharging or undercharging of daily politics: they fail to accommodate their own historical contingencies. Krleža perceives an inability of either of these positions to take into account the historical contingencies of other cultures that they enter. He sees both Soviet art and aestheticism as politically incorrect, so to speak, because of their inadequacy for exchange with the traditions of the cultures to which they are imported as foreign-made cultural products. Their deconstruction begins with their act of border crossing.

In view of Krleža's obsession with border crossing, the positions of aestheticism and social realism are charted in a peculiar symbolic geography. Krleža locates the pro-communist and the pro-Marxist discourse of social realism in Russia, but in the Russia of loosely defined boundaries, which operates as a convenient synecdoche for all the other, non-Russian discourses featuring social realism or decreed revolutionary subjects. Rather predictably, aestheticism is located in great Western European literatures of the nineteenth century, but the symbolic boundaries of Western Europe are perceived as equally loose and unstable insofar as they contract and expand in order to accommodate the symbolic raw material and the imaginary spaces of their colonies.

The figure of Oscar Wilde operates as a synecdoche of Krleža's idiosyncratic mapping of European aestheticism and determines Krleža's perception of Pre-Raphaelitism. For Krleža, Wilde is the representative of the end-of-the-century cult of beauty, not least because of the symbolic geography of his performance, which includes not only the predictable spaces of Ireland, England, and France, but also the ornamental Orient of his *Salome*. In other words, Wilde is conveniently far-reaching. Insofar as Wilde can be perceived as the synecdoche of aestheticism, his figure is determined by the surplus value of the symbolic capital invested in his performance, as opposed to other, comparatively deflated instances of aestheticism. According to Krleža, these deflated instances of aestheticism include, for instance, the works of Joachim Hermann Bang and Hermann Bahr, but also—rather paradoxically—Krleža's own early writings. As a young man before World War I, Krleža wrote several plays influenced by Wilde's poetics (including his own version of *Salome*), admitting in 1917 that "Wilde is not the worst role-model one could have had."[11]

Krleža's construction of Wilde relies on a plethora of metonymies organizing more precisely the scope of his performance, with Pre-Raphaelitism as one such formatting attribute. In other words, Pre-Raphaelitism, as surfacing in the discourse of Miroslav Krleža, derives its own symbolic value from the synecdochic surplus value invested in the aestheticist performance of Oscar Wilde—as its attribute, metonymy, or symbol. Indeed, the passage of Krleža's "Foreword" featuring the Pre-Raphaelites—with its rhetorical excess, akin to expressionism and intended to scandalize—is a synecdoche of Krleža's rhetoric:

> At the end of the last century, petty bourgeois decadents attempted to neutralize the concept of Beauty by declaring it immortal and elevating it above all reality, in the form of a mysterious deity made of crystalline Egyptian calcite: a cold greenish female body shrouded in precious alabaster cloth, with the eyes of onyx or of chrysoprase. That one-dimensional Pre-Raphaelite ornament or the allegory in the style of John Keats, that tapestry-like Wildean abstraction interwoven with gold, it stood amidst the European powder-room and slaughterhouse like a sublime statue made of ivory, one of the many metaphysical monograms by which God has sealed us into a sign of "our divine origin," . . . sending us to graves and caskets as heroes of the international epics, turning us into idealist *Schöngeists* or blue stockings or proponents of *l'art-pour-l'art*.[12]

This indicates that Krleža suppresses all the elements of Pre-Raphaelitism that he cannot use as tropes of Wildean aestheticism, in favor of "[t]hat one-dimensional Pre-Raphaelite ornament," "one of the many metaphysical monograms." His handling of Pre-Raphaelitism is therefore itself involved in an economy of synecdoche, as a figure operating in terms of repression and capitalization of discourse: complex and intricately diversified practices of Pre-Raphaelitism come to be represented in Krleža only by the way in which Pre-Raphaelitism structures and uses symbol and ornament. The figural economy of Pre-Raphaelitism in Krleža concentrates rhetorical value: the Pre-Raphaelite structuring of symbol comes to symbolize Pre-Raphaelitism in general, only to be used as a trope of Wildean aestheticism.

Moreover, Krleža uses Wildean aestheticism itself as a trope, a synecdoche, of a more general cultural framework. The "Pre-Raphaelite ornament" symbolizes the elaborate Western cultural construction entering "the European slaughterhouse"—the space of violence resisting representation and of extreme cultural hybridity. The nesting tropology of Pre-Raphaelitism in Krleža thus reverts the symbolic boundary back to a seemingly demarcated position (of Krleža's articulation). In his view, the cultural history and cultural geography of Croatia are determined by their cultural indeterminacy. As such, the cultural frame of Krleža's articulation is not a location but the positioning of indeterminacy.

Krleža sees the place of articulation, the birthsite of discourse, as the continuous performance of intersecting modalities and positionalities, which—instead of a place—yield only the unstoppable process of displacement. Hegedušić's art, according to Krleža, is effective specifically because it manages to relate to this impossibility of autonomous local tradition, source, and groundwork. Furthermore, it is effective because Hegedušić's own synecdoche of Croatia is the Northern Croatian region of Podravina, the territory of various borderlines and contact zones, which for a long time staged political and economic violence as the Western frontier toward the Ottoman East and its recruitment region—as a "European slaughterhouse." In Krleža's words,

> When I was (once again) writing, some eight years ago, about our unresolved issue, how to represent, in art and in literature, our obstinate, dark and unknown reality, it seemed to me—in that search for our own creative stronghold, for that hypothetical groundwork that Dostoevsky calls *pochva*—that Brueghel was the author whose creation of Brabant was so similar to our upper-Croatian region situated along the strategic historical counter-Turk bases between the cities of Karlovac and Koprivnica.[13]

Yet,

> [d]espite Brueghel's Flanders and the degenerated Berlin of George Grosz, Hegedušić's painting is local and related to this ancient recruitment region, in which baroque and feudal tributes, rates, tithes, chimney-taxes, bridge- and road-tolls shaped those serf and frontier conditions in stables, in barracks, and in churches, in human souls and physiognomies. The melancholy of an unsung elegy hangs above these open local issues.[14]

Krleža's references to the paintings of Brueghel and of George Grosz signal that the figures of foreignness in Hegedušić's paintings enter the very coreless core of Croatian cultural synecdoche, to be used as the figures of its radical displacement: they come closest to the intractable place of origin, resisting representation. As such, the paintings by Brueghel and Grosz are—symbolically—as far away as possible from Krleža's notion of aestheticism and Pre-Raphaelitism. At one point Krleža defines George Grosz and his poetics specifically as the opposite of Pre-Raphaelitism. In his 1926 essay on George Grosz, Krleža says that "compared to George Grosz, Svidrigailov, for instance, would be as mild and as romantic as a Pre-Raphaelite, if only he knew how to express visually his most perverse observations."[15]

Still, references to Brueghel and Grosz are common enough in Krleža—so common that they lose their aura of historical or cultural otherness: they acknowledge, once and again, the overriding otherness of Croatian culture itself. Paradoxically enough, it is their repeated affinity with the coreless core of Croatian culture that renders them central and authorizing, in the same way that Krleža's works—capitalizing precisely on the indeterminacy of Croatian culture—have become its present-day groundwork, its twentieth-century pochva.

As a result, marginal figures (here, the tropes of Pre-Raphaelitism) prove more efficacious in outlining the symbolic work of the boundary than the figures contracted for the positions of centrality, even in cultures conditioned by miscellaneous margins and boundaries. Krleža perceives social realism and—especially—aestheticism as having been imported into Croatian culture of the 1920s and 1930s. Their performance is bilateral: though figures of foreignness, of the outside, they still manage to enter, as foreign bodies of discourse, the disturbed symbolic space of Croatian culture. Their impact is crucial for the organization of the Croatian cultural perimeter in that they generate clusters of local satellites whose discourse production continually transfigures the outside as the inside, and vice versa.

In Krleža's essays of the late 1920s and 1930s—the eight years of his writing "about our unresolved issue"—Antun Gustav Matoš represented Croatian aestheticism. Matoš was for Krleža as synecdochic as Wilde: Matoš is a figure of the symbolic surplus value of symbolism itself, but one who traces the movement of Wildean tropes toward the difficult boundary separating Europe from its eastern colonies. As he does with Wilde, Krleža uses Pre-Raphaelitism as a trope to organize the symbolic function of Matoš and his work in terms of symbolic geography.

While Krleža's "Foreword" remains the interpretive center of this cultural decentering, his essay "On Marcel Proust" ("O Marcelu Proustu," 1926) paves the way for the paradoxical resolution of the unresolved in Croatian culture by organizing symbolically not only its Western outside but also Croatian cultural boundaries. Pre-Raphaelitism enters once again as a trope of Oscar Wilde and Anglo-French aestheticism, but also as the foreign body within the nesting, bilateral boundaries in Croatian culture— here, as an attribute of Matoš and his circle:

> Tunisia, India, Peru, Schubert, and Chopin, that is the subject matter of those aristocratic Wilde's Pre-Raphaelites, that is the prop which fascinated international artists and bohemia, blossoming profusely, it seems, in all European literatures (here, for instance, in Matoš's Toledo-style Barrèsism or in the Ragusan pieces by Count Ivo Vojnović).[16]

Krleža's mapping of foreignness is an interesting example of different kinds of symbolic profit made out of cultural otherness. While Western Europe provides the symbolic capital for Wildean Pre-Raphaelite production in the form of Schubert and Chopin (elaborate, pre-produced, and individualized symbolic constructions), the symbolic colonies of Tunisia, India, and Peru are used as semiotic raw materials. Croatian literature is represented as an expanse of void in-betweenness, which merely registers the transit of foreign traces.

The same rhetorical gesture is repeated in Krleža's essay on Ljubo Wiesner, a Croatian poet whom he describes as a minor member of Matoš's circle ("Lirika Ljube Wiesnera," 1927). According to Krleža, the poetry of Ljubo Wiesner is conditioned by

> that yearning for discoveries and for the sensation of a romantic journey that knows no return, . . . that chase for a way out of the "European gloom," that fascination with the Ganges, the Madonna cult, or the ideals of St. Francis of Assisi (typical imports of the end-of-the-century Western neo-Catholicism, Pre-Raphaelitism, *Sezession, Moderna*,[17] etc.)[18]

The writing produced by Matoš and his circle, in Krleža's view, seems to do less than what Walter Benjamin describes as the task of the translator, the mission of "watching over the maturing process of the original language and the birth pangs of its own"[19] and a "coming to terms with the foreignness of languages."[20] Still, Krleža's description of Matoš in terms of foreignness is problematic: Matoš produced not only symbolist poetry and short *Moderna*-style narratives, but essays, reviews, and travelogues in which he set about demarcating the boundaries of Croatian culture. Moreover, he critically dismissed many writers whom Krleža denotes as his followers, specifically because of their uncritical use of foreign literary traditions—most poignantly, Milan Begović and his imitation of D'Annunzio. Apart from this, Matoš wrote extensively about Croatian politicians and was later, in socialist Yugoslavia, criticized in the official cultural programs as a Croatian nationalist, and only a sanitized selection of his work was taught at schools. This selection included some Matoš's symbolist poetry and his *Moderna*-style stories (precisely the kind of texts that Krleža defines as void of political responsibility) and omitted his essays on politics. By the time Krleža started writing, just before World War I, Matoš's works had already performed as the semiotic groundwork of Croatian culture, as its tentative twentieth-century pochva. The nesting in Krleža's discourse is not merely the layered foreignness of Croatian culture but also its preceding mappings. This overlapping suggests that Krleža's writing stages both the mapping of culture and the process of its own authorization. In other words, the construction of cultural identity in Krleža is at the same time the construction of the right to construct, represent, and identify, based on a deconstruction of previous mappings and representations. Or, in the words of Pierre Bourdieu, symbolic properties generally, "even the most negative, can be used strategically according to the material but also the symbolic interests of their bearer."[21]

Krleža's deconstruction of Matoš and his symbolism appears to be flawed once again in its handling of tropology. Though I have already located the flaw in Krleža's deconstruction of symbol and its modus operandi (because Krleža capitalizes on the figural economy of symbol while simultaneously performing its critique), the flaw widens if one examines Matoš's own analysis of symbol and its modus operandi, which Krleža repressed in order to produce an operable synecdoche. In other words, Krleža's critical use of symbol contains, as its repressed material, Matoš's subtle historicizing of symbol and—through that historicizing—its own deconstruction.

Pre-Raphaelitism surfaces in Matoš as a useful material of both symbolism and historicism, yielding auto-deconstruction. Unlike Krleža's writing, Matoš's discourse on symbol in general, and Pre-Raphaelitism in particular, tends to desymbolize them in order to contain their rhetoric in terms of their historical and cultural contingencies.

Matoš's tendency to historicize the use of symbol and to localize its effect is perhaps best seen in his essay "The Obsolescence of Literary Terms" ("Zastarjelost literarnih termina," 1909). Matoš uses Pre-Raphaelitism as an example of a rhetoric that continually fails to sustain its genealogy:

> Pre-Raphaelitism in England is actually an episode of late romanticism, degenerating in some painters into pure realism, as in Ruskin's writing about art, and then into symbolism and mysticism, tendencies seemingly opposite to romanticism.[22]

It follows that as early as 1909, Matoš saw Pre-Raphaelitism as an obsolete literary term because of its inability to accommodate the evolution of its rhetoric. What is more, genealogies themselves, as seen by Matoš, may be multiple and overlaying. Thus, the Pre-Raphaelite use of symbol in Matoš is granted its own culturally and historically contingent genealogy, which goes back to Dante Alighieri. According to Matoš, "Dante is the purest and the most famous symbolist of all, the best painter of thoughts with material signs, and the modern Pre-Raphaelites are his direct descendants."[23] In addition, Matoš's own trope of symbolism and aestheticism is Pre-Raphaelitism. In his 1904 essay on Charles Baudelaire, for instance, Matoš singles out "Wagner, D. G. Rossetti, Ruskin, Taine and Nietzsche" next to Baudelaire as "the most powerful components of modern aestheticist tendencies."[24] Two years earlier, moreover, Matoš defined modernism as historically contingent, with Pre-Raphaelitism as one of its performances:

> Modernism is merely a new style, a search for the new idiom, the evolution of style. All the new schools and styles were at the moment of their emergence a reaction against old patterns and routines, i.e. modernisms. Victor Hugo, the beginnings of Romanticism, the Parnassians, the Pre-Raphaelites, Poe, naturalists and verists, Symbolism—these are all modernisms until they start declining.[25]

In view of Krleža's zealous politics of discourse and its tropology, it is worth noting that as early as 1900, Matoš analyzes the difficult relation of symbol and ornament in European symbolisms and aestheticisms in terms of their figural charge—in terms of their effect rather than their formal differences. Thus fin-de-siècle symbol and ornament, according to Matoš, differ: symbol facilitates the trespassing of its figural boundaries, while ornament tends to fortify the bounds of representation. Pre-Raphaelitism is constitutive for this evolution of symbol and ornament, which finds its representation in the visual art of Alphonse Mucha:

> Mucha is generally primitive, and the stillness and the abstract shapes of his simple figures remind me of Byzantine icons, of the Rhine school and the Pre-Raphaelites. It is through this that his posters . . . acquire certain mannerism, certain monotony which the artist manages to avoid by means of extraordinary, luxurious ornamentation. The contrast between the central, hieratic, primitivized, symbolic figure and the luscious, tropical yet simple ornaments yields in his works that saturation, that pure fin-de-siècle quality, which in the greatest modern artists appears as the combination of "too much" and "too little"—a consequence of clogged ennui and an insatiable desire for simplicity and liberation. That rich ornamentation makes most Mucha's symbols decorative, symbol passes into ornament (as in Carlos Schwabe), ornament into symbol, and this is certainly not the least original trait of this artist.[26]

Matoš's remarks seem to anticipate current views on Pre-Raphaelitism and its effect on Mucha and Schwabe. Alicia Craig Faxon, for instance, says that "Rossetti's beautiful and enigmatic women, as in his *Astarte Syriaca* . . . can be seen echoed in such popular images as Alphonse Mucha's poster advertising Sarah Bernhardt."[27] Also, Craig Faxon identifies Carlos Schwabe as an imitator of the Pre-Raphaelites, who "perpetuated the ideal of late Pre-Raphaelitism in the realms of myth, legend, allegory, and the dream,"[28] while Susan P. Casteras describes his poster for the 1892 Rosicrucian salon in Paris as "decidedly Pre-Raphaelite in spirit."[29] Sarah Phelps Smith notices in Mucha "the transformation of Rossetti's women and flowers into Art Nouveau," as well as the tension between symbol and ornament.[30]

Matoš often uses Pre-Raphaelitism as a figure of speech that enables him to delimit foreign tropes in the symbolic boundaries of Croatian culture. Since Krleža uses Matoš as a trope of his cultural geography, it is relevant that Matoš's travel writing, too, contains references to symbolism and Pre-Raphaelitism—especially the instances when Matoš uses Pre-Raphaelitism as a trope to represent Croatian locations. Matoš's mapping of Croatian regionality and spatiality contracts Pre-Raphaelitism as its trope-generating mechanism, yet in a way which invalidates Krleža's criticisms.

Matoš's travelogue "Around Lobor" ("Oko Lobora," 1907) is one of the most sophisticated twentieth-century Croatian travelogues, in that it traces the tradition of the nineteenth-century Croatian travelogues and maps the Croatian space in terms of its history and cultural geography.[31] It charts the village of Lobor in the region of Hrvatsko Zagorje—a predominantly rural region in northwestern Croatia, in many respects comparable to Krleža's Podravina. This unlikely venue elicits a reference to Pre-Raphaelitism. When describing his visit to the old castle, Matoš compares the ghosts of its past to a painting by Edward Burne-Jones:

> Or maybe this thing in the branches is no wind at all, maybe it is not a dryad, that lover of rivulets and Pan-like, shepherd dreamers? That must be some lost sound of Lobor, a countess or a pale little duchess, living in the sadness of eternal green shades, like a princess in that painting by Burne-Jones,[32] who whispers sweet, melancholy, enervated little stories to unexpected visitors, the stories for which she has no words.[33]

Matoš's reference to Burne-Jones in this context operates as an intrusive trope, a foreign body of discourse, facilitating the location of Croatian culture only in terms of its constant displacement. Yet, unlike Krleža's aggressively overstepping tropes involving Pre-Raphaelitism, Matoš's comparison of the local Lobor ghosts to a painting by Burne-Jones tends to reduce and localize its figural activity: it utilizes Pre-Raphaelitism not as an overriding trope of aestheticism but as a specific, delimited reference to a particular painting by Edward Burne-Jones. Also, this localized reference operates as a trope of mute ghosts and an old castle, of a difficult local past that cannot communicate itself to the present and thus fails to constitute an operable local genealogy. It is a trope of the past that itself operates as a foreign body in the given frame.[34]

Matoš's art criticism on Croatian subjects features Pre-Raphaelitism in a similar manner. His review of Bela Csikos (1864–1931) and his exhibits in the 1900 Paris World Exhibition is a vivid example of this negative inclusion of the Pre-Raphaelites in the Croatian cultural space. Matoš describes Csikos's paintings of the crucial events in Croatian history as similar to "the Munich dreamers rather than to Burne Jones, the Burne Jones of fairy tales, legends and artless quivering."[35] Burne-Jones's visuality thus helps delineating the outside of the Croatian cultural space—what it is *not*—yet at the same time appears inscribed in this space because organizing its boundary.

In his review of a 1908 Zagreb exhibition of Croatian and other South Slav painters, Matoš describes Branko Šenoa's paintings of flowers and plants as done "in the romantic manner of the Pre-Raphaelites."[36] Still, though he finds Šenoa's "Pre-Raphaelite" flowers pleasing, Matoš excludes Šenoa from what he considers the best Croatian painting by describing his focus on plants and gardens as "too sweet" and "too feminine."[37] Also, Matoš is careful to localize Šenoa's visual interests to botany and a detailed portrayal of Croatian gardens and parks, a kind of mapping of the local space that is conveniently small-scale and femininely Other (Figure 5.1).[38] Thus Šenoa's interest in a detailed representation of the botanical world renders him "Pre-Raphaelite," but at the same time deflates his cultural impact and renders him marginal.

Matoš's description of a decorative panel by Tomislav Krizman (1882–1955; Figure 5.2), exhibited in Zagreb in 1910, contains another localized reference to Pre-Raphaelitism in Croatian visual arts:

> Tomislav Krizman is under a foreign influence whenever not painting straight from the nature. His drawing technique is lovely, but his eye and his imagination are not original. . . . His grand panel *Prince Marko and the Fairy (Kraljević Marko i vila)*[39] offers: a splendid drawing of two *pinzgauer* horses with two naked riders in the striking manner of Rubens-Stuck. The forest, the silent forest with trees, naked trees, in the manner of Böcklin. A fairy in the branches, painted very naively, in the manner of Burne-Jones; adding to this Pre-Raphaelite naiveté, there are animals down below, without any fear of humans, as if in the first naiveté of Eden: a squirrel and a bird—a feathery cross of a goldfinch and a parrot. And above all the Krizman-style blue sky with the eternal rainbow on a still horizon. Five different styles in a single painting![40]

According to Matoš, Pre-Raphaelitism surfaces in Krizman's decorative panel as only one of the four distinctly foreign styles (Rubens, Stuck, Böcklin, Burne-Jones). Also, Matoš restricts its presence to a single figure (the fairy), and thus further limits its participation in the organization of pictorial space.

The Pre-Raphaelite fairy helps organizing the space similar to Lobor of Matoš's travelogue: it is the immaterial space of the legendary local past, featuring Prince Marko, the figure far more significant in folklore and literature than history and historiography. Of the five styles that

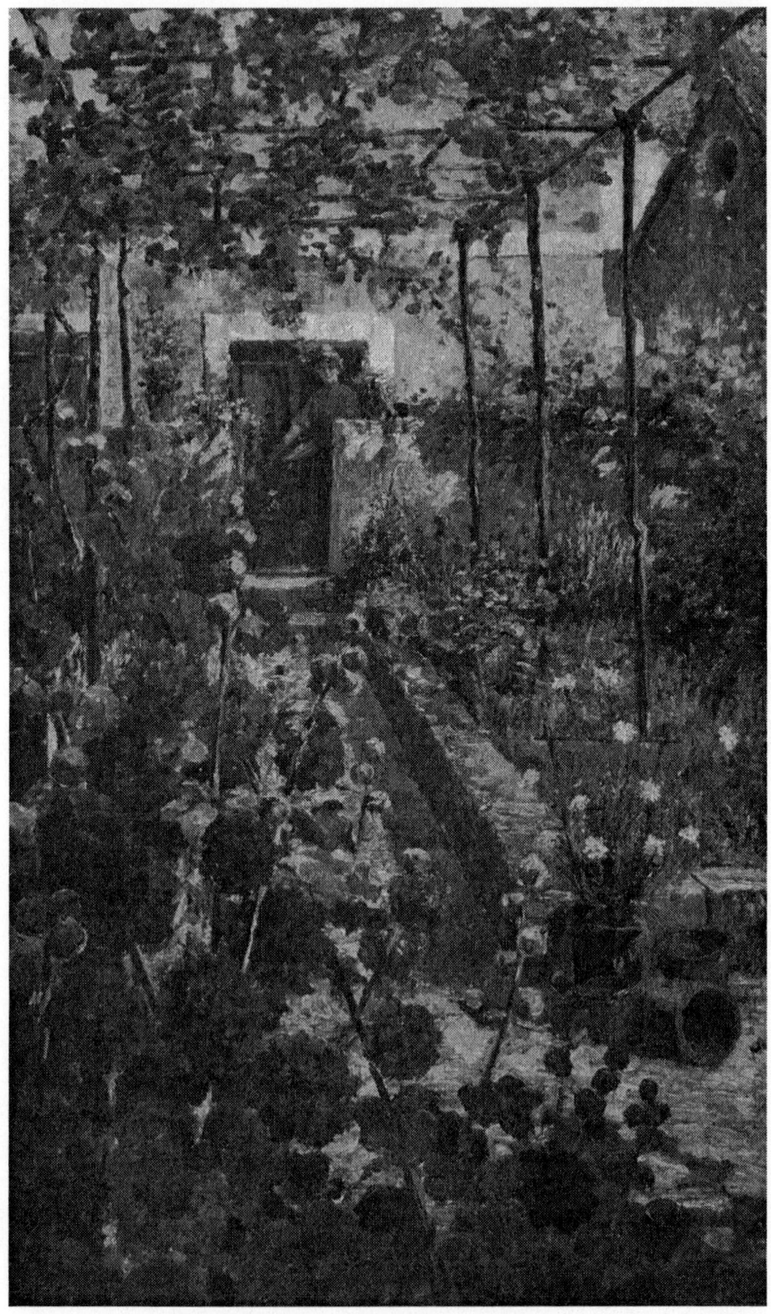

Figure 5.1. Branko Šenoa, *Iz Kraljevice* "From Kraljevica" (1908). Used by kind permission of the Modern Gallery, Zagreb.

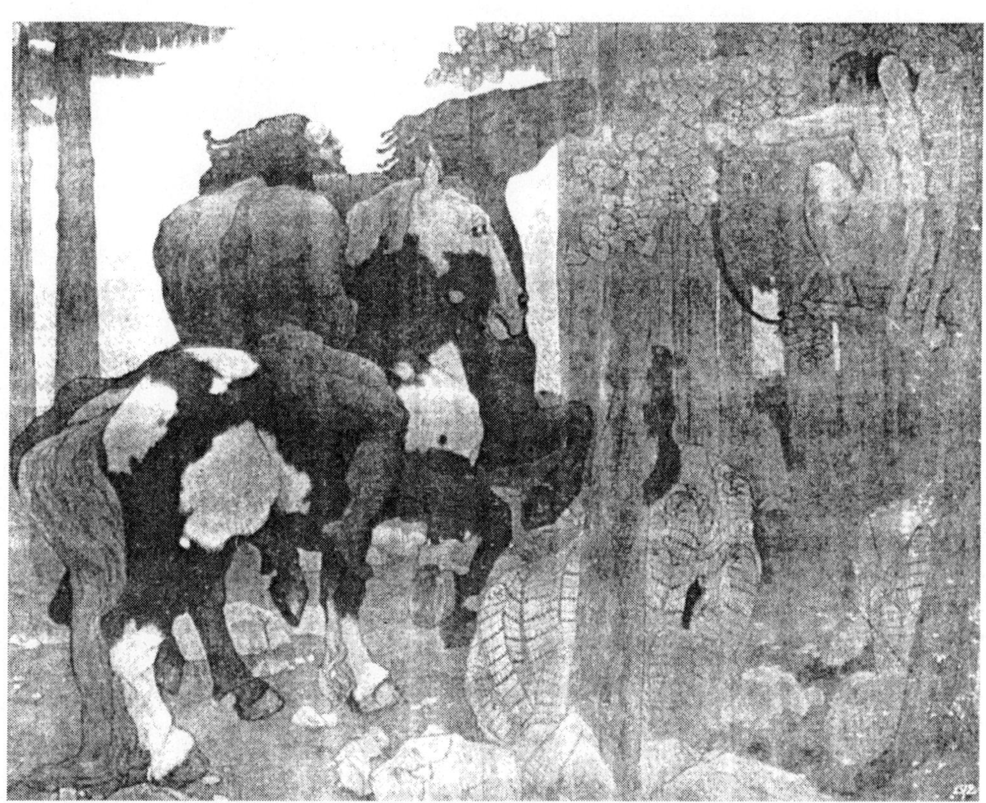

Figure 5.2. Tomislav Krizman, *Kraljević Marko i vila* "Prince Marko and the Fairy."
The original work is presumed lost; figure reprinted from Izložba Medulića,
Nejunačkom vremenu uprkos (Zagreb: Umjetnički Paviljon, 1910), by kind
permission of the Archiv za Likovne Umjetnosti, Zagreb.

Matoš enumerates in his review of Krizman's panel, Pre-Raphaelitism is the only one signaling improbability of this past as naive and downright fantastic. Further, the imaginary quality of this past performs through the Pre-Raphaelite woman, enveloped in foliage and suspended between sensuality and incorporeality—in other words, the figure that proved to be the most profitable Pre-Raphaelite import into Continental art. Next to Matoš's Lobor ghost, Krizman's fairy can thus be seen as another echo of the Pre-Raphaelite woman figure in Croatian context, functional as a trope of the controversial local past. After all, Krleža's reference to "that one dimensional Pre-Raphaelite ornament" too outlines the Pre-Raphaelite ornament as an exotic goddess figure.

As a result, Matoš's handling of Pre-Raphaelitism effects the deconstruction of trope that Krleža later calls for. Yet, in Krleža's writing about Croatian culture Matoš's Pre-Raphaelitism is constructed into a synecdoche of the excess of symbolism. Matoš's delimited and localized use of Pre-Raphaelitism and its symbols, careful of their cultural and historical contingencies, performs as the repressed of Krleža's cultural politics of the late 1920s and 1930s, facilitating Krleža's overvaluation of figurality.

Another symptom of Krleža's cultural politics in the late 1920s and the early 1930s is the very phrasing that shapes his references to the Pre-Raphaelites. Krleža refers to Pre-Raphaelitism in the adjectival form (as in "Pre-Raphaelite ornament"), or he uses it as an vague umbrella-term, "the Pre-Raphaelites."[41] Unlike Matoš, whose texts feature in addition to the general terms such as "Pre-Raphaelite," "the Pre-Raphaelites," and "Pre-Raphaelitism," the names of William Holman Hunt, Dante Gabriel Rossetti, John Ruskin, William Morris, and Edward Burne-Jones, as well as many references to their idiosyncratic practices.

Matoš refers to Holman Hunt as "the last Pre-Raphaelite"[42] and to having seen "the Pre-Raphaelite's" self-portrait in Uffizi, in Florence.[43] He comments on Burne-Jones as the author of "the famous *Golden Stairs* and *The Mirror of Venus*."[44] Also, Matoš emphasizes the interaction of literature and the visual in Pre-Raphaelitism, especially in Rossetti.[45] When describing, in 1898, the work of Leon Kojen, a Serbian painter living in Munich at the time, Matoš says that his painting resembles Pre-Raphaelitism because of its brilliant color and its narrativity.[46] Further, Matoš implies that Pre-Raphaelitism contains elements of hallucination and neurosis, "being the school of D. G. Rossetti, a morphinist," and criticizes a Croatian art critic who described Pre-Raphaelite paintings as "not nervous."[47] On the other hand, Matoš says that "spiritualism and explicit pro-Catholic sentiments" of "the Pre-Raphaelite poets" should appeal to what he identifies as the Jesuit streak in Croatian art and literary criticism.[48]

In addition, Matoš was a keen analyst of the social impulse of Pre-Raphaelitism and its medievalism, especially in John Ruskin and William Morris. In his essay "Modern symbols," he says that Pre-Raphaelitism failed to accomplish its goal—"democratizing arts"—because it "blindly imitated primitive Italian arts" instead of constructing new symbols, adequate to the social circumstances of the nineteenth century.[49] Matoš was equally sensitive of the role that this misconceived medievalism of the Pre-Raphaelites played in popular culture. In his story "After a New God," which he wrote in Paris in 1902, Matoš perceives the impact of Pre-Raphaelitism in terms of fashion and the new ideal of female beauty: he describes his heroine with a mass of thick auburn hair combed in the hairstyle fashionable in Croatia in the 1890s, initiated by the craze for "Botticelli, the Pre-Raphaelites and Cléo de Mérode, a dancer from Paris."[50]

Krleža's few references to Pre-Raphaelitism, on the other hand, are vague and unspecific. Krleža's adjectival use of the term renders it relational, defined by the need for another, defining term. It opens up Pre-Raphaelitism as a symbolic space of unceasing metaphor production, the space whose mapping depends on the instability of its conceptual borders.

By transfiguring Matoš and his cultural knowledge into a symbol, Krleža produces the kind of cultural geography that Matoš himself had first identified as lacking—the symbolic groundwork out of gaps and discontinuities, a genealogy necessarily defective, a strangely repressive narrative of cultural evolution. These negative symbolic properties produced at the same time Krleža's position as the position of cultural authority, authorizing Krleža to represent and identify Croatian culture. This process resembles what Gillian Beer describes as the way in which most discourses concerning scientific discoveries operate in terms of rhetoric transfiguring anomaly into law. According to Beer, the transfiguration of what has been perceived as anomaly into law requires yet another rhetorical operation: a conversion of the old law into a gray domain of metaphor. The word "transfiguration" here is far from contingent: Beer argues that most major scientific theories "disturb assumed relationships and shift what has been substantial into metaphor."[51] Troping and figuring are the principal operations in the process of negotiating a marginal position into a position of centrality and legitimacy.

Krleža's use of Pre-Raphaelitism in the 1940s and the 1970s—after his writing had acquired a central position in Croatian culture—seems to support the above proposition. Once again, Pre-Raphaelitism functions as a trace, a visible trope of an entire modus operandi, now helping to negotiate what appears to be an aberration in Krleža's discourse into a protocol of its interpretation. In his essay about G. K. Chesterton, written in 1942, Krleža describes Chesterton's views on religious orthodoxy by associating them with Pre-Raphaelite practices:

> How is one to confront these "superhuman paradoxes,"[52] like the one when Chesterton claims that West European fashion, for instance, is the element that separates us from the Asiatic civilizations, or the one when he regally refutes the liberal assumption that European art is becoming less religious, for European art is traveling as fast as the tank-engine towards the Supernatural? All that was written in the 1890s, in the sign of P. R. B.[53]

Krleža's use of Pre-Raphaelitism in 1942 seems no different from his use of the trope in the late 1920s and the 1930s. Pre-Raphaelitism is still seen as a generalizing set of practices—a conveniently all-inclusive "P. R. B."—open to potentially limitless trope production. What is more, the very phrase "in the sign of P. R. B." suggests an agile rhetorical productivity of Pre-Raphaelite discourse and recognizes its effect as generative of various other Victorian discourses.

Yet, Krleža's 1942 reference to Pre-Raphaelitism as the "P. R. B." implies a different kind of cultural knowledge, a more positive identification of a trace instead of a potentially boundless production of tropes, the inclusion of the insider information missing from his essays of the late 1920s and the 1930s. Once in the position of symbolic centrality and legitimacy, Krleža no longer needed the authorization-providing labor of tropes and could afford to adopt "assumed relationships" of cultural knowledge. Also, it suggests a shift in what is perceived as the dominant genealogy of Pre-Raphaelitism. While in his earlier essays Krleža perceived Pre-Raphaelitism as a practice related to various Anglo-French aestheticisms and symbolisms, criticizing its lack of political responsibility, in 1942 he describes it as the cultural institution productive of the nineteenth-century religious controversy and of deeply ethical issues.

Krleža's essay on Chesterton remained an unpublished fragment for decades and was published only in 1971, accompanied by footnotes that date from the late 1960s and comment on the text written in 1942. Thus, what in 1942 were the somewhat enigmatic initials, "P. R. B."—a trace of cryptic inscription defying deciphering—received in 1971 a footnote, in which Krleža interpreted the initials and the cultural genealogy of Pre-Raphaelitism and set a seal on its figural productivity:

> P. R. B. Pre-Raphaelite Brotherhood. Rossetti, Hunt, Brown, "the Pre-Raphaelite Brotherhood," a pendant of Overbeck's Nazarene "Lukasbund." A group of English and German painters, predecessors and descendants of Romanticism, who were inspired by traditional Catholicism, and who found their role models in the religious inspiration of the pre-Raphaelite period. At the time when Chesterton wrote his *Orthodoxy*, when conversion was fashionable among artists, there was an entire phalange of converts: Hofmannsthal, Hermann Bahr, Rilke, and so on to Papini and Panaiotus Istrati.[54]

This difficult genealogy of Krleža's "P. R. B." can be seen as a symptom of the difficult genealogy of Krleža's own discourse, covering the span of nearly sixty years. Also, it is a trace of the discourse that was itself in many ways symptomatic of the difficult genealogy of Croatian culture at the time. Thus, in the late 1920s and the 1930s, Krleža used the term "Pre-Raphaelite" as a trope of the colonizing Anglo-French aestheticisms and of politically irresponsible art. In 1942—when official Croatia was a German ally and when Krleža, though a famous writer and a known leftist, risked staying in Zagreb—"Pre-Raphaelitism" surfaces as a cryptic trope of Anglo-Catholic doubt, burdened by the legacy of unacknowledged German romanticism. In 1971—when Krleža was the head of the central state Encyclopedic Institute and by far the most authoritative Croatian writer—Pre-Raphaelitism divulges its complicated genealogy of the 1940s, but suppresses its preauthorized figural activity of the 1920s and the 1930s. The term "Pre-Raphaelitism" in Krleža (and in Croatian culture) remains vague and displacing, tracing equally the symbolic interests of Krleža's writing and of Croatian culture.

Finally, whatever the interests invested in this project of mapping and border crossing, they ultimately testify to the lasting performance of Pre-Raphaelitism as a trope and the abiding circulation of its Victorian symbolic capital. Its performance as a symbol-generating foreign body within other cultures and within the discourses of Others testifies to the cultural grafts in what is today perceived as Pre-Raphaelitism, demanding a new critical analysis of the act of border crossing. Pre-Raphaelitism, now as at the time of its (ever-displaced) origination, keeps performing Other-wise.

NOTES

1. Alicia Craig Faxon, "Introduction: A New View of Pre-Raphaelitism," in *Pre-Raphaelite Art in Its European Context* eds. Susan P. Casteras and Alicia

Craig Faxon (Cranbury, London, Mississauga: Associated University Press, 1995), 24.

2. Faxon, 11.

3. Matoš was pardoned and allowed to return to Zagreb in 1908.

4. Antun Gustav Matoš, "Nove simpatije Marka Cara," in *Djela. Knjiga XI* (Zagreb: Binoza, 1940), 7.

5. Morana Čale, "Begovićev dramski let iznad D'Annunzijevog nadčovjeka," in *Umjetnost riječi*, 42.1 (1998): 60.

6. Nikola Batušić, Zoran Kravar, and Viktor Žmegač, *Književni protusvjetovi. Poglavlja iz hrvatske moderne* (Zagreb: Matica Hrvatska, 2001), 201–2.

7. Miroslav Krleža, "Predgovor 'Podravskim motivima' Krste Hegedušića" in *Eseji III. Sabrana djela* (Zagreb: Zora, 1963), 318. The translations of all passages from Krleža and Matoš are my own.

8. Ibid., 332.

9. Ibid., 313.

10. Ibid., 334.

11. Miroslav Krleža, *Davni dani. Zapisi 1914–1921. Sabrana djela* (Zagreb: Zora, 1956), 244.

12. Krleža, 313.

13. Ibid., 330.

14. Ibid., 336.

15. Miroslav Krleža, "O njemačkom slikaru Georgeu Groszu" in *Eseji I. Sabrana djela* (Zagreb: Zora, 1961), 247.

16. Miroslav Krleža, "O Marcelu Proustu" in *Eseji I. Sabrana djela* (Zagreb: Zora, 1961), 63.

17. *Moderna* designates turn-of-the-century Croatian literature, akin to symbolism and aestheticism.

18. Miroslav Krleža, "Lirika Ljube Wiesnera" in *Eseji III. Sabrana djela* (Zagreb: Zora, 1963), 90.

19. Walter Benjamin, "The Task of the Translator" in *Illuminations: Essays and Reflections*, ed. Hannah Arendt (New York: Schocken, 1969), 73.

20. Ibid., 75.

21. Pierre Bourdieu, "Identity and Representation: Elements for a Critical

Reflection on the Idea of Region," in *Language and Symbolic Power* (Cambridge, MA: Harvard University Press, 1991), 221.

22. Antun Gustav Matoš, "Zastarjelost Literarnih Termina," in *Djela. Knjiga XVI* (Zagreb: Binoza, 1940), 260.

23. Antun Gustav Matoš, "Baudelaire," in *Antun Gustav Matoš II. Pet stoljeća hrvatske književnosti* (Zagreb: Matica hrvatska, Zora, 1967), 64.

24. Ibid., 80.

25. Antun Gustav Matoš, "Sintetična kritika" in *Djela. Knjiga IV* (Zagreb: Binoza, 1937), 159.

26. Antun Gustav Matoš, "Dojmovi s Pariške izložbe" in *Djela. Knjiga VI* (Zagreb: Binoza, 1940), 171.

27. Faxon, 24.

28. Ibid., 24.

29. Susan P. Casteras, "The Pre-Raphaelite Legacy to Symbolism: Continental Response and Impact on Artists in the Rosicrucian Circle," in *Pre-Raphaelite Art in Its European Context*, eds. Susan P. Casteras and Alicia Craig Faxon (Cranbury, London, Mississauga: Associated University Presses, 1995), 41.

30. Sarah Phelps Smith, "From Allegory to Symbol: Rossetti's Renaissance Roots and His Influence on Continental Symbolism" in *Pre-Raphaelite Art in Its European Context*, eds. Susan P. Casteras and Alicia Craig Faxon (Cranbury, London, Mississauga: Associated University Presses, 1995), 62–64.

31. See Dean Duda, *Priča i putovanje. Hrvatski romantičarski putopis kao pripovjednižanr* (Zagreb: Matica Hrvatska, 1998), 129.

32. Possibly *King Cophetua and the Beggar Maid* or the *Briar Rose* series of panels.

33. Antun Gustav Matoš, "Oko Lobora" in *Djela. Knjiga IV* (Zagreb: Binoza, 1937), 12.

34. Another of Matoš's references to Burne-Jones in the context of Croatian culture supports such a reading of his tropology. In 1908, Matoš says that the supremely talented infantile naiveté of Croatian aestheticist poetry, including the poetry of Ljubo Wiesner, would "no doubt fascinate Burne-Jones and Verlaine." Yet this possibly laudatory comment lapses into irony by virtue of its textual framing—it is part of Matoš's text which features two farcical characters, the Hairy and the Hunchback (*Rutavac* and *Guravac*), who comment on Croatian culture and politics from a provincial, *petit bourgeois* perspective. See Antun

Gustav Matoš, "Literarni dialozi" in *Djela. Knjiga XVI* (Zagreb: Binoza, 1940), 205.

35. Antun Gustav Matoš, "Dojmovi sa pariške izložbe" in *Djela. Knjiga VI* (Zagreb: Binoza, 1938), 140.

36. Antun Gustav Matoš, "Izložbene impresije. Treća jugoslavenska umjetnička izložba saveza 'Lade' u Zagrebu" in *Djela. Knjiga XVI* (Zagreb: Binoza, 1940), 161. Šenoa (1879–1939) exhibited two paintings in the 1908 "Lada" association of painters' exhibition in Zagreb: *Spring* (*Proljeće*, location unknown) and *From Kraljevica* (*Iz Kraljevice*, Figure 1).

37. Antun Gustav Matoš, "Dojmovi s umjetničke izložbe" in *Sabrana djela. Svezak XI. O likovnim umjetnostima. Putopisi* (Zagreb: JAZU, Liber, Mladost, 1973), 61.

38. Ironically, Šenoa is nowadays remembered for his cityscapes and the paintings of representative Croatian buildings, for the most part painted after World War I.

39. Presumed lost. There survives a reproduction in the exhibition catalogue (*Nejunačkom vremenu uprkos. Izložba Medulića*, Zagreb: Umjetnički paviljon, XI-XII, 1910, Figure 2). See a catalogue raisonné in Smiljka Domac Ceraj, *Slikarsko i grafičko djelo Tomislava Krizmana* (MA thesis, Faculty of Philosophy, University of Zagreb, 1999).

40. Antun Gustav Matoš, "Povodom izložbe 'Medulića' " in *Sabrana djela. Svezak XI. O likovnim umjetnostima. Putopisi* (Zagreb: JAZU, Liber, Mladost, 1973), 92.

41. As, for instance, in his 1926 essay on George Bernard Shaw, when he says that Hogarth and Voltaire are closer to Shaw "than his contemporaries, the Pre-Raphaelites, than Kipling's lyricism or Beardsley's perverse decorativeness." See Miroslav Krleža, "George Bernard Shaw" in *Eseji I. Sabrana djela* (Zagreb: Zora, 1961), 205.

42. Antun Gustav Matoš, "Engleske siluete" in *Djela. Knjiga XII* (Zagreb: Binoza, 1940), 146.

43. Antun Gustav Matoš, "Od Firence do Zagreba" in *Antun Gustav Matoš III. Pet stoljeća hrvatske književnosti* (Zagreb: Matica hrvatska, Zora, 1967), 325.

44. Antun Gustav Matoš, "Dojmovi s Pariške izložbe" in *Djela. Knjiga VI* (Zagreb: Binoza, 1938), 228; and "Napomene" in *Djela. Knjiga VI* (Zagreb: Binoza, 1938), 247.

45. Antun Gustav Matoš, "Dojmovi s umjetničke izložbe" in *Djela. Knjiga XVI* (Zagreb: Binoza, 1940), 267, and "Književnost i književnici" in *Sabrana*

djela. Svezak III. Ogledi. Vidici i putovi. Naši ljudi i krajevi (Zagreb: JAZU, 1955), 398.

46. Antun Gustav Matoš, "Od Münchena do Ženeve" in *Djela. Knjiga VI* (Zagreb: Binoza, 1938), 89–90.

47. Antun Gustav Matoš, "Šmokovi" in *Djela. Knjiga XVI* (Zagreb: Binoza, 1940), 179.

48. Antun Gustav Matoš, "Jezuitska kritika" in *Djela. Knjiga XVI* (Zagreb: Binoza, 1940), 56.

49. Antun Gustav Matoš, "Moderni simboli" in *Djela. Knjiga XVI* (Zagreb: Binoza, 1940), 20. In an essay on Rousseau and his concept of nature, Matoš remarks that "Ruskin and the Pre-Raphaelites, too, dislike big cities" ("Dvjestagodišnjica Jeana-Jacquesa Rousseaua" in *Antun Gustav Matoš III. Pet stoljeća hrvatske književnosti*, Zagreb: Matica Hrvatska, Zora, 1967), 151.

50. Antun Gustav Matoš, "Za novim bogom" in *Sabrana djela. Svezak II. Novele, humoreske, satire, scenski tekstovi* (Zagreb: JAZU, Liber, Mladost, 1973), 70.

51. Gillian Beer, *Darwin's Plots: Evolutionary Narrative in Darwin, George Eliot and Nineteenth-Century Fiction* (London: Routledge & Kegan Paul, 1983), 3.

52. Krleža refers to a phrase used by Chesterton, who—according to Krleža—"declared that his liberal essays were the book of superhuman paradox." See Miroslav Krleža, "Chestertonova knjiga o ortodoksiji. Fragment rukopisa iz kasne jeseni 1942," in *Dijalozi i ideje. Studije. Knjiga 5. Sabrana djela* (Sarajevo: Oslobođenje, 1985), 271.

53. Krleža, "Chestertonova knjiga o ortodoksiji," 271.

54. Ibid., 271n.

Chapter 6

SYMBOLIST DEBTS TO PRE-RAPHAELITISM: A PAN-EUROPEAN PHENOMENON

Susan P. Casteras

The legacy of Pre-Raphaelitism was truly pan-European in the late-nineteenth century, and its impact on Symbolist art was particularly strong.[1] France and Belgium, main venues for the Rose+Croix salons, were the primary sites where this was manifested, and there were also waves of influence that flowed into Austria, Switzerland, Spain, Holland, Germany, Finland, Italy, Hungary, and eastern Europe.[2] This topic has only recently begun to be plumbed, from definitions of what British symbolism encompassed in terms of adherents and influence to the far-reaching ramifications for modern art.[3]

One of the major factors for this cross-fertilization was the ascendancy on the Continent of the reputations of Dante Gabriel Rossetti and Edward Burne-Jones (and, to a lesser extent, John Everett Millais and William Holman Hunt), for it was primarily these Pre-Raphaelite brethren who inspired members of the Rose+Croix salon, Les XX (les Vingt), La Libre Esthetique, and the Salon d'Art Idéaliste. Among the artists most deeply moved by Pre-Raphaelite constructions of feminine beauty, self-conscious reverie, and enigma were Edmond Aman-Jean, Jean Delville, Carloz Schwabe, Ferdinand Hodler, Gustav Klimt, Gustave Moreau (already famous but still not immune to Pre-Raphaelitism), and, above all, Fernand Khnopff. Critics too responded to the phenomenon of the Pre-Raphaelite Brotherhood, especially in France, with a melange of applause, disapproval, and astonishment. Overall, it was the image of the fin-de-siècle female that united these diverse individuals and groups, all of whom recast their own visions of dreamy Burne-Jonesian and Rossettian feminine icons.

In terms of the years leading up to the Symbolist "explosion" of art and artists in the 1880s and 1890s, the appeal of Pre-Raphaelite art had actually surfaced in the artistic sensibility of the Continent long before then, beginning in the mid-1850s in the seminal responses registered in various journals in France especially.[4] A major figure who wrote about this "British invasion" throughout the entire period was Ernest Chesneau, who corresponded with John Ruskin from 1864 to 1893 and penned *L'art et les Artists Modernes en France et en Angleterre* in 1864. Chesneau is moreover notable because, like fellow critic Robert de la Sizeranne and others, he actually saw Pre-Raphaelite art in France at various exhibitions and expositions. Chesneau's book also communicated what became the classic, fluctuating complaints about Pre-Raphaelitism, its original yet eccentric style and unique, prismatic colors, and its alleged lack of awareness of and homage to modern—that is, French—art.

Regarding the relationship with Ruskin, the great cultural arbiter of the Pre-Raphaelite Brotherhood and of Victorian art in general, Chesneau admired Ruskin's writings *Pre-Raphaelitism* and *The Two Paths* and even tried to convince his colleague to permit the former to be translated into French. Ruskin returned this compliment, commissioning him to write about English landscape for French audiences and writing an endorsement for the preface of the English version of Chesneau's 1885 *The English School of Painting*.[5] Chesneau reminded his readers that it was at the Universal Exposition in Paris in 1855 where the Pre-Raphaelites made their French debut. Prophetically, this form of "world's fair" exposition turned out to be the first major means for Pre-Raphaelite art to be seen and transmitted abroad. Eugene Delacroix and Théophile Gautier were among those who saw and responded to this new type of British art, in Delacroix's case with positive words about John Everett Millais' *Order of Release, 1746* (1853, Tate Gallery). Gautier was more confounded than complimentary, but he too acknowledged this painting's sincerity of technique. To him, Millais' *Return of the Dove to the Ark* (1851, Ashmolean Museum) and *Ophelia* (1851–52, Tate Gallery), along with Holman Hunt's *Light of the World* (1851–54, Keble College Chapel, Oxford), *Claudio and Isabella* (1850–53, Tate Gallery), and *Our English Coasts (Strayed Sheep*; 1852, Tate Gallery), were all riveting examples of an unheralded (and to the French, bizarre) order of English painting. *Le Journal pour Rire*, for example, wittily suggested regarding Millais' canvas that "the title should be changed to 'The Joy of the Straw on the Return of the Dove,' since it is obvious that M. Millais lavished most care on his depiction of the hay!"[6] *Ophelia* was described as having the "air of a doll who drowns herself in a basin" in a fantastic realm replete with prodigious botanical details.[7] The same air of "charming childishness" and mimetic, but excessive, realism Gautier ascribed to Hunt.

In the late 1850s and 1860s, Gallic responses remained both pro and con of the new breed of English art, although some comments were quite acidic. Among these were the judgments of Prosper Mérimée on Hunt's *Awakening Conscience* (1853–54, Tate Gallery) in the *Révue des Deux Mondes*.[8] When Hunt, Millais, and Arthur Hughes contributed to yet another Universal Exposition in 1867, they encountered more contradictory reactions. Millais' *Eve of St. Agnes* (1863, Collection of Queen Elizabeth the Queen Mother) gained almost cult-like stature, being praised by the poets Arthur Rimbaud and Paul Verlaine after seeing it in London in 1872–73. It was also cited in Joris-Karl Huysmans' famous 1884 "decadent" novel *A Rebours* (*Against the Grain*).[9] Thus, the literary appeal to the Symbolist poets was clearly established, along with the suggestive metaphors they created for the hypnotic beauty and power of women.

Interest in the work of Hunt and Millais was soon overshadowed, however, by focus on another member of this formidable contingent, when in the late 1860s, Chesneau in *Rival Nations of Art* and Philippe Burty in the *Gazette des Beaux-Arts* were among those who turned their attention to the paintings of Dante Gabriel Rossetti. In words and on canvas, Rossetti's love affair with female pulchritude struck a responsive chord, even though his paintings were not on public view in France. It obviously did not hurt his cause that his poetry was sometimes compared with *Les Fleurs du Mal* by Charles Baudelaire, who himself sanctioned aspects of Pre-Raphaelite art in an 1859 review of the Paris Salon in *La Revue Francaise*.

The 1870s witnessed yet more Continental appearances by members of the Pre-Raphaelite circle when Millais and Edward Burne-Jones contributed various paintings to the 1878 Universal Exposition. George F. Watts, an older friend of the band who was frequently identified by French critics as being Pre-Raphaelite in spirit, also sent works.[10] This labeling attests to a decided looseness with which the term was applied at this time in Europe. Rossetti also fared well and might have exerted even more impact, but he usually preferred not to send works for public exhibition, whether in Europe or on his home turf. (Later, he and Burne-Jones would be represented often by photographic reproductions in lieu of original canvases.) Much as Burne-Jones had garnered attention and praise in London at this time when his works were shown at the avant-garde Grosvenor Gallery, he also met with favor with French audiences.[11]

As a result of the huge successes and notoriety he scored at the Grosvenor Gallery, Burne-Jones's celebrity sparked attention as well from European critics and artists. Sir Coutts Lindsay, founder, owner, and proprietor of the Grosvenor Gallery, was highly instrumental in promoting *The Beguiling of Merlin* (1873–77, Lady Lever Art Gallery) and others abroad. Coutts Lindsay was the one who brought Burne-Jones and second-generation Pre-Raphaelites to the notice of the public in the first exhibition of his gallery in 1877, and his innovations in an open (non-juried) invitational policy with considerable artist involvement, novel display practices and ways of publicizing events and painters, and a carefully crafted interior design for art to be shown in all had considerable impact abroad.[12] The Gallery's deputy director, Joseph Comyns Carr, further fueled these fires by serving as the English correspondent for *L'Art* from 1877 to 1883 and consciously promoting British art. Engravings of works by Burne-Jones, Watts, and others advertised their talents, and Comyns Carr produced specific columns on both those artists from the Grosvenor (for which illustrated catalogues were available at the Paris offices of *L'Art*).[13] He devoted numerous passages (written in French) extolling Burne-Jones's paintings and has been cited as the chief catalyst that enabled the *Beguiling of Merlin* to be "recognized in France as one of the first post-Pre-Raphaelite masterpieces and as a key work in the new aesthetic dialogue that was developing, with his enthusiastic support, between the two countries."[14] The next year, the French exposure to Burne-Jones at the Universal Exposition (where Coutts Lindsay was one of the British jurors who selected the art) marked a turning point in late Victorian art and reiterated the rise of this type of venue serving as an important outlet for the dissemination of Pre-Raphaelite art.

The 1878 public display was a breakthrough for Burne-Jones (and others in his circle) and for those artists with Symbolist leanings who saw their art. Comyns Carr was undoubtedly pleased that the French principally focused on *The Beguiling of Merlin*, on which Edmond Duranty, Charles Blanc, and other French reviewers centered their encomia. Duranty ardently christened Burne-Jones the leader of the second-generation Pre-Raphaelites, an accurate assessment, and also enumerated among the new followers Watts, Marie Spartali Stillman, and John Melhuish Strudwick. Blanc, on the other hand, simply lavished superlatives on *The Beguiling of Merlin*, hailing it as "to my sense the most astonishing painting we can see from London . . . a quintessence of the ideal and a sublime poetry that touches me to the very core."[15] Chesneau, writing in *La Peinture Anglaise* in 1882, had already embraced it (and other works) as remarkable for the richness of color and poetic conception, underscoring an "adoration of the truth . . . in the service of a high imagination . . . which gives these interpreted things a sort of singular extra value, an emotion, a poetic transfiguration."[16]

In the 1880s, Continental esteem for Pre-Raphaelitism mounted, along with the marked ascent of Burne-Jones and Rossetti in general. Huysmans and others made pilgrimages to London and saw Pre-Raphaelite art, thereby solidifying the link between Burne-Jones and his circle with literary Symbolists. Even before Jean Moreas issued his revolutionary manifesto of Symbolism in 1886 in *Le Figaro*, comparisons were being drawn by Gallic critics between the Pre-Raphaelites and artists such as Gustave Moreau—for example, his *Salome* (1855, Louvre). Duranty had already dubbed Burne-Jones a kindred spirit to Moreau and in an 1879 review credited Burne-Jones's *Pygmalion* series as recalling the sensitive poetry of the Frenchman's artistry.[17] Furthermore, Moreau knew Burne-Jones, owned a reproduction of his *Days of Creation*, had seen British art at the 1855 exposition and at the Galerie Anglaise in Paris in 1867, and like him, had exhibited at the inaugural exhibition of the Grosvenor Gallery.[18] Numerous visual affinities can be found between the two artists, for example, between Moreau's *Sappho* watercolor (ca. 1884, Victoria & Albert Museum) and Burne-Jones's *Psyche and Pan* (1869–74, Fogg Art Museum) or the *Rock of Doom* (1886–87, Staatsgallerie, Stuttgart). Years later, in 1893, author Léon Balzagette paid a backhanded compliment to Burne-Jones's *Perseus* series (on view at the liberal Salon du Champ de Mars) when he asserted that although this was not as powerful as a work by Moreau, it was nonetheless impressive on its own merits.

It was also in the 1880s that the rise of the occult author Joséphin Péladan occurred. Péladan, who had written about French salons and praised both Moreau and the Pre-Raphaelites, produced his Symbolist manifesto in 1886 and five years later founded the Rose+Croix society. By the mid-to-late 1880s, the adulation of Rossetti seemed to peak, with both Chesneau's book and Edouard Rod's two articles in 1887 in the *Gazette des Beaux-Arts* serving as Continental testimony at its zenith. Chesneau had even corresponded with Rossetti about a book he was working on (apparently never published) entitled a *History of the Pre-Raphaelite School in England*, stating that Rossetti had sent him lists of his paintings just before he died in 1882.

Among the stellar achievements of Rossetti that proved perennial favorites among the Symbolists and French writers alike were *Beata Beatrix* (1864, Tate Gallery) and *Sibylla Palmifera* (1866–70, Lady Lever Art Gallery). The transcendent state of consciousness in *Beata Beatrix* especially appealed to Symbolists, and one author estimated that at least five hundred people owned reproductions of this painting—along with Burne-Jones's *St. Cecilia* (ca. 1874 watercolor version, private collection) and Moreau's *Salome* (ca. 1875, Musée Gustave Moreau, Paris).[19] Fernand Khnopff drew an analogy between *Beata Beatrix* and Edgar Allan Poe's "Oval Poetry," a poem that explored the magical relationship between a painted image and its living sitter.[20] Other popular images were Rossetti's *Lady Lilith* (1868, Delaware Art Museum) and *La Ghirlandata* (1873, Guildhall Art Gallery), the latter often described in terms of its Moreau-infused sense of suspended motion and musicality. Rod's articles ascribed visionary qualities to these works, and one passage in particular captured the essence of Pre-Raphaelite influence on the Symbolist vocabulary: "These figures have an immobility, a silence, a pose almost suspended, a slow hesitation in their rare movement, which make them resemble something like sleepwalkers."[21]

In 1891, Péladan issued a special doctrine as a pendant to the secretive mystic order of the Rose+Croix he had founded. This document hinged on articles of faith that made specific references to the Pre-Raphaelite Brotherhood, and, rather like that group, the members of Péladan's radical fraternity were to be known by abbreviated initials, in this case "artistes R+C."[22] Other shared traits were an appreciation for "primitive" art before Raphael and an explicit desire to revolt against official art, mundane history painting, genre pictures, and anecdotalism.[23] As Péladan enunciated this creed, the aim was to "ruin realism, reform pedestrian taste, and create a school of ideal art."[24] Less interested in Ruskinian naturalism than the early Pre-Raphaelites had been, Péladan preferred subjects relating to legend, myth, religion, dream, and poetry, themes that were also consistent with Pre-Raphaelite proclivities and especially Rossetti's and Burne-Jones's works. Rossetti's works of the 1860s clearly personified R+C goals to aspire to a less literal, more *idéaliste* level of art and to champion beauty.

Péladan also demonstrated another link to the Rossettian legacy in the form of Félicien Rops. Péladan had praised Rops as a contemporary master in an 1885 article and was among the first to defend the modern eroticism of his nude, crucified women, as in *The Temptation of St. Anthony*

(1878, Cabinet des Estampes, Bibliotheque Royale, Brussels), and even the alleged satanism (as in the rather lurid plate entitled "The Sacrifice" from *Les Sataniques*) in his oeuvre.[25] In 1887, he wrote to Rops and encouraged him to send a work to Clemence Couve, whom Péladan had met that year and who translated Rossetti's "House of Life" poems into French (for which Péladan wrote the preface).[26] Péladan was able to overlook the shock value of Rops's images and to understand them as emblems of modernity, perversity, and sexuality. He thus wrote in 1885 of Rops's visual tendencies in his *Sataniques* series from 1882—in explicit pictorial hallucinations—to obsess about the topic of man possessed by women, a theme that also preoccupied the Rosicrucian salons.[27]

In addition, Péladan envisioned international participation for the Rose+Croix organization, including in his manifesto the names of Khnopff and Moreau (the latter did not join in the group but encouraged some of his students to do so). Moreover, Péladan hoped to solicit direct contact and "go to London to invite Burne-Jones, Watts, and five other Pre-Raphaelites" (although this affiliation never materialized).[28] Burne-Jones spurned Péladan's offer because he was busy preparing *King Cophetua and the Beggar Maid* (1884, Tate Gallery) for the 1889 Universal Exposition, where the canvas would win him the coveted cross of the Legion of Honor (and would also pique the curiosity of Khnopff, among others).

Burne-Jones also had an opportunity in 1888 to contribute to the Belgian group Les XX (in existence from 1884–93) but turned down that invitation as well. (Like many other progressive groups, Les XX deliberately cultivated an international contingent of participants—among them Dario de Regoyas, Khnopff, James Ensor, and other artists such as James Whistler and Walter Crane.) However, the following year Burne-Jones sent *King Cophetua* to La Libre Esthetique, yet another avant-garde outgrowth (six years later, Hunt and Watts exhibited their individual portraits of Rossetti at the same venue).[29] Privately, he dismissed Péladan's Rosicrucian treatise, in a letter to Watts, as a "disgracefully silly manifesto."[30] In spite of the absence of the Pre-Raphaelite circle, the first Rose+Croix salon (which ended in 1897) opened in March of 1892 with sixty-nine contributors, including Odilon Redon, Alexandre Séon, Ferdinand Hodler, Edmond Aman-Jean, Armand Point, and Carloz Schwabe. It met with considerable acclaim and generated nearly 20,000 visitors. In early 1892, editor Marion H. Spielmann of the *Magazine of Art* commented on the Rosicrucian development and compared it directly with the Pre-Raphaelites:

As the Brotherhood was a protest against the inanities, conventions, and the generalisations of the day, and braved ridicule in carrying out the tenets of "sincerity," so the new Rosicrucians exist to proclaim by the work of their hand against the triumph of brushwork and the excess of realism. To them, technique or excellence of execution is no longer paramount; Religious Fervour and the "Beautiful" are what they care for.[31]

The *Magazine of Art*'s commentator was trenchant in his perceptions, for Péladan and likeminded compatriots all held the concept of soulful beauty very high in their aesthetic credo. In his 1894 edict titled *L'art idéaliste et mystique*, Péladan further articulated a quasi-worship of Dantean themes, which clearly reinforced connections with Rossetti's art. Like some earlier French critics, Péladan too understood that there were affinities between Moreau's art and Burne-Jones's, and that these shared—as did Rossetti's work—a preoccupation with certain themes besides that of the hauntingly beautiful woman.

One of these common denominators was the sexually ambiguous sphinx, a motif that appeared in the oeuvres of all three artists and that also surfaced, as critic Walter Shaw Sparrow discerned in an 1890 *Magazine of Art* article, in the empathetic distillations of Rossetti's and Moreau's art evident in Khnopff's work. Péladan also was interested in androgyny and expounded on the fluidity of gender identity in his first novel *Le Vice Supreme*. At the same time, writers like Jean Lorrain were drawn to this concept and applied it to the Rosicrucian artist Leonard Sarluys. Lorrain even cited a passage from Péladan's *L'Androgyne*, in which the female protagonist combines a *Mona-Lisa* smile of a DaVinci with a long Rossettian neck.[32]

The French critic de la Sizeranne, a frequent visitor (like Khnopff) to Burne-Jones's home, cemented other connections among Pre-Raphaelite and Symbolists both by his personal knowledge of Burne-Jones and his professional championing of Pre-Raphaelitism. De la Sizeranne wrote at length about the interlinking of the Rosicrucian and Pre-Raphaelite artists and goals, above all their mutual desires to renew contemporary art with serious subject matter. However, in his 1892 article and his 1895 book *English Contemporary Painting 1844–1894*, he questioned whether the Continental group could ever sustain as much influence as their earlier British counterparts. To him, the Symbolists lacked the ardent moralizing force, were perhaps too literary, and did not embody the well-timed blend of radical content and technique. Thus, he moaned, while "our Rose+Croix want to be Pre-Raphaelites; they will only be aesthetes."[33]

Like his compatriots, de la Sizeranne singled out Rossetti and particularly Burne-Jones as the reigning luminaries of British art. Burne-Jones's *Beguiling of Merlin* again was the dominant star, but other contenders were *Love Among the Ruins* (1870–1, Wightwick Manor Collection, Wolverhampton)—which was shown at the Universal Exposition in 1878—and the ever-controversial *Laus Veneris* (1873–75, Laing Art Gallery). At the 1889 Universal Exposition, Burne-Jones's *King Cophetua* rose to challenge *Merlin* as the work most favored by viewers. For Khnopff, who wrote frequent columns for the *Magazine of Art*, this painting hovered on "the threshold of the Absolute," for it absolutely transfixed spectators and personally left him "enwrapped in an atmosphere of dream . . . carried away to an intoxicating level of the soul."[34]

Like the *Beguiling of Merlin*, *King Cophetua* was a keystone to Burne-Jones's European success. Antonin Proust approved of it, while Moreau (who supported Burne-Jones receiving a gold medal at the 1889 Universal Exposition) seems to have been inspired by the painting in his own *Orestes and Erinyea* (1892, private collection). Similarly, Moreau's watercolor entitled *The Glorification of Helen* (1897, Musée Gustave Moreau) evokes comparison with Burne-Jones's *Depths of the Sea* (1887, Fogg Art Museum), which was exhibited in Paris in 1893, and with another "hit" abroad, *The Wheel of Fortune* (1875–83, Musée d'Orsay).[35] During this same period, Burne-Jones earned the confidence of various curators, who hoped to acquire his canvases for assorted French national museums, and was moreover increasingly the subject of articles and books, for example, Georges-Oliver Destrées's *Les Préraphaélites: Notes sur l'Art Décoratif et la Peinture en Angleterre*, published in 1894.

In Belgium, critical response vacillated less, with Emile Verhaeren ranking Burne-Jones (and Watts) along with Moreau as among the greatest of the nineteenth century.[36] As in France, Burne-Jones was represented at times by photographic reproductions: at the 1888 exhibition of Les XX (where Rossetti too was seen only in photographic form), at the Galerie Dumont in Brussels, and at the Salon d'Art Idéaliste in 1896 (where Rossetti and Watts were also seen in "surrogate" photographic form).[37] Further Belgian bonds were strengthened when two of Burne-Jones's greatest successes, *The Wheel of Fortune* and *Love Among the Ruins* went to the 1895 Exposition of Fine Arts in Brussels and traveled two years later to another Belgian venue.

The spellbinding immobility and self-absorption of Burne-Jones's figures were well matched by those of Belgium's highly gifted Fernand Khnopff. Much as this artist had swooned over Burne-Jones' work, so too did the critic Paul Leprieur in his remarks in 1892–93 for the *Gazette des Beaux-Arts*. For him, Burne-Jones's *Briar Rose* series (1870–90, Faringdon Collection Trust, Buscot Park) was the source for Leprieur's own epiphany. The panel depicting sleeping figures moved him to exclaim, "I shall never forget the deep impression made on men, not only by the work itself, but by the attitude of the public who crowded to see it, waiting till the picture had delivered its message, and then carefully carrying away its revelation." He then speculated that the metaphor of slumber was paralleled by the artist's state and accordingly wrote that Burne-Jones seemed to have "slept in the depths of some enchanted places, preserving through his slumbers all the exquisite and primitive refinement of the Tuscan painters."[38]

During the five years that its salon existed (1892–97), the Rose+ Croix contributors were particularly receptive to these moods and modes of late Pre-Raphaelitism. Among those who experimented with Pre-Raphaelite motifs and styles was Edmond Aman-Jean, who had been invited to join the Rosicrucian artists in 1892–93 and admired Millais, Rossetti, and Burne-Jones. On the most obvious levels, his poster titled *Beatrix* (1892, private collection) for the second salon of the Rose+Croix reused the Dantean subject so dear to Rossetti. An unidentified author in the *Magazine of Art* viewed the Frenchman as "an apostle of the modern diaphanous movement" for whom "it is clear that the English Pre-Raphaelite school has influenced him."[39] Rossetti's string of voluptuous, anesthetized-looking female stunners were a visual touchstone for Aman-Jean, who produced his own proliferation of images of beautifully inert and mysterious women among flowers. Among prominent examples in his oeuvre are a color lithograph titled *Under the Flowers* (1897, private collection) and *Hair* (1898, Musée de Dijon), the latter a commission from Ambroise Vollard for the third *Album des Peintres Graveurs*.[40]

This formula of enigmatic, listless, long-haired women with blossoms, appealed to other Symbolists too, particularly Khnopff. He tapped into Rossettian influence in various works such as the *Necklace of Medallions* (1899, private collection). Another Rosicrucian devotée, the German-born but Swiss national Carloz Schwabe, also interpreted this phlegmatic female holding emblematic flowers. His poster for the 1892 Rose+Croix opening, for example, is decidedly Pre-Raphaelite in style and overall composition, and other works like his pastel *Silence Interieur* (1908,

Barry Friedman Ltd., New York) borrow from the Rossettian mold of introspective, isolated, rather androgynous figures. This could also be said of the work of the French artist Armand Point, who emerged as a Pre-Raphaelite following a trip to Italy in 1894 and later founded a William-Morris-like decorative arts workshop. Point's *Eternal Chimera* (ca. 1895, private collection), like Burne-Jones's delicate drawing to illustrate "Summer Snow" in *Good Words* of 1863, places a female protagonist alone in a garden full of blossoms. Similarly, his drawing of *St. Cecile* (1896, Barry Friedman Ltd., New York) recalls the exquisite lassitude, lack of expression, and motionlessness often captured by Rossetti, Hughes, and Burne-Jones.

Another artist affected by Pre-Raphaelitism was Edgar Maxence, one of Moreau's protégés who briefly exhibited at the Rose+Croix from 1895 to 1897. Although subsequently better known for his biblical subjects, his oil panel *In the Orchard* (1900, private collection) belongs within the Rossettian context of intimate glimpses of pensive women amid flowers. The figure's face, however, owes more to Burne-Jones's blend, but here with a certain androgynous, Mona Lisa-like character with distinctly contemporary touches. This New Woman/Eve is an emblem of modernity who essentially straddles both centuries, in one hand holding a lit cigarette while posing against an archetypal, densely floriated Pre-Raphaelite backdrop. The widespread use of this juxtaposition of women and flowers in various media and posters soon became a cultural joke, however, and was ridiculed in England in *Punch* under the guise of the aesthetic female and in the French press in the 1890s, by Octave Mirbeau among others. In *Le Journal* in 1895, Mirbeau mocked English and French Pre-Raphaelite types: "See in this precious flower the symbol of an entire aesthetic. Ah! their princesses with lanky bodies and faces like poisonous flowers—who pass on cloud-like stairs to banks of silly moons."[41]

The Symbolist artist who most consistently and brilliantly displayed a debt to Pre-Raphaelitism was undoubtedly Khnopff, who exhibited with the Rose+Croix and other avant-garde groups. By 1890, the British critic Sparrow had already noted the correspondences between this artist's oeuvre and those of Rossetti and Burne-Jones. In Khnopff's own Belgium, various journalists also detected this tendency.[42] This indebtedness can be explained partly in terms of the artist's genuine Anglophilia. Not only did he often exhibit his work (sometimes with English titles or allusions) between 1890 and 1906 in London at the Hanover, New, and Grafton galleries, but he also served as a prolific correspondent for *The Studio* from

1895 to 1914 and intermittently contributed to other periodicals. He married an Englishwoman and owned an extensive private library of English art books. More importantly, he personally befriended some of the most celebrated artists of this period—Rossetti, Burne-Jones, Watts, Ford Madox Brown, and Valentine Prinsep, as well as Frederic Leighton and Lawrence Alma-Tadema. Even more persuasively, throughout Khnopff's long career, there was continuous evidence of his adaptation of the Pre-Raphaelite ideal female, a subject that bordered on near-obsession in his case, as it had—for other reasons—with Rossetti.[43]

Visually, Khnopff reflected the complex aesthetic perspectives of Rossetti and Burne-Jones, whose home he frequented and with whom he occasionally exchanged drawings. For example, in 1890, Burne-Jones inscribed to Khnopff a drawing of a woman's head, while in ca. 1896, Khnopff gave Burne-Jones the head of a woman, a work that had held a prominent place in the Belgian's studio, near the portrait of his beloved sister/model/muse Marguerite. Khnopff was inspired by Burne-Jones's androgynous facial type—squarish forehead, fixed gaze, somewhat masculinized features—heightened by a softly descriptive style. This blurred sexuality and the *sfumato* effects in eyes, mouths, and faces are found in Khnopff's own drawings, for example, in his ca. 1887 *Study of a Woman* and *Ygraine a la Porte* of 1898 (both, Barry Friedman, Ltd., New York). Burne-Jones was a constant point of reference, and in his memorial tribute, Khnopff extolled the Englishman's "virgin forms of delicate and pensive gesture . . . the exquisite curve of innocence of their lips, and . . . their limpid gaze."[44]

Arguably the most salient example of a Burne-Jonesian imprint is found in Khnopff's English-titled *Memories (The Lawn Tennis Party*; 1889, Royaux Musées des Beaux-Arts de Belgique, Brussels), in which each figure in a human chain is oddly isolated and based on a single sitter, the artist's sister. Perhaps, as has been suggested, *Memories* (seen in London in 1890) was intended as a kind of horizontal homage to Burne-Jones's vertical *Golden Stairs* (1880, Tate Gallery).[45] In fact, Khnopff's own description of the latter as "an array of our most tender and precious memories in the progress of life" also applies to his own pursuit of ambiguity and memory. The format and mood of *Golden Stairs* and *Memories* alike also are reminiscent of Rossetti's provocative depictions of soulful female multiples in his chalk version of *Rosa Triplex* (1867, Tate Gallery) or *The Bower Meadow* (1850–72, Manchester City Art Gallery). As in the *Golden Stairs,* the lyrical insularity and sense of stasis in *Memories,* what Sparrow termed "a hush, an hour of dreaminess" generated by the females, may owe something to the reincarnated spirit of Burne-Jones's *The Mill* (1870, Victoria & Albert Museum), with its frieze-like order and aura of allegory and timelessness. Of such borrowings, fellow artist (but of decidedly untamed images of femininity) Felicien Rops mockingly wrote of Khnopff's entries in the 1893 Rose+Croix salon that he "no longer imitates the French; he has sunk up to the chin in the boots of the Englishman Burne-Jones."[46]

In addition, Khnopff may have assimilated a rather Whistlerian approach, his *Silence* (1890, Royaux Musées des Beaux-Arts de Belgique, Brussels) evoking comparisons with Whistler's *Symphony in White No. 1: The White Girl* (1862, Freer Art Gallery) and with Rossettian antecedents of inscrutability in preternaturally attenuated figures like those in *The Maids of Elfen-Mere* (1855 drawing, Yale Center for British Art). On the other hand, imagery such as Khnopff's *Britomart* (1892, private collection) seem to adapt the elongated, narrow format, bewitched hair, and slightly closed eyes prefigured in Rossetti's *Damsel of the Sanct Grael* (1857, Tate Gallery) and overlay these with a Burne-Jonesian cast evident in *St. George* (undated, H.R.H. Princess Ludwig of Hesse and the Rhine) and other works.

Another outstanding example of Khnopff's homage to Pre-Raphaelitism is *I Lock the Door upon Myself* (1891, Neue Pinakothek, Munich), which was criticized by some reviewers when shown at Les XX in Brussels in 1892 as being too Pre-Raphaelite. The English title came from lines in Christina Rossetti's poem "Who shall deliver me?" but the figure type—solitary, brooding, beautiful, with partly lowered eyes and an alienating, willful glance—is one made famous by the poet's brother. This painting was exhibited at the Rose+Croix in 1893, when its enervated protagonist was hailed as "La Lady." The woman's semi-lowered eyelids, massive hair, withdrawn mood, and hermetic interior all drew on Rossettian prototypes, such as *Pandora* (1879, Fogg Art Museum), in which Jane Burden Morris's crane neck, beetle brow, and crinkly hair are all idealized. Interestingly, both Rossetti and Khnopff selected as models women who personified their own preconceived notions of femininity and beauty—Khnopff choosing his sister, Rossetti his paramours.[47] Moreover, as if to add a reference to Burne-Jones in *I Lock My Door*, Khnopff placed in the background a crystalline orb recalling one that appears in Burne-Jones's *Days of Creation* watercolor series (1872–76, Fogg Art Museum). In contrast, the clutter of objects behind this strangely inaccessible female is more of a tribute to Rossetti's seemingly endless chain of women-in-niches with their indolent, almost drugged, demeanors.

Coincidentally, the same verse by Christina Rossetti inspired Khnopff's *Who Shall Deliver Me?* (1891, Nourhan Manoukian Collection, Paris), which, in turn bears a striking resemblance to Rossetti's fallen-woman picture *Found* (begun 1853, Delaware Art Museum), a work that was well known in the late nineteenth century despite its unfinished state. A red-haired protagonist, an urban backdrop with a brick wall, and a gutter are shared elements, although Khnoppf's wayward female is very different in her confrontational, candid gaze. Both figures wear wilted flowers—Rossetti's in the pattern of the dress and Khnopff's in the hair—as emblems of defloration. However, Khnopff's creature seems more of a seer than a harlot, and her eyes, like her curious brooch, project an infinite void, inviting viewers to stare within and portend future events and omens.

A last example by Khnopff that synthesizes Rossettian and other Pre-Raphaelite visual sources is *The Head of a Woman* (ca. 1899, private collection), which continues the visual heritage of Rossetti's myriad wild-haired, aloof stunners. Khnopff's recycling of this kind of haunting, mesmerizing figure was noted by Sparrow as capturing the elusive "heart of womankind—fascinating us at a distance, repelling us on drawing closer, tempting us half-cruelly, half spiritually."[48]

Another artist with a Belgian background was Georges Lemmen, who was elected to Les XX in 1888 and, like Khnopff, was interested in the art of Whistler and the Pre-Raphaelites (as well as in the writings of Ruskin and William Morris). He was part of the Vingtiste initiative that petitioned the Pre-Raphaelites to participate in Les XX, and at his behest, Walter Crane's books were included in the 1891 exhibition.[49] A fellow Vingtiste was the Dutch artist Jan Toroop, who was in contact with members of the Pre-Raphaelite circle when he visited London in the 1880s. His pastel *Illusion* (ca. 1893, private collection), singled out by Sparrow in *The Studio*, depicts a woman with flowing locks that seem of Pre-Raphaelite origin.[50]

There were further permutations that appeared in other Rosicrucian works, for example, by Jean Delville and Lucien Lévy-Dhurmer.[51] Delville, who knew Khnopff and actively exhibited at the R+C salons from 1892 to 1895, began his own Salon (d'Art Idéaliste) in 1896 with the statement that "in its analogies with the Rose+Croix in Paris and with the Pre-Raphaelite movement in London, this new group attempts to continue the great tradition of idealist art from the ancient masters to contemporary ones."[52] He declared that the Belgian Idealist school was "analogous if not identical to the one in Paris and the Pre-Raphaelite movement."[53] Delville knew Péladan well, having been encouraged by him to move to Paris, where Delville lived in the Bourbon quarter among many other Rosicrucian disciples and became actively engaged in organizing Rose+Croix exhibitions.[54] Delville also remarked in his *Autobiography* that Péladan helped the artist by giving center stage to Delville's *Death of Orpheus* (1893, private collection) and by exhibiting some of his drawings.

Delville sent several notable works to the Rose+Croix venue. Besides those mentioned, *The End of the Reign* (1893, private collection), *The Love of Souls* (1900, Musée d'Ixelles, Brussels), *The Angel of Splendors* (private collection), and a portrait of Péladan appeared there. Concurrently he also was a part—with Emile Fabry and Xavier Mellery—of the salon "Pour l'Art," for which he designed the emblem of a sphinx. Other Rosicrucians like Schwabe and Rops exhibited there as well, and there was significant crossover among these avant-garde coteries. Schwabe and Khnopff, for example, contributed to Kumris, a Belgian branch of the salon Pour l'Art. After this dissolved in 1895, the next year Delville founded the Salon d'art Idéaliste (which lasted until 1898). This organization deliberately attracted many of the same artists and extended the reach of the Rosicrucians, with Point and Alexandre Séon among the new additions. To further attest to his loyalties, Delville printed the idéaliste catalogue on mauve paper, a nod to Péladan's ideas, and in his text saluted both Péladan's Rose+Croix group and the Pre-Raphaelites.[55]

In his *Portrait of Madame Stuart Merrill* (1892, private collection), included in the 1892 R+C salon, Delville made one of his clearest allusions to Pre-Raphaelitism, especially to Millais' *Ophelia* and *The Bridesmaid* (1851, Fitzwilliam Museum), both renowned for their eerie poses, magic net of tresses, and open-eyed trance of otherworldliness. Partial inspiration derives too from Rossetti's *Beata Beatrix*, universally adored in Symbolist circles and translated by Delville into an amazing mass of hair that functions as a near-parody of electrical force—with a magnetic field of red locks, upturned eyes, and mystic triangle all heightening the intensity of the figure's state of psychological stupor and ecstasy. Another spiritual offspring is *Eve* (1896, Michel Perinet Collection, Paris) by Lévy-Dhurmer, who admired the Pre-Raphaelites and was invited by Péladan to join the Rosicrucians. The siren with entwining hair pictured in *Eve* reforges the dense foliate background typical of Rossettian icons and retains a smolderingly mysterious female protagonist.

Not surprisingly, even more malevolent Symbolist manifestations of the femme fatale multiplied, usually seen frontally and even more transmogrified into a horrifying, deadly incarnation. The omniscient, serenely emotionless temptress surfaced in Khnopff's drawing of *The Blood of the*

Medusa (ca. 1895, Bibliothèque Royale Albert Ier, Brussels), which echoes the Pre-Raphaelite archetype of Rossetti's killer-woman, perpetuated as well in Frederick Sandys' earlier *Medusa* (ca. 1875, Victoria & Albert Museum), with her stony expression, magnetic (literally red-eyed and demonic) stare, and sinuous ringlets-cum-snakes.

The Symbolist phenomenon was by no means exclusive to France and Belgium.[56] Ferdinand Hodler of Switzerland exhibited in Paris in the 1890s and produced paintings like *The Dream* (ca. 1897–1903, private collection), whose serpentine, red-haired woman rapt with blossoms evokes parallels with Pre-Raphaelite predecessors like Rossetti's *Blessed Damozel* (ca. 1875–78, Fogg Art Museum). However, the difference in style and tone is palpable, as is the incorporation in the lower predella not of a noble knight but a languid, nude male who retains the pose of his Rossettian counterpart dreaming of a rendezvous. Kneeling amid flowers, Hodler's "blessed damozel" also evokes Rossetti by embodying the ideal state of dreams for the hallucinating male and perhaps for the artist himself.

In a related vein, Austrian artist Gustav Klimt, who at one point contributed (like Hodler) to the Vienna Secession (where Khnopff also exhibited), also assimilated both Rossettian and Burne-Jonesian pictorial idioms. Klimt's *Salome* (1909, Galleria d'Arte Moderne, Venice) is only one of numerous works that qualify as more sinister variations of Rossetti's sexy, soulful, yet dangerous women, for example, the protagonist in *The Blue Bower* (1865, Barber Institute of Fine Arts, University of Birmingham, U.K.). Yet, while Rossetti's embowered beings often seem restrained by barriers or walls in their niches, Klimt's creatures are captives literally locked into the surface of the painting, which becomes both a gilded prison and a tabernacle enshrining love and peril together. The resulting claustrophobic backdrop of pattern and ornament also recurs in Klimt's famous *Kiss* (ca. 1909, Musée d'Art Moderne, Strasbourg). In some respects a descendant of Rossetti's densely packed, almost spaceless scenes of amorousness, as in *The Wedding of St. George and Princess Sabra* (1857, Tate Gallery), Klimt's work nonetheless escalates the tone and stylized composition into a mosaic-like plane. In addition, Burne-Jones's pictures also loom in Klimt's imagination, as reflected in the latter's *Sea Serpents* (1904–7, private collection), which in its vertical format reinvents the underwater fantasy blending love and death with feminine watery seduction communicated by Burne-Jones's *Depths of the Sea.*

In Germany, Burne-Jones received attention as well, ranging from honors bestowed at exhibitions in 1893 and 1897, the latter a gold medal given to his *Saint George* series at the Munich International Exhibition, to a monograph written on the artist in 1901 by Otto von Schleinitz.[57] The Grand Duke of Hesse positioned a version of *Saint George* (1897–98, Collection Hessische Hausstiftung, Kronberg) in his art nouveau-decorated chamber at Darmstadt.[58] Innumerable artists bore testimony to the Rossettian heritage, too, among them Franz von Stuck, as seen in his earlier works such as the *Guardian of Paradise* (1889, Villa Stuck Museum, Munich). In addition, members of the progressive Jugendstil group admired Burne-Jones and esteemed him as a leader in modern art. The independent, nonacademy-sanctioned standards of exhibition reform personified by the Grosvenor Gallery was another inspiration, as was its focus on showcasing little-known artists who had made bold or unprecedented kinds of art.

Elsewhere in Europe, artists such as the Dutch painter Matthijs Maris reacted to later permutations of figural Pre-Raphaelitism conveyed in the works of artists such as Sidney Meteyard and in numerous *Lady of Shalott* canvases (for example, the 1888 version at the Tate Gallery) by John W. Waterhouse.[59] There were, moreover, reverberations conveyed by Walter Crane's and William Morris's art on Hungarian artists, particularly members of the early twentieth-century Godollo Art Colony.[60] Austro-Hungarian artist Alphonse Mucha also was indebted in the female "pinups" for his posters by Rossetti, Schwabe, and Burne-Jones. Italian painter Giovanni Segantini tapped into Millais' *Ophelia* and Burne-Jones's sleeping beauty motifs—as well as Rossetti's red-haired stunners—in works such as *The Punishment for Lasciviousness* (1891, Walker Art Gallery, Liverpool). Exposure to art by Burne-Jones at the Biennale exhibitions and appreciation of the general Pre-Raphaelite indebtedness to earlier Italian Renaissance painting (e.g., Bottecelli) further strengthened Anglo-Italian links. Alfredo Melani was among the critics to respond, while artists included Antonio Sartorio in *The Gorgons and the Heroes* (Rome, National Gallery of Modern Art), illustrator Giuseppe Cellini, Leonardo Bistolfi, and Adolfo De Carolis, for example, in his vestal-virgin-like *Le Castaldi* (Rome, National Gallery of Modern Art).[61] Farther afield, in Finland, Alfred William Finch was a founding member of Les XX, and his English origins heightened his receptivity to Pre-Raphaelite art, Ruskin's writings, Crane's books, and Morris's Arts and Crafts movement.[62] Even in Russia there were hints of Burne-Jones's presence, quite literally in a painting of St. George created for an aristocratic patron.[63]

In Spain there was also a Pre-Raphaelite fallout effect, particularly on Symbolist and decadent artists who explored the sexual, occult, spiritual, mystic, and other esoteric and aesthetic strands of imagery.[64] Overall, the impact of the British antecedents seems to have gone more in the direction

of Decadence and often resulted in rather morbid subjects and supersexu-
alized Rossettian femmes fatales. The hermetic and narcissistic qualities
inherent in Rossetti's stunners are amplified, almost histrionically exaggerated, in many Spanish constructions of femininity. As elsewhere, all this
transpired at a time parallel to the Continental fin-de-siècle (el fin del siglo
in Spain), but there it seems to have proliferated well into the early twentieth century, beyond World War I into the 1920s.[65] The writings of Huysmans and Pater were known in Spain, and Spanish writers such as Ramón
Casellas, Santiago Rusinol, and Juan Romano Jimenez absorbed Pre-
Raphaelite influences through those authors, Rossetti, and the writings of
Ruskin, Oscar Wilde, and others.[66] Some critics in *Luz*, *La Illustración
Catalana*, and *La Ilustración Iberica o Pel & Plum* were highly aware of
these interpenetrations of literary and visual dimensions. For example,
Balsa de la Vega wrote in 1895 about the repercussions in Spain among "re-
alists, naturalists, symbolists, decadents, mistico-idealists" in a battle be-
tween excessively scientific realism and the primacy of the Aesthetic
Movement's notions of the beautiful.[67] Four years later, he was still exploring these interchanges, and other critics followed suit, including *Il Globo*'s
comments in 1906 that Spanish art imitated Burne-Jones, Rossetti, and
Moreau in an archaistic, perhaps even slavish, manner.[68] Even more than
Rossetti, Burne-Jones and especially Aubrey Beardsley triggered—or at
least stimulated—this decadent strain of Spanish visual production. Works
that support this development include *Buitre* (*Vulture*) by Eduardo Chicarro
and Rogelio Dalmau's *Nochas Solitarias* (*Solitary Nights*), the former a
nude descendant of Rossetti's sultry stunners and the latter a somewhat
cloying Beardsleyesque embodiment.

 While there are other examples, this sampling of French, Belgian,
Austrian, Swiss, Dutch, Italian, and Spanish artists seals the general indebtedness of artists throughout Europe to Pre-Raphaelite ideals and
themes. Ironically, this happened at precisely the time when Pre-
Raphaelitism had begun to decline and to be neutralized, in part under-
going a "natural" death due to the advent of more avant-garde art and also
hastened by the attacks of detractors like Mirbeau and others in the late
1890s who castigated the group and their imagery. Robert de Montesquiou, for example, in "Le Spectre Burne-Jones" of 1894 embodied
the shift in taste when he remarked of Burne-Jones's art that his "dolor-
ous yet passionate canvases" featured both "cold reason in the conception" and meticulous execution.[69] To de Montesquiou, this resulted in
creating more decorative tapestries than paintings and thus mirrored

changing notions of what art—and the beautiful—had become by the end of the nineteenth century.

For all these artists of various countries, it was not style that united them, but rather certain recurrent motifs of femininity (sleeping, tempestuous, languid, world-weary, spiritual, transcendent) that so preoccupied the end of the century. In fact, one writer, Léon Balzagette, specifically identified such alterations as part of a definite Pre-Raphaelite demise; in his *New Spirit in Artistic, Social, and Religious Life* (1898), he complained that the failure of Pre-Raphaelitism in France was attributable to the malaise projected by a glut of female imagery, a supposedly unhealthy penchant for fleshly lips, and a morbid mysticism that bordered on the oppressive and nightmarish.[70]

In his 1888 book on aesthetic decadence, Péladan had maintained that a woman was the most perfect form to convey the tangibly real through the paradox of dreams. Indeed, the imagery in his Rosicrucian salons endorsed this belief and virtually enthroned the female as a quasi-priestess, an ethereal symbol of the triumph of dream and mystery over materialism, over the everyday in life and art, and over the realistic style itself. From a heritage of Pre-Raphaelite icons, the equally esoteric Rosicrucians pushed concrete detail and dreaminess to new limits, aspiring to another level of reality and extending the languorous nostalgia of Rossetti and Burne-Jones into a different key of poetic allegory and sensuousness. Rosicrucian images parted company with the chafing restrictions of morality and storytelling typically inherent in early Pre-Raphaelitism and moved beyond the visible to aim for the transient and unseen, charged with erotic, emotional, aesthetic, or spiritual undertones.

In creating their own paradigmatic icons, both Pre-Raphaelite and Symbolist artists evolved rather disturbing—even chilling—notions of the cult of the beautiful. Even more than their forerunners, Symbolist women were simultaneously personified as visionary, overpowering, inscrutable quasi-divinities of the canvas as well as enervated, tantalizing, languishing sexual beings. Reigning from their artificial, escapist realms in a state of unremitting torpor, it is small wonder that they so unnerved Sparrow, who nonetheless approved of the Symbolists' aversion to "the vivisection of naturalism" and search for answers to "the immense algebra" inherent in the problematic hierarchies of art and representation."[71] Yet, ultimately he wondered whether such an art of anti-reality—peopled almost exclusively by occult sages and not common laborers (whom Péladan disdained as unworthy subjects)—had perhaps gone too far.

Accordingly, Sparrow exhorted fin-de-siècle painters to "remember our 'strikes' and the life in every alley and street, . . . the colliery, the ship-yards, and the slate-quarry . . . art of the religion of daily toil."[72] Despite Sparrow's urging urban reality on artists as an antidote, the Symbolists generally identified more with the relentless allure of femininity implicit in Pre-Raphaelitism and thus became an integral part of the dawning of a new erotic revolution and legacy to the twentieth century.

Symbolist artists in Europe increasingly rejected the more timid Pre-Raphaelite female type and unleashed her tempestuous Other, mak-ing her more graphic, full of libido, and sensual indulgence, withdrawn yet paradoxically exulting in her female power, and even violent at times. Such icons presaged the bohemian femme fatale of the cinema as well as the liberated ideas and behavior of the New Woman. This infusion of innovative nuances served a vital function, for in many senses, Pre-Raphaelitism had become too predictable, stagnant, and sanctimonious about its technique and even its fixation with femininity. Spectacular suc-cesses followed by dilution of their original aims in the end ironically threatened to deaden the already moribund Pre-Raphaelite movement, which had, after all, lasted for more than fifty years as a constant pres-ence. It could not remain full of adolescent spirit and freshness forever, and its viability had actually been greatly enhanced, revived, and invig-orated by the locally and individually idiosyncratic flavors given it by artists in the European avant-garde. These artists had absorbed—not just copied—Pre-Raphaelitism, then appropriated and transformed it into something different, original, and typically more sensuous. Without this input, the waning of this phenomenon and disillusionment with its evolu-tion might have been far more swift.

As for the "sexual revolution" in imagery engendered by Pre-Raphaelitism, insight on this issue was provided years later, in 1936, by the Surrealist artist Salvador Dali, who aptly analyzed what he perceived as a bequeathing of neurotic femininity by Pre-Raphaelitism to twentieth-century art. Praising their sensationalizing of the "eternal feminine" and listing specific traits (long hair, sad eyes, lassitude—as well as the seminal images of Ophelia and Beatrice), Dali ironically pinpointed some of the principal strengths and weaknesses of this legacy.[73] It is equally interesting that today, Pre-Raphaelite—and Symbolist—paintings still retain their nos-talgic appeal to vast international audiences who, unlike their forebears, do not seem to weary of these phenomena. Instead, the public endlessly clam-ors for yet more greeting cards, refrigerator magnets, posters, books, adver-tisements, fashion designs, and other visual ephemera that nevertheless affirm the inescapable and seemingly inextinguishable tenacity, even sovereignty, of paradigmatic Pre-Raphaelitism.

Notes

1. Some of the text and information for this essay has been culled, rewritten, and significantly added to from one I published in 1995 in *English Pre-Raphaelitism in Its European Context* eds. Susan P. Casteras and Alicia Faxon (London: Associated University Presses), 33–49. Since then, other scholars have pursued this material, notably Laurence des Cars, who makes some of the same points about Burne-Jones, in particular in Andrew Wilton and Robert Upstone, *The Age of Rossetti, Burne-Jones, & Watts: Symbolism in Britain 1860–1910* (London: Tate Gallery Publications, 1997).

2. On the wider implications of this phenomenon in Spain alone, for example, see Lola Capparós Masegosa, *Prerafaelismo, Simbolismo y Decadentismo en la Pintura Espanola de Fin de Siglo* (Granada: University of Granada, Monographica Arte y Arqueologia, 1999), especially 14–23.

3. For the English phenomenon, the best example is the 1997 exhibition and accompanying catalogue entitled *The Age of Rossetti, Burne-Jones & Watts: Symbolism in Britain 1860–1910*. Another useful exhibition/catalogue source is John Christian et al., *The Last Romantics: The Romantic Tradition in British Art, Burne-Jones to Stanley Spencer* (London: Lund Humphries, 1989), especially Mary Anne Stevens, "Towards a Definition of Symbolism," 33–37.

4. See, for example, Howard D. Rodee, "France and England: Some Mid-Victorian Views of One Another's Paintings," *Gazette des Beaux Arts* 6th ser. 91 (Jan. 1978): 39–48. Another useful source is Mary Ball Howkins, *The Victorian Example: French Critical Response to Mid-Victorian Paintings in Paris, 1850–1870* (Ph.D. diss., Columbia University, 1985). A general guide to Symbolism, richly illustrated and annotated, is the Montreal Museum of Fine Arts, *Lost Paradise: Symbolist Europe* (Montreal, 1995).

5. Ruskin, for example, asked Chesneau to "write a life of Turner, prefaced by a history of previous landscape." See Ernest Chesneau, *The English School of Painting*, trans. Lucy N. Etherington (London: Cassell, 1885), ix.

6. The comments about *The Return of the Dove to the Ark* are from *Le Journal pour Rire*. *Journal L'Union* also commented on this work, and I am grateful to Thomas J. Tobin for providing the precise details for this reference.

7. The full text of Gautier's remarks (and also of Delacroix on 111–12) are reprinted in Laurence des Cars, *Les Préraphaélites: Un Modernisme à l'Anglaise* (Gallimard: Réunion des Musées Nationaux, 1999), 112–14.

8. See Prosper Mérimée, "Les Beaux-arts en Angleterre," *Révue des Deux Mondes* 11 (15 Oct. 1857): 11.

9. This elevated status for the painting is suggested by Theodore Reff, "Degas's *Tableau de Genre*," *Art Bulletin* 54 (Sept. 1972): 332–37.

10. Concurrent with Burne-Jones, Watts was a linchpin in the spread of British influence among the Symbolists, and he also enjoyed considerable popularity with French critics. Based on Watts' works at the 1878 Universal Exposition, de la Sizeranne saw him as part of the Pre-Raphaelite coterie and later hailed him as a modern master for some key works displayed at the 1889 Universal Exposition. Like Burne-Jones, Watts exhibited at the liberal Salon du Champ de Mars and in 1893 lent twenty-four works to Munich for a highly successful one-person show. The best source on Watts' career is Barbara Bryant, "G. F. Watts and the Symbolist Vision," in Wilton and Upstone, 65–81.

11. On this recognition of talent, see "Edward Burne-Jones and France," a chapter by Laurence des Cars in *Edward Burne-Jones: Victorian Artist-Dreamer*, eds. Stephen Wildman and John Christian (New York: Metropolitan Museum of Art, 1998), 25–39.

12. Colleen Denney, "The Role of Sir Coutts Lindsay and the Grosvenor Gallery in the Reception of Pre-Raphaelitism on the Continent," in Casteras and Faxon, *Pre-Raphaelitism in its European Context*, 66 and throughout this highly informative essay.

13. See, for example, J. Comyns Carr, "'La Grosvenor Gallery' à Londres," *L'Art* 9 (1877): 265; and "La Saison de l'Art à Londres. VI. La 'Grosvenor Gallery,'" *L'Art* 10 (1877): 77–83.

14. des Cars, 27.

15. Charles Blanc, *Les Beaux-Arts à l'Exposition de 1878* (Paris: Renouard, 1878), 335.

16. This is my translation from a passage reprinted in des Cars, *Les Préraphaélites*, 115.

17. Edmond Duranty, "Expositions de la Royal Academy et de la Grosvenor Gallery," *Gazette des Beaux-Arts* ser. 2, 20 (1879): 372.

18. On the parallels between Moreau and Pre-Raphaelite adherents, see Robin Ironside, "Gustave Moreau and Burne-Jones," *Apollo* 101 (March 1975): 173–82.

19. Camille Mauclair, *L'art en Silence* (Paris: Société d'Editions Littéraires et Artistiques, 1901), 173.

20. Fernand Khnopff, "Les Oeuvres d'Art Inspirées par Dante,"

Le Flambeau 4 (1921): 358. See also Ronald W. Johnson, "Dante Rossetti's *Beata Beatrix* and the New Life," *Art Bulletin* 57 (Dec. 1975): 548–58.

21. Edouard Rod, "Les Pré-raphaélites Anglais," *Gazette des Beaux-Arts* ser. 2, 36 (Nov. 1887): 405.

22. Quoted in Robert Pincus-Witten, *Occult Symbolism in France: Joséphin Péladan and the Salons de la Rose+Croix* (Ph.D. diss., University of Chicago, 1976), 119.

23. On his remarks about Raphael, see da Silva, 39.

24. My translation from the full text is reproduced in Jean da Silva, *Le Salon de la Rose+Croix, 1892–7* (Paris: Editions Syros-Alternative, 1991), 12.

25. This article originally appeared in *La Jeune Belgique* in 1885 and was reprinted in *Le Plume* in 1896. See Josephin Péladan, *Félicien Rops/Joséphin Péladan Correspondance*, reuniée, presentée, et annotée par Hélène Védrine (Paris: Séguier Nouvelles Editions, 1997), especially information in the footnote on 12–13.

26. June 1887 letter from Péladan to Rops and its accompanying footnote in ibid., 217.

27. Ibid., 14.

28. Quoted in Pincus-Witten, 92.

29. For additional information, see Bruce Laughton, "The British and American Contributors to Les XX, 1884–1893," *Apollo* 86 (Nov. 1967): 375.

30. Quoted in Penelope Fitzgerald, *Edward Burne-Jones, A Biography* (London: Michael Joseph, 1975), 221.

31. See "The Chronicle of Art," *The Magazine of Art* 15 (1892): xiii.

32. "Raitif de la Bretonne" [Jean Lorrain], "Pall Mall," *Le Journal* (2 Apr. 1896), n. p.

33. My translation from Robert de la Sizeranne, "Rose + Croix, Pre-Raphaelites et Esthetes," *Le Correspondant* 40 (Mar. 1892): 1140.

34. Fernand Khnopff, "A Memorial Tribute to Burne-Jones," *The Magazine of Art* 22 (1898): 522.

35. These points of comparison are made in des Cars, "Edward Burne-Jones and France," 30.

36. Emile Verhaeren, "L'Essor," *La Nation* (1892), reprinted in Paul Aron, compiler/ed., *Emile Verhaeren: Ecrits sur l'Art (1881–1892)* (Brussels: Editions Labor, 1997), 412.

37. This point is made in des Cars, "Edward Burne-Jones and France," 32, 34.

38. Quoted in de la Sizeranne, "A Memorial Tribute to Burne-Jones," 519.

39. "Exhibitions," *The Magazine of Art* 16 (1893): xxi.

40. Patrick-Gilles Persin, *Aman-Jean, Peintre de la Femme* (Paris: Bibliothèque des Arts, 1993), 47.

41. Quoted in Jacques Letheve, "La Connaissance des Peintres Pré-Raphaélites Anglais en France (1855–1900)," *Gazette des Beaux-Arts* ser. 6, 53 (May–Jun. 1959): 323–24.

42. An 8 Apr. 1893 review by M. Broadley is quoted in Walter Shaw Sparrow, "English Art and Fernand Khnopff," *The Studio* 2 (1894): 207.

43. In his art, Rossetti was often preoccupied with the faces of women he loved—Elizabeth Siddal, Jane Burden Morris, Fanny Cornforth, etc.—while Khnopff frequently used his sister Marguerite as a model (at least until she married in 1890).

44. Fernand Khnopff, "In Memoriam: Sir Edward Burne-Jones," *The Magazine of Art* 22 (1898): 524.

45. This point is made in Jeffrey Howe, *The Symbolist Art of Fernand Khnopff* (Ann Arbor: UMI Research Press, 1982), 119–20.

46. Felicien Rops, "Lettre à Armand Rassenfosse du 5 avril 1893," quoted by Laurent Busine, "From Edward Burne-Jones to Fernand Khnopff," in *Burne-Jones, 1833–1898: Déssins du Fitzwilliam Museum de Cambridge* ed. Jane Munro (Nantes: Musée des Beaux-Arts de Nantes, 1992), 60.

47. Howe, 123–24 suggests that there may have been an incestuous relationship between Khnopff and his sister.

48. Sparrow, "Fernand Khnopff," 43.

49. On Lemmen, see Stephen H. Goddard, ed. *Les XX and the Belgian Avant-Garde: Prints, Drawings, and Books ca. 1890* (Lawrence, KS: Spencer Museum of Art, 1992), especially Jane Block, " 'Soyons Nous': Les XX and the Cultural Discourse of the Belgian Avant-Garde," 37.

50. Robert Siebelhoff, "Three Brides, a drawing by Jan Toroop" *NKJ* 27 (1976): 230n28.

51. On Delville's Rosicrucian affiliations, see Maria Luisa Frangia, *Il Simbolismo di Jean Delville* (Bologna: Casa Editrice Patron, 1978), 45–49.

52. Quoted in "Symbolist Paintings, Drawings, and Watercolors," *Christie's London Auction Catalogue* (Dec. 1989), lot entry 1153.

53. As quoted in Pierre Mathieu, *The Symbolist Generation 1870–1910* (New York: Rizzoli Publications, 1990), 131.

54. My translation from passages of Delville's *Autobiography*, quoted in Frangia, 49.

55. See da Silva, 94.

56. For more on Belgian variations, see Laurence Brogniex, "Les Préraphaélites en Belgique: d'Étranges Reveurs," in *Splendeurs de l'Idéal: Rops, Khnopff, Delville et Leur Temps* (Liege: Musée de l'Art Wallon, 1996), 123–29. Also note Brogniez's "L'Exemple Préraphaélite en Belgique: Barbares, Primitifs et Modernes," in the colloquium proceedings for *France-Belgique, 1848–1914: Affinitiés—Ambiguitées* (Brussels, 1997), 196.

57. See Denney, 71.

58. Wildman and Christian, 202.

59. See, for example, the essay titled "A Dutch Lady of Shalott" by Linda Groen in this volume.

60. For details on this hitherto unknown offshoot, see the essay titled "Pre-Raphaelitism in Hungary" by Éva Péteri in this volume. Commentary on the linguistic impact on Croatian writers is found in the essay by Tatjana Jukić in this anthology.

61. On the links to Italy, see Rossana Bossaglia, "Note Sulla Fortuna Italiana di Burne-Jones," in Maria Benedetti and Gianna Piantoni, *Burne-Jones: Dal Preraffaelismo al Simbolismo* (Milan: Mazzota, 1986), 82–85.

62. Goddard et al., 229.

63. Wildman and Christian, 202. For a Russian review of the Pre-Raphaelite influence (kindly shared with me by Thomas J. Tobin), see V[ladimir] V[iktorovitch] Chuiko, "Dorafaelisty I Ikh Posliedovateli eh Angeli," *Vestnik Iziashchnykh Iskutstv* 4 (1886): 271–304.

64. See, for example, Masegosa as well as J. V. Selma, *Los Prerafaelistas: Arte y Sociedad en el Debate Victoriana* (Barcelona: Montesinos, 1991). Another useful source is C. Reyero, *Apariencia e Identidad Masculina: De la Ilustración al Decadentismo* (Madrid: Catedra, 1996). Wildman and Christian, 202, also remind readers that in Barcelona, the young Picasso saw a reproduction of works by Burne-Jones and supposedly had planned to go to London to see these when he was detained in Paris.

65. For visual examples, see Masegosa, 710–18 especially.

66. On this literary connection, see Masegosa, 18.

67. De la Vega's words (in my translation) from a piece he wrote on 19 May 1895 for the Madrid *El Liberal* are quoted in Masegosa, 21. Other commentary on Spanish reviewers is found in ibid., 19–23, passim.

68. From a 12 May 1906 review Orbaneja wrote for *El Globo*, as quoted in Masegosa, 23.

69. Robert de Montesquiou, excerpts of "Le Spectre Burne-Jones" translated by me and reprinted in des Cars, *Les Preraphaelites*, 115.

70. Léon Balzagette, *L'Esprit Nouveau dans la vie Artistique, Sociale et Réligieuse* (Paris, 1898).

71. Sparrow, "Fernand Khnopff," 42.

72. Walter Shaw Sparrow, "English Art and M. Fernand Khnopff," *Studio* (1894), 203.

73. Salvador Dali, "Le Surréalisme Spectral de l'Éternel Féminin Préraphaélite" in *Le Minotaure* no. 8 (1936): n. p. This excerpt was translated by me from text reproduced in des Cars, *Les Préraphaélites*, 116–7.

Chapter 7

William Morris's Later Writings and the Socialist Modernism of Lewis Grassic Gibbon

Florence S. Boos

Many critics and commentators in the twentieth century seemed to consider William Morris's principal gifts to their century artistic and ideological rather than literary and linguistic, and assume that he manifested them most directly in the form of influences on the Arts and Crafts movement, several generations of Labourites, and other members of the British left. His passionate invocations of the "Social-Revolution," for example, seemed remote from the skeptical detachment or elitist conservatism of such writers as Conrad, Eliot, and Pound, and his translations, epic poetry, historical romances, and revolutionary-utopian writings seemed "archaic" and irrelevant to later authors' more avant-garde experimentation with imagism, stream of consciousness, multiple points of view, and achronological patterns of cyclical recurrence.

More recently, however, there has been a partial reassimilation of Victorian and early-twentieth-century writers, as the modernity of "modernism" gradually receded from critical view. Several recent books and articles have examined literary filiations between Morris and H. D., Orwell, and Auden, as well as earlier figures such as Yeats, Chesterton, and Wilde.[1] But few writers—and no Morris critics—have commented on the rather striking affinities that might be traced between Morris's prose romances and the neglected trilogy *A Scots Quair* (1932–1935), one of Britain's greatest modernist works, written under the pseudonym of Lewis Grassic Gibbon.

James Leslie Mitchell, its author, published ten novels, seven works on history, biography, travel, archaeology and cultural criticism, and scores of uncollected short stories and essays before he died at age thirty-four in

1935.[2] Born to a family of limited means in 1901, Mitchell struggled to escape a life of penury and farm labor through early attempts at journalism (he was a reporter at sixteen), then spent ten years in Mesopotamia, Palestine, Egypt, and London with the Royal Army Service Corps (1919–23) and the R. A. F. (1923–29). According to his biographer, Douglas Young, he "hated army life with an intensity that comes out in almost everything that he wrote," and his military experiences also exacerbated the deep hatred of war manifested in his writings.[3]

He had also read voraciously from earliest youth, especially works of history, science, and science fiction by Jules Verne, Rider Haggard, and H. G. Wells. Wells—whom he later described wrly as "the inspirer and bamboozler of youth"[4]—also personally encouraged his interests in science as well as socialism, and helped him find a publisher for his first novel.[5] More precisely, Wells and others encouraged Leslie Mitchell to leave the military service he hated at twenty-eight, and settle in southern England, first in London and later in Welwyn Garden City, and undertake the precarious project to support himself, his wife Ray (whom he had married in 1925), and two children, Rhea and Daryll, through the authorship of books.

Stained Radiance (1930), *The Thirteenth Disciple* (1931), *Three Go Back* (1932), and *The Lost Trumpet* (1932) appeared under his own name and enjoyed a measure of success. He adopted the pseudonym "Lewis Grassic Gibbon" for *Sunset Song*, a novel of Scottish rural life, as a tribute to his mother Lelias Grassic Gibbon. For the rest of his short life, Mitchell/Gibbon published concurrently under both names, and added *Cloud Howe* (1933) and *Grey Granite* (1934) to *Sunset Song* to complete the trilogy *A Scots Quair* before his death in 1935.

The principal works of D. G. Rossetti, William Morris, and other Pre-Raphaelites were found in Mitchell's library after his death, and one of his favorite books was Morris's socialist romance *News from Nowhere*.[6] Collateral evidence of Mitchell's interest in Pre-Raphaelitism might also be found in "The Road," a short story he published in 1929, whose narrator praised the Brotherhood for its (comparatively) enlightened views of women's social roles, more particularly an aunt who had given Jane, the tale's heroic protagonist, an

> education and . . . freedom beyond that decade even in England . . . [and] was a member of some society of the painters that may have been your Pre-Raphaelite Brotherhood; she was a friend of Ruskin and Morris and the

gentle rebels of those days. The New Age was nigh when all men would be free and kindly and happy, and all women not only the equals of men, but the goddesses to inspire. . . . Except in the brown lands of the Nile, . . . where women were the cattle-slaves and dolls, where the light Pre-Raphaelite had never shone.[7]

Mitchell's own "gentle rebellion" and lifelong left-wing politics derived from his deeply ingrained sympathy with the victims of grinding labor and cynical injustice. Criticized for the brutality and pain portrayed in his 1933 novel *Image and Superscription*, which included a description of the lynching of a pregnant black woman, he explained his priorities in a letter to his friend, the poet Helen B. Cruickshank:

Ancient Greece is never the Parthenon to me: it's a slave being tortured in a dungeon of the Athenian law courts; ancient Egypt is never the Pyramids: it's the blood and tears of Goshen: Ancient Scotland is never Mary Queen: it's those serfs they kept chained in the mines of Fife a hundred years ago. And so with the moderns. I am so horrified by all our dirty little cruelties and bestialities that I would feel the lowest type of skunk if I didn't shout the horror of them from the housetops.[8]

His angry sympathies extended to other sentient beings as well. In an autobiographical essay, "The Land" (1934), Mitchell reflected that

[w]hen I hear or read of a dog tortured to death, very vilely and foully, of some old horse driven to a broken back down a hill with an overloaded car of corn, of rats captured and tormented with red-hot pikers in bothies, I have a shudder of disgust.[9]

Mitchell's socialist inclinations and generally dissident views found encouragement from his older neighbor (and later father-in-law) Robert Middleton, who later became the original for Long Rob of the Mill in *Sunset Song*. They were also confirmed by his two years as a reporter, assigned first to the harbor beat of Aberdeen and later to the Gorbals district of Glasgow, and he drew on his experiences as a speaker and member of the Aberdeen Soviet for his portrait of the young socialist activitist Ewan Tavendale, hero of the *Scots Quair*'s third novel *Grey Granite*.

Malcom Maudslay, moreover, the hero of Mitchell's earlier autobiographical novel *The Thirteenth Disciple* (1931), immersed himself in the works of impassioned socialist authors such as William Morris:

> Here were people who, like himself, had shuddered in sick horror at sight
> of the dehumanized and wandering crucified . . . and seen solution of
> all the earth's bitter cruelties in a gigantic expedition against the World's
> Walls. . . . He discovered with them a splendid, romantic hope which
> coloured his days and nights. . . . William Morris led [him] into the jungle
> and without apparent qualms abandoned [him] to . . . Lafargue . . . Hynd-
> man . . . Blatchford . . . Karl Liebknecht . . . Shaw, the incomprehensible
> Marx, and . . . H. G. Wells.[10]

Like Morris, Mitchell has also been variously described as an orthodox
Marxist and an irremediably "romantic" pastoral anarcho-communist.
William K. Malcolm, for example, remarks that "Mitchell himself contributed to the uncertainty by using different terms—principally those of
anarchist and communist—to describe his personal standpoint, and definition is made more complicated by the keen interest he also took in Scottish affairs."[11]

Like many activist intellectuals, Morris included, Mitchell may also
have found the torturous verities of "party discipline" hard to take, for he
wrote his fellow novelist and leftist Neil Gunn in 1934 that "[b]y the way
I'm not an official Communist. . . . They refuse to allow me into the
party!"[12] But until the day he died, he consistently advocated communism
as the only practicable path to revolution, however flawed and makeshift
he found those turns to be.

Another, distinctly idiosyncratic but rather Morrisian aspect of
Mitchell's distaste for rigid orthodoxies might be found in Mitchell's
attraction to "Diffusionism," a view of ancient societies popularized
by Grafton Elliot Smith (*The Migration of Early Cultures*, 1915) and
H. J. Massingham (*The Golden Age*, 1927). "Diffusionists" held that hu-
mans had originally lived in free and genuinely egalitarian communal societies, a state of secular grace of the sort Morris might have described as
"mutualist or communist anarchism." Mitchell spoke of "the clean anarchy which is the essence of life" in his essay "Glasgow" (1934),[13] and argued in the anarchist periodical *The Twentieth Century* (1932) that our
ancestors once "co-operated in matters of mutual group life as a colony of
modern anarchists might co-operate—without the merging of individuality in any group-consciousness."[14] Malcolm later characterized the persistent anarchist qualities of Mitchell's political ideals as follows:

> His ideal, in which all men live in happy communal freedom, endures un-
> changed throughout his work. Thus he, like Kropotkin, ultimately demands

the abolition of property rather than the Marxist redistribution of wealth, and finally, in accordance with the original meaning of the word anarchy, he calls for the abolition of all constitutional and legislative ruling, eventually seeking what is effectively an apolitical state.[15]

The allusion to Peter Kropotkin is accurate, of course, but so also might have been a more "literary" comparison with the limiting ideals of Morris's *News from Nowhere* (1890), an anarchist kingdom-of-ends in which political parties and insititutions of the nineteenth and twentieth centuries have vanished altogether.[16]

Against the canvas of these ideals, the tensions between Mitchell's anarcho-communist views and the communist orthodoxies of the period may also be compared with Morris's vexed interractions in the 1880s and 1890s with the social democrats of the Social Democratic Federation (SDF) and the more doctrinaire anarchists of the Socialist League,[17] and one can find strong affinities between Mitchell's views and convictions Morris expressed in essays such as "Communism," "Why I Became a Socialist," "The Society of the Future," and "True and False Society." Both men were motivated by "the humanistic principles of communism," as Malcolm put it, and resisted then-current forms of orthodoxy and doctrinal rigidity. And both sought to envision transformed—not simply ameliorated—social orders, which they hoped would fulfill natural human aspirations in unanticipated ways.

A closely related analogy with Morris's views might be found in the historicist qualities of Mitchell's displacement of utopian aspirations into a remote (and perhaps partially preagrarian) pastoral past. Marx, Engels, and Reclus, among other nineteenth-century socialists, had sought to find anticipations in "primitive" societies of anti-capitalist social structures they valued,[18] and Morris's *News from Nowhere* was one of a series of historical or quasi-historical recreations Morris wrote in the 1880s and early 1890s—among them *The House of the Wolfings, The Roots of the Mountains,* and *A Dream of John Ball.*[19]

Mitchell took pains to set his account of the devastating local consequences of the First World War I against a background of reconstructed Scottish history, from its ancient Pictish past to the early-twentieth-century present, and a number of other "historicist" aspects of Mitchell's "diffusionist" or populist and socialist readings of history paralleled views Morris had set forth in essays such as "Feudal England," "The Art of the People," "Art and Architecture," and the co-authored *Commonweal* series, "The Roots of Socialism."[20]

In "How I Became a Socialist," for example, Morris himself decried industrial "civilization" for its "mastery of and its waste of mechanical power, its commonwealth so poor, its enemies of the commonwealth so rich, its stupendous organization—for the misery of life . . . [i]ts contempt of simple pleasures which everyone could enjoy but for its folly[.]"[21] Morris likewise sought to recover in history and prehistory an absence of class-hierarchy, a more just and long-overdue regard for the aspirations and accomplishments of women, and a more honest and equitable respect for simple human needs and desires, not least among them the love of beauty.

All of these, Morris had argued, had been distorted or effaced by forms of civilization that worshiped technique over art, profit over value, power over cooperation, and repression over simple natural pleasures:

> I demand a free and unfettered animal life for man first of all: I demand the utter extinction of all asceticism. If we feel the least degradation in being amorous, or merry, or hungry, or sleepy, we are so far bad animals, and therefore miserable men. And you know civilization does bid us to be ashamed of all these moods and deeds.[22]

All of Leslie Mitchell's works bear witness to his shared preoccupations with exploration, heroism, social injustice, historical evolution, and the search for an unrealised "golden age" of human dignity, but the late works of "Lewis Grassic Gibbon" manifested some of his most striking echoes of Morris's aesthetic ideals and historicist as well as socialist ground-motives. In particular, *Sunset Song* and the other novels of *A Scots Quair* resonate with poetic celebrations of the beauty of nature, the sorrows of life lived near the soil, the difficulties and limitations of political effort, and a secular faith in cyclical renewal. They express the sort of elegiac epiphanies and heightened moments of visionary prophecy Morris had evoked in *The Earthly Paradise, A Dream of John Ball*, and *News from Nowhere*. In the closing scene of *Sunset Song*, for example, the local minister, Robert Coloquohoun, preaches a war-memorial sermon that hauntingly echoes the doomed revolutionary priest's climactic "sermon at the Cross" in Morris's *A Dream of John Ball*.

For simplicity and brevity I confine myself here to the trilogy's first novel, *Sunset Song*, and consider only four of the detailed resemblances that might be traced between the literary work of Morris and Gibbon: (1) their experiments with languages and their historical and regional inflexions; (2) their shared anticapitalism, calls for revolutionary action, and appeals for stoic resilience, charitable "fellowship" and utopian hope; (3) their common beliefs in the sacredness of nature and expressions of deep reverence for its enduring spirit; and, finally, (4) their attempts to find in "new women"—reflective, determined, independent and unrepressed— emblems of continuity between an idealised past and a desired future.

Morris in his later writings and Mitchell/Gibbon in his Scottish fiction both sought to find new forms of poetic prose outside the boundaries of standard English, though Mitchell's was more autochthonous, more innovative and less "formulaic." Influenced by several years of study of Old Norse and by his early readings in Chaucer, Malory, Froissart, and other Medieval authors, Morris infused a variety of germanicisms and archaisms into much of his later poetry, translations, and late romances.

> There was a lord named Thorir, a man of mighty power in Norway, a man of fame, and wedded to a noble wife: this earl begat on his wife a woman-child, Olof by name, who was wondrous fair-mannered from her youth up; and she was the fairest fashioned of all women of Norway, so that her name was lengthened and she was called Olof Sunbeam.[23]

Morris sacrificed part of the nineteenth- and early-twentieth-century rhetorical diapason in this diction; many translation scholars have criticized it, but others have noted its ability to evoke forms of ethos and plainspoken cadences lost in modern English.[24] It also has its declamatory and narrative charms, which Morris systematically exploited in the later prose romances to suggest their placement in a hypothetical atemporal niche and quasi-Scandinavian region, somewhere beyond (and well to the north of) the Isles of the Blest. Consider, for example, the following passage in *Water of the Wondrous Isles*, in which Habundia the wise-woman tells her protege Birdalone that

> [t]hou art the beloved child of my wisdom; and now I see of thee that thou wilt be faithful and true and loving unto me unto the end. . . . And whatsoever thou wilt of me that I may do for thee or thy friends, ask it freely, and freely shalt thou have it.[25]

Or the tale's conclusion:

> Now when all this hath been said, we have no more to tell about this company of friends, the most of whom had once haunted the lands about the *Water of the Wondrous Isles*, save that their love never sundered, and that they lived without shame and died without fear. So here is an end.[26]

Morris's own everyday prose—in his letters and essays, for example—
actually had something of this style's straightforward underpunctuated
lilt, and the quasi-medievalism of the late romances sustained a kind of
liminal detachment and evoked a carefully modulated sense of loss. At
their best, moreover—in Ball's sermon, for example—they were hauntingly beautiful.

The language of *Sunset Song* and its companions was *sui generis* and
experimental in different ways. It was not archaic, but it was historically
evocative, and it was also "artificially" designed to bridge two rather dis-
parate cultures. Mitchell himself explained his purposes in a prefatory
note, in which he used the relationship between Dutch and German as a
metaphor for the problems a Scot writing for early twentieth-century Scottish and English audiences faced.

> If the great Dutch language disappeared from literary usage and a Dutch-
> man wrote in German a story of the Lekside peasants, one may hazard he
> would ask and receive a certain latitude and forbearance in his usage of
> German. He might import into his pages some score or so untranslatable
> words and idioms—untranslatable except in their context and setting; he
> might mould in some fashion his German to the rhythms and cadence of
> the kindred speech that his peasants speak. Beyond that, in fairness to his
> hosts, he hardly could go: to seek effect by a spray of apostrophes would be
> both impertience and mis-translation.

The courtesy that the hypothetical Dutchman might receive from German
a Scot may invoke from the great English tongue.

Several critics have admired the effect of Gibbon's synthetic attempt to reconcile the nationalist goals of the Scottish Renaissance with
his desire to reach a wider international audience. Douglas Young, for example, praised his achievement of a "personal and distinctive style which
is neither standard English nor broad Scots, but attempts to reproduce the
rhythms of Scots speech whilst avoiding an excessive use of dialect
words."[27] In Ian Campbell's view, Gibbon's prose also had a clear secondary
meaning to Scots readers, who

> can recognise vocabulary items which make the story recognisably attrac-
> tive, and . . . read . . . silently or aloud will betray familiar sentence-
> patterns, or ambiguous words such as "brave" and "childe" which mean
> one thing to a Scot, another to an English reader coming new to the prose.
> The mixed response . . . conveys a different impression to different readers:

the Scots are communicated to with an immediacy simply not possible through prose in standard English.[28]

Above all, the narrative voice of *Sunset Song* is remarkably flexible—alternately authoritative, mock-credulous, resistant and openly ironic, as the values of the author weave in and out of the speech of the folk narrator, a dweller in the Mearns of northeast Scotland.

A sweep of history—real and imagined—is also conveyed in the book's initial section, "The Untilled Field," which evokes the fictive Kinraddie's misty past in the "days of William the Lyon, when gryphons and such-like beasts still roamed the Scots countryside," then ranges forward into the lives of the present inhabitants, whom the narrator introduces one by one in knowing tones that shift abruptly from kindred feeling to demotic *Schadenfreude*:

> *Out of the World and into Blawearie* they said in Kinraddie, and faith! it was coarse land and lonely up there on the brae, . . . and some said there was no bottom to it, the loch, and Long Rob of the Mill said that made it like the depths of a parson's depravity. That was an ill thing to say about any minister, though Rob said it was an ill thing to say about any loch. . . . nearby the bit loch was a circle of stones from olden times. . . . They were Druid stones and folk told that the Druids had been coarse devils of men in the times long syne, they'd climb up there and sing their foul heathen songs around the stones; and if they met a bit Christian missionary they'd gut him as soon as look at him. And Long Rob of the Mill would say what Scotland wanted was a return of the Druids, but that was just a speak of his, for they must have been awful ignorant folk, not canny. (12–13)

At other times, the voice of the knowing bystander/narrator blends together with that of a particular character's stream of consciousness, most often that of the heroine's central protagonist Chris Guthrie, as in the following passage about her divided linguistic identity:

> So that was Chris and her reading and schooling, two Chrisses there were that fought for her heart and tormented her. . . . You saw their faces in firelight . . . you wanted the words they'd known and used, forgotten in the far-off youngness of their lives, Scots words to tell to your heart how they wrung it and held it, the toil of their days and unendingly their faith. And the next minute that passed from you, you were English, back to the English words so sharp and clean and true—for a while, for a while, till they

slide so smooth from your throat you knew they could never say anything
that was worth the saying at all. (32)

This interweaving voice is often polyphonic, in part-writing as well
as Bakhtinian senses, and sometimes blends viewpoints within the same
sentence, alternating the meanness, ignorance, and narrow-mindedness
of neighbors' gossip with moments of epiphanic celebration of the land
and the struggles of the people who have passed over it. Another instance
of such choral writing occurs when Chris learns that she has inherited her
father's farm, and is overpowered by a sense of love as well as dread:

> she could never leave it, this life of toiling days and the needs of beasts and
> the smoke of wood fires and the air that stung your throat so acrid, Autumn
> and Spring, she was bound and held as though they had prisoned her
> there. . . . The kye were in sight then, they stood in the lithe of the free-
> stone dyke that ebbed and flowed over the shoulder of the long ley field,
> and they hugged to it close from the drive of the wind, not heeding her as
> she came among them, the smell of their bodies foul in her face—foul and
> known and enduring as the land itself. Oh, she hated and loved in a breath!
> Even her love might hardly endure, but beside it the hate was no more than
> the whimpering and fear of a child that cowered from the wind in the lithe
> of its mother's skirts. (120)

In more autochthonous counterparts of Morris's cadences, Gibbon sought
to express in a single passage the consolations of reflection, the passions
of freedom and bondage, the desire to range over the world, and the
yearning for home.

Sunset Song traces the origins and inner life of Chris Guthrie, born
somewhere south of Aberdeen around 1890 to the dourly autocratic
crofter John Guthrie and his meekly forbearing wife Jean Murdoch. Her
father's already puritanical temperament had been hardened in the backbreaking labor of marginal tillage when his pride and stubborn resistence
to local authorities cost him his lease and forced him to move his family
further south to "Blawearie," a farm in Kinraddie in the Mearns.

After the birth of three sons and a daughter, Jean Murdoch pled with
her husband for a break in childbearing, but he "thundered at her, that
way he had. *Fine? We'll have what God in His mercy may send to us, woman.
See you to that*" (28), and she gave birth to twins. When she poisoned the
two infants and herself, "[i]t was not mother only that died with the[m],
something died in your heart and went down with her to lie in Kinraddie
kirkyard—the child in your heart died then" (63).

Guthrie's ranting threats and physical cruelty alienate his eldest son, Will, who lacks the money to marry his sweetheart, Mollie, until her mother helps him find work in Argentina. After Will's departure, John Guthrie is left alone to work the farm, and Chris must stoically endure his verbal abuse and sexual harassment when he becomes paralyzed and needs incessant care. After his death three years later, Chris struggles to temper her relief with a sense of pity for the harshness he suffered as well as inflicted, and is surprised to learn that John has left the farm entirely to her—an anomalous event in rural Scotland. His two younger sons are adopted by his childless sister and her husband, and Chris marries the highlander Ewan Tavendale soon after she assumes ownership of the farm, in a ceremony enlivened by communal good wishes and warm speeches of her neighbors Chae Strachan and Long Rob the Miller. Chris and Ewan work the land peacefully for several years, and bring their son Ewan into the world before the "Great War" and its social pressures and legal compulsions separate them.

Moved neither by patriotism nor belief in the war, Ewan succumbs to local social pressures to enlist, but does not tell Chris at first, misdirects his bitterness at her and their son later on, and finally leaves home in shame and anger at the end of his last miserable leave before departure for the front. Stunned and hurt by his uncharacteristic behavior, Chris maintains the farm with the help of a hired man and Long Rob, until she learns first of Ewan's death in France, and then from Chae, who is home on leave, that her husband had in fact been shot as a deserter after an abortive effort to return home. Chris climbs up to "the Standing Stones," a Druid circle on a hill near the farm and her favorite retreat, and consoles herself with a vision of her husband's reconciliation and return.

Chae himself, a hopeful man with socialist convictions, is killed later in France, and leaves behind his wife and young children. Even Long Rob, the area's wise skeptic and a principled opponent of the war, finally enlists in despair and misguided solidarity with the dead, leaving behind his mill farm and devoted friend Chris. The son of the region's one wealthy family is also blinded in the war, which is "won" in the region only by outsiders who invested heavily in assorted industries, among them deforestation for "the war effort" of old-stand trees. This clearcutting further degrades the land, and damages in consequence its already-marginal economy.

The novel ends with the dedication ceremony for a war memorial on the site of the ancient Standing Stones, at which the new minister Robert Coloquohoun, himself returned from the war with damaged lungs, preaches an unpatriotic but utopian sermon in which he appeals for a transformed community: "With them we may say there died a thing older than themselves, these were the Last of the Peasants, the last of the Old Scots folk. . . . the crofter is gone, the man with the house and the steading of his own and the land closer to his heart than the flesh of his body" (256). He advocates not the ravaged present but something "beyond it and us [where] there shines a greater hope and a newer world, undreamt when these four died" (256). In hope if not expectation of that day, the novel's folk-narrator observes that "you can do without the day if you've a lamp quiet-lighted and kind in your heart" (258).

Morris's most moving and universal critiques of war and capitalist exploitation may not have appeared in his overtly political writings but in the medieval and future-contingent cadences of *A Dream of John Ball* and *News from Nowhere*—for example, in the doomed rebel priest John Ball's "sermon at the Cross":

> Yes, forsooth, once again I saw as of old, the great treading down the little, and the strong beating down the weak, and cruel men fearing not, and kind men daring not, and wise men caring not; and the saints in heaven forbearing and yet bidding me not to forebear. . . .
>
> And how shall it be then when these are gone? What else shall ye lack when ye lack masters? . . . then shall no man mow the deep grass for another, while his own kine lack cow-meat; and he that soweth shall reap, and . . . he that buildeth a house shall dwell in it with those that he biddeth of his free will; and the tithe barn shall garner the wheat for all men to eat of when the seasons are untoward, and . . . all shall be without money and without price. (54, 59)

Or more prosaically in chapter XV of *News*, in which old Hammond explains to the revenant Guest that

> the appetite of the World-Market grew with what it fed on: the countries within the ring of "civilisation" (that is, organised misery) were glutted with the abortions of the market, and force and fraud were used unsparingly to "open up" countries outside that pale. . . . [accompanied by] the use of hypocrisy and cant to evade the responsiblity of vicarious ferocity. When the civilised World-Market coveted a country not yet in its clutches, some transparent pretext was found—the suppression of a slavery different from, and not so cruel as that of commerce; the pushing of a religion no longer believed in by its promoters; the "rescue" of some desperado or homicidal madman whose misdeeds had got him into trouble amonst the natives of the "barbarous" country—any stick, in short, which would beat the dog at all. (278)

Mitchell/Gibbon's socialism—as befitted a novelist—emerged most often in assessments of economic forces that underlay plot events, and in *Sunset Song*, he often cast these assessments as laconic or angry remarks by Chae or Long Rob. Subtitles in the trilogy's first volume also make literal as well as symbolic reference to the cyclical labors of that society: "The Unfurrowed Field" (a prelude); "Ploughing," "Drilling," "Seed-Time," and "Harvest" (a song-cycle); and finally an "epilude" or return to "The Unfurrowed Field." In "Ploughing," for example, we see the psychological scars of the sternly religious John Guthrie's grinding efforts to work the land:

> when things went clean over him, as that day in the sowing of the park below Blawearie when first the car-shaft had broken and then the hammer had broken and then he'd watched the rain come on, and he'd gone nearly mad, raging at Will and Chris that he'd leather them till they hadn't enough skin to sit a threepenny bit on; and at last, fair skite, he'd shaken his fist at the sky and cried *Ay, laugh, you Mucker!* (59)

When Chris and Ewan courted, they traveled to see the ruins of Dunnottar Castle in Stonehaven (Aberdeen), where

> down below, in the dungeons, were the mouldering clefts where a prisoner's hands were nailed while they put him to torment. There the Covenanting folk had screamed and died while the gentry dined and danced in their lithe, warm hall, Chris stared at the places, sick and angry and sad for those folk she could never help now, that hatred of rulers and gentry a flame in her heart, John Guthrie's hate. Her folk and his they had been, those whose names stand graved in tragedy. (125)

Mitchell knew well (and hated) the postwar British army, and anatomized with a certain care and bitter interest the pretensions of military rhetoric and forms of psychological as well as physical and economic destruction the war had wrought in a once-cohesive if poor rural society. Not even membership in the "gentry" had provided protection against small rotating projectiles of milled metal that shattered skulls. When Chae had visited Mistress Gordon of Underhill,

> she told him the news of her blinded son in the hospital in England. . . . he'd drawn back the bandages when she went to see him and shown her the great red holes in his head; and syne he'd laughed at her, demented like, and cried: *What think you of your son now, old wife?—the son you wanted*

to make a name for you with his bravery in Kinraddie? Be proud, be proud, I'll be home right soon to crawl around the parks and I'll show these holes to every bitch in the Mearns that's looking for a hero. He'd fair screamed the words at his mother and a nurse had come running and soothed him down, she said he didn't know what he said, but Mistress Gordon had never a doubt about that. And she told Chae about it and wept uncovered, her braveness and her Englishness all fair gone. (204–205)

Shortly before he was to be shot as a deserter, Ewan told his friend Chae what had made him leave:

Ewan looked at him and shook his head, *It was that wind that came with the sun, I minded Blawearie, I seemed to waken up smelling that smell. And I couldn't believe it was me that stood in the trench, it was just daft to be there. So I turned and got out of it. . . .* So out he had gone for that, remembering Chris, wanting to reach her, knowing as he tramped mile on mile that he never would. . . . And young Ewan came into his thoughts, he'd so much to tell her of him, so much he'd to say and do if only he might win to Blawearie. (238)

For Mitchell, there were no "just wars." The brutal mutilations that the war had inflicted were not "tragedy," but "desertion" of a much deeper sort, of one's kindred and land.

Thus deserted, the land and mills of Blawearie and the surrounding Kinraddie farms eroded away in the wind, and could be bought for a pittance:

that was the way things went in the end on the old bit place up there on the brae, sheep baaed and scrunched where once the parks flowed thick with corn, no corn would come at all, they said, since the woods went down. And the new minister when he preached his incoming sermon cried *They have made a desert and they call it peace*; and some had no liking of the creature for that, but God! there was truth in his speak. (251)

Such passages recall the tonal parallels mentioned earlier between Coloquhoun's sermon and the thoughts and cadences of John Ball's reflections at the crossroad:

Therefore, I tell you [cf. "Verily, verily, I say unto thee. . . ."] that the proud, despiteous rich man, though he knoweth it not, is in hell already, because he hath no fellow; and he that hath so hardy a heart that in sorrow he thinketh of fellowship, his sorrow is soon but a story of sorrow—a little change in the life that knows not ill. (52)

When Guest ponders the priest's "dream" in Morris's work, he also reflects on the complex evolution of ideals such as Ball's" fellowship," which recede and reemerge again and again in new forms:

> how men fight and lose the battle, and the things that they fought for comes about in spite of their defeat, and when it comes turns out not to be what they meant, and other men have to fight for what they meant under another name. (53)

Ball listens stoically to Guest's report that his people's exploitation will continue in ever-subtler forms for centuries, and the two men meditate quietly together in the symbolic light of dawn on a limiting ideal that seemed for a moment so close: "by such grey light shall wise men and valiant souls see the remedy, and deal with it, a real thing that may be touched and handled, and no glory of the heavens to be worshipped from afar off " (18).

Coloquohoun's elegiac sermon also invokes the eternally recurrent imagery of sunset and dawn, the cycles of season and weather, and what Morris—in the voice of Ellen in *News from Nowhere*—called the "love of the earth":

> *it was not in them to tell in words of the earth that moved and lived and abided, their life and enduring love. And who knows at the last what memories of it were with them, the springs and the winters of this land and all the sounds and scents of it that had once been theirs, deep, and a passion of their blood and spirit, those four who died in France?* (255–56)

Indeed, his elegy—like all good elegies—mourns not only the dead, but also the loss and neglect and dispersion of what they had loved and cared for:

> *And the land changes, their parks and their steadings are a desolation where the sheep are pastured, we are told that great machines come soon to till the land, and the great herds come to feed on it. . . . They died for a world that is past, these men, but they did not die for this that we seem to inherit. . . .* (256)

And it is at this point that Mitchell and Coloquohoun invoke the secular-millenarian "dream" Guest and Ball had shared for a moment in the gray medieval dawn:

Beyond it and us there shines a greater hope and a newer world, undreamt when these four died. But need we doubt which side the battle they would range themselves did they live to-day, need we doubt the answer they cry to us even now, the four of them, from the places of the sunset? (256)[29]

In *Cloud Howe* and *Grey Granite*, the second and third volumes of *A Scots Quair*, Chris, Robert, and young Ewan encounter the obstacles Coloquohoun had predicted. As in *A Dream of John Ball* and *News from Nowhere*, the kingdom of ends the minister evoked remained as Kant himself described it—"only an ideal." The very power to evoke it, however, gives it its guiding, regulative, and even programmatic force. The kingdom of ends—to vary a phrase—is within you.

Common to Morris and Gibbon were their abandonment of religious orthodoxies (Anglican and Presbyterian, respectively), and a dialectical desire to redress the evils of the world with a meditative or metaphysical appreciation of its resilient natural beauty through endless processes of physical and social change.

Morris, for example, explicitly advocated a "religion of humanity," based on social ethics and a respect for the rituals of communal history, in his coauthored *Socialism: Its Growth and Outcome* and such romances as *The Roots of the Mountains*.[30] Extended critiques of hypocrisies and intolerance were essential ground-motives of Mitchell's work as well, but he also shared Morris's devotion to complementary ideals of near-mystical contemplation and meditative acceptance of cyclical succession in "the sign of Earth, its . . . steadfastness and change."

This expression of Morris's metaphysical views appeared in fact quite early on in his work, in the lyrics of his 1871 masque, *Love Is Enough*, where an allegorical figure of "Love" points the tale's deferred and bittersweet resolution:

> Lo, for such days I speak and say, believe
> That from these hands reward ye shall receive. . . .
> —What sign, what sign, ye cry, that so it is?
> The sign of Earth, its sorrow and its bliss,
> Waxing and waning, steadfastness and change";
> Too full of life that I should think it strange
> Though death hang over it; too sure to die
> But I must deem its resurrection nigh.
> —In what wise, ah, in what wise shall it be?
> How shall the bark that girds the winter tree

> Babble about the sap that sleeps beneath,
> And tell the fashion of its life and death?. . . . (115–16)

An equally passionate and no less beautiful aspect of this duality appears in Ellen's affirmation of nature in *News from Nowhere*, when she and Guest arrive at the old house at river's (and journey's) end, depicted in a woodcut as Morris's beloved Kelmscott Manor:

> She led me up close to the house, and laid her shapely sun browned hand and arm on the lichened wall as if to embrace it, and cried out, "O me! O me! How I love the earth, and the seasons, and weather, and all things that deal with it, and all that grows out of it—as this has done!" (391)

Many of Chris' reflections in *A Scots Quair* are refracted through comparable moments of heightened emotion, recollected not in tranquillity but "under the aspect of eternity," as Spinoza put it. Such epiphanies occur when she meditates at the Standing Stones in youth, and on a similarly isolated hilltop in middle age. In *Sunset Song*, for example, when she learns that she has inherited Blawearie, this leads not to thoughts of possession, but to a vision of her own impermanence:

> And then a queer thought came to her there in the drooked fields, that nothing endured at all, nothing but the land she passed across, tossed and turned and perpetually changed below the hands of the crofter folk since the oldest of them had set the Standing Stones by the loch of Blawearie. . . . Sea and sky and the folk who wrote and fought and were learned, teaching and saying and praying, they lasted but as a breath, a mist of fog in the hills, but the land was forever, it moved and changed below you, but was forever, you were close to it and it to you, not at a bleak remove it held you and hurted you. (119)

An equally poignant sense of loss and detachment hovers at her wedding—an oddly gentle and elegiac understanding of the impermanence of human love itself:

> Strange and eerie it was, sitting there, she couldn't move from the frozen flow of thoughts that came to her then . . . that this marriage of hers was nothing, that it would pass on and forward into days that had long forgotten it, her life and Ewan's, and they pass also, and the face of the land change and change again in the coming of the seasons and centuries till the last lights sank away from it and the sea came flooding up the Howe, all her

love and tears for Ewan not even a ripple on that flood of water far in the times to be. (146)

A similar vision passes through her in *Cloud Howe* and *Gray Granite*, when she contemplates the worthy social and political projects of her husband and son.

> And she thought then, looking on the shadowed Howe with its stratus mists and its pillars of spume, . . . that men had followed these pillars of cloud like lost men lost in the high, dreich hills, they followed and fought and toiled in the wake of each whirling pillar that rose from the heights, clouds by day to darken men's minds—loyalty and fealty, patriotism, love, the mumbling chants of the dead old gods that once were worshipped in the circles of stones, christianity, socialism, nationalism—all—Clouds that swept through the Howe of the world, with men that took them for gods: just clouds, they passed and finished, dissolved and were done, nothing endured but the Seeker himself, him and the everlasting Hills. . . .
>
> The men of the earth that had been, that she'd known—the hunters of clouds that were such as was Robert: how much was each wrong and how much each right, and was there maybe a third way to Life, unguessed, unhailed, never dreamed of yet? (II, 142–43)

After Robert's death, Chris struggles to maintain herself; she blends sympathy with Ewan's communist commitments with sorrow at his lack of personal attachments. When in middle age she returns to her birthplace in the Bennachie mountains, she climbs a nearby hill to make another meditative offering to her private religion of dialectical sublation and stoic understanding:

> No twilight land anywhere for shade, sun or night the portion of all, her little shelter in Cairndhu a dream of no-life that could not endure. And that was the best deliverance of all, as she saw it now, sitting here quiet—that that Change who ruled the earth and the sky and the waters underneath the earth, Change whose face she'd once feared to see, whose right hand was Death and whose left hand Life, might be stayed by none of the dreams of men, love, hate, compassion, anger or pity, gods or devils or wild crying to the sky. He passed and repassed in the ways of the wind, Deliverer, Destroyer and Friend in one. (III, 203)

In the novel, this Job-like passage may presage Chris's death and understanding of it in universal and apostrophic terms, as the formulation of it may have foreshadowed Mitchell's own. Both Morris and Mitchell, in any event, saw such invocations of loss, change, acceptance and detachment not as relativisations or negations of utopian socialism, but as affirmations of its values.

Another distinctive attribute of Morris's and Mitchell's works appears in their common efforts to write empathetic portrayals of the experiences of independent and sexually assertive women—"new women" in fin-de-siècle terminology—who formed points of moral reference in their respective narratives.

Morris sketched early versions of such figures in "The Defence of Guenevere" and "The Lovers of Gudrun." Later, his personal experiences as a husband, his study of socialism, and the rise of the woman's movement in Great Britain during the 1880s prompted him to formulate views of sexual ethics and the "socialist new woman" in more systematic terms in works such as *News from Nowhere* and *The Water of the Wondrous Isles*.[31]

On paper at least, socialists pioneered advocacy of certain forms of equality for women: August Bebels's *Women and Socialism* (English translation, 1885) and Eleanor Marx and Edward Aveling's *The Woman Question* (1886) express the view that property claims and forms of scarcity endemic to capitalism were the primary sources of what John Stuart Mill and Harriet Taylor had called "the subjugation of women." Women freed from such constraints would no longer be defined in relation to men or their reproductive roles, but be liberated to choose partners and raise any children they might have free of economic anxieties—a radical program in Victorian Britain, but one which also left clearly presupposed certain views of childraising and "definition in relation to men."

In their roles as coauthors of the 1885 manifesto of the Socialist League, for example, Morris and Ernest Belfort Bax proclaimed that

> Under a Socialistic system contracts between individuals would be voluntary and unenforced by the community. This would apply to the marriage contract as well as others. . . . Women also would share in the certainty of livelihood which would be the lot of all; . . . so that economical compulsion could be no more brought to bear on the contract than legal compulsion could be. Nor would a truly enlightened public opinion, freed from mere theological views as to chastity, insist on its permanently binding nature in the face of any discomfort or suffering that might come of it.[32]

Morris embodied this view in Ellen, the un-aetherial Beatrice-figure of *News from Nowhere*, who, as we have seen, expresses the ardent love of nature characteristic of the inhabitants of an ideal future society. But she also values Morris's (and Mitchell's) "people's history," and she is well aware that in past ages "[m]y beauty and cleverness and brightness . . . would have been sold to rich men, and my life would have been wasted. . . ."[33] Ellen views the attentions of men as matter-of-factly inevitable circumstances of her life, but desires children for their own sakes, as beings to whom she will impart the values that are important to her:

> I shall have children; perhaps before the end a good many—I hope so. And though of course I cannot force any special kind of knowledge upon them, yet, my friend, I cannot help thinking that just as they might be like me in body, so I might impress upon them some part of my ways of thinking; that is, indeed, some of the essential part of myself; that part which was not mere moods, created by the matters and events round about me. (383)

This is exactly what Gibbon's Chris accomplishes in her education of her only child, her son Ewan. More than Morris, in fact, Mitchell/Gibbon was distinctive among male writers of the early twentieth century for his ardent feminism as well as (hetero)sexual egalitarianism, and for the striking authenticity of his principal work's primary narrative voice.

Chris Guthrie, in particular, carries the principal narrative counterpart of Grassic Gibbon's authorial voice in *Sunset Song*, as I have mentioned. In *Cloud Howe* and *Grey Granite*, she shares this role with her second husband, Robert Coloquohoun, and son, Ewan, but it is she who expresses the final poetic and metaphysical judgments which frame all three works.

Mitchell shares his fellow modernists' desire for explicitness and honesty in the portrayal of sexual matters, but he also focuses truthfully on the special pains which sexuality imposes on women, as well as evoking concrete experiences of awakening sexuality, pregnancy, birth, miscarriage, aging, and anticipated death. In puberty, for example, the young Chris looks at herself reflectively, and without any particular narcissism:

> Below the tilt of her left breast was a dimple, she saw it and bent to look at it and the moonlight ran down her back . . . And Chris saw the brown glimmer of her face grow sweet and scared as she thought of that—how they'd lie together, in a room with moonlight, and she'd be kind to him, kind and kind, giving him all and everything, and he'd sleep with his head here on her breast or they'd lie far into the mornings whispering one to the other, they'd have so much to tell! (71)

Other scenes conveyed the young couple's intense lovemaking, her shifts of mood during pregnancy, and the birth of her son Ewan:

> Mrs Ogilvie [the midwife] sat down and next minute jumped to her feet again, *Don't do that, Mrs. Tavendale, don't grip yourself up! Slacken and its easy, wish it to come, there's a brave girl!*
>
> Chris tried: it was torment: the beast moved away form her breasts, scrabbled and tore and returned again, it wasn't a beast, red-hot pincers were riving her apart. Riven and riven she bit at her lips, the blood on her tongue, she couldn't bite more, she heard herself scream then, twice. And then there were feet on the stairs, the room rose and fell, hands on her everywhere, holding her, tormenting her, she cried out again, ringingly, deep, a cry that ebbed to a sigh, the cry and the sigh with which young Ewan Tavendale came into the world in the farm-house of Blawearie. (190)

The same laconic and nonjudgmental straightforwardness characterizes the account of Chris's brief sexual interlude with Long Rob after her husband's death, and her second marriage to the socialist minister Robert Coloquohoun.

Gibbon also manages to express with visceral but matter-of-fact immediacy the blunt, crude, and sometimes bizarre forms of damage and alienation male sexual impulses inflicted on women who became their "objects": a pathetic episode, for example, in which the retarded "dafty" Andy embraces Chris in the woods; or a sexual assault on her by two men from a neighboring region; or her mother's forced childbearing and deranged suicide-murder; or, finally

> a worse thing [that] came as that slow September dragged to its end, a thing she would never tell to a soul, festering away in a closet of her mind the memory lay . . . those evening fancies when father lay with the red in his face and his eye on her, whispering and whispering at her, the harvest in his blood, whispering her to come to him, they'd done it in Old Testament times, whispering You're my flesh and blood, I can do with you what I will, come to me, Chris, do you hear?
>
> And then she'd slip down from his room, frightened and frightened, quivering below-stairs while her fancies raced, . . . seeing father somehow struggling from his bed, like a great frog struggling, squattering across the floor, thump, thump on the stairs, coming down on her while she slept, that madness and tenderness there in his eyes. (109)

Chris managed to evade him, but his domineering lust made it harder to find the measure of detached forgiveness she sought in her meditations by the grave.

> Sadder, because a greater betrayal, is the the marital rape Ewan inflicted on her in a frenzy of shame and drunken fear the last night before his departure for the front.
>
> She remembered that now, lying in the darkness the while he slept, why he had left the lamp alight; and at memory of that foulness something cold and vile turned and turned like a wheeling mirror inside her brain. For there had been other things than his beast-like mauling that had made her whisper in agony, Oh Ewan, put out the light! The horror of his eyes upon her she would never forget, they burned and danced on that mirror that wheeled and wheeled in her brain. (224–25)

Chris Guthrie survived her marriages and shifts of location, fortune, and occupation with her sense of identity and integrity intact, something like what Morris's Ellen called "the essential part of myself; that part which was not mere moods, created by the matters and events round about me." This affirmation of an integral female human self—beyond marriage, beyond love, beyond "relationships"—was essentially unique in the work of male authors of Mitchell's time.

The aim of this essay has been to trace a number of strong parallels between the writings of William Morris and Leslie Mitchell, and interpret them as common reflections of a shared commitment to concrete social action, visionary utopian socialism, evolving feminist awareness, and an elegiac sense of the evanescence of human life.

Both writers, for example, cherished a vision of an ideal society based on harmony with the earth and human fellowship, which must be reimagined and fought for in successive ages under different names. In poetic prose which they tried to free from turgidity and infuse with history, both writers also sought to temper a complex sense of transcendence with a belief in the essential goodness of sexual desire, and the conviction that any reformed society would respect women as sources of unique forms of wisdom and bearers of life. Both writers passionately believed, finally, that one must "love well what thou must leave" (as Shakespeare put it).

A first part of what they enjoined us to "love" was what Mitchell called the "speak of the place," in all its illimitable variety and nuanced diversion. A second was the "place" itself—its recurrent cycles and fleeting natural beauties, the histories of those who passed over it, and the lost memories of their most ardent efforts and hopes. A third, however—and perhaps the deepest of all—was the "love" itself. This they enjoined us to cherish the more dearly, for it expresses our lingering regret that it (and we) will vanish from the face of the earth.

Notes

1. One of the first books to deal with this subject was C. S. Lewis, *The Allegory of Love* (Oxford: Oxford University Press, 1936). More recent discussions have appeared, for example, in Cassandra Laity, *H. D. and the Victorian Fin de Siècle: Gender, Modernism, Decadence* (Cambridge: Cambridge University Press, 1996); Norman Kelvin, "Morris, the 1890s and the Problematic Autonomy of Art," *Victorian Poetry* 43.3 (1996): 425–33; Robert MacFarlane, "At the World's Waning: William Morris and the Sources of the Wasteland," *Times Literary Supplement* (16 November 2001); and Norman Kelvin, "Many Mansions, Many Filiations: Modernist Appropriations of the Pre-Raphaelites," MLA paper, William Morris session, 2001.

2. A bibliography of Leslie Mitchell's works may be found in William K. Malcolm, *A Blasphemer and Reformer: A Study of James Leslie Mitchell/Lewis Grassic Gibbon* (Aberdeen: Aberdeen University Press, 1984). Perhaps the best known of his works not mentioned in this article are *Spartacus* (London: Jarrolds, 1933), a novel; and *The Scottish Scene, or The Intelligent Man's Guide to Albyn*, with Hugh MacDiarmid, (London: Jarrolds, 1934), a collection of essays. Two posthumous collections appeared: *A Scots Hairst*, ed. and intro. Ian S. Munro (London: Hutchinson, 1967) and *Smeddum: A Lewis Grassic Gibbon Anthology*, ed. and intro. Valentina Bold (Edinburgh: Canongate, 2001).

3. Douglas F. Young, *Beyond the Sunset: A Study of James Leslie Mitchell (Lewis Grassic Gibbon)* (Aberdeen: Impulse Books, 1973). Other biographical and critical discussions have appeared in Ian Campbell, *Lewis Grassic Gibbon* (Edinburgh: Scottish Academic Press, 1985); Malcolm, op. cit.; Ian S. Munro, *Leslie Mitchell: Lewis Grassic Gibbon* (Edinburgh: Oliver and Boyd, 1966); and *A Scots Quair*, ed. and intro. Tom Crawford (Edinburgh: Canongate, 1995). All citations to *A Scots Quair* are from this edition.

4. Notes for unpublished autobiography, cited in Young, 5.

5. See ibid. for a discussion of Wells's influence on Mitchell. Nearly all of the parallels Young cites can be applied to Morris as well.

6. Ibid., 24.

7. *Cornhill Magazine* 67 (1929): 341–52, reprinted in Bold.

8. Letter dated 18 Nov. 1933, cited in Munro, *Leslie Mitchell*, 107.

9. "The Land," *Scottish Scene*, 79.

10. *The Thirteenth Disciple* (London: Jarrolds, 1931), 60: "For, led to them through a strange love for the limpid, childish verse of William Morris, he had discovered the socialists and their gigantic, amorphous literature."

11. Ibid., 1.

12. Malcolm, 25.

13. "Glasgow," *Scottish Scene*, 141.

14. "The Prince's Placenta and Prometheus as God," *Twentieth Century* 2.12 (Feb. 1932): 17.

15. Malcolm, 21.

16. *News from Nowhere and Other Writings*, ed. with intro. Clive Wilmer (Penguin, 1998), chapter X. See also "The Society of the Future," *William Morris: Artist, Writer, Socialist*, ed. May Morris, 2 vols. (Oxford: Blackwell's, 1936).

17. Treatments of Morris's relationships with other Victorian socialists have included E. P. Thompson, *William Morris: Romantic to Revolutionary*, rev. ed. (London: Merlin P, 1977); *William Morris's "Socialist Diary,"* ed. and intro, Florence Boos (London: Journeyman Press, 1985); Fiona McCarthy, *William Morris: A Life for Our Time* (London: Faber and Faber, 1994); and *Journalism: Contributions to Commonweal: 1885–1890*, ed. and intro Nicholas Salmon (Bristow: Thoemmes Press, 1966) and *Political Writings: Contributions to Justice and Commonwealth, 1883–1890* (Bristow: Thoemmes Press, 1994).

18. Frederick Engels, *The Origin of the Family, Private Property and the State*, intro. Eleanor Burke Leacock (New York: International Publishers, 1972); Ellie Reclus, *Primitive Folk: Studies in Comparative Ethnology* (London: Walter Scott, 1899). See also Florence and William Boos, "Victorian Socialist Feminism and William Morris's *News From Nowhere*," *Nineteenth-Century Contexts* 14.1 (1990): 3–32 and "Gender Division and Political Allegory in *The Sundering Flood*," *Journal of Pre-Raphaelite Studies* n.s.1.2 (1992): 12–23.

19. See Florence Boos, "Morris's German Romances as Socialist History," *Victorian Studies* 27.3 (1984): 321–42, and Michael Holzman's "The Encouragement and Warning of History: William Morris's *A Dream of John Ball*," in *Socialism and the Literary Artistry of William Morris*, ed. Florence Boos and Carole Silver (Columbia: University of Missouri Press, 1990), 98–116.

20. 1886; revised and enlarged for republication as William Morris and E. Belfort Bax, *Socialism: Its Growth and Outcome* (London: Swan Sonnenschein, 1893).

21. "How I Became a Socialist," *The Political Writings of William Morris*, ed. A. L. Morton (London: Lawrence and Wishart, 1984), 243.

22. "The Society of the Future," 193.

23. "The Story of Viglund the Fair," II.

24. See E. R. Eddison, "Terminal Essay: On Some Principles of Translation," *Egil's Saga* (Cambridge: Cambridge University Press, 1930); Stefán Einarssón, "Eirikr Magnussón and his Saga Translations," *Scandinavian Studies and Notes* 13 (1934): 17–24; Karl Litzenberg, "The Diction of William Morris: A Discussion of his Translations from the Old Norse," *Arkiv for Nordisk Filologi* 53 (1937): 327–63 and "The Victorians and the Vikings," *University of Michigan Contributions in Modern Philology*, 3 (April 1947): 101–124; Karl Anderson, "Scandinavian Elements in the Works of William Morris" (Dissertation, Harvard University, 1940); Linda Gallasch, *The Use of Compounds and Archaic Diction in the Works of William Morris* (Berne: Peter Lang, 1979); and Gary Aho, "William Morris and Iceland," *Kairos* 1.2 (1982).

25. *The Collected Works of William Morris*, ed. May Morris (London: Longmans, 1913), 20: 378.

26. Ibid., 387.

27. See Young, 82, which cites a 1933 letter to Cuthbert Graham: "It's the old problem of dialect or no dialect. I see three ways out. The first is to write in Scots, synthetic Scots for preference—everything in the book, all the descriptive and narrative matter as well as the conversations of the characters. The second way is to write in English—everything in English—so that, names apart, the story might well take place in Cornwall. The third method is what I myself employ: writing everything, descriptive matter and all, in the twists of Scottish idiom but not in the actual dialect except for such words as have a fine vigour or vulgarity, and no exact English equivalents" (*Aberdeen Bon Accord*, 15 Feb. 1935).

28. Campbell, 53. About Mitchell's uses of this technique to effect register-shifts, Campbell further remarks that "the decision making on attitude, response, emotional temperature is left to the reader, who has frequently the material for a complex or highlighted response, embedded in a passage which is perfectly capable of being read at a simple level."

29. The imagery suggests Tennyson's "Ulysses," the text of which hung over the fireplace of the Mitchell home in Welwyn Garden City (Young, 15).

30. See Boos, "Morris's German Romances, as Socialist History," *Victorian Studies* 27.3 (1984): 321–42.

31. This subject has been discussed by several critics, including Sylvia Strauss, "Women in Utopia," *South Atlantic Quarterly* 75 (1976): 115–31; Linda Richardson, "William Morris and Women: Experience and Representation" (Dissertation, Oxford University, 1989); Jan Marsh, "Concerning Love, News

from Nowhere and Gender," *William Morris and News from Nowhere: A Vision for Our Life,* eds. Stephen Coleman and Paddy O'Sullivan (Green Books, 1990): 1–20; Norman Talbot, "Heroine as Hero: Morris's Case Against Quest Romance in *The Water of the Wondrous Isles," The Nameless Wood* (St. Lucia, Queensland: Mythopoeic Literature Society, 1986); Florence and William Boos, "An (Almost) Egalitarian Sage: William Morris's Later Writings and 'The Woman Question,'" *Victorian Sages and Cultural Discourse,* ed. Thaïs Morgan (New Brunswick, NJ: Rutgers University Press, 1990): 187–206; and Florence Boos, "The Socialist New Woman in William Morris's *The Water of the Wondrous Isles," Victorian Literature and Culture* 23 (1995):159–75.

32. Norman Kelvin, ed., *The Collected Letters of William Morris* (Princeton, NJ: University Press, 1987), 2: Appendix A.

33. *News from Nowhere,* chapter XXXI, 394.

Chapter 8

PRE-RAPHAELITISM'S FAREWELL TOUR: "ISRAFEL" [GERTRUDE HUDSON] GOES TO INDIA

Margaret D. Stetz

If, as Elizabeth Prettejohn has said, "it is difficult to pinpoint the beginning of the Pre-Raphaelite movement," that "is trivial compared to the problem of locating an end for it."[1] The title of my essay invokes the concept of the farewell tour, which often proves an unreliable way of marking the conclusion to a career. Influential figures in the music world may announce their final appearances, but frequently resurface on the public stage via the "master class." Instructing a new generation of artists, great originals pass along their own principles of style and technique and continue to dominate those who learn from them. Their principles, however, will necessarily be altered by these protegées, who are responding to different cultural conditions and to new social and economic imperatives.

Pre-Raphaelitism failed to "retire" completely once its founding Brothers ostensibly had left the stage. The echo of its voice could still be heard at the end of the nineteenth century, as Pre-Raphaelitism gave its own master classes to new students—especially to the British painters, decorative artists, and writers associated with the aesthetic movement. It continued to occupy a central place in the world of art and literature, although in changed—sometimes in greatly changed—incarnations. By the 1890s, the public identity of Pre-Raphaelitism bore not only the early impress of John Everett Millais and Dante Gabriel Rossetti, or the mark of later contributions from Edward Burne-Jones and William Morris, but also the effects of adaptations introduced by new successors, such as Walter Pater, Oscar Wilde, and even Aubrey Beardsley.

Yet the list above wrongly suggests that Pre-Raphaelitism's end-of-the-century interpreters and practitioners were chiefly men. In recent years, scholars of Victorian art and literature such as Debra N. Mancoff and Jan Marsh have focused on the importance of the "sisters" among the Pre-Raphaelite Brotherhood at every stage of its development, even as Talia Schaffer and Kathy Psomiades have highlighted the range and number of women participants in the aesthetic movements of the late 1870s and 1880s, from "Vernon Lee" and "Ouida" to Mary Haweis.[2] As we reach the 1890s, late-stage Pre-Raphaelitism and late-stage aestheticism—with the latter, in some ways, a movement already shaped by the former—interweave their strands in the works of new sets of women writers, publishing in new venues.

Among these new venues were books from the Unicorn Press, the publishing firm run by Ernest J. Oldmeadow, as well as Oldmeadow's magazine, *The Dome*. Started as a quarterly in 1897, *The Dome* later turned into a monthly, while maintaining over the course of its three-year-long span its original mission to offer "Examples of All the Arts."[3] Both the Unicorn Press and *The Dome* reflected their owner's devotion not only to the aesthetic present, but to the Pre-Raphaelite past. John Dixon Hunt long ago asserted the importance of that past to late-Victorian artists and writers, recognizing that it gave them "a repertoire of basic themes and vocabularies in which to talk about them. By the 1890s the Pre-Raphaelite imagination was still a dominant attraction, rivaling that of the French arts."[4] Perhaps more surprisingly, the same principle held true for a new generation of publishers. In a 1957 article for *The Book Collector*, Paul West noted Oldmeadow's interest in carrying

> into the new century a tradition of publishing which had been based on the aesthetic ideals and practice of William Morris. It [the Unicorn Press] produced works which, if they were not important or memorable, were at least exquisite and original. As the century drew to an end, the Unicorn Press became increasingly interested in publishing de luxe limited editions. It published, at five guineas, a reprint of *Hand and Soul*, a story by Rossetti which had appeared in *The Germ* and which was re-published in *The Dome*.[5]

Althea Gyles, the Irish-born book designer, illustrator, poet, and disciple of Pater—who, like "Pater's Marius the Epicurean . . . never committed herself to any 'faith' besides that of art"—became a contributor to *The Dome*.[6] So, too, did Nora Hopper, also a prose and verse writer of Irish extraction. The periodical flourished through its connections with a woman-dominated social circle that centered on another contributor, Alice Meynell—perhaps a predictable choice, since Ernest Oldmeadow, like Meynell, was an adult convert to Roman Catholicism.

But the woman author whose career at the turn of the century proved most closely associated with Oldmeadow's ventures was Gertrude Hudson. Working pseudonymously and calling herself "Israfel" or "Israfel Mondego," Hudson developed an ornate, heavily descriptive, sometimes arch style for her prose pieces, which combined art and music criticism with the contours of the personal essay and then added touches of fictional narrative. Walter Pater was certainly her master and model in this genre, but her work also looked back further to the prose of John Ruskin and Rossetti, whose names appeared both as touchstones and as points of departure throughout her writings. Hudson published regularly in *The Dome*, particularly in its last two years (from 1898 to 1900). At the same time, Oldmeadow was bringing out her work in book form, with the appearance first of *Ivory, Apes and Peacocks*, which was issued "At the Sign of the Unicorn" in 1899, to be followed by *A Little Beast-Book* in 1902.

Gertrude Hudson unambiguously turned away from one of the paths where late-stage Pre-Raphaelitism led—that is, toward the embrace of British Socialism via the political and artistic efforts of William Morris. Her preference instead was for the sort of aestheticism associated with "the notion of the artist as enclosed consciousness and of art as a realm separate from the world of politics and economic production."[7] The aesthetic practice of her prose divorced the ideal of design, the ideal of The Beautiful, from the critical examinations of nineteenth-century labor associated with an earlier generation of Pre-Raphaelite social thought. Yet, as Jon Whitely has pointed out, even this apolitical or antipolitical version of aestheticism often was embedded within and dependent upon its Pre-Raphaelite origins:

> Although many of the younger generation, the aesthetes, who followed Pater into a cult of pure art, tended to reject the earnestness of the Pre-Raphaelites and although the neo-Renaissance taste which they cultivated had other sources apart from Morris and his circle, the cult of design, which affected all aspects of public life in late Victorian England, would not have existed and would not have taken the form it did without the example of the Pre-Raphaelites.[8]

In her fin-de-siècle publications for Ernest Oldmeadow, however, Hudson's choice of aesthetic stance and creation of a persona through which to convey her thoughts on the arts were determined by gender-based pressures to which her male counterparts in the "younger generation" were not subject, as the men around her decided which aspects of Pre-Raphaelitism to preserve. One of these pressures was the need to distance herself from the increasingly controversial and reviled figure of the New Woman. Hudson's use of the pseudonym "Israfel" might have seemed merely to reflect a preference for an androgynous, gender-blurring persona. In *Ivory, Apes and Peacocks*, on the contrary, Hudson deliberately presented her voice as that of a man, inventing a masculine identity and referring to herself throughout as a gentleman. Talia Schaffer has explained the preference for masculine pseudonyms found among a number of late-Victorian female aesthetes as a release "from the particular culture and expectations of women writers."[9] During the decade of the 1890s (and especially during its first half), New Women authors used autobiographical fiction as the site for political debate over women's social roles. Male literary critics, in response, attacked and dismissed work by contemporary women in general as nothing but a confessional, shapeless literature of protest. "Female aesthetes rebelled against the autobiographical fallacy by constructing fanciful, nonrealistic texts," as Schaffer says. By "treating art as an autonomous region," they "escaped the inhibiting demand that they produce confessional writing," as well as the opprobrium that would fall upon them for being labeled either as inartistically personal or political or, worse yet, as both.[10] Presenting herself in her essays as a gentleman allowed Gertrude Hudson to appropriate a gentleman's freedom to be read and reviewed as a prose artist, rather than as a propagandist. At the same time, it enabled her to invade a sphere to which nineteenth-century British women's access had been strictly limited—the world of the professional art critic.

The exclusion of women from the ranks of art critics was not accidental but rather, as Pamela Gerrish Nunn argues, endemic to the process by which men asserted their own right to inhabit those positions: "Men's proprietorial attitude to art criticism, that is to say their jealousy of the critical faculty and their claim to its practice, was often based on showing women's opinion to lack knowledge, good sense, objectivity—in short, authority."[11] Susan Casteras adds, "Since women were very rarely art dealers, curators, or judges on important art juries in the contemporary art world, they had little access to authority (except in the rarefied confines of the Society of Female Arts)."[12] Thus, the cycle was self-perpetuating. Yet, as Claire Richter Sherman has suggested, women found ways around the barriers constructed to deny them access and, in "the period from 1890" onwards, "maintained a high level of activity in art criticism" nevertheless.[13] One means for doing so was by producing anonymous or—as in the case of Gertrude Hudson's "gentlemanly" disguise as "Israfel"—pseudonymous submissions for the burgeoning number of periodicals inspired by the aesthetic movement, which were too eager to fill their quarterly or monthly issues to worry about exposing and exploding the identities of their contributors.

The publishers and editors of these magazines were, like Ernest Oldmeadow, deeply devoted to the principles of beauty (including those of beautiful book design) that they had received from the Pre-Raphaelites and from the Pre-Raphaelites' disciples and immediate successors. But they were also men of business. Aestheticism had opened up a fresh area of business, as Jonathan Freedman demonstrates in his 1990 study, *Professions of Taste*, for anyone who wished to lay claim to superior discernment and to make this superiority the basis of his livelihood, "by forging a career for himself out of the imparting of knowledge about this 'new' field to an awed and appreciative public."[14] If this commodification of an ideal seemed problematic or even a trifle unsavory to those who engaged in it, then there was certainly a Pre-Raphaelite precedent to which they could cling. After all, had not William Morris, who was dedicated to the principles of handicrafts and to socioeconomic egalitarianism, made money from Morris and Company by selling machine-printed textiles for the drawing rooms of the upper-middle classes?

Ernest Oldmeadow appears to have had little compunction about sacrificing exaggerated notions of aesthetic "purity" where profit was concerned. *The Dome* began by limiting the advertising at the back of each issue to announcements by booksellers, much as John Lane's quarterly, *The Yellow Book*, had done before it. But *The Yellow Book* had gone under just as *The Dome* was starting up, and Oldmeadow took warning. Before long, as Paul West reports, "there appeared on the outside of the back cover an advertisement . . . for 'Calvert's Carbolic Ointment.' "[15] Thus, we may liken the entry into *The Dome* and into the lists of the Unicorn Press of "Israfel" to the acceptance of the Carbolic Ointment advertisement—a decision motivated by business concerns. The market for aesthetic criticism and (to use Jonathan Freedman's phrase) for "professions of taste," whatever their source, overrode any reservations Oldmeadow might have had about accepting a woman art critic as an "authority." As for Gertrude Hudson herself, the construction of her pseudonym "Israfel," and later of "Israfel Mondego," seems to have signaled a wish to confess the very deception in which she was engaged, for both the Semitic-sounding given name and the surname with its allusions to Portuguese geography, of her masculine persona alerted English readers to the presence of something alien, something not quite "gentlemanly."

Yet the vaguely factitious, foreign-seeming pseudonym might also have prepared readers for another feature of Hudson's aesthetic practice. It was indeed through her knowledge of the foreign that Gertrude Hudson would stake her claim to authority. Like the Wandering Jew, "Israfel" was a globetrotter. "Mondego" created a professional identity by carrying a well-developed ego/I/eye to the far corners of the world, deliberately seeking out the sites and sights where male predecessors in the Pre-Raphaelite and aesthetic movements had not been. "Inevitably," as Claire Richter Sherman notes of the late-Victorian women who attempted art criticism, "they responded in various ways to the leading male critics of the nineteenth century, among whom Ruskin was a prominent and inescapable presence."[16] So Hudson, too, paid her obeisance to him. But Ruskin had never been to India; neither had Walter Pater; nor, for that matter, had Oscar Wilde.

William Morris had, of course, used India both as a political paradigm and as a source of artistic inspiration. In the catalogue for the exhibition *The Victorian Vision*, the Victoria & Albert Museum's recent reconsideration of Victorian art from the perspective of a century afterwards, Tim Barringer has elaborated on the importance of India to latter-stage Pre-Raphaelitism, which had created its own "imperial vision":

> Ruskin and his follower William Morris looked back to the Middle Ages as a golden age of craft production, in which labour was a creative, expressive act rather than the repetitious, dehumanised industrial wage-slavery which they perceived in the Victorian city. India, commonly thought of as an unchanging society, preserving traditional craft skills, offered interesting parallels to the Europe of the Middle Ages. . . . It followed, then, that Indian art, as William Morris declared, was "founded on the truest and most natural principles." His own designs for textiles, eschewing both naturalism and geometry, but based on organic forms, drew on Indian models as well as medieval European ones.[17]

Although Morris may have appropriated India as a trope for his political arguments and his decorative arts, that appropriation had not taken the form of a traveler's direct observations. In going to India by way of the "Peninsular and Oriental"—the title of the first of the essays in *Ivory, Apes and Peacocks*, as well as the name of the steamer that carried her across the Suez Canal—Gertrude Hudson set out to establish her own literary terrain by making the East her aesthetic territory.

What she chose to describe was influenced by what she had read as well as by what she knew the audience for Unicorn Press publications would want to "see" through her eyes. William Morris had decided that the decorative arts of India were still unspoiled and organic in origin, while those of England had been corrupted by mass production and by the preference for machine-made perfection over natural irregularity. Hudson would emphasize similar conclusions, using firsthand observations that Morris had not been in a position to make. Throughout her Indian sketches—at least one of which, "Jeypore," also appeared in *The Dome*—she would play off scenes of native Indian beauty against the ugliness of imported objects of English manufacture, as well as appreciations of the physical beauty of the populace against the ugliness of the British colonials. *Ivory, Apes and Peacocks* draws its biblical title from I Kings, seemingly a complimentary allusion to the British monarchy as Solomon-like and as receiving a similar bounty of exotic merchandise sent to it from abroad. But the title, which retained a comma between the first and second words in advertisements for the book bound into the back of other Unicorn Press publications, had no such punctuation on the volume's cover or title page. Instead, readers were confronted with a configuration of words that turned the initial noun into an adjective and produced a highly unflattering phrase. In the context of the essays that followed, "Peacocks" seemed to refer to the gorgeous Indian people themselves and the "Ivory Apes" to the less-than-gorgeous white colonials who ruled them. Hudson's prose pieces reinforced and endorsed Morris's Pre-Raphaelite perspective, but also ventured beyond it, raising questions not only about the supposedly Solomon-like wisdom of the earlier imperialist conquest of India, but about contemporary British reform movements that were attempting to remake Indian culture in the guise of "civilizing" it.

Concepts drawn from the decorative arts dominated Hudson's portrait of India, a land that she likened repeatedly to a "mosaic." Thus, the Jeypore (Jaipur) she offered to English audiences was not merely a "colorful" place but one deliberately unified through color, albeit chosen from a palate unfamiliar to readers in London:

> For the wonderful town is a shimmer of rose-jacynth throughout; its wide, grand streets all pink! its fine houses—in the Hindu style of architecture, varied and picturesque, and all different in design though uniform in colour—pink. These Arabian-Night-like houses of the Bazar [*sic*] have soft green shutters to their lowest storey, where the merchants display their wares; and they have overhanging balconies, with pink and white carved lattices. The mingled turquoise and sapphire of the Indian sky, seen

> through those rose-coloured screens, must make an exquisite mosaic. But
> this rose-coloured city is not too monotonous of hue; sometimes the ubiq-
> uitous pink is all overbroidered—one can use no other word—with other
> colours—green and blue and white—images of god, flowers, horses.[18]

Here, nature and artifice blend seamlessly into an "overbroidered" spec-
tacle in which the smallest features of interior design serve both as independent objects of interest and as a fitting frame for the sky, to which they
are linked. Gertrude Hudson creates an image of an Indian city spilling
over with art, especially with the sorts of applied arts that were being lost
or degraded in England through mass production: "Now the roof and
crown of Jeypore art is its brass-work—its wrought and enamelled brass
vases and tables and trays. This is very seductive, and the whole town
teems with it."[19] At the same time, Hudson shows no interest in attributing such art to particular artisans or in investigating the conditions of
their labor, as William Morris might have done. Pre-Raphaelite attention
to detail mixes in her essay with an aestheticism so arrogant and insular
that the resulting vision of the indigenous population scarcely distinguishes between the human and the nonhuman:

> The natives all get drunk on this auspicious occasion [a festival honoring
> Krishna], and they also cover themselves with rose-coloured paint. I chanced
> to meet a great procession of the revellers in the Bazar [*sic*]—several huge
> elephants, with gorgeous caparisons and painted ears and foreheads, their
> white tusks banded with brass; camels and Turkoman horses, all gaily
> adorned, and crowds of brilliant natives. The effect in the pink bewilder-
> ing Bazar [*sic*] of Jeypore was most beautiful, mad, and impossible.[20]

Her view of India is at once a cruelly dehumanizing and an appreciative
one, in which every sight can be reduced to part of a pattern and judged
according to whether or not it suits the overall design. And it is, of course,
Hudson herself, in the role of the enlightened aesthetic tourist, who determines that design and exercises the power of deciding what does or
does not fit.

Hudson's notions of cultural appropriateness and incongruity were
based on the stereotype of the Indian subcontinent as a place out of time
and as "unchanging" as a medieval village, much as it had seemed to
William Morris (who was, however, reflecting on it from far across the
sea). Gertrude Hudson preferred an India without visible signs of modern
Western influence, regardless of whether those influences were being

embraced by Indian leaders for the good of their subjects. When she looked, for instance, at recent civic projects instituted by the Maharajah of Jeypore, she could only bemoan the coming of "a Museum, a Zoo, and also a School of Art" as signs of corruption; to have "streets . . . paved, and lit with gas" meant that "now Jeypore is like a fairy-tale with an unfortunate veneer of Parisian boulevard."[21]

The ideal of India that Hudson's work articulates could be dismissed nowadays, perhaps, as merely another expression of what Susan Horton calls "the imperial nostalgia for unspoiled natives characteristic of so much writing by nineteenth-century male travelers,"[22] though produced in this case by a woman impersonating a male narrator's voice. Yet Hudson's version of this romantic devotion to the "unspoiled" also seems to have allowed her to stand back from the British imperialist project in India and to critique it in unusually harsh terms. Throughout *Ivory, Apes and Peacocks*, the imperial occupation of India figures as an unlovely, wrongheaded effort by English philistines to import their own tastelessness into a culture that would have been better off without their intervention. In Calcutta, Hudson finds "the trail of the Englishman is over the town. It is terribly depressing to find fine shops, where you can get . . . shirts and socks and Kodaks."[23] The colonials prove physically unattractive to the point of being comical, with "the complexion of either a kippered herring or a boiled sole," as well as provincial and emptyheaded: "The Calcutta woman, you may take as a foregone conclusion, has never read anything, heard anything, or thought anything; and instead of this blissful state of vacuity making her quite charming, it only makes her dull."[24] The architecture of British colonial government buildings and of private residences bespeaks a dullness, too, deserving of such inhabitants. In terms of beauty, the exchange between England and India has been all one-sided, to the advantage of the former. At the sight of a tomb in Agra, Hudson rhapsodizes:

> Never before have I seen a building mosaiced over the whole of its surface. And the workmanship is so exquisite! How is it that the Orientals, left to themselves, are so infinitely artistic? Whence do we get all our modern friezes and dados and designs for house decoration, if not from these old palaces and tombs of the Mogul emperors?[25]

According to the "British imperialist world view," as Ruth Roach Pierson has noted in her introduction to *Nation, Empire, Colony*, "civilization emanated out from centers of learning and culture in England, located at the heart of civilization, to the outposts of civilization, Britain's colonies."[26] Yet, Hudson's depiction of the relation between the arts in Britain and those in India is based not on hierarchy, but on equivalency. If art represents the peak of civilization, then India appears to have reached that summit through a different course, utilizing different media, but to have achieved it nonetheless. The finest products of nineteenth-century English and Continental culture are matched and mirrored in the objects created by the Indian artisans whom Hudson encounters in Delhi:

> Here you see marvellous and exquisite Oriental things thick-wrought with gold as the Prelude of "The Meistersingers" . . . combinations of colours daring and magnificent as Mr. Swinburne's alliteration, chuddahs costly and chaste as the diction of Walter Pater, embroideries delicate and rare as the cadenzas in Chopin's nocturnes, little table centres perfect as Heine's lyrics. I saw one (it might have been a Rossetti sonnet, so exotic and strangely exquisite it was) of yellow satin broidered—oh! so faultlessly!— with peacocks,—peacocks in iridescent blue, green, and gold thread.
>
> What patient, passionate artists these Eastern embroiderers must be! Their works are poems and pictures and symphonies, they are not mere embroideries.[27]

The absence of condescension in Hudson's evaluation of Indian cultural productions and her readiness to accord them elite status, equal to that of contemporary Western examples of High Art (including Pre-Raphaelite examples), marked *Ivory, Apes and Peacocks* as almost unique. Neither in late-Victorian travel narratives nor in works of art criticism did such judgments often occur. What John Ruskin had done in the 1850s for Gothic cathedrals—lifting from them the stigma of being seen as the barbaric expressions of a supposedly primitive society—Gertrude Hudson attempted in the 1890s to do for the arts of India. That she met with less success in her efforts was not surprising, for the continued political domination of India depended on assertions of British superiority in every area of endeavor, and suggestions of equality remained unwelcome.

Almost as radical was the handling of gender in Hudson's text. Her impersonation of a gentleman's narrative voice freed her from one of the constraints that might otherwise have bound her—that is, the need to demonstrate what Barbara N. Ramusack has termed "maternal imperialism" toward Indian women. "Preaching a gospel of women's uplift," late-Victorian Englishwomen who traveled to the subcontinent "were frequently

referred to as mothers or saw themselves as mothering India and Indians."
The accounts of Indian life that they published for English audiences featured "the goals of promoting female education, raising the minimum age
of marriage for women, and improving the situation of Hindu widows."
Most of all, they hoped "to mold the life-style of Indian women according
to Victorian ideals that reflected Christian influence, as in their campaign
for modest dress."[28] By the 1890s, so common were these tales of the
oppression of Indian women, written by Englishwomen allegedly determined to improve their lot, that the result was a somewhat clichéd journalistic genre. As Antoinette Burton puts it, "The recital of woes usually
began with a description of the inside of the *zenana* [i. e., women's segre-
gated living-spaces], followed by . . . commentary on the practice of child-
marriage, culminating in . . . the treatment of widows as outcasts"[29]—a
pattern that became increasingly "formulaic" in its own objectification of
"'the Oriental woman'" as little more than the occasion for white feminist
outrage.

"Israfel"—Gertrude Hudson's raffish masculine alter-ego—was un-
interested in lecturing Indian women or in stirring up English readers
to interfere in their cultural practices; still less did "he" wish to see
them cover themselves in drab and modest Western garb. Instead, "he"
assumed the stance of a Rossettian worshipper of The Beautiful, focusing on the beauty of Indian women. Just as Gertrude Hudson's Pre-
Raphaelite antecedents had sought their feminine ideal among outcast
Englishwomen—working-class shop girls, professional models for artists,
prostitutes, and other specimens of "the fallen"—and had redefined for
their contemporaries both where beauty was to be found and what forms
it might take, so "Israfel" made claim to connoisseurship through prose
appreciations of Indian women as visual spectacles, as figures "in gaudy
saris, with silver anklets clinking lazily on their dusky limbs, silver studs
in their noses, and lustrous soulless kohl-ringed eyes."[30] "In Jeypore,"
wrote Hudson, "I saw a nautch-girl who was the spirit of Dance incarnate—
she moved with such a wanton, wicked grace; her tinselled skirts were
glorious with mock jewels." Conjuring this picture of sexually suggestive
glamour, Hudson asked her English readers pointedly, "Do you think she
will ever wear a false fringe and high-heeled shoes?" Indeed, Hudson argued explicitly against the movement to force Indian women into the prim
costumes of British ladies: "A welcome eye-resting sight was the smart
Ranee in her native splendours of pink and green satin and silken
gauze. . . . Robed in diaphanous yellow, with languid kohl-darkened

eyes . . . a native woman becomes symbolic and attractive; in European dress she is a horror!"[31]

Nonetheless, it would be wrong to see Gertrude Hudson's aesthetic tourism as a repudiation of what Tim Barringer labels "imperial vision," for *Ivory, Apes and Peacocks* offered, in the end, little more than a modification of that perspective. The "native woman" was still a silent and speechless figure throughout Hudson's text; so, for that matter, was the "native man," reduced to a mere picturesque element—the "majestic beggar" with "his ragged, imposing turban."[32] By taking late-stage Pre-Raphaelite ideals of beauty on a farewell tour, so to speak, at the end of the century, Hudson made India visible to English readers in a new way, as something other than an administrative problem or a sphere of social practices in need of reform. The India that she constructed through her prose sketches was a culture dominated by art and by artists and, therefore, deserving of respect. Yet this version of India still called out for an aesthetically sophisticated British traveler to define it; the "mosaic" of India could be seen only by one sweeping across the landscape, in passing. And such tourism was possible only with a permanent colonial presence that guaranteed Hudson's passage on ships, trains, and carriages, one that safeguarded her stays at the "good" European-style hotels on which Hudson's narrative depended and which it faithfully recorded.

Sarah Bilston has noted that "As historians and critics have uncovered the Englishwoman's role as a 'civilizing' agent in the imperial project, so too they have recognized that late-Victorian British women used imperialism as a means of developing a 'legitimate' political role."[33] Hudson's *Ivory, Apes and Peacocks* suggests the existence of a more complicated story, in which some British women also used imperialism as a way to develop a legitimate aesthetic space for themselves, especially in the male-dominated world of Victorian art criticism. Certainly, that seems to have been Gertrude Hudson's professional goal as she packed her bags and boarded the "Peninsular and Oriental" steamer, fully intending to write about her perceptions for *The Dome*. But her way of seeing India and, thus, of presenting it afterwards to English readers, would be shaped by what she carried with her: not just a new identity, as "Israfel," but an older Pre-Raphaelite vision of The Beautiful. As *Ivory, Apes and Peacocks* proves, it was a vision still adaptable to new circumstances and scenery, and still surprisingly distinct and bright at the century's end.

NOTES

1. Elizabeth Prettejohn, *The Art of the Pre-Raphaelites* (Princeton, NJ: Princeton University Press, 2000), 87.

2. See, for instance, Jan Marsh, *The Pre-Raphaelite Sisterhood* (New York: St. Martin's, 1985); Jan Marsh and Pamela Gerrish Nunn, *Women Artists and the Pre-Raphaelite Movement* (London: Virago, 1989); Debra N. Mancoff, *Jane Morris: The Pre-Raphaelite Model of Beauty* (San Francisco: Pomegranate, 2000); Kathy Alexis Psomiades, *Beauty's Body: Femininity and Representation in British Aestheticism* (Stanford, CA: Stanford University Press, 1997); Talia Schaffer, *The Forgotten Female Aesthetes: Literary Culture in Late-Victorian England* (Charlottesville and London: University Press of Virginia, 2000); and Talia Schaffer and Kathy Alexis Psomiades, eds., *Women and British Aestheticism* (Charlottesville and London: University Press of Virginia, 1999).

3. Paul West, "*The Dome*: An Aesthetic Periodical of the 1890s," *Book Collector* 6.2 (1957): 160.

4. John Dixon Hunt, *The Pre-Raphaelite Imagination, 1848–1900* (London: Routledge & Kegan Paul, 1968), 6.

5. West, 163.

6. Bonnie J. Robinson, "Gyles, Althea (1868–1949)," in *The 1890s: An Encyclopedia of British Literature, Art, and Culture*, ed. G. A. Cevasco (New York and London: Garland, 1993), 250.

7. Psomiades, *Beauty's Body*, 9.

8. Jon Whiteley, *Oxford and the Pre-Raphaelites* (Oxford: Ashmolean Museum, 1989), 71.

9. Schaffer, *The Forgotten Female Aesthetes*, 14.

10. Ibid., 14.

11. Pamela Gerrish Nunn, "Critically Speaking," in *Women in the Victorian Art World*, ed. Clarissa Campbell Orr (Manchester and New York: Manchester University Press 1995), 108.

12. Susan P. Casteras, "From 'Safe Havens' to 'A Wide Sea of Notoriety,'" in *A Struggle for Fame: Victorian Women Artists and Authors*, eds. Susan P. Casteras and Linda H. Peterson (New Haven, CT: Yale Center for British Art, 1994), 14.

13. Claire Richter Sherman, "Widening Horizons (1890–1930)," in *Women as Interpreters of the Visual Arts, 1820–1979*, ed. Claire Richter Sherman with Adele M. Holcomb (Westport, CT; London: Greenwood, 1981), 40.

14. Jonathan Freedman, *Professions of Taste: Henry James, British Aestheticism, and Commodity Culture* (Stanford, CT: Stanford University Press, 1990), xix.

15. West, 161.

16. Sherman, 40.

17. Tim Barringer, "Imperial Visions: Responses to India and Africa in Victorian Art and Design," in *The Victorian Vision: Inventing New Britain* (London: V & A Publications; Harry N. Abrams, 2001), 329.

18. Israfel [Gertrude Hudson], *Ivory, Apes and Peacocks* (London: At the Sign of the Unicorn, 1899), 87.

19. Ibid., 92.

20. Ibid., 90.

21. Ibid., 92.

22. Susan R. Horton, *Difficult Women, Artful Lives: Olive Schreiner and Isak Dinesen, In and Out of Africa* (Baltimore, MD and London: Johns Hopkins University Press, 1995), 149.

23. Israfel, 123.

24. Ibid., 51.

25. Ibid., 66.

26. Ruth Roach Pierson, "Introduction," in *Nation, Empire, Colony: Historicizing Gender and Race* (Bloomington: Indiana University Press, 1998), 8.

27. Israfel, 75–76.

28. Barbara N. Ramusack, "Cultural Missionaries, Maternal Imperialists, Feminist Allies: British Women Activists in India, 1865–1945," in *Western Women and Imperialism: Complicity and Resistance*, eds. Nupur Chaudhuri and Margaret Strobel (Bloomington: Indiana University Press, 1992), 132–33.

29. Antoinette M. Burton, "The White Woman's Burden: British Feminists and 'The Indian Woman,' 1865–1915," in *Western Women and Imperialism: Complicity and Resistance*, 147–157.

30. Israfel, 29.

31. Ibid., 132.

32. Ibid., 28.

33. Sarah Bilston, "A New Reading of the Anglo-Indian Women's Novel, 1880–1894: Passages to India, Passages to Womanhood," *English Literature in Transition*, 44.3 (2001): 321.

Chapter 9

PRE-RAPHAELITISM IN HUNGARY[1]

Éva Péteri

The year of the formation of the Pre-Raphaelite Brotherhood, 1848, saw the outbreak of revolutions throughout Europe, of which the Hungarian proved to be the longest and most resolute, turning into an all-out war of independence against the ruling Hapsburg dynasty of Austria.[2] Following its suppression in 1849, there was no more hope of attaining full political independence for Hungary in the foreseeable future. However, Hungarian national identity and national character were as strong as ever; the period after 1849 saw a rise in the study and cultivation of Hungarian cultural traditions, especially the language. Artists preferred historical subjects advocating the heroism of the Hungarian people, the readiness of great men and ordinary citizens alike to make sacrifices for the country's freedom and advancement. Austria's defeat at the hands of the Prussians in 1866 and Hungary's gradual acceptance of the impossibility of independence led to the Compromise of 1867 and the establishment of the Austro-Hungarian Monarchy. This ended the centuries-long conflict between the two states and brought political stability and steady economic and cultural development to Hungary.

An important aspect of Hungarian cultural life in the late nineteenth and early twentieth centuries was that painters, designers, and architects wanted to free themselves from German-Austrian influence and create an independent Hungarian style. What the architect Ödön Lechner writes in his "Önéletrajzi vázlat" (Autobiographical Sketch) indicates the general attitude:

In the course of my endeavours and experiments I had to realize that German culture . . . kept me in its unrelenting hold, weighed heavily on me, and quenched all my free artistic thoughts. . . . I felt as if being engulfed by enormous waves against which I stretched out my arms for protection to no avail; and that against this huge current a powerful and big bar had to be set.[3]

At first Lechner, like many, turned to France in the hope of attaining a culture "strong enough to shield [him] against the German,"[4] but by the end of the nineteenth century, England was an equally popular alternative; in certain fields, especially in the applied arts, it became the preferred choice. Many of the ideas advocated by John Ruskin and William Morris proved to be both compatible with Hungarian objectives and also highly stimulating, creating an awareness of and enthusiasm for English culture that had rarely been experienced in Hungary before.

The ideas of Ruskin and Morris started spreading in Hungary in the 1880s and became common in artistic circles during the first few years of the twentieth century. As part of the government's policy after the 1867 Compromise, much attention was given to the improvement of the taste and artistic standards of Hungary as a means to stimulate intellectual independence. The foundation of the Museum of Applied Arts in 1878 and the subsequent establishment of the Hungarian Applied Art Society by Ágoston Trefort, then Minister of Education, marked the beginning of a systematic promotion of "modern" applied art. When one of the founding members of the Society, the connoisseur and former ministerial deputy Jenô Radisics became director of the museum—which was housed in 1896 in a magnificent purpose-built palace designed by Lechner—his veneration for the English and their achievements was clearly manifest in its program. He had spent considerable time in England in the 1890s, and was well acquainted with the English Arts and Crafts movement; he wished it to influence the artistic development of his country. As a result, some of Morris's printed cottons and velveteens were among the first artefacts purchased by the museum, and due to Radisics's effort and enthusiasm, several award-winning exhibits of the English National Competition were put on display in Budapest in November 1898. In addition, a catalogue was published, with extracts from the evaluation and the critical observations of the English jury. These years also brought an important English theoretical work to Hungary: in 1896, Ruskin's *The Stones of Venice* appeared in Hungarian in the translation of Sarolta Geôcze, a sociologist and pedagogical writer, making Ruskin's ideas widely available for the nation.

The real breakthrough came, however, with Walter Crane's exhibition and visit to Hungary in 1900. Kálmán Rozsnyai, the Hungarian actor and journalist, who had been living in London as Crane's guest, served as a mediator between the Master, as he referred to Crane, and his compatriots. He seemed to have made Crane acquainted with the work of the Applied Art Society and with the current trends and achievements in the development of the applied arts in Hungary, and had persuaded him to bring a collection of his works to exhibit in Budapest.[5] Rozsnyai's letter introducing Crane and describing his preparation for the exhibition was published in *Magyar Iparmûvészet* (Hungarian Applied Art), the magazine of the Applied Art Society and the leading arts organ at the time, and his enthusiastic words set the tone for the writings on Ruskin and Morris to be published in Hungary in the following years: "The names Ruskin, Morris, Rossetti, and Crane mean a history of art in themselves, and they are the brightest names in the history of applied art."[6]

Crane's subsequent letter to the Hungarians was published in the same periodical[7] and created a general feeling of gratitude. He had been presented by the Society with its prestigious book *Applied Art in 1896*, published on the occasion of Hungary's millennium, which illustrated numerous products from the various applied arts in Hungary. Crane describes his impressions and praises the nation's achievements. Though he admits detecting traces of German and French influence on Hungarian products, he emphasizes—with good instincts or a delicate understanding of the country's position and objectives—the dominant Hungarian character. He praises most of all the beauty of the embroideries and the traditional flower patterns and colors of peasant art. Crane's appreciation and his heartwarming words gave a significant boost to Hungarian self-confidence and to the nation's cultural attachment to England.

Crane's exhibition in October 1900 was a great success. He visited Hungary and delivered a lecture based on extracts from his book *Line and Form*, which ten years later was published in Hungarian.[8] *Magyar Iparmûvészet* paid tribute to Crane with an issue dedicated to him; it was bound in a cover designed by the artist for the occasion. As Crane's popularity grew, so did the awareness of and devotion to his own masters, Ruskin and Morris, as well as to his predecessors in painting, the early Pre-Raphaelites.

With the resolution to promote applied arts in Hungary and with the English regarded as the most advanced in the world in these, the Museum of Applied Art housed a British Applied Art Exhibition in September–November 1902. Radisics introduced the catalogue of the exhibition with the following words:

The role and significance of English applied art in the establishment of modern art is well-known, there is basically no study, no article discussing the recent changes concerning the applied arts starting otherwise than with the praise of English art.[9]

The reviews published on the occasion of the exhibition justify Radisics's words. Among these, an article by Frigyes Spiegel, a noted architect and artist-craftsman, is of special interest in relation to Ruskin, Morris and the Pre-Raphaelites.[10] Spiegel writes about Ruskin as the "fire-spirited apostle" who was the first to realize that "the ever more preponderant mechanical industry could be counter-balanced only by the revival of the handicrafts." Morris is described as the man who put Ruskin's theories into practice, who "seeded the fallow field of applied arts once again." Spiegel is aware of Morris's devotion to the Middle Ages and his observance of the inherent two-dimensionality of the decorative arts, and of the importance of structure and functionality in the applied arts. And though Pre-Raphaelite paintings are seen as too mannered and too heavily dependent on symbolic references, he finds that the Pre-Raphaelites played a crucial role in the development of the principles of ornamentation.

Another critic, József Diner-Dénes, likewise praises the English initiative in the development of the applied arts. "England started his fight against tastelessness two generations earlier than any other European nation."[11] As well as being an art historian, Diner-Dénes was also a sociologist and a committed social democrat; his view of Morris thus had a political aspect, too. While he accepted Morris's claim that factory-made products were always aesthetically inferior to the handmade, he remained critical of Morris's achievements for its social bearings: Morris's beautiful handmade works were mostly affordable only to the wealthy privileged classes. Here Diner-Dénes draws attention to an issue that much concerned Morris's Hungarian followers: they wished to create a powerful national art, but they had to take the people's moderate means strongly into consideration.

A year after the British Exhibition, Geôcze's book *Ruskin élete és tanításai* (The Life and Teachings of Ruskin) came out with lengthy extracts translated from *Modern Painters* and *The Seven Lamps of Architecture*, and a seventy-two-page introduction presenting Ruskin's life and thoughts.[12] Geôcze has a surprising knowledge of Ruskin; her devotion to the man she is writing about is obvious throughout. Ruskin appears as a kind of Christ figure, a man of virtue and moral teaching, the helper of those in need, the lover of children: he is even described as "the saviour of the English nation." In order to be faithful to this ideal, she deviates from the truth at certain points—for example in her presentation of Ruskin's divorce from Effie Gray—whether out of ignorance or deliberate idealization cannot be known. Nevertheless, a Hungarian reader could hardly have been provided with a more thorough account of Ruskin's life and views at the time. Geôcze writes about the past and marriage of Ruskin's parents, about his childhood—including the Bible readings with his mother and the journeys in the family carriage—about his education and his emotional relationships. She explains Ruskin's aesthetic views and social theories by quoting from several of his works, *Fors Clavigera* among them; she also mentions his foundation of the St. George's Guild. The words with which she recommends the study of Ruskin's works to the Hungarians show her dedication:

> I would like to imbue the Hungarian mentality with Ruskin's noble idealism. I would like his noble views of life to take root in each Hungarian soul. I have written a book on his life and teachings for that purpose. But it happened that, as if walking in a field of flowers, I wished to take the whole field home. But it cannot be. One might be content with a bunch of them. . . . Nevertheless, it still has the color, the scent and the freshness of the whole field. Thus, instead of the whole Ruskinian field, behold a bunch. Come to love it, my Hungarian reader.[13]

Besides the significance of the information given in Geôcze's book, it is also important because it contained black and white illustrations, Rossetti's *Ecce Ancilla Domini*, Millais's *The Huguenot*, Hunt's *The Light of the World*, and Burne-Jones's *The Mirror of Venus* among them. This is especially noteworthy since few Pre-Raphaelite pictures were accessible in Hungary at the time. In the 1901 Spring International Exhibition at the Mûcsarnok (Exhibition Hall), Millais's *Mrs. Louise Jopling* was shown with a work by Hunt referred to in the catalogue as *Night over the Sea*, and Philip Burne-Jones's portrait of G. F. Watts; these could hardly give an impression of what Pre-Raphaelitism actually meant. However, in the same year, the Burne-Jones volume of the German *Künstler Monographien* series was published. This was widely circulated in Hungary; it is easily available in secondhand bookshops even today. The Rossetti book in the same series came out in 1905, and Hunt's volume even later, all with numerous black and white illustrations. No wonder, therefore, that the thoughts and ideas of Ruskin and Morris made a stronger impact in Hungary at the very beginning of the century than the pictorial style of the

Pre-Raphaelites. These, however, became generally known within a few years. As early as 1904, István Dömötör, an art journalist, wrote in an article "Ruskin nálunk" (Ruskin Here) that "Ruskin has a very good name in Hungary today,"[14] an indication of how quickly and easily he had been accepted as the country's aesthetic apostle. Dömötör adds,

> I do not want to give a prophecy, and it cannot even be calculated how and what [Ruskin's influence] will germinate. Maybe just a few forlorn traces will mark its former presence and efforts [in Hungary]. It passes by and nothing remains but the remembrance of a flash in the pan. But perhaps the whole Hungarian nation will settle on a new culture in which Ruskin's teaching is vivid and thriving.[15]

Although Dömötör's desired all-embracing assimilation of Ruskin's views never came to pass, Ruskin's ideas spread throughout the artistic circles of Hungary in the early twentieth century.

In 1905, Géza Supka, a young art historian, made an attempt to give an overall view of Pre-Raphaelitism in his essay "Költôk—Iparmûvészek: az Angol Preraffaelisták" (Poets—Craftsmen: the English Pre-Raphaelites).[16] He expressed regret that Hungarians knew sadly little of the Pre-Raphaelites, yet his article is mostly restricted to a discussion of Morris and Ruskin. He gives a brief but precise account of Morris's work: his poetry, essays, involvement in the various applied arts, and his socialism. In relation to the Pre-Raphaelites, he observes that they can be regarded as the first Secessionist group who, advocating individualism in art, broke away from its traditional schools. He describes the Pre-Raphaelites as basically naturalists, yet adds that "while the execution is always strictly realistic, the meaning is always embedded in a profound symbolism."[17]

The most significant Hungarian publication on the Pre-Raphaelites also came out in 1905.[18] *Ruskinról s az Angol Preraffaelitákról* (On Ruskin and the English Pre-Raphaelites) was written by the Hungarian painter, Aladár Körösfôi Kriesch, and it contained four lectures he had delivered to a select audience somewhat earlier. The book is a significant achievement. It is, first of all, comprehensive: giving a view of Ruskin's and Morris's theories, the latter's achievements in applied arts, of the Pre-Raphaelites' literary works as well as their paintings. It is accurate, and its evaluations show a unique understanding and sound judgment. It is enthusiastic, yet purposeful, even in style, and in language often reminiscent of Ruskin and Morris. Like Geôcze, Körösfôi emphasizes that his aim in presenting Ruskin's ideas and works is for his fellow-countrymen to profit by them. We should be aware, he says, that all the progressive thoughts and achievements of new art owe their existence to Ruskin, thus "We are all his disciples, whether we have read a line of him or not."[19] His devotion is similar to Geôcze's, though he concentrates on Ruskin's works, referring only occasionally to biographical details. Ruskin is described as a "prophet," a "seer" who declared that art is the ultimate guide, "the flaming torch and lighting tower, the shine of which illuminates the way of humanity towards happiness and understanding."[20] He begins his praise of Ruskin with a reference to his emphatic perception of nature:

> Surely there were poets before him, too who had been moved by the lily dancing on the waves at the shore, or the summit of the Alps bathed in crimson. But one has to read Ruskin suddenly to realise how much it was mere looking and not seeing, that we might have paid attention yet heard nothing, and that our souls were neither large enough, nor pure and peaceful enough to reflect the surrounding universe as truly as a mirror.[21]

Körösfôi shares Ruskin's admiration for Medieval art: for the simplicity, piety, and humility of the Medieval artists, and claims that Ruskin was the one who "realized that the last true, the last living art was that of the Middle Ages."[22] To him, however, the essence of Ruskin's teaching is the idea that "everyone has the right to and need for art as much as for air or daily bread, and that the happiness of every age and society is in proportion with whether it grants it to its people or deprives them of it."[23] In connection with the role of art in man's life, he adds that Ruskin was the first who made it evident that "the moral and artistic truths stem from one and the same source and that the latter cannot be without the first."[24]

As Ruskin is seen as the intellectual promoter of noble art, Morris is regarded as the one who "with practical variety and inexhaustible working capacity gives form to Ruskin's great Word: that every manifestation of life must be endowed with artistic quality."[25] Morris's work in the applied arts are presented by Körösfôi in detail. For him, Morris's works in stained glass brought a complete regeneration of the craft, according to which the transparent color of the glass itself and the thick line of the lead create the image and not the heavy painting on the glass. The products of the Kelmscott Press are likewise praised, described as generating a "spiritual communication with the reader in the course of which one feels as if holding in his hands a constituent of his own soul."[26] Körösfôi writes extensively on textiles, noting Morris's thoroughness in everything related to the craft: in finding the best materials, in his experimenting with natural dyes, in studying ancient techniques, and in supervising the whole process of production. He praises Morris's printed cottons for their honest simplicity, and his carpets and tapestries for the quality of their execution. Furniture- and tile-making are also referred to with an emphasis on Morris's wish to refine the "home" in general. In Körösfôi's words, Morris's work assumes divine dimensions; Morris "lays his powerful creative hand onto every single object of our dismal homes and breathes art into them."[27] "When we see somewhere," he adds, "a simple, modern piece of furniture which serves its function entirely, which is clear in its structure, noble in its proportions, and honest in its making; or a modern piece of fabric or a tapestry, in which the depth and power of every single color contributes to the delicate harmony of the whole—then we should be aware that whosoever the designer might have been the spirit of Morris dwells there."[28]

Ruskin and Morris are likewise appreciated in connection with the protection of old buildings, with the advocacy of the moral and aesthetic superiority of handiwork as compared to mechanized work, and with the consequent concern for the working classes. Their efforts made for the preservation of their country's architectural heritage and for the improvement of working conditions, and the reestablishment of noble and pleasurable work are regarded as so fundamental that they are set as examples to be followed in Hungary. Körösfôi quotes long passages from Ruskin's *Unto this Last*, which he describes as a "modern gospel,"[29] and from Morris's "Socialism in Art" and a brief section from "How I became a Socialist." Nevertheless, Morris's socialism is treated with reserve. In Körösfôi's view, it was a mistake, though a noble one, that Morris joined the socialists; Körösfôi is convinced that "ideal aims can never be achieved with political alliances."[30] In his opinion, Morris's political disillusionment was unavoidable, and his understanding that "the happiness of humanity depends solely on intellectual and moral cognizance"[31] should be regarded as his ultimate message.

Körösfôi writes in the third part of his book that it is indeed curious that he, a painter, takes on the task to write about the literary achievements of the Pre-Raphaelites. Yet, in his literary evaluation he proves to be as successful and well versed as in his aesthetic. Regarding prose and poetic works as of equal importance, he writes here on Ruskin, Morris, Rossetti, and Swinburne. According to him, Ruskin's literary greatness lies in his realization that aesthetic refinement is as vital in prose as it is in poetry, and in his ability to write accordingly. He is seen as a master of his language, who "builds fortresses, towers, and pleasant bowers with his sentences and clauses," and "as if he was walking amidst a host of flowers, he picks the most beautiful ones from here and there to bedeck his thoughts, till the charm of the fragrant brunch slowly captivates all the faculties of our spirits."[32] Compared to Ruskin's, Morris's prose is found inferior, where ordinary, simple statements and deductions create a dry language. Körösfői sees Morris at his best as an epic poet and as a medievalist, the descendant of Chaucer and Keats. His medievalism as well as his Icelandic interest and translations are regarded as part of the same inclination, his indebtedness to his country's Teutonic cultural heritage.

Rossetti, on the other hand, is described as a lyric poet, who was able to integrate the aristocratic, refined Latin culture he inherited into the English literary tradition. He is seen as the descendant of Dante, Petrarch, and Michelangelo, for "clearly feeling the great transcendental and metaphysical concerns of omniscient and omnipotent love,"[33] the love that "derives from the all-embracing divine reason."[34] Körösfői finds no contradiction in the simultaneous presence of sacred love and overt sensuality in Rossetti's sonnets. On the contrary, he claims that the latter makes the poems even more fervent, more ethereal. He also praises Rossetti's command of the language and his perfect use of the strict Italian sonnet form. To Swinburne, he explains, he devotes only a few paragraphs, simply because he belonged to the Pre-Raphaelites only for a brief period. His poems are nevertheless praised for their musicality and refined language.

About the Pre-Raphaelite painters—or as he calls them "picture-writers"—Körösfői writes in abundance. Reading his estimate, it is interesting to see how aware he was of the diversity within the movement, even within the Pre-Raphaelite Brotherhood. Though he knows how the Pre-Raphaelites were inspired by Medieval art, how they wished to be realists in their "truth to nature," and how they searched for noble ideas to express, he seems to view Pre-Raphaelitism from a wider perspective. To him the common aim of the Pre-Raphaelites was "the absolute sincerity and independence of their endeavors."[35] In his opinion, it was the idea that brought them together and also what brought about the dissolution of the Brotherhood so soon; since after a brief period of joint work each artist started following his own style, his own conviction. Accordingly, after giving the story of the formation of the Brotherhood and its aims and interests, he discusses the painters Ford Madox Brown, Rossetti, William Holman Hunt, John Everett Millais, and Edward Burne-Jones individually. Brown is described as the unfairly unappreciated artist, whose works, though "often rough in composition,"[36] reveal the sincere mind and honest craftsmanship of the painter. Rossetti is seen as an artist whose "career is like that of a stupendous meteor from some other world that has fallen to us" and as "the greatest individuality" of the circle "in his force and in his one-sidedness alike." In Körösfôi's view, Rossetti has a "real artistic disposition," which means that "the spiritual impulse and sensual piety of his art is very difficult to apprehend," but, Körösfôi prophesies, "in the course of time it will diffuse ever greater and greater light."[37] Hunt is characterized as a man of biblical profundity. "He was the first painter," writes Körösfôi, "who, after so many centuries, approached the Bible once more with a pure, unspoiled spirit and exerted himself to become a Christian painter." He is described as an indefatigable master, the only conscientious realist in the group, whose intellect is governed by a "relentless sincerity," whose works are yet endowed with a deep symbolic significance. Millais is "the temporary Pre-Raphaelite,"[38] who, inspired by his friends as a young man, took on their views and aims, but, as early as *The Huguenot*, started deviating from the Pre-Raphaelite creed. Burne-Jones, however, though he soon developed his own individual style, is believed to belong strongly to the Pre-Raphaelite movement. "His figures constitute a distinct world, a mysterious and dreamy one where, as it seems, there is no room for violent and spontaneous deeds. Nevertheless, they always profess the great truths of humanity," says Körösfôi.[39] Besides the above-mentioned painters discussed in detail, Körösfôi knows James Collinson and many of the followers: Arthur Hughes, Walter Deverell, Simeon Solomon, Frederick Sandys, William Bell Scott, William Shakespeare Burton, and Crane are all referred to. Yet, it is not so much the extent of his knowledge that takes the reader by surprise, but his full understanding of these painters and their works, his insight into their spiritual concerns and intellectual dilemmas. "What is then the significance of Pre-Raphaelitism?" he asks in the final part of his last essay.

> We have seen, how Madox Brown endows his historical characters with real feelings instead of the conventional platitudes, . . . how Holman Hunt wishes to elaborate on the essence or faith instead of the ecclesiastic dogmas and stereotypes in his religious works, . . . how Rossetti opens up an entirely new world in the light of the Dantesque celestial love,[40]

and "how Burne-Jones populates this world with his figures imbued with Christian benevolence." Thus, according to Körösfôi, the Pre-Raphaelites were all realists in the sense that they depicted what they felt or lived through, and that this sincerity and honesty is the very thing that makes all their works modern and great at the same time.

Körösfôi's advocacy of Pre-Raphaelitism was not only theoretical. Under the influence of Ruskin and Morris, he, together with his friend and colleague, Sándor Nagy, became much involved in the applied arts, and to a certain extent the influence of the Pre-Raphaelites can also be seen in his, as well as in Nagy's pictorial works.

The two young art students, Körösfôi and Nagy, first met abroad, in Rome in 1891. As Katalin Gellér observes,[41] it can be seen as symbolic that the two scholars first met at the home of the later Nazarene painter, Ferenc Szoldatits, when both happened to be visiting the master. At Szoldatits's studio, they admired the bright colors of the works of the old painter and the way he prepared his paints and primed his canvases himself. After his return from Rome, Nagy left for Paris; there he stayed for more than seven years and discovered the art of the Pre-Raphaelites. By that time they, especially Burne-Jones, had captivated the French capital and during Nagy's stay there were significant exhibitions of Pre-Raphaelite works in Paris. Moreover, Nagy made friends with the Canadian-born Percival Tudor-Hart, who, having studied in England, was well acquainted with Pre-Raphaelite works and ideas, and further excited Nagy's interest. Also in Paris he came to know the art of the Rosicrucian group, which in certain respects was also inspired by the Pre-Raphaelites.[42] In 1895, Körösfôi made a short visit to France, where he met Nagy and his new friends, and two years later Nagy and Tudor-Hart visited Körösfôi in Transylvania.

Exploring the traditional Hungarian villages of the area, they found that the folk art and the different crafts were still practiced in their ancient forms there, and through their discussions with Tudor-Hart, they realized that this type of work and this way of life were much in accordance with the Ruskinian-Morrisian vision of the unity of art and life and of man's joy in everyday work. They discovered that the English ideal, which was based on a Medieval model, had a living counterpart in the folk art and home-industry of Transylvania. Thus the small villages of Transylvania, especially those of the region of Kalotaszeg, which had remained mostly unaffected by the industrial innovations of the time, became regarded by Körösfôi and Nagy as "Ruskinian lands." Körösfôi's admiration for this area went to such an extent that he adopted the name of one of these villages, Körösfô, and became known as an artist by this name, just as his architect friend, Ede Torockai Wigand took on the name of another Transylvanian village, Torockó, somewhat later.

Given its richness in traditional folk art, ethnographers and artists had been visiting this region since the 1880s, collecting data and making drawings of the folk costumes, traditional architecture, peasant embroidery, and wood carvings, with attention given to techniques, motifs, and materials. Körösfôi and some of his friends joined in the Ruskinian spirit. Most of their work was done also as a contribution to Dezsô Malonyai's great enterprise, a five-volume book *A Magyar nép Mûvészete* (The Art of the Hungarian People), which, as Malonyai's words in the foreword reveal, was intended as an important and valuable product of the country's efforts to promote its national identity. When the first volume came out in 1907, dealing solely with Kalotaszeg, it was greeted with enthusiasm and, for quite understandable reasons, seen in a Ruskin-Morris perspective:

> And now a book has come out. What is its content? Everything. Since it is life itself, the one which was dreamt about by Ruskin walking under the arcades of the cemetery in Pisa, and for which the fanatic Morris had been fighting till the end of his life. The one which is the ideal of everyone striving for culture.[43]

The association of national heritage with the Ruskinian ideal of art and life is, however, not unique to Hungary. As Ákos Moravánszky points out, the Poles, Czechs, and Finns all had their own Ruskinian lands: Zakopane, Slovaco, and Karelia respectively.[44] In Körösfôi's mind, too, the interrelation of folk art and the ideas of Ruskin and Morris is decisive: Transylvanian folk art should be regarded as our master that teaches us that life cannot be without art. "All the formal manifestations of life must have an artistic purport—if there is not, then they are corrupt. Since in a way—however latently—it is harmful to humanity."[45] To him, folk art means something like the Gothic to Ruskin and Morris. In an essay "A Népmûvészetrôl"[46] (On Folk Art), he praises it as a form that is in full harmony with life; it satisfies the needs of daily life in the most perfect way, since the one who practices it knows these needs best. In structure and execution it always relies on the natural qualities of the materials used, and it is also of a high aesthetic standard, since the maker has the time and the willingness to make it beautiful. Consequently, folk art should be protected against the steady spread of mass production, which destroys all of the values mentioned previously. For Körösfôi, the artist has an important role, or even a duty, in relation to this process. This is, however, not the menial copying of folk motifs, but the thorough understanding of the nature and the principles of folk art. Supplying designs for the home industry movement, learning and practicing traditional methods of different crafts, and education, passing on experience, may come after that.

But Körösfôi went one step further. Establishing himself and his family in Gödöllô, a small town some twenty miles away from Budapest, he tried to live a full, creative life in accordance with the principles he promoted. Soon many of his friends and colleagues followed him, and this is how the Gödöllô Art Colony evolved.

The Gödöllô artists were involved in almost all the crafts Morris had practiced. These included weaving, stained glass, furniture, and even interior design, book illustration, and leather work. Most important was the weaving workshop, which under Körösfôi's dedicated direction acquired international fame within a few years. In the 1890s, Körösfôi and Nagy started making designs for weaving workshops, and some of their works even won prestigious awards at international exhibitions: in Paris in 1900, in Torino in 1902, and in St. Louis in 1904. Taking over one of these workshops in 1903, Körösfôi started the work with the aims of promoting home industry by producing high quality and aesthetically pleasing tapestries and carpets, along with the aim of giving work to local girls and women, which was much in need in the area. Work in the weaving workshop was based on traditional techniques, such as the Hungarian Kilim or Torontál technique, the originally Swedish Scherebeck and the Caucasian Szumák looping techniques, but they also made old Gobelins and knotted carpets.

Local girls were trained for the work by a woman of unusual talent in the field, Valéria Kiss, who had studied weaving and bone-lace making in several parts of the world: Persia, Arabia, Turkey, Venice and Brussels. She was also experienced in the making and use of natural dyes; on her initiative the Gödöllô men started growing plants in the garden of the weaving workshop for this purpose. Körösfôi, convinced of the superiority of natural dyes, did much to raise the nation's awareness of the devastating effect synthetic dyes have on quality. In his opinion, the introduction of cheap aniline dyes did more harm to the weaving industry than that of machine work: they impair the fabric and destroy its natural character. His Morrisian principle was that "the material determines the quality" and that "only with fine materials can one create something really fine and noble."[47] He wrote several articles to promote his views, and in certain cases offered practical solutions for producing and distributing natural dyes and making them more attractive for the consumers. To improve the quality and extend the variety of their products, Leo Belmonte, the Swedish-born member of the colony, was sent to Paris to study traditional weaving techniques and methods of dyeing. On his return, Belmonte was entrusted with the execution of the most demanding designs, for example Körösfôi's *A Jó Kormányos* (The Good Helmsman, Figure 9.1). This tapestry, which can be seen as the manifestation of Körösfôi's Huntian artistic creed, depicts the boat of humanity sailing on the sea of life, driven by the allegorical figures of Determination, Benevolence, Love, and Understanding and steered by the attentive, haloed figure of Christ.

In most cases, however, the patterns and motifs of Gödöllô woven works were taken from folk art sources, the themes mainly from the ballads and legends of the Hungarians, which, as Katalin Gellér observes, is akin to the Pre-Raphaelites' preference for Arthurian legends.[48] Körösfôi was familiar with Morris's *Holy Grail* tapestries, and described them as perfect both in the "harmony of their deep colors as well as in the delicacy of the outlines."[49]

Körösfôi's workshop regularly contributed to national exhibitions and fairs, and given its steady development and the high standard of its products, it became the appointed training workshop of the School of Applied Arts in 1907. In 1908, they were invited to the Cannes textile exhibition; they took part, with great success, at the Hungarian Exhibition at Earl's Court in London, and they served as interior decorators at the International Architectural Exhibition in Vienna. As the reminiscences of those associated with the workshop reveal, many of the Gödöllô carpets and tapestries were foreign commissions, mainly English and American, and many were sold in Spain.[50] In 1914, their works were taken as far as the San Francisco World Exhibition.

Stained glass and mosaics were another important part of the applied arts practiced by the artists of Gödöllô. They were lucky to find an excellent craftsman for the execution, Miksa Róth, to whom the country owes the rebirth of stained glass in Hungary, just like its revival in England is due to Morris. Róth, like Körösfôi and Nagy, held the work of Morris and the Pre-Raphaelites in very high esteem, and tried to follow the example set by them. In his essay "Az Üvegfestészet 40 Éve" (Glass-Painting in the Last Forty Years), he attributes the liberation of stained-glass art from its nineteenth-century degraded state to Morris and Burne-Jones:

> Burne-Jones, the great artist of England, deals with the problems of glass-painting with devotion and enthusiasm. Understanding the real nature of glass-painting he penetrates its spirit. . . . In his compositions he always remains two-dimensional, avoiding depth and superfluous plasticity, and, at the same time, he strives for a mosaic-like effect with his forceful lead-lines.[51]

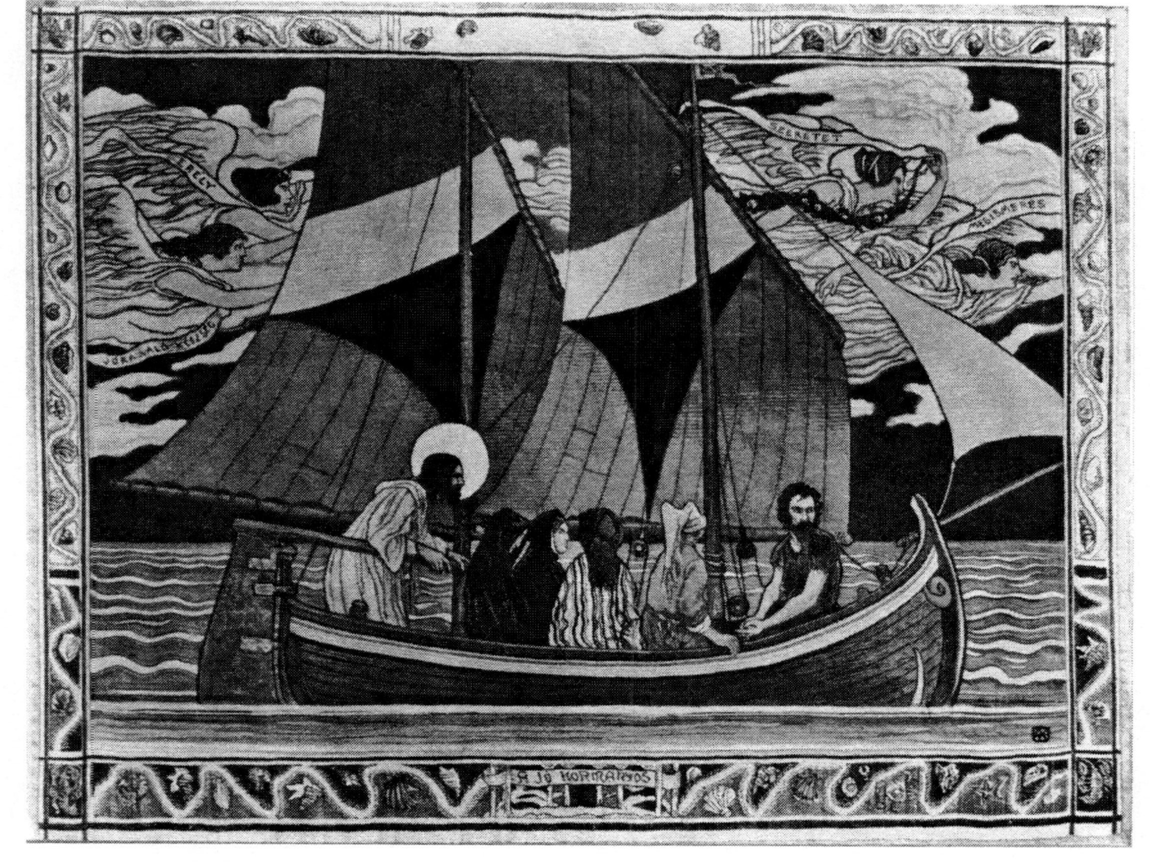

Figure 9.1. Aladár Körösfôi Kriesch: *The Good Helmsman* (1907). Gobelin-style tapestry, woven by Leo Belmonte. Reprinted from *Magyar Iparmûvészet* (1907), iv.

Morris is described by Róth as the "congenial executor" of Burne-Jones's designs, who, going back to the techniques of the Middle Ages and re- garding the appropriate use of the material as his basic principle, re- duced the amount of painting on the glass to the minimum and relied on "the proper application of the colored glass made in the foundry" in- stead.[52] Róth worked along the same principles, and the Gödöllô artists supplied him with suitable designs. The most important examples of their work are the windows made for the Palace of Culture in Marosvásárhely, Transylvania, and the windows made for the chapel of the Mental Asylum in Lipótmezô, Budapest. In the case of the former, in accordance with the function of the building, the designers took their themes from the folk bal- lads of the area; for the latter, Nagy relied on the Bible as his source.

Vera Varga writes in her recent book on Róth[53] that in the case of the Lipótmezô windows the original plan was to make two windows for the chancel, representing two Hungarian saints, in accordance with the cur- rent German and Hungarian custom. Nagy, however, decided on breaking with this tradition and making rather a coherent, systematic series of win- dows for the chapel based on traditional and individual iconographic ref- erences. Accordingly, the windows of the nave represent the Tree of Life in the highly stylized image of the Christmas tree and its symbolic can- dles and presents—the child Jesus, the Eucharist, the Holy Ghost and seraphs—all within a frame of wheat-ears, which stands for the Host. The two chancel windows present "Fall and Redemption" and "The Last Judgment"; in both cases the concept is based on an ascent from Earth to Heaven, which suits the tall and narrow shape of the windows perfectly. Nagy tried to revive the traditions of Christian iconography while incor- porating his individual findings in these windows; it echoes Hunt's simi- lar attempts in painting: his traditional iconography being complemented with his original emblems and types, such as the breastplate and the lantern in *The Light of the World*, or the unique visual type of the cruci- form shadow of Christ in *The Shadow of Death*. In technique, in style, and in effect—especially in the glowing, bright colors—these works defi- nitely recall Burne-Jones's and Morris's works in the same medium, most of all the ones made for St. Philip Cathedral, Birmingham. Nagy's "The Last Judgment" window is reminiscent of the Birmingham window of the same subject even in delineation and composition.

Just as in the case of woven textiles, the stained-glass works of Gödöllô artists and Miksa Róth brought appreciation, praise, and further commissions, such as the decoration of the National Salon and the Hun- garian pavilion in Venice. The success of the Lipótmezô windows is also indicated by the fact that the cultural attaché of the United States wished them to be taken to the San Francisco International Exhibition. Finally, however, the Hungarian government did not give consent because of the outbreak of World War I. Nevertheless, Róth's works had been taken as far as Mexico City, where the huge 1500-square-foot dome designed by Géza Maróti and the proscenium mosaic by Körösfôi in the Teatro Nacional (today the Palacio de Bellas Artes) are the work of Hungarian craftsmen.

Though the Gödöllô artists had no press of their own, they were involved in making book illustrations under Morrisian guidelines. In 1904, when the poems of the minor Hungarian poet Koronghi Lippich Elek were published with Körösfôi's and Nagy's drawings, borders, and initials, it was greeted as "the first Hungarian book made with real artistic decoration" and as the fruit of the influence of Morris's Kelmscott Press in Hungary.[54] "It is due to Morris and his Kelmscott Press," wrote the prominent art historian, Béla Lázár, in 1904 that "the book has become once again an artistic product" and "is seen in its whole organic unity."[55] In typography, it lacks Morris's devoted attention and taste, but the volume does show a regard for the harmony of content and form, and the proper proportions of the print on the pages are based on the view of the open book, the two facing pages regarded as forming an inseparable unit.

Furniture design, leather work, and ceramics were also among the products of Gödöllô. Inspired by the English sense of "home" and their belief in the unity of the arts as well as in the interdependence of art and a happy life, they also designed complete interiors (Figure 9.2). Like Morris beginning by decorating his own home, they started with the furnishing of the Gödöllô home of Körösfôi; this was followed by Nagy's house in Gödöllô that, designed by his architect friend, István Medgyaszay and built of red brick, can be seen as an interesting parallel to Morris's Red House. In the first two decades of the twentieth century, they regularly contributed interiors to the Hungarian pavilions at international exhibitions. Besides the basic Morrisian principles of functionality and the appropriate treatment of materials, their interiors were much inspired by Hungarian folk art, with structural as well as decorative elements taken from that source. One of the most important designers was the architect Ede Torockai Wigand, who never moved to Gödöllô but worked in close collaboration with the members of the colony.

In style, the painters of the colony did not strictly follow the naturalism of the early Pre-Raphaelites, and the details of their paintings are rarely minute in execution, yet the Pre-Raphaelite influence on most of the Gödöllô paintings is undeniable. Though they often depicted literary

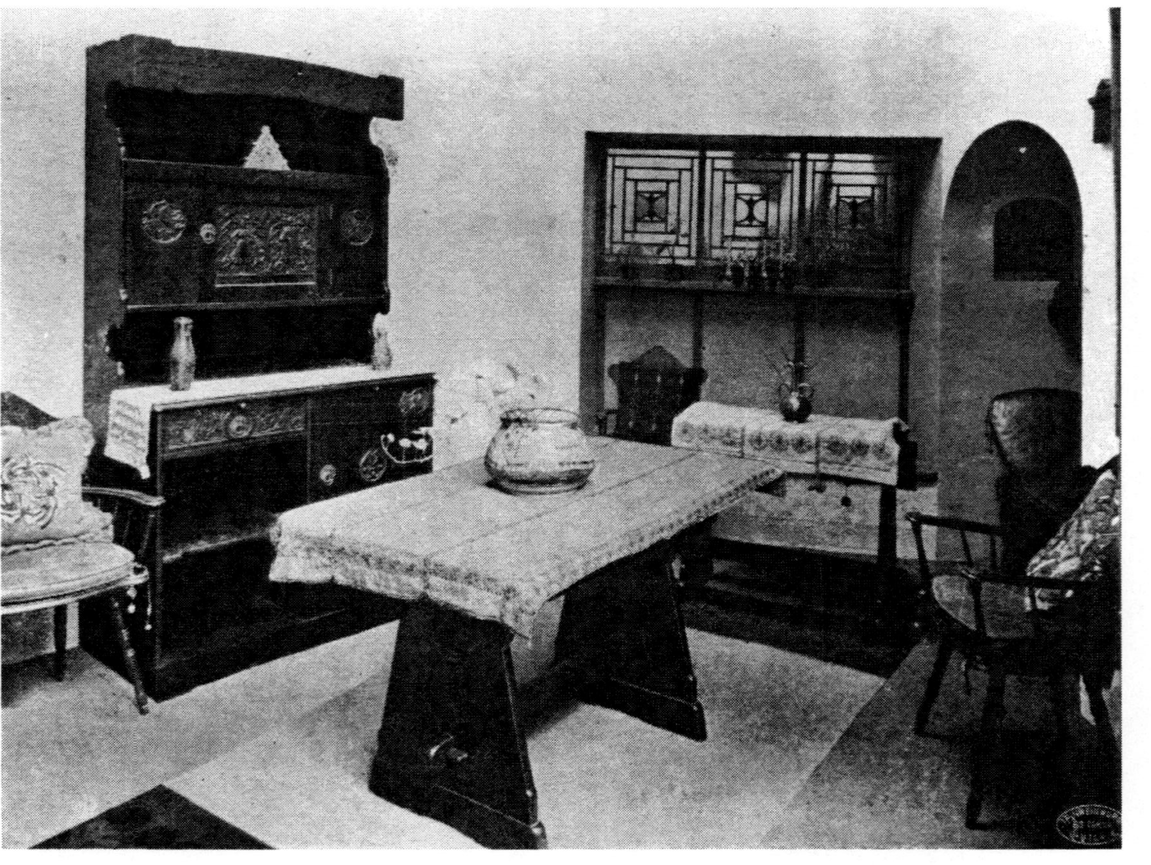

Figure 9.2. Ede Torockai Wigand: Dining-room at the World Exhibition in Milan (1906). Reprinted from *Magyar Iparmûvészet* (1906), 203.

themes and made portraits of their families and other members of the colony, the Pre-Raphaelite influence appears mostly in their religious paintings. Many of these can be seen as in line with Hunt's moral allegories, based on a formulaic message that is supported by symbolic references. To get the meaning through, they, just like their English predecessors, occasionally relied on inscriptions: thus Körösfői's allegorical fresco *A Művészet Forrása* (The Spring of Art), made for the Academy of Music in 1907, in which the text "Those in search for life make a pilgrimage to the spring of Art" makes the allegorical reference easy to perceive. In a few instances, even the frame is endowed with symbolic significance, just as in several Pre-Raphaelite pictures.

The most noteworthy and individual of these is Körösfői's *Ego sum Via, Veritas et Vita* (Figure 9.3). This painting is, perhaps, the best known of his works in Hungary, though regarded as artistically not the most successful. It depicts the artist and his wife mourning over their dead son, held by the allegorical black figure of Death standing on his gravestone, while an angel is standing behind the grieving parents and tries to turn their attention to the figure of Christ dressed in white and surrounded by a mysterious golden light and holding the same child, who is smiling and full of life. Around Christ, the members of the colony are depicted sitting in a circle on the ground and looking at Christ or at each other. In the background, the peasants of Kalotaszeg are watching all this, dressed in traditional folk costumes, and even the famous carved wooden gate so typical of eastern Transylvania is incorporated into the image. The picture itself meant something similar to Körösfői as *The Light of the World* to Hunt; he depicted in it his experience of divine revelation. The result is similar, an allegorical and didactic image that aims at transmitting the illumination presented to him to those looking at it. The frame of Körösfői's work recalls the shape of a ship, an old symbol of the journey of the spirit into the other world. It is decorated with twelve stars, which may refer to the twelve gates of the Heavenly Jerusalem, and with a decorative pattern indicating the form of a tulip growing out of a stream on each side; the water stands for eternal life and the tulip, a traditional symbol in Hungarian folk art, for the "gate of life." Uniquely, the frame incorporates a smaller, separate painting, which repeats the theme of the main one in a more general form, without direct autobiographical references. The spiritual revelation depicted in *Ego sum Via, Veritas et Vita* also declares Körösfői's recognition of the priestly role of the artist. As his friend Nagy put it in his memorial speech in 1922, two years after Körösfői's death, "Ruskin was given a new follower" then.[56]

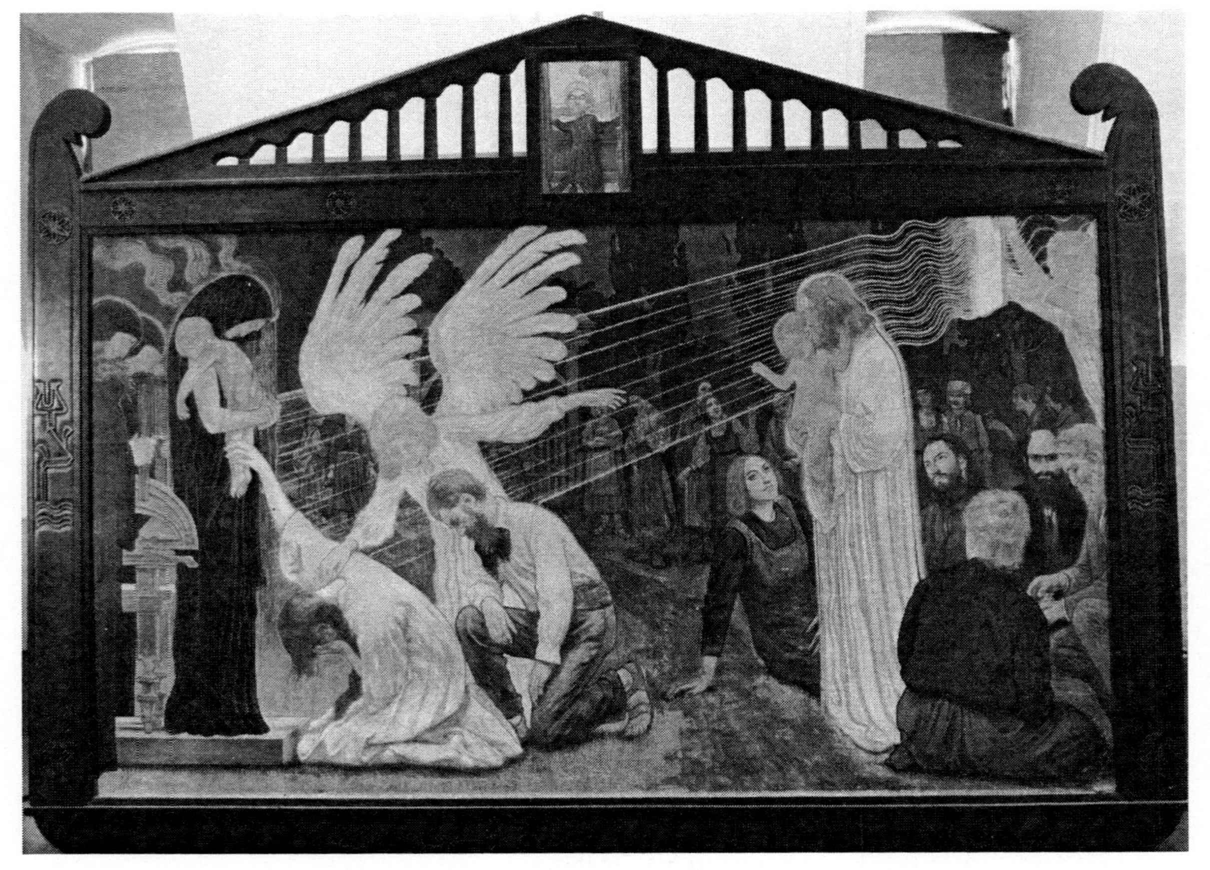

Figure 9.3. Aladár Körösfôi Kriesch, *Ego Sum Via, Veritas et Vita* (1903). Used by kind permission of the Hungarian National Gallery, Budapest.

For Ruskin, the artist's duty is like that of the preacher: "to express and illustrate every lesson which can be received from God's creation,"[57] and he found a devoted advocate in Nagy. Nagy realized the moral responsibility of the artist in Paris, where he was disillusioned by what he found "in the sacred entrance-hall of the Arts," as he described the city.[58] He was disappointed to find art education mechanical and routine, concentrating on technicalities; various competitions had a devastating effect on the process of painting and on the pictures themselves: "what struck me was the moral sting of the decaying spirit."[59] Hunt rejected the late-nineteenth-century art of Paris similarly on moral grounds:

> [It proclaims] the bare idea that art is only admirable when severed from moral ideals, and is alone worthy to be wildly extolled when the artist, degraded in mind and crippled in all his powers of representation and expression, has produced on his canvas . . . the inevitable result of idleness, dissipation, and corrupted taste.[60]

In his series of drawings, *Paris Reminiscences* (1920), Nagy shows the process of his self-understanding and spiritual enlightenment through different stages, from his departure for Paris to his vision in his Paris studio, in which a Christ-figure akin to that of Hunt's in *The Light of the World* overpowers demons. To Nagy, Hunt's image of Christ carrying the light of the world became the emblem of the sacerdotal role of the artist: "First of all you should give light to those who walk in darkness, and lead them towards the light with words and deeds. . . . busy yourself, make a way, so that the light should radiate from you, since till then you speak to no avail."[61]

Moral responsibility never became burdensome for Nagy and Körösfôi. On the contrary, it showed the only way to attain happiness. Körösfôi's words might be taken as the creed of the whole Gödöllô community, as the basis of their work and of their daily life:

> As the artist creates, he presents in small the surrounding great, divine law. Thus every product is a living testimony to the everlasting divine law. The feeling, the realization or the awareness of this great divine law gives the purest happiness. In this sense can we say that art makes us happy and noble. . . . This is, thus, the great import of doing even our minor works with artistic demand, with a regard to this great law. Thus it is not the same, whether we put a gray or a richly, harmoniously colored carpet under our feet, or we drink out of an ugly jug. It is not without consequence concerning the one who uses these objects, let alone the one who makes them.[62]

The flourishing work and steady development of the Gödöllő colony suffered a fatal blow with the outbreak of World War I. Many of the men were called up, some never to return. Some of the survivors decided to leave Gödöllő; the way of life based on the philanthropic ideology of common incentives became hard to believe in and even harder to restore after what they had gone through. Körösfői tried to keep the work going, especially in the weaving workshop, where production never stopped during the war. Yet, during the brief period of the Hungarian Soviet Republic after the war in 1919, the workshop was taken away from him and brought under full state control. Once more, his friend Nagy turned to Morris and his views for help in formulating their deep disillusionment and their faint hope for a better world. In his article "Bolshevism and Art" published after the short sway of the Soviet Republic, he wrote that the only right form of socialism was Morris's concept of love, fellowship, and humanity.[63] With Körösfői's death in 1920, however, there was no more hope for the revival of the colony.

In 1979, when in an interview Körösfői's daughter gave her reminiscences of her father and the colony, she described the loss it meant in relation to Ruskin and Morris:

> How beautiful it used to be! It was a long time ago, and only a few of us can still remember it. And then came the First, and then the Second World War. What could have been, if the ideas of Ruskin and Morris—which were so whole-heartedly adopted and promoted by my father—had filled humanity instead.[64]

Pre-Raphaelitism had another important adherent in Hungary. The painter Lajos Gulácsy was a follower of Rossetti and Burne-Jones rather than of Ruskin, Morris, or Hunt. Unlike the Gödöllő artists, he had no concerns with the moral function of art. Nevertheless, he—like Burne-Jones—could never accept the notion of art purely for art's sake, holding that "art is the revelation . . . of the simple, yet sublime essence hidden in nature."[65] This essence is always the soul, and his art is the projection of his own spirit in its entranced intensity: "My works might be called my children. I put into them a part of myself. Thus my works give away my entire being; its weaknesses and its worth, its mystic spirituality and its sensual body."[66] His creed answers that of Rossetti as expressed in *Hand and Soul* by the beautiful woman who appears to Chiaro: "I am an image, Chiaro, of thine own soul within thee. . . . paint me thus, as I am, to know me: weak, as I am, and in the weeds of this time."[67] Gulácsy writes that

"With intention and with force no great work of art can be created,"[68] which can be seen as analogous with what is revealed to the young painter about the nature of true art as an answer to his sense of failure after "put[ting] his hand to no other works but only to such as had for their end the presentment of some moral greatness that should influence the beholder."[69] "How is it that thou, a man, wouldst say coldly to the mind what God hath said to the heart warmly? . . . In all that thou doest, work from thine own heart, simply; for his heart is as thine, when thine is wise and humble."[70] Thus, as Rossetti's art is alien from that of Hunt in its disregard of didactic purpose, so is Gulácsy's from that of Nagy and Körösfôi. In his evaluation of modern art, Gulácsy writes:

> Modern art will find greater favor in the sight of our successors than the art of the previous era. Burne-Jones, Millais, Whistler, Rossetti, Turner, and Gauguin created their works with much more inwardness than the great artists of the Renaissance, and though as masters they are inferior, their souls, and the sensory vibration and the essence of their art are much deeper than those of their predecessors.[71]

It is noteworthy how much the Pre-Raphaelites dominate Gulácsy's list, and noteworthy that Hunt is not included. The naturalistic and didactic early Pre-Raphaelite style did not appeal to him, but the emotionally charged, intense later phase. Although Gulácsy appreciated Ruskin for the efforts he had made to purge art of academic clichés, he found Ruskin mistaken in his rejection of Whistler.[72] Gulácsy, the aesthete believed that a good painting is always musical, its tune being evoked by the harmony of the colors and the rhythm of the lines. Accordingly, even his paintings that contain no reference to music at all are called "songs" by him.

Gulácsy belonged to no Hungarian artistic school. This could be due to his strong reliance on his personal feelings and impressions, but the fact that he spent more time in Italy during his active years than in Hungary may also have contributed to his alienation from the cultural movements of his native land. His first visit to Italy in 1902, when he was captivated by its beauty and artistic spirit, made him a Latin in spirit for life. A man of wide reading and considerable literary talent, he developed a deep admiration for Dante in Italy, which brought him closer to an understanding of Rossetti. In 1904–7 he painted his *Dante és Beatrice Találkozása* (The Meeting of Dante and Beatrice) in Florence, and his earlier *Elhangzott dal Régi Fényrôl, Szerelemrôl* (Song that has Been Sung about Remote Light and Love, 1904) seems to depict the same scene. In the latter, the figures—a man and three women who are just about to cross each other's paths—are hardly identifiable; they are indicated only by patches of colors. Yet the male figure, ascending some steps, clad in red and carrying a book under his right arm is very reminiscent of Rossetti's figure in *The Salutation of Beatrice* (1859). The tension of the moment is expressed in Gulácsy's composition by the glowing golden light of the early morning sunshine, which is intensified by being reflected on the dreamy Mediterranean buildings in the background. Rossetti's influence can be seen in many of Gulácsy's female portraits, too. Though his figures are rarely detached from their natural surroundings, the pictures do not tend to decoration or flatness; the captivating, mysterious beauty of *Helena* (Figure 9.4), *Veszta Szűz* (The Vestal), or *Dal a Rózsatőről* (Song about the Rose-Tree) indicate an affinity with Rossetti's works, softened in the works of the Hungarian painter by a Burne-Jonesean ethereal vagueness.

Gulácsy's writings display a similar spiritual intensity. His heroes and heroines are all endowed with an artistic sensitivity typical of early twentieth-century literature. Sometimes they are charming, fabulous creatures, the inhabitants of the artist's imaginary dreamland, Na'Conxypan. But even when they are ordinary men and women, they are surrounded by an air of mystic vibration. Gulácsy viewed and perceived the world so strongly in the terms of art that in one of his stories, *Nasi*, much of the spiritual meaning is delivered by direct references to Ruskin and Rossetti. The story tells how a beautiful blind girl, Nasi, finds her love and happiness in the son of her father's usurer. The young man is an aesthete, who has adopted as his principle Ruskin's love of beauty and benevolence. Nasi, who by her fate has been deprived of concerns of the outer world and consequently of human vanity, is a Rossettian beauty with thick dark hair and a sense of mystery enshrining her delicate figure. The union of the lovers has an obviously transcendental quality, the characters being above the ordinary concerns of physical reality as indicated by Nasi's lack of external vision. As in Gulácsy's paintings, the narrative itself is only of secondary importance: feelings, impressions, and the strong atmosphere captivate the reader and indicate Gulácsy's "sublime essence."

Nasi, like some of Gulácsy's other writings, was first published only in the late 1970s, so the real scope of Gulácsy's art could not be fully assessed by his contemporaries. Unfortunately, many of his paintings have disappeared or have been destroyed in the wars, no more remaining of them than the beautiful, lyric titles the painter gave them, preserved in the exhibition catalogues from nearly a hundred years ago. What has

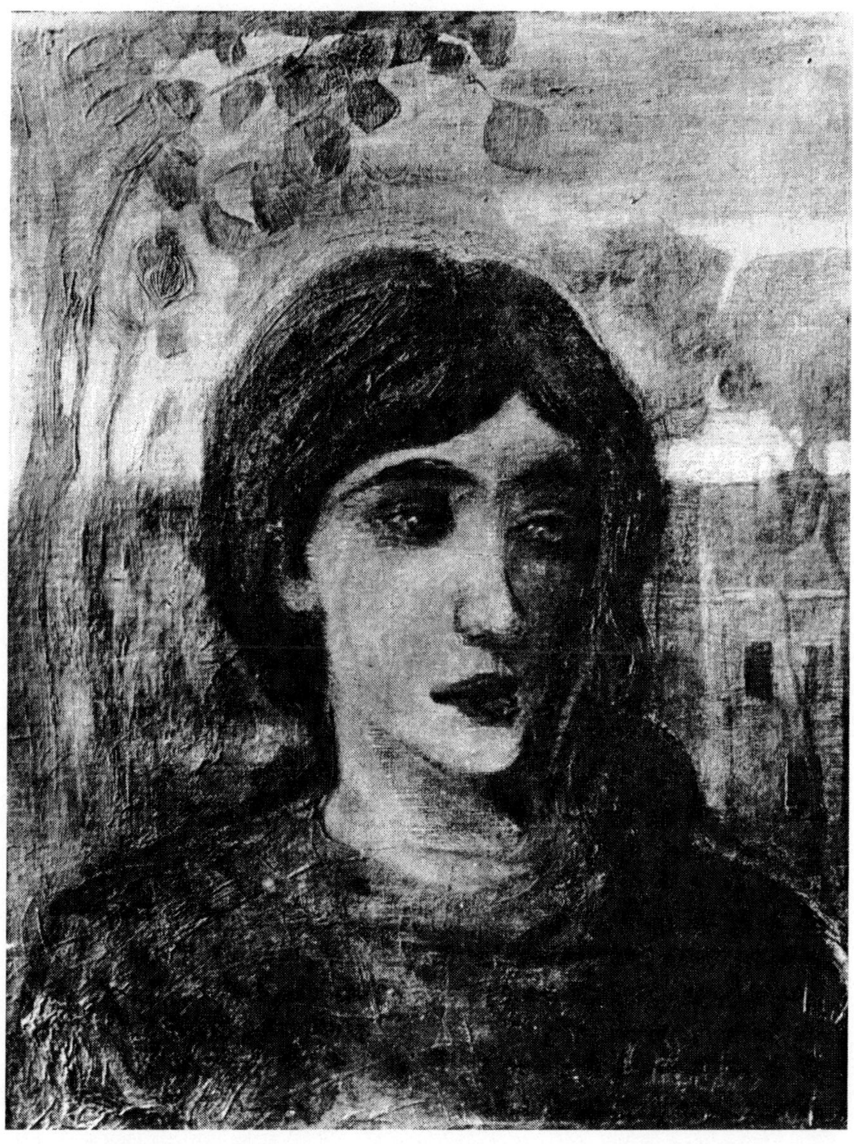

Figure 9.4. Lajos Gulácsy, *Helena* (1904). Used by kind permission of the Hungarian National Gallery, Budapest.

been left, however, calls for ever more attention, and Gulácsy is regarded nowadays as one of Hungary's greatest twentieth-century artists.

Disillusionment in the old values and disappointment in Britain for its role in the separation of more than seventy percent of the country's territory—including Transylvania—after World War I brought about a sharp turn in Hungary's cultural life. Though neither the Gödöllô artists nor Gulácsy were completely forgotten by the generations after them, considerable attention started being given to their work only in the late 1960s. Exhibitions have since been held, critical articles and monographs have been published, and a search was launched for the works and reminiscences still traceable. Likewise, an interest in Pre-Raphaelitism has never disappeared in Hungary. There were artists working under their spell in the internal period, too, like Kacziány Aladár, whose *Dante Álma* (Dante's Dream) (1921), for example, combines Rossetti's Dante images, his *Beata Beatrix* and late Pre-Raphaelite decoration in a strange, individual way; and the former Gödöllô artist, Sándor Nagy, who painted religious frescoes for the Szent Erzsébet (St. Elizabeth) Church in Pesterzsébet, Budapest (1938–41), still much in the Huntian-Ruskinian spirit.

The last twenty years have brought an escalation in Hungary's interest in Pre-Raphaelite art. Though Körösfôi's book is still the only comprehensive work on the Pre-Raphaelites in Hungarian, 1983 saw a brief biography on Burne-Jones published;[73] in 1996, as part of an exhibition of the huge collection of a Hungarian-born art collector living in Basle—Károly Lászl—a small group of Pre-Raphaelite works were put on display in the Mûcsarnok in Budapest. In 2001, the Museum of Applied Arts held a Walter Crane memorial exhibition, and the centenary of the Gödöllô Colony was celebrated with publications, exhibitions, and an academic conference with numerous references to Ruskin, Morris, and the Pre-Raphaelites.

NOTES

1. This essay was sponsored by an OTKA Postdoctoral Research Grant (D34578).

2. The desperate struggle of a small central European nation brought Hungary international attention, and Dante Gabriel Rossetti commemorated his thoughts in a sonnet "On Refusal of Aid between Nations" (1849). See Rossetti's letter to his brother William on 26 August 1869, in Oswald Doughty and John Robert Wahl, eds., *Letters of Dante Gabriel Rossetti* (London: Oxford University Press, 1960), 721.

3. Ödön Lechner, "Önéletrajzi Vázlat" (1911), in Tibor Bakonyi and Mihály Kubinszky, *Lechner Ödön* (Budapest: Corvina, 1981), 185. Unless otherwise noted, all translations are my own.

4. Ibid.

5. This was, however, not the first exhibition of Crane's works in Hungary. In 1895, a small collection was shown in the Mûcsarnok (Exhibition Hall), which, however, had little effect.

6. Kálmán Rozsnyai, "Walter Crane," *Magyar Iparmûvészet* (1900): 155.

7. Walter Crane, "Néhány Szó a Magyar Iparmûvészetrôl" [A Few Words on the Hungarian Arts and Crafts], *Magyar Iparmûvészet* (1900): 151–54.

8. Walter Crane, *Vonal és Forma* [Line and Form] (Budapest: Lampel R Kk, 1910).

9. Jenô Radisics, foreword to *Brit Iparmûvészeti Kiállítás Katalógusa: Budapest 1902 Szeptember–November* [Catalogue to British Arts and Crafts Exhibition, September to November 1902 Budapest] (Budapest: Franklin, 1902).

10. Frigyes Spiegel, "Brit Iparmûvészet Budapesten" [British Arts and Crafts in Budapest], *Magyar Iparmûvészet* (1902): 97.

11. Jóesef Diner-Dénes, "A Brit Iparmûvészeti Kiállítás" [The British Applied Art Exhibition], *Mûvészet* [Art] (1902): 325.

12. Sarotta Geôcze, *Ruskin Élete és Tanításai* [The Life and Teachings of Ruskin] (Budapest: Athenaeum, 1903).

13. Ibid., foreword.

14. István Dömötör, "Ruskin Nálunk" [Ruskin Here], *Magyar Iparmûvészet* (1904): 24.

15. Ibid., 33–34.

16. Géza Supka, "Költôk-Iparmûvészck" [Pocts and Craftsmen], *Magyar Iparmûvészet* (1905): 29–41.

17. Ibid., 31.

18. Aladár Körösfôi, *Ruskinról s az Angol Preraffaelitákról* [On Ruskin and the English Pre-Raphaelites] (Budapest: Franklin, 1905).

19. Ibid., 8.

20. Ibid., 6–7.

21. Ibid., 9–10.

22. Ibid., 17.

23. Ibid., 21.

24. Ibid., 22.

25. Ibid., 30.

26. Ibid., 60.

27. Ibid., 31.

28. Ibid., 62.

29. Ibid., 22.

30. Ibid., 59.

31. Ibid., 60.

32. Ibid., 69.

33. Ibid., 104.

34. Ibid., 105.

35. Ibid., 135.

36. Ibid., 129.

37. Ibid., 135–36.

38. Ibid., 139.

39. Ibid., 140–41.

40. Ibid., 147–48.

41. Katalin Gellér and Katalin Keserû, *A Gödöllôi Mûvésztelep* [The Gödöllô Art Colony] (Budapest: Cégér, 1994), 25.

42. See the essay by Susan P. Casteras in this volume.

43. Ernô Margitay, "A Magyar nép Mûvészete" [The Art of the Hungarian People], *Magyar Iparmûvészet* (1907): 218.

44. Ákos Moravánszky, *Versengô Látomások: Esztétikai Ujîtás és Társadalmi Program az Osztrák-Magyar Monarchia Epîtészetében 1867–1918*, trans. Katalin M. Gyöngy (Budapest: Vince, 1998); originally published as *Competing Visions: Aesthetic Invention and Social Imagination in Central European Architecture, 1867–1918* (Cambridge, MA: MIT Press, 1988), 208.

45. Aladár Körösfôi, "Mit Jelent hát a Kalotaszegi Mûvészet?" [What is, then, the Art of Kalotaszeg?], *Magyar Iparmûvészet* (1903): 250.

46. Aladár Körösfôi, "A Népmûvészetrôl" [On Folk Art], *Magyar Iparmûvészet* (1913): 351–55.

47. Aladár Körösfôi, "A Fonalak Festésérôl" [On Yarn Dyeing], *Díszítô Mûvészet* [Decorative Art] (1914): 38.

48. Katalin Gellér and Katalin Keserû, 132.

49. Körösfôi, *Ruskinról*, 46–47.

50. Péter Polónyi, ed. *Emlékezések a Gödöllôi Mûvésztelepre* [Reminiscences of the Gödöllô Art Colony], *Studia Comitatensia 10* (Gödöllô: Helytörténeti Gyûjtemény, 1982), 16, 23.

51. Miksa Róth, "Az Üvegfestészet 40 Éve" [Glass-Painting in the Last 40 Years], *Magyar Iparmûvészet* (1924): 41.

52. Ibid.

53. Vera Varga, *Róth Miksa Mûvészete* [The Art of Miksa Róth] (Budapest: Helikon, 1993), 37.

54. Béla Lázár, "Egy Könyvrôl, Mely Mûvészet" [On a Book that is Art], *Magyar Iparmûvészet* (1904): 34.

55. Ibid.

56. Sándor Nagy, "Körösfôi Kriesch Aladárról—Emlékbeszéd" [On Aladár Körösfôi Kriesch—Memorial Speech], *Magyar Iparmûvészet* (1922): 39.

57. John Ruskin, *Modern Painters* (London: J. M. Dent & Sons, 1923), 1:59.

58. Sándor Nagy, "Levelek a Képírásról" [Letters on Picture-Writing], *Huszadik Század* [Twentieth Century] (1903): 326.

59. Ibid.

60. William Holman Hunt, *Pre-Raphaelitism and the Pre-Raphaelite Brotherhood*, 2 vols. (London: Macmillan, 1905), 2:475.

61. Sándor Nagy, "Levél Egy, Több, Sok Kollégához" [Letter to One, More, Many Colleagues], *Mûvészet* (1903): 58.

62. Aladár Körösfôi, "Mûvészet és Mûvelôdés" [Art and Culture], *Mûvészi Ipar* [Industrial Arts] (1906): 3.

63. Sándor Nagy, "Bolsevizmus és Mûvészet" [Bolshevism and Art], *Magyar Iparmûvészet* (1919): 48–49.

64. In Péter Polónyi *Emlékezések a Gödöllôi Mûvésztelepre* [Memoirs of the Gödöllo Colony] (Budapest, 1900), 10.

65. Lajos Gulácsy, "Mûvészetrôl" [On Art], in *Gulácsy Lajos ed.*, Béla Szíj, (Budapest: Corvina, 1979), 132.

66. Ibid., 130.

67. Dante Gabriel Rossetti, "Hand and Soul," in *The Works of Dante Gabriel Rossetti*, ed. William M. Rossetti (London: Ellis, 1911), 553, 555.

68. Gulácsy, "Mûvészetrôl," 130.

69. Rossetti, "Hand and Soul," 551.

70. Ibid., 554.

71. Gulácsy, "Mûvészetrôl," 131.

72. Lajos Gulácsy, "A Jövô Mûvészete" [The Art of the Future], in *Virágünnep Vége* [The End of the Flower Feast], ed. Judit Szabadi (Budapest: Szépirodalmi Könyvkiadó, 1989), 56–57.

73. Ilona Sármány, *Burne-Jones* (Budapest: Corvina, 1983).

Chapter 10

Pre-Raphaelitism in Colonial Australia

Juliette Peers

Pre-Raphaelite paintings in twenty-first-century Anglo-American culture represent romance and poetry to the popular audience and continue to inspire scholarship. Yet in a world where Pre-Raphaelitism has attained art historical respectability, the Australian experience of the movement stands apart. In white Australian critical writing, beginning in the nineteenth century, Pre-Raphaelitism has been a metaphor for mistaken or deluded artistic values. James Smith (1820–1910), writing in the Melbourne *Argus* in 1870, exemplifies this view:

> Vor-Raffaellismus had its first, and perhaps its most congenial home in Germany. It commenced there long before the corresponding art-revolution to which we have given the name Pre-Raphaelitism took place in England. Cornelius, with . . . Overbeck, were the predecessors of Ruskin and the disciples who followed the creed he so eloquently taught. It is not, therefore, astonishing that even in this colony the sole artist of any pretensions who has adopted the new doctrine should be a son of the Vaterland, and a belted knight of Franz Josef. M. Eugen von Guerard is our local apostle of that microscopism in pictorial delineation which was the extravagance wherein the indignant protest of the German "purists" first took shape. His landscapes may not present quite fifteen hundred different grasses, as there are not generally so many to be found in the bush scenes with which his pencil is familiar, but they offer a minutely laborious description of almost every leaf upon the gum trees, and of every vein and crevice in the rocks, which would make them delightful illustrations of a treatise on the botanical and geological features of the colony.[1]

Smith's denunciation is typical of the interchange between the avant-garde and the conservative during the 1870s and prefigures the terms of modernist debate over Pre-Raphaelitism in the twentieth century. The date of Smith's text illustrates the separateness of Australian critical thought: although Pre-Raphaelitism encountered hostility in England during the 1850s, by the 1870s the movement was largely accepted in Europe and America.

Smith was an influential conservative Australian critic, and his article should not be dismissed as marginal ranting. By naming the style "Vor Raphaellismus," he identifies it as alien (and German) rather than as worthy (and British). His denunciation is rooted in the idea of naturalist *plein air* landscapes as the "proper" expression of white Australian identity. Australian *plein air* artists circa 1900 saw Pre-Raphaelitism as antithetical to "true" art. Members of the Australian *plein air* school, for instance, turned their backs on the popular fervor surrounding the Australian tour of William Holman Hunt's *Light of the World* in 1906.[2] Eugen von Guerard drafted a lengthy reply to Smith's article, which remained unpublished:

> If the noble Art Critic which took so much trouble to show his erudition in Art literature accuses the style of painting of Mr. G. as pre-Raffaelite, this artist can assure the Public that it was the first time that he heard of that school in the year 1854 when he exhibited his first pictures of Australian scenery in Melbourne and that the only reason for which he adopted that so-caled [sic] style was that he finds nature so infinitely pre-Raffaelite and with all the exacting difficulties he wished to paint so closely as he saw the details and effects of nature.[3]

Like the better known English artists Thomas Woolner (1825–92), Bernhard Smith (1820–85), and Edward LaTrobe Bateman (ca. 1815–79), Guerard had been drawn to Australia by promises of riches from gold mining and, like Bateman and Bernhard Smith, stayed for several decades after the immediate excitement of the 1851 gold rush. Guerard is now acknowledged to have close affinities to the German Romanticism of the early nineteenth-century Düsseldorf Academy, where he first trained as a painter.

Sixty-four years after James Smith denigrated Pre-Raphaelitism as a sub-par foreign import, Max Meldrum, writing in 1934 on "The Literary Idea in Painting," also sees little merit in Pre-Raphaelite art as represented by Edward Burne-Jones:

> One more type is worth noting, for it possess in marked degree the characteristics of a diseased state of mind—a fear of the visual truths of nature

which are never to be found in pure art . . . at the same time they are clearly an expression of that diseased state of mind which always developed in decadent and dying civilisations—the fear of the truth. Particularly in "The Wheel of Fate" [by Burne-Jones] do we observe this horror of naked nature. The lady in angular and carefully adjusted drapery was accepted as being beautiful when this kind of art enjoyed its vogue; but today we, who can at least regard dispassionately the artistic fashions of forty years ago, can only see a stiff, elongated, microcephalous and most undesirable female.[4]

Classifying a Burne-Jones painting as a symptom of clinical psychosis is unmistakably the argot of the day. Denouncing Burne-Jones's Pre-Raphaelite paintings is both a prophylactic against corruption in modern times and a modernist rejection of the Pre-Raphaelites' refusal to face pragmatic reality.

Representing locally Australian taste, these texts by Smith and Meldrum might seem to have parochial rather than international relevance. The Pre-Raphaelite connection with Australia is often only a footnote: a few years in the career of Thomas Woolner.[5] This essay will outline how the Pre-Raphaelite movement spread throughout Australia, first through Woolner's friendship with the Australian artists Bernhard Smith and Edward LaTrobe Bateman, then via the Howitt, Bateman, and LaTrobe families, and finally through the return of Woolner's sculptures (but not Woolner) to Australia.

Woolner, a member of the original Pre-Raphaelite Brotherhood, spent three years during the 1850s in Australia, where he developed patron links that were sustained throughout his later successful years in Britain. Bernhard Smith and Edward LaTrobe Bateman were two Australian artists close to Woolner, the Rossetti family, and the rest of the "inner circle" of the Pre-Raphaelite movement; later, Australian artist Florence Williams showed an informed knowledge of the group's stylistic aims and adhered to them.

One cannot, however, talk about an Australian Pre-Raphaelite "school." Pre-Raphaelitism's visual legacy in Australia was intermittent, seen as alien or irrelevant to local art. One reason may be that white Australian artists and critics like Smith and Meldrum favored landscape as the most authentic Australian art. Also, Australian radical culture frequently sees England as foreign and draws heavily on the rhetoric of Irish and Scottish liberation and resistance to British rule: in the early twentieth century, the Irish formed the driving cultural and political elites. In this scenario of cultural antipathy toward Britain, Pre-Raphaelitism's British associations tended to render it a spurious artistic entity.

The marginalization of Pre-Raphaelitism in Australia also has an art historical basis. The ideals of the New English Art Club, established in London in 1886, found an enthusiastic response in Australia. Throughout the first half of the twentieth century, its taste dominated collecting policies at public institutions and guided Australian artists. The Art Club validated realism in both modern artists such as Manet, and historical artists such as Rembrandt and Velasquez, who were placed above the quattrocento and Medieval artists favored by the Pre-Raphaelite Brotherhood. Pre-Raphaelitism was anathema to the New English Art Club: its poetical inspiration and pictorial eccentricity offended the conservative Art Club's philosophy.

Australian Pre-Raphaelitism adds dark, uncomfortable, awkward elements to the Pre-Raphaelite canon. It is a twentieth-century vision of Pre-Raphaelitism as representing not angelic maidens but existential alienation and the bleakness of the human condition. This strangeness is conveyed through the accounts of Australian art writers and in the experience of the two members of the Pre-Raphaelite circle who traveled to Australia in 1852, Thomas Woolner and Bernhard Smith.

Woolner and Smith did not find easy fortunes in Australia. From Woolner's diary, we learn that the drowning of Henry Pinchus, a member of the mining party, which Smith and Woolner had joined, was especially traumatic for Smith, who had caught hold of his drowning friend but was forced to release him due to the strength of the current. Woolner saw Pinchus rise briefly to the surface before disappearing, and he recorded Smith's sense of shock after his friend sank.[6]

Of the two artists, Woolner was the more forthcoming about his experiences. His diaries provide a candid account of the tensions of colonial expansion, the keeping of gentlemanly standards among social inferiors and in trying circumstances, the backbreaking labor, the profiteering, and cheating. Class issues thread through the diary: Woolner is concerned about the roughness and uncongeniality of his surroundings. When he first set out on his journey to the gold fields, Australia was a "splendid country" that resembled an English park.[7] A few days later, the roughness of the land and people was symbolized in the shabby town of Kilmore: "the most hideous place that I have ever seen. The people look like maggots wriggling over corruption: a scab on the face of Australia."[8] Woolner found the land "a brutal—worse than brutal sight," further declaring, "I like or dislike this country according to the mood I am in."[9] By

30 November 1852, a month into his diary, Woolner realizes he will not find a windfall. "I see no very sparkling fortune in the future,"[10] but in Australia, "nothing but primitive necessities are understood and those of the coarsest kind, sleeping, eating, working, eating and sleeping again, this on and on without a change unless for a fight or drunkenness."[11] Woolner later concludes that gold prospecting would not provide even a steady income:

> So this gold digging is dead unless successful: in all other occupations labor tells directly or indirectly sometimes to one's profit, but in this if you fail obtaining gold there is so much life wasted, time, loss of friends, money, enjoyment, instead of good, positive harm is effected.[12]

Woolner carried his combativeness, jealousy, and insecurities throughout his career, such were the lasting consequences from his Australian experience.

To emphasize only the darkness, however, is to distort the nature of the relationship. Australia was, on occasion, a stimulus to creative ideas around the Pre-Raphaelite group. Woolner's travels provided the plot of Tennyson's "Enoch Arden,"[13] for example. Also, the "idea" of Australia produced *The Last of England* by Ford Madox Brown, who was inspired by the sight of the departing Woolner, Smith, and Bateman. William Howitt recalls how Britons of all classes were obsessed with tales of easily gained wealth in the Australian gold fields:

> The most wonderful statements appeared continuously in the English newspapers of the prolific finds of gold, much of it lying on the surface. . . . Men of all ranks and classes [went] to this Eldorado. Even to me it appeared a fine opportunity to make a substantial sum at the same time that I gave myself release for a time from the long-worn harness of literary work.[14]

Perhaps gold mining was seen as exemplary of the turning away from the paradigmatic and complacently overrefined that marked early Pre-Raphaelite thought. If so, Woolner and Smith found their idealistic preconceptions set at naught when they confronted the rigors of physical labor in Australia.

The Australian Pre-Raphaelites connect to a wider series of fellow travelers. Woolner was the only "official" member of the Brotherhood to arrive in the country, but his traveling companion Bernhard Smith appears in William Michael Rossetti's 1901 list of sympathizers.[15] Edward

LaTrobe Bateman was known in the Pre-Raphaelite circle, as was one of Bernhard Smith's brothers, Alexander, whom Dante Gabriel Rossetti visited in 1854.[16] Alexander Smith served as a commissioner governing the gold fields' residents. Bernhard Smith opted to join the commission, as did Alfred Howitt, son of notable British literary critic William Howitt. Both father and son were in Australia mining for gold at the same time as other members of the Pre-Raphaelite circle. Bateman had sailed with Smith and Woolner but worked mining claims with the Howitt family, all of whom remained in close contact with the other Pre-Raphaelite voyagers.

The Howitts were a major conduit between Australia and the Pre-Raphaelite movement. William and Mary Howitt were Quakers with an openminded attitude toward artistic innovation. As literary critics, consciously aiming to bringing high culture to a popular readership, they had developed wide literary connections in early Victorian Britain, which appear to have played a part in validating the Pre-Raphaelites' literary ambitions during the 1840s. They introduced the artists to notable literary figures on occasion.[17] William and Mary Howitt were neighbors of Edward LaTrobe Bateman's parents and met the other Pre-Raphaelite artists through Bateman.[18] The Howitts were in frequent communication with Australia even before William and Alfred emigrated, since William's younger brother, Dr. Godfrey Howitt, had settled in Melbourne in 1840. The Melbourne Howitts and their colleagues formed a cultural elite in the fledgling city. Woolner was pleasantly surprised at the luxurious conditions in which the Melbourne branch of the family lived, commenting especially on their produce garden as being as fine as anything in England.[19] Later, it was recognized in the *Melbourne Morning Herald* that "Dr. Godfrey Howitt had done his best to bring Mr. Woolner's talents to the knowledge of the Victorian world."[20] When the males of the family were on the gold fields with Bateman—and in close contact with Smith and Woolner—Mary Howitt and her two daughters stayed in Bateman's London house, where Rossetti had been a previous resident.[21]

A more minor family connection is Florence Williams, who was the daughter of an early patron of Millais. A London-based artist, she married, came to Australia, and lived and painted in Tasmania and New South Wales. When writing a biography of his father, John Guille Millais painted a highly unflattering picture of Williams's father, London barrister Ralph Thomas.[22] In later life, Williams and her brother compiled a publication to defend her father's honor,[23] stressing the supportive nature of the family's relationship to Millais.[24] Perhaps these Australian associates felt that their stories had been overwritten by those in London and that their contributions to Pre-Raphaelitism were being marginalized. Williams had been taught by the young Millais, who had loaned her his paint box and given her a lay figure. Like Millais, Williams's talents matured early, and, following his example, she was soon submitting works (in her maiden name, Florence Thomas) to exhibitions in London and getting them accepted. Her oil paintings, held now in private hands and rarely seen in public since the 1870s, display the deep bright azures, greens, and mauves of the early Pre-Raphaelites as well as intense concentration on detail and fidelity to nature. Her exquisite *Doll's House* (ca. 1875, private collection) is painted with the dogged truth to reality seen in the works of Holman Hunt: the unexpected juxtaposition of colors, the telescoped perspective, and the stress on awkward and clumsy angles of outline and pose. Yet Williams's beautiful paintings inspired no local artists to explore their innovations, and few in Australia recognized her artistic pedigree. Joanna Kerr mentions that Sydney critic James Green described Williams's fruit paintings as "perfect of their kind," and a now-lost work titled *Ophelia* (1880?) was once praised for the realism of the painting of flowers, grasses, and water.[25] Williams, whose works have been documented fully only since 1995, should be added to the canon of female artists around the Pre-Raphaelite circle.

The decorative artist and applied designer Edward LaTrobe Bateman was another of the Australian Pre-Raphaelite circle. His interest in Medieval art during the 1840s brought him in contact with the members of the future Brotherhood, and he brought a Ruskininan sensibility with him to Australia when he emigrated in 1852. His cousin was the colonial governor Charles Joseph LaTrobe. An early success of Woolner's, a statuette of Little Red Riding Hood, stood on C. J. LaTrobe's drawing room mantel and was the governor's favorite ornament.[26] This sculpture actually preceded Woolner to Melbourne: the presence of Howitt, Bateman, and LaTrobe family connections in Melbourne may have made a Pre-Raphaelite expedition to the Antipodes seem less daunting. Both C. J. LaTrobe and Godfrey Howitt had been resident more than a decade in Melbourne by the time the first gold discoveries were made in 1851.

Edward Bateman enjoyed a diverse artistic career in Australia. His concentration on decorative and applied arts reflected radical ideas emerging from the idealization of Medieval society's integration of art, life, and everyday objects. He even trimmed ladies' bonnets and provided the decorations for grand balls,[27] which included not only floral displays but ephemeral art works such as wall decorations and painted designs on the dance floor.[28] Bateman's oeuvre included decorations and illuminations in books, book cover designs, designs for woven shawls in Australian wool, stenciling and decoration in interiors, building design, and landscape gardening for both municipal and private projects. The University of Melbourne, for instance, was originally surrounded by grounds laid out by Bateman.[29]

The few of Bateman's works that have survived are mostly meticulous landscape drawings documenting large homes and estates. Some architectural designs for rugged neo-Medieval houses, including Heronswood on the lower slopes of Arthur's Seat on Port Phillip Bay, are attributed to him (although some nineteenth-century sources assign him only the interiors). After injuring his arm in an accident while designing a garden for a wealthy landholder, Bateman returned to Britain and worked as a landscape garden designer. Bateman and the Howitts constituted an important circle of art patronage in colonial Melbourne.[30] Among these connoisseurs, Woolner was accepted by Melbournians not as a Pre-Raphaelite per se, but as a talented artist promoted by the Howitts.

Australia played a central part in shaping Woolner's career. It provided a means for him to gain an advantage over his competitors in a sculptural marketplace that was—following Woolner's own pessimistic accounts—cutthroat and treacherous, with sculptors fighting over infrequent commissions. His Australian connections provided a crucial backbone of support for Woolner's career. Rather than finding gold, Woolner survived on his earnings as an artist. His small portrait medallions were extremely popular, and through the Howitts he found a ready-made series of sitters. When he left Australia in order to secure a commission for a statue of William Charles Wentworth, he left enough work in hand to offer it to Bernhard Smith as a livelihood.[31] Despite the unnerving aspects of his Australian experience, Woolner also capitalized on the venture, noting that his accomplished series of Australian portrait medallions created favorable attention. He used his traveler's tales and collection of Australian stones and minerals to great effect in order to open social doors to potential patrons. For example, a satisfied Australian portrait sitter, Sir Charles Fitzroy, procured an introduction for Woolner to show his statue of *Love* in a gallery in Pall Mall.[32] Woolner regarded the medallions as his capital, the pay-dirt, the "stock of seed" that he brought home. Woolner expressed consternation when he thought that his Australian portrait medallions had not been freighted with him on his return to England.[33]

Australia gave Woolner important patrons, among them Henry Parkes, for whom he executed one major work, *Captain Cook*, and a number of bronze busts of British prime ministers. Parkes was an important confidante with whom Woolner had a strong relationship. Thousands of miles away in London, Woolner could, in his letters to Parkes, pour out the fears and jealousies that hedged his career. Australia also provided a solace to Woolner. When professional reverses became intolerable in 1879, Woolner asked Parkes to seek out a piece of land to which the Woolner family could emigrate,[34] although he never actually took that dramatic step.

Woolner's letters to Parkes are full of the business of art making, of ingratiating oneself to possible patrons, of listening out for possible commissions, of bitter denunciations when a buyer would not close an expected deal or a committee awarded a commission to another and (in Woolner's eyes) inferior hand. There is even a degree of camp—despite Woolner's somewhat hearty masculinity—in this constant exchange of news and gossip about the famous and artistically well connected. Perhaps Woolner trimmed his pen and his name-dropping narratives to suit Parkes's taste. Parkes was a collector of autographs who wrote to well-known nineteenth-century figures, creating a remarkable cache of letters from eminent Victorians, now in the State Library of New South Wales.

Woolner also acquired professional validation as a cultural go-between for Australians coming to Britain and wishing to mingle with notables. Most famously, he facilitated a friendship between Tennyson and Parkes, who had literary ambitions and had published a number of books of verses.[35] Woolner's facilitation of Parkes's access to High Victorian culture confirmed Parkes's belief in the northern hemisphere as the true art center, the model to which Australia must lean. A letter to Robert Browning indicates something of Woolner' *modus operandi*. The tone is similar to those written to Parkes, with its combination of warm personal greetings and detailed accounts of contemporary art and cultural politics. Although these narratives are mostly directed toward Woolner's own interests, he also seems engaged in mapping his contemporaries' professional activities as much for their own sake as for any careerist gain. He enjoyed keeping his correspondents informed about current events and personalities:

As I know you always say what you really mean, and as you gave me permission to give a friend an introduction, I did so and gave my friend Sir Charles Nicholson a line to you: he started in November for Egypt intending to take Italy on his return and rejoiced at the notion of seeing you and Mrs. Browning. He was a very kind friend to me during my sojourn in Sydney, in fact he did for me all that he could. He is Chancellor of the Sydney University and ex-Speaker of the Legislative Council: a patron of literature, science, art, and all that tends to the advancement of his adopted country, where he is a great magnate. I think that you will be pleased with his society, for he is a man of great knowledge, good nature and amiable to the highest degree.[36]

In some ways, Woolner was more influential among Australians as a networker than through any stylistic influence of his sculptures. Throughout the nineteenth century, there is little of the expected influence from teacher to pupil, from center to province. Not only was sculptural patronage in nineteenth-century Australia regional, with few commissions outside of a sculptor's hometown, but sculpture in Australia depended on the presence of dominant local personalities: the trade frequently dissipated with the deaths or removals of particular sculptors.

Woolner's attitude toward the aspirations of Australia-based sculptors was harsh. He seems to have had no desire to inspire or assist local sculptors—who would then become rivals—thus ensuring that he begot no loyal school of either "truth to nature" or Pre-Raphaelite sculpture. For example, when he described himself as the "only sculptor in Sydney,"[37] he brushed aside at least one competent local professional, W. G. Nicholls.[38] His plea to Parkes to be placed at the top of the line for commissions, above "native roughness,"[39] indicates the scant regard Woolner gave to Australians. In defining Australian sculptors as "native roughness," he blackened them, reduced them to a sub-European level, and belittled their executive ability. "Native roughness" was, in the narrative of Empire, naturally expected to cede to more advanced British refinement and skill. Woolner's works helped to further the glorification of the colonial empire even after he had left Australia.

Two works that the artist and his family regarded as masterpieces eventually found their way to Australia—the Cook statue and the mature, or "bearded," Tennyson bust. Woolner's works had a potent symbolic presence in late-nineteenth- and early-twentieth-century Australia. They were the focus of patriotic public displays, demonstrating the important role that Pre-Raphaelite art could play in cultural debate. The *Captain Cook* statue was decorated on ceremonial occasions with flowers, flags, bunting, and electric lights.[40] It was the subject of numerous early photographs, lithographs, and postcards until as late as the 1920s. Henry Parkes claimed that a crowd of 70,000–80,000 people gathered to watch the unveiling of *Captain Cook* in 1879.

Woolner's bust of the mature Tennyson (1872, Art Gallery of South Australia) was unveiled by the Duke of York (later King George V) in 1901 as a new acquisition for the fledgling Art Gallery of South Australia.

Unveiling the sculpture was part of a highly political royal visit by the Duke and Duchess of York, who were the most exalted Britons yet to set foot in the country. Poets and artists were seen as worthies well-suited to conveying British cultural glory: "His Royal Highness . . . graciously consented to honour the poet, the sculptor, the donor, and the country by unveiling it in the New Art Gallery."[41] The Tennyson bust was "a piece of work which [Woolner] did not wish to part with."[42] The Woolner family were reluctant to part with it but were swayed by the assurance that the bust would be in a public gallery rather than hidden in the home of a collector. Unlike the first bust for which Tennyson sat for Woolner, no replicas were made of the 1872 portrait. The bust presented both "the poet and the sculptor at their prime."[43]

With such vocabulary, Woolner's sculptures were invested with the spiritual power of the Pre-Raphaelite movement. Likewise, the *Captain Cook* statue, which is now regarded as a straightforward portrait, was understood in the nineteenth century also to have a transcendent quality, which Woolner described as "an animated figure filled with wonder and delight at the moment of discovering a new country. Smitten by the sun he would always stand a shining welcome to comers to the fair Australian land."[44] Henry Parkes claimed that "when the flag was drawn off the statue" during its unveiling, "the genius of the thing quite thrilled me as if a living man had sprung forth from a great achievement."[45] Woolner's sculptures operated for his contemporaries as a form of typological symbolism, where everyday reality was invested with symbolism. Discussing the Tennyson portrait bust in 1901, Harry P. Gill makes reference to Woolner's ability in capturing the "truth to nature" aspects of the Pre-Raphaelite vision, commenting on "the detailed treatment of the features, hair and beard, each assisting the other by its opposition in contrast."[46]

Woolner is often considered a "minor" Pre-Raphaelite. Bernhard Smith is even less visible. Smith's Pre-Raphaelitism is claimed solely by his daughter Minnie Bernhard Smith's biography of 1917, wherein she argues that he was a member of the original Pre-Raphaelite Brotherhood, a "fact" clearly incorrect. Sadly, other inaccurate statements made by his relatives even before the release of Minnie Smith's book diminished Smith's status as an artist.[47] A little-known letter sent by William Michael Rossetti to Bernhard Smith Jr. after his father's death affirms the respect that the Rossetti family accorded to him as friend and artist: "few indeed have I known to match him, either in geniality of character and bearing, or in the striking manly mould of his face and person."[48] The eccentricity and inaccuracy of his daughter's manuscript overshadows the fact that

Smith provided a backbone of artistic professionalism to the incipient Pre-Raphaelite group in late-1840s London.

Apart from Ford Madox Brown, Bernhard Smith was one of the most experienced artists in the proto-Pre-Raphaelite circle during the 1840s.[49] He first studied at the Royal Academy School. In the early 1840s, Smith went to France to study in the atelier of the sculptor Etienne Jules Ramey, to research historical manuscripts, and to visit notable towns. He had a wide art historical knowledge: a small surviving sketchbook dated 1844 is full of drawings of gothic architecture and decorative arts.[50] Afterward, Smith provided technical assistance to Woolner in finishing bronzes. Most importantly, Smith brought French ideas to the circle, including his interest in the work of French sculptor David d'Angers, associated with the revival of medallion portraits in the Romantic period.[51] The medallion portrait was favored by the sculptors associated with the Pre-Raphaelites: Woolner, Alexander Munro, and John Hancock. Thus, Smith's Francophile interests helped to create a key Pre-Raphaelite sculptural format. Smith should be noted as a potentially major conduit of ideas, whose presence has been rarely acknowledged in scholarship. He seems to have known the work of the Nazarenes working in Germany, of which he saw reproductions in France in the early 1840s. He also researched Medieval artworks and architecture first hand in France.[52]

Once Smith emigrated, he came in contact with a number of artists, architects, and classical musicians in 1880s Melbourne. Like Bateman, Smith chose to work in media, illustration, and graphics that for much of the twentieth century were defined as minor art forms in relation to oil painting, and this choice also colored his subsequent reputation. His line drawings and graphics are less identifiably Pre-Raphaelite in style than those of Bateman, which can be assimilated relatively easily into the movement. In subject, Smith's works draw on the mid-Victorian fashion of "fairy painting," a genre tangential to Pre-Raphaelitism. The strongest indication of a stylistic precedent in Smith's oeuvre is to John Flaxman. Scholars have suggested that Flaxman was an influence on both French and Pre-Raphaelite artists, opening up subjects from Dante as fit subjects for modern art,[53] again demonstrating how congruent Smith's ideas were to the context and origins of the Pre-Raphaelite group.

While Woolner, Bateman, and Smith formed a nexus of late-nineteenth- and early-twentieth-century Pre-Raphaelitism in Australia, several minor figures around that center deserve at least passing mention here. Despite the forces ranged against the movement, some Australian artists occasionally deliberately chose the Pre-Raphaelite style. Most extraordinary is George Coates's *Motherhood* (1893, National Gallery of Victoria), a normalizing and sentimentalizing of the erotic dream of Rossetti's *Blessed Damozel* (1875–79, Lady Lever Art Gallery Port Sunlight). Coates follows Rossetti's Italian altarpiece format to indicate two different worlds, the earth and the afterlife. A scene of motherless children bravely carrying on in the face of their bereavement is rendered Pre-Raphaelite by the small oil of the mother peering out from heaven— like the Blessed Damozel—to watch the loved ones on earth below. *Motherhood* has a customized neo-Italian gilt frame, again indicating the Pre-Raphaelite intention of the work. Coates would also later reference Pre-Raphaelite art when depicting Australian soldiers bearing their wounded comrades as, in effect, Pre-Raphaelite angels in strange drag, and placing them in a shallow quattrocento space in his painting entitled *Casualty Clearance Station, 1918* (Australian War Memorial).

Another minor Australian Pre-Raphaelite is Blamire Young, who trained as a commercial artist in Britain in the 1890s. Young was regarded as one of the most radical of turn-of-the-century poster designers active in Australia. His large watercolor *Tennyson and His Friends* (c. 1905, Australian National Gallery) presents an imagined Pre-Raphaelite universe, realized in Art Nouveau style, in which Tennyson reads from his works to the members of the Pre-Raphaelite Brotherhood. Possibly drawing on the cartoons of Max Beerbohm, which had forged a connection between mythologizing the biographical details of the Pre-Raphaelites and drawing in a contemporary graphic style, Young's work seems also inspired by Alphonse Mucha's decorative *panneaux*, which inform elements of *Tennyson and His Friends* such as its horizontal format, its grand artwork, its commercial-poster images, and the cloisonné attention to outline and shape in the drawings. In the subject of a public reading, Young possibly was inspired by Ford Madox Brown's *Chaucer at the Court of King Edward* (1847–51), a well-known exhibit at the Art Gallery of New South Wales. Each face in Young's painting is recognizable as a portrait, including an impossibly glamorized Lady Tennyson, as well as Jane Morris.

In the 1920s and 1930s, Violet Teague echoed the quattrocento revival, the early Pre-Raphaelite religious scenes, and the later decorative expressions of the movement as seen in works by Evelyn de Morgan and Kate Bunce. However, with the exception of her *Coleraine Altarpiece* (1926), she does not replicate the linear control associated with the work of the last quarter of the nineteenth century, although she certainly references the high color palette, the neo-Medieval costume, and even the types of beauty associated with Pre-Raphaelitism. Her most remarkably Pre-Raphaelite work is the *Altarpiece for Saint James the Less* (1931, Mount Eliza, Victoria), which stretches across the full width of the rear of the church. In it, she records the likenesses of many friends and community members, with the local children posing for the angels. As a collective portrait of the ethos and the identity of a small rural Australian community in the early 1930s, a Pre-Raphaelite altarpiece is an unexpected but eloquent choice of format. Despite Max Meldrum's 1934 denunciation of the Pre-Raphaelites, Teague saw their style as appropriate to 1930s Melbourne. Teague also arranged a series of *tableaux vivants* for a charity fundraising event, photographed and published in Australia's most glamorous fashion and social magazines in 1930 and 1931.[54] There are the expected Old Master compositions, but there are also tableaux of Millais's *My First Sermon* and Rossetti's *Monna Pomona*, the latter a strange meeting of Hollywood glamour with the then-highly unfashionable Pre-Raphaelite style.

We must move forward to 1962 to pick up the thread of Pre-Raphaelitism in Australia, after decades of it largely being ignored. Pre-Raphaelitism returned to Australia as a hybrid of self and Other, as something not wholly English or Australian, but a link between the two cultures. This homage to Pre-Raphaelitism reflects colonial mimicry, the margin's somewhat eccentric rereading of the center. Australia in 1962 provided one of the first scholarly recapitulations of Pre-Raphaelitism in light of twentieth-century art historical practice and one of the first exhibitions of Pre-Raphaelitism anywhere informed by modern museum techniques. Exhibits were sent to Adelaide from major British collections, including the Tate Gallery and the Victoria and Albert Museum. The Pre-Raphaelite Exhibition of 1962 was part of the second Adelaide Festival of the Arts and celebrated the opening of new extensions of the Art Gallery of South Australia. It was one of a series of ambitious exhibitions that consciously proclaimed a desire for Australia to perform culturally at an international and cosmopolitan level. Australian critics refashioned the Pre-Raphaelites as proto-beatniks:

> Pre-Raphaelitism is at the opposite pole to the contemporary vogue of abstraction and *tachisme*—the chuck–it–onsky method of painting. Yet fundamentally both are revolutionary. The Pre-Raphaelite Brotherhood was the banding together of a group of young art students in London in protest at the stodgy, dark, academics of the Victorian era.[55]

A report from the *Sydney Morning Herald* again emphasizes the ambiguity that Pre-Raphaelitism has raised in an Australian context. The Pre-Raphaelite exhibition was named explicitly as the "most interesting and important" of the several exhibitions at the expanded Art Gallery of South Australia. Moreover, the Brotherhood was again partly cast in an explicitly modernist light. It was "formed as a protest against the dull academic tradition in art of the period" and even "sought in principal, a reality—an acceptance of nature," but at the same time it was roundly criticized for its failure in the modernist stakes:

> The paintings failed to register any spark of life even if they did escape the heavy turgid bonds of the prevailing academic school. Wrapped in story telling allegory and scriptural illustration, the brotherhood's paintings remained schematised and sweetly sexless. A mannered decoration was the final result.[56]

If Australia is famous in international culture as a location of anomalies and topsy-turveydom, the land down under, with unique animals, with seasons out of step with the Northern Hemisphere, with films that defy accepted genre narratives, then Australia's interaction with the Pre-Raphaelite movement is by no means "straight," either. Those Australians who embraced Pre-Raphaelitism did so despite mainstream disfavor. Australian gestures of love and homage seem faintly off-center, yet are insightful about the movement. If one seeks to contextualize Pre-Raphaelitism and how it appeared to its audiences, both historic and present day, the Australian experience adds an unfamiliar dimension to the much-related story of Pre-Raphaelitism.

NOTES

1. [James Smith], "Mr. Von Guerard's New Picture," *The Argus* (13 Jul. 1870): 7.

2. Jeremy Maas, *Holman Hunt and the "Light of the World"* (London and Berkley: Scholar, 1984), 141–63.

3. Eugen von Geurard unpublished letter to *The Argus* (ca. Jul. 1870), reprinted in *Eugen von Guerard* ed. Candice Bruce (Canberra: National Gallery of Australia and Art Gallery Directors' Association, 1980), 134–35.

4. Max Meldrum, "The Literary Idea in Painting," *Pandemonium* (2 Apr. 1934): 9.

5. Woolner has consistently been treated as an afterthought in histories of Pre-Raphaelitism, apart from Benedict Read, "Was There a Pre-Raphaelite Sculpture?" in *Pre-Raphaelite Papers*, ed. Leslie Parris, (London: Tate Gallery, 1984), 97–110.

6. Thomas Woolner, "Australian Diary 1852–1854" (Bodlean Lib. Ms. Facs. d152, Australian Joint Copying Project reel 1926), 18 Dec. 1852. A photocopy of the diary is also held by the Australian National Library (Ms. 2939).

7. Ibid., 3 Nov. 1852.

8. Ibid., 7 Nov. 1852, (cf. 4 Jan. 1853): "Kilmore, that charming town of shabbiness and filth."

9. Ibid., 8 Nov. 1852.

10. Ibid., 30 Nov. 1852.

11. Ibid., 25 Jan. 1853.

12. Ibid., 17 Apr. 1853.

13. Ian Ousky, ed., *Cambridge Guide to Literature in England* (Cambridge: Cambridge University Press, 1992), 322; also Leonee Ormond, "Thomas Woolner and the Image of Tennyson," in *Pre-Raphaelite Sculpture: Nature and Imagination in British Sculpture, 1848-1914*, eds. Benedict Read and Joanna Barnes (London: Henry Moore Foundation in association with Lund Humphries, 1991), 45.

14. William Howitt, unpublished memoirs. Quoted in Mary Howitt Walker, *Come Wind Come Weather: A Biography of Alfred Howitt* (Melbourne: Melbourne University Press, 1971), 21.

15. William Michael Rossetti, "Introduction," in *The Germ: Thoughts Towards Nature in Poetry, Literature and Art: Being a Facsimile Reprint of the Literary Journal of the Pre-Raphaelite Brotherhood Published in 1850* (London: Elliot Stock, 1901), 8. See also William Michael Rossetti, *Some Reminiscences*, 2 vols. (London: Brown and Langham, 1906), 1:145–46.

16. Letter, Thomas Woolner to Bernhard Smith (13 July [1854]), private collection, Melbourne.

17. The Howitts' relationship to the Pre-Raphaelite Brotherhood is discussed in Mary Howitt Botham, *Mary Howitt: An Autobiography: Edited by her Daughter Margaret Howitt* (London: Isbister, 1889), 71–75.

18. Ibid., 26–27, 71–75.

19. Woolner, "Diary," 9 Jan. 1853. See also a letter from Woolner to his

father (28 Oct. 1853), quoted in Amy Woolner, *Thomas Woolner, R. A.: Sculptor and Poet* (New York: Dutton, 1917), 18.

20. "Mr. Woolner and the Statue," *Melbourne Morning Herald* (13 Jul. 1853): 6–7.

21. George Paston, *Little Memoirs of the Nineteenth Century* (London: Grant Richards, 1902), 367.

22. John Guille Millais, *The Life and Letters of Sir John Everett Millais by his Son John Guille Millais*, 2 vols. (London: Methuen, 1899), 1:33–34.

23. Williams published *Sergeant Thomas and J. E. Millais* privately in London in 1901 under the name "Ralph Thomas." See Joanna Kerr, "Florence Elizabeth Williams," in *Heritage: The National Women's Art Book: 500 Works by 500 Australian Women Artists from Colonial Times to 1955*, eds. Joanna Kerr and Anita Callaway (Roseville, East NSW: Craftsman House, 1995), 65–66, 476.

24. Bernhard Smith's daughter Minnie would likewise write and self-publish a memoir in order to write her father back into the story of the movement. See Minnie Bernhard Smith, *Bernhard Smith and His Connection With Art; or, The Seven Founders of the Pre-Raphaelite Brotherhood* (Melbourne: The Author, 1917).

25. Kerr, 476.

26. Amy Woolner, 18.

27. Walker, 74–75.

28. Anita Callaway, *Visual Ephemera: Theatrical Art in Nineteenth Century Australia* (Sydney: University of New South Wales Press, 2000), 25, 124–27.

29. Louisa Anne Meredith, *Over the Straits—A Visit to Victoria* (London: Chapman and Hall, 1862), 93. Meredith mentions the "exquisite taste and ability" shown by Bateman's design.

30. Caroline Clementi, "Artists in Society: A Melbourne Circle, 1850s–1880s," *Art Bulletin of Victoria* 30 (1989): 44–57.

31. Letter, Thomas Woolner to Bernhard Smith (13 Jul. [1854]), private collection, Melbourne.

32. Letter, Sir Charles Fitzroy to Thomas Woolner (27 Sept. 1856), Bodlean Lib. Ms. Eng. Lett. d292; Australian Joint Copying Project reel 1826.

33. Juliette Peers, "Beyond Captain Cook: Thomas Woolner and Australia," in Reed and Barnes, 36.

34. Letter, Thomas Woolner to Henry Parkes (13 Apr. 1879), Parkes Papers A722, Mitchell Library, State Library of New South Wales.

35. Peers, "Beyond," 36.

36. Letter, Thomas Woolner to Robert Browning (5 Jan. 1857), quoted in A. N. L. Munby, "Letters of British Artists of the 18th and 19th Century—Part IV," *The Connoisseur* (December 1948): 71–72.

37. Amy Woolner, 64.

38. Peers, "Beyond," 34, 38.

39. Letter, Thomas Woolner to Henry Parkes (undated [ca. 1883]), Parkes Papers A722, Mitchell Library, State Library of New South Wales.

40. See the picture from the Mitchell Library collection reproduced in Peers, 37.

41. Draft of undated letter, Harry P. Gill to unknown recipient (1901), with heading "Marble bust of Alfred Lord Tennyson by T. Woolner The Painting *Love and Death* by G. F. Watts, R. A. to be unveiled in the National Art Gallery by His Royal Highness the Duke of Cornwall and York." Original manuscript in the Archives of the Art Gallery of South Australia (File GRG 19/51: Letters Sent by the Curator, 1901).

42. Ibid.

43. Ibid.

44. Letter, Thomas Woolner to Henry Parkes (23 Nov. 1874), Parkes Papers A722, Mitchell Library, State Library of New South Wales. An early copy of this letter is preserved in the State Archives of New South Wales (New South Wales Colonial Secretary: Special Bundles, Captain Cook's Statue 1876–79, AONSW ref. 4/859.1).

45. Letter, Henry Parkes to Thomas Woolner (26 Feb. 1876), Bodlean Lib. Ms. Eng. Lett. d.293; Australian Joint Copying Project reel 1926.

46. Draft of undated latter, Harry P. Gill to unknown recipient (1901).

47. See, for example, William Michael Rossetti's letter to the *Pall Mall Gazette* (10 Sept. 1886): 3; and Minnie Bernhard Smith.

48. Letter, William Michael Rossetti to Bernhard Alexander Smith (undated [ca. 1890]), LaTrobe Collection, State Library of Victoria, Ms. 10626, b2f25. This letter survives in several fragments, in which William Rossetti's positive comments about Smith, his ratification of Smith's presence in the Pre-Raphaelite circle, and the respect accorded Smith by the formal members of the Brotherhood. According to Rossetti, the title "Pre-Raphaelite" was applied to Smith on occasion "by my brother and others in a spirit of artistic sympathy." Smith signed works in the late 1840s as "Bernhard Smith, P. R. B."

49. For a detailed overview of Smith's artistic career, see Juliette Peers "Bernhard Smith: 'The Missing Brother,'" in Read and Barnes, 21–20, and Juliette Peers, "Bernhard Smith," *Dictionary of Australian Artists*, 733–36.

50. In the collection of the LaTrobe Library, State Library of Victoria.

51. Benedict Read, "Introduction," Read and Barnes, 8.

52. Letter, Bernhard Smith to Edward Smith (30 Nov. 1841, private collection, Melbourne).

53. For Ramey's advocacy of Flaxman as a source for sculptural students, see Letter, Bernhard Smith to Edward Smith (30 Nov. 1841, private collection, Melbourne).

54. *Table Talk* (20 Nov. 1930): 5–6; and *Home* (2 Jan. 1931): 26–27.

55. *Adelaide Advertiser* (17 Mar. 1962): 2.

56. *Sydney Morning Herald* (22 Mar. 1962): 2.

Chapter 11

"Lo, here is felawschipe": Morris, Medievalism, and Christian Socialism in America

Paul Hardwick

> Lo, here is felawschipe:
> One fayth to holde,
> One truth to speake,
> One wrong to wreke,
> One loving-cuppe to syppe,
> And to dippe
> In one disshe faithfullich,
> As lamkins of one folde.
> Either for other to suffre alle thing.
> One songe to sing
> In swete accord and maken melodye.
> Right-so thou and I good-fellowes be:
> Now God us thee!

With this verse, Florence Converse (1871–1967) dedicates her 1903 novel, *Long Will*, to her former tutor and lifelong companion, Vida Scudder (1861–1954), the Boston scholar, critic, and Christian socialist.[1] *Long Will* is a historical novel set in England during the 1380s, which imaginatively re-creates the events leading up to and immediately following the "Peasants' Revolt," drawing on figures such as Richard II, Wat Tyler, John Ball, Chaucer, William Langland (the "Long Will" of the title), and his daughter Calote. Ultimately, it is a story of the survival of Christian social ideals in the face of hypocrisy and self-interest. It is singularly apt that the dedication should extol the virtues of lasting "fellowship" and make use of archaic forms in which to do so. This essay will explore Scudder's thinking on William Morris, whose own work combined Medievalism and social concern. From an initial position of ambivalence, Scudder came to respond to Morris's Medievalized yet forward-looking vision of social change and socialist "felawschipe."

Scudder's admiration of England was not reciprocated in Morris's feelings about the United States. Morris had, as Fiona MacCarthy has put it, "an ingrained resistance to America."[2] While pursuing business interests in the United States, invitations were consistently refused. Indeed, in a letter to John Coleman Kenworthy, conjecturally dated to May 1890, Morris makes his position emphatically clear: "I don't think I am likely to go to America: I certainly would not go unless under compulsion. Yet I thank you for considering me in the matter."[3]

By the 1890s, Morris was a writer, designer, and social thinker greatly esteemed in the United States. The foundations of this reputation had been laid in the 1860s by the patronage of literary critics who were among the earliest American purchasers of his decorative designs. As Lindsay Leard-Coolidge has discussed, nowhere was Morris more immediately and fervently embraced than in Boston, by influential critics such as Charles Eliot Norton, Henry James, and William Dean Howells.[4] As first president of the Boston Society of Arts and Crafts, Norton was particularly influential in promoting the craftsman ideal embodied by Morris, which informed the Arts and Crafts movement that flourished in America in the last quarter of the nineteenth century.[5]

Vida Scudder was raised and educated as a member of New England Society, and took the obligatory sojourns in Europe fashionable for young American ladies.[6] Born in India, Julia Davida Scudder returned to the United States in infancy with her mother, Harriet, on the tragic death of her missionary father, David. On her father's side, her relatives included Samuel Scudder, entomologist and president of the Boston Association of Natural History, and Horace Scudder, author, editor of the *Atlantic Monthly*, and literary advisor to the Houghton-Mifflin Company. Her mother's family included Edward Dutton, head of the publishing firm E. P. Dutton, and her favorite uncle Horace Dutton, who "had a varied career, but his best and happiest years perhaps were spent in city mission work."[7] The twin family traits of intellectual vigor and Christian philanthropy would characterize Scudder's life, admixed with a passion for history engendered by four years of extensive travels throughout Europe following the death of her grandparents in 1867. As she would later recall,

> How those European years nourished my small being! . . . and I know,
> looking back, that they determined what sort of person I should be. Two in-
> fluences had pervaded me which were always to control my instincts and
> in large measure to shape my conduct: devotion to beauty, and awed intu-
> ition of the human past.[8]

As Linda Parry, among others, has noted, Morris also developed "an early affinity with historic romance, landscape and buildings" in childhood.[9] In this reverence for beauty and history, we see the same passions by which both would be driven throughout their lives. Like Morris, too, Scudder did not allow her devotion to beauty and history to draw her into an idyll of bourgeois medievalism; instead she drew on the past as a basis for future social reform. This became clear to her during her postgraduate studies in literature at Oxford, as she would later reflect in her autobiography, *On Journey* (1937): "To me [Oxford] brought a passionate sense which has never faded, that the middle ages rather than the nineteenth century were my natural home, but she also paradoxically brought initiation into the mood of prophecy."[10]

The chief catalyst in this awakening was John Ruskin, whose last lecture series Scudder attended in 1884. Indeed, she had a letter of introduction to Ruskin, although a sense of deference prevented her from presenting herself. Although widely criticized in his later years, Ruskin's impact on Scudder was immense, as she recalled in the *Atlantic Monthly* in 1900, the year of his death:

> New questions began to form in his hearers' minds. Were political econ-
> omy and art so far separated, after all? Could either be wisely considered
> apart from the laws of righteousness? Could a nation play beautifully that
> did not work healthfully? Could art flourish as the monopoly of the privi-
> leged? Is it delicate, is it courteous, is it Christian, is it even just to rejoice
> in the descriptions of nature or contemplation of art, while throngs of those
> to whom we owe our fine sensibilities and the leisure to enjoy them are shut
> off from art and nature alike? What should idealism play upon—dreams,
> abstractions, the study of the past, or the big crude world of modern fact?
> These questions are obvious enough now; then, they meant to many a
> hearer a new point of view.[11]

Late in his life Morris also acknowledged the pivotal role of Ruskin in his development:

> [Ruskin], before my days of practical Socialism, was my master towards
> the ideal aforesaid, and looking backward, I cannot help saying, by the
> way, how deadly dull the world would have been twenty years ago but for
> Ruskin! It was through him that I learned to give form to my discontent,
> which I must say was not by any means vague.[12]

While it is important to note that Morris moved beyond Ruskin's sphere
into "practical Socialism," we see that, like Scudder, he ascribes to
Ruskin the impetus behind his subsequent development.[13] Indeed, when
listing his "Hundred Best Books" for the *Pall Mall Gazette* in February
1886, "Ruskin's Works (especially the ethical and politico-economical
parts of them)," presumably including *Unto This Last*, which Scudder was
to hold in particularly high esteem, are included.[14]

Ruskin's 1884 lectures on art and politics awoke in Scudder an "intolerable stabbing pain" when she considered the "plethora of privilege"
that had been her lot.[15] This initially led her to join the Salvation Army,
the first of many organizations in which she immersed herself throughout
a life dedicated to the alleviation of social ills. Her appointment to the
teaching faculty at Wellesley College in 1887 coincided with her meeting
William D. P. Bliss and becoming a charter member of his Christian Socialist group. And, although the "intolerable stabbing pain" of class
awareness became merely a "dull chronic ache," Scudder continued to
work with the poor and immigrant communities throughout her forty-one
years at Wellesley, and she imbued her teaching with an intensity not always welcomed by more conservative students' parents.[16] The close interaction between the diverse strands of Scudder's work may be seen,
in differing proportions, in the books she produced throughout her long
career.

Scudder's earliest discussion of William Morris is to be found in her
first major critical work, *The Life of the Spirit in the Modern English Poets* (1895). This discussion of the "disciple of Ruskin" is somewhat am-
bivalent, for while Morris's socialism is in harmony with Scudder's own
views, it is, nonetheless, an "irreligious communism."[17] After abandoning
early aspirations to enter the church, Morris rarely alluded to his own religious views, although Sydney Cockerell, in his "Notes of a Biographical
Talk by William Morris at Kelmscott House, Nov. 28, 1892," records his
famous assertion that "in religion I am a pagan."[18] In his reminiscences of
Morris, J. Bruce Glasier recalls a conversation late in Morris's life, in
which he declared

> So far as I can discover from logical thinking, I am what is called bluntly
> an Atheist. I cannot see any real evidence of the existence of God or of im-
> mortality in the facts of the world—amazing as is the whole phenomenon
> of the universe. And of this I am absolutely convinced—that if there is a
> God, He never meant us to know much about Himself, or indeed to con-
> cern ourselves about Him at all.[19]

Such pragmatic lack of concern with the unseen is at odds with Scudder's
own religious temper.[20]

Writing in the year before Morris's death, however, Scudder concedes
that "so far, socialism has no poet but Morris, whose voice is too faint to
carry far."[21] Indeed, there seems to be a contradiction in her assessment of
Morris, for she separates "Morris the poet" from "Morris the socialist." The
former she sees as lacking the passion of his mentor, Rossetti:

> The world of Morris is a world of forms and dreams, lacking the substantial
> variety even of emotion. Alone among modern poets he rests for poetic ma-
> terial entirely upon the past, and his inventive faculty is sterile.[22]

The latter "prophet and champion of the social democracy" is a separate
entity, who finds a true voice by "breaking loose from all traditions of æs-
theticism, and by flinging himself full on life."[23] It is interesting, in view
of her own forward-looking view of the past, that Scudder did not at this
point recognize the same in Morris, instead perceiving the two elements
at odds—a contradiction that, as Ruth Kinna has recently noted, lies at
the heart of most discussions of Morris.[24] Indeed, with ironic prescience
in 1896, Scudder declared that "Morris the poet died long ago, to give
place to the prose-writer and social reformer."[25] Within the year, Morris
the man would be dead, and in J. W. Mackail's authorized biography of
1899,[26] it is the social reformer who is in a sense buried, for, as Mac-
Carthy has observed,

> Mackail was the originator of the view, widely accepted over the next few
> decades, that Morris's membership of, first, the revolutionary Democratic
> Foundation, then the Socialist League, were aberrations from which he
> soon recovered to enjoy a golden twilight of renewed artistic and literary
> activity.[27]

Along with Rossetti and Swinburne, Morris is firmly defined by
Scudder as a Pre-Raphaelite, one of that "group of poets to whom escape

from the present is almost a battle-cry,"[28] whose works exist in a nostalgic "dream world of art."[29] Although Morris's self-characterization as an "idle singer of an empty day"[30] may be hard to integrate with his later socialist persona, we may expect from Scudder a greater sympathy with Morris's utopian romance, *News from Nowhere* (1890). Set within the Medieval form of the dream-vision, this work is Morris's most forward-looking meditation on the past. Curiously, Scudder fails to see beyond the picturesque:

> He does not mind inconvenience, but the ugliness of modern civilization haunts him like a nightmare; and with his mind stored with memories of all that has been most beautiful in the past, he dreams a fair dream for us of a lovely future, where architecture shall be redeemed from sordidness to dignity, and people from vulgarity to grace. His dream is a decorative frieze, without depth or movement; seek to penetrate below aspect to soul, and the beauty flees.[31]

"The artist," concludes Scudder regretfully, "could create only an artistic ideal."[32] While not explicitly stated, we may perhaps see here her earlier antipathy toward Morris's "irreligious communism." In his concern with the material causes and effects of social change, he has neglected the "world of experience and emotion," which she finds, for example, in Rossetti's work, albeit in his case at the expense of "intellectual conviction."[33]

In looking at Morris's future society, however, Scudder is guilty of inverting causality, rhetorically placing artistic reform before social reform. For while beauty may be an ideal for Morris, his text asserts that this end will be achieved only as a result of radical social change. As old Hammond makes plain to Guest,

> The art or work-pleasure, as one ought to call it, of which I am now speaking, sprung up almost spontaneously, it seems, from a kind of instinct amongst people, no longer desperately tied to painful and terrible overwork, to do the best they could with the work in hand—to make it excellent of its own kind.[34]

The art of Morris's utopian state naturally grows from improved social conditions. In failing to acknowledge this, Scudder negates the hopeful exhortation that closes *News from Nowhere*—"if others can see it as I have seen it, then it may be called a vision rather than a dream"[35]—instead characterizing it as a dream "without which the world would be poor indeed."[36] It is a beautiful dream, but nothing more.[37] If Scudder has praise for Morris, it is very faint praise indeed:

> Nobody would dream of calling William Morris a thinker, yet he is something better than the most picturesque figure of the modern movement. Charm, fervor, self-surrender,—these have always counted at least as much as ideas, despite the discontent of the philosopher, in determining the onward march of men. The fascination of Morris' work is so great that one forgets its lack of thought-values; or rather, let us say that the mere spectacle of this winsome "dreamer of dreams, born out of his due time," driven by stress of events and emotions to "strive to put the crooked straight" by organizing socialist leagues and haranguing irreverent street audiences on political economy which he did not understand, is evidence of the irresistible impulse forcing the modern dreamer on to act, evidence all the stronger on account of the weakness of the dreamer's theories.
>
> Anarchist and inveterate idealist, Morris is one with socialism on its critical side, but absurdly far from it in constructive ideas. His thought is in the main, literally [a] de-moralized derivation from Ruskin.[38]

In spite of this, Scudder recognizes in the last chapter of *A Dream of John Ball* (1886)—that other late dream-vision, still more firmly anchored in the medieval past—a "profoundly stirring and troubling passage . . . of social idealism."[39] While Scudder sees no prophecy in this retrospect, the perfect expression of "the long and weary struggle for freedom which stretches out in phase after phase through the passing generations," as the narrator consoles the doomed rebel leader, cannot help but strike a chord in Scudder, the socialist Medievalist.

Indeed, as Morris noted in a letter to his wife of 25 November 1886, his *Dream of John Ball* had "been much admired by people of various opinions."[40] It has retained its appeal through successive generations of the political left, independent of Morris's broader cultural standing and, indeed, changes within the field of left-wing politics. As Fiona MacCarthy has observed, "the reason is surely the sheer strength of Morris's argument for fellowship," and this is true of its appeal for Scudder.[41] Morris may be no "thinker," but his "wistful retrospect-prophecy" stirs thought in others.[42]

In Scudder's next major work, *Socialism and Character* (1912), we are hard pressed to recognize the same William Morris, whom she praises for his "valiant work" in bringing socialism to a position in which it could not be ignored.[43] It would appear that, following a period of reflection, Scudder found sympathy with Morris, viewing both the Medievalist writer-artist and the socialist as necessary parts of the whole person. In *Socialism and Character*, Scudder recognizes her own "prophetic" relationship with the past as part of a broader movement to which Morris is central:

> The mediæval revival in literature, religion, and art, which has persisted against such heavy odds for the past hundred years, has had real significance; and we need to learn that the ages of romance have as much to teach the sociologist as to the artist or the priest. We shall never get at their worth to us through prim or sentimental imitations; we cannot profit by the past through copying it. . . . We want no dilettante Pre-Raphaelitism in ethics; yet the curiously common union of mediæval enthusiasm with social radicalism is no sentimental folly; and all good socialists should catch the point of that orthodox Marxian, William Morris, who contended that ever since the Middle Ages the race has been on the wrong tack, and that we must go back to recover the trail.[44]

While still implicitly critical of Morris's wholly earthly focus,[45] Scudder becomes part of the same ideological "fellowship"—a term that, as noted by Teresa Corcoran, was to become increasingly important in her later writings.[46] She no longer categorizes Morris as one of "the poets of art," along with Rossetti and Swinburne,[47] but places him in opposition to the lack of social engagement epitomized by "dilettante Pre-Raphaelitism." "Pre-Raphaelite *pastiches*" are dismissed as worthless.[48] While Morris's works are not discussed in detail, Scudder detects something beneath his "decorative frieze" that she does not find in other Pre-Raphaelite writers. Although Morris may espouse "irreligious communism," it is imbued with a moral depth that points to something more substantial than "only an artistic ideal."

Socialism and Character, which Scudder later opined "contained some of my best thinking," is separated from *Social Ideals in English Letters* by a gap of twelve years.[49] It is a period that began in turmoil, with Scudder embroiled in an ideological controversy at Wellesley. At a "struggling college, dedicated to the pious education of young women," any resistance to gifts from benefactors was viewed as disloyal.[50] Yet, a number of the Wellesley faculty were opposed to accepting a donation by John D. Rockefeller of "tainted money" from Standard Oil, whose business practices had been criticized in Henry Demarest Lloyd's book, *Wealth Against Commonwealth* (1894). The gift was ultimately accepted, with the money being spent, as Scudder was to recall many years later, on a "much needed central heating plant, with an ugly tower which intrudes into our fair landscape to this day."[51] However, the conflict was not so easily resolved within Scudder herself. As Morris would always remain uncomfortable with the knowledge that his reforms in the arts and his workers' conditions were funded by catering to the "swinish luxury of the rich," so Scudder could never fully reconcile her social and educational ideals with the necessity of compromise in order to gain financial support. The "intolerable stabbing pain" engendered by Ruskin's lectures remained a goad to her conscience.

The self-confessed "most violent" opponent of the Rockefeller gift, Scudder eventually acquiesced following a lengthy period of both inner and outer conflict, precipitating a nervous illness that required a two-year sabbatical. This period saw a further trip to Europe with her mother between 1901 and 1903, this time accompanied by Florence Converse, whom she referred to as "the dearest of my students . . . by this time my close friend."[52] Indeed, she singles out Converse in the "Friends" section of *On Journey*:

> I calculate that I have taught between two and three thousand girls; apart from the genuine if sometimes exasperated affection I have borne to them *en masse*, I have admitted between thirty and forty to my "inner mansions,"—a large proportion, to my mind. One has entered the inmost region in my power to open.[53]

The relationship between Scudder and Converse within the broader context of women's friendships and their representation in literature has been discussed by Nan Bauer Maglin.[54] In *Socialism and Character*, dedicated "To Florence Converse, Comrade and Companion," we observe the intellectual fruits of the exchange of ideas between the two women, which led to Scudder's more integrated vision of Morris and, indeed, of herself. The dedicatory preface refers to the book's genesis at some time in the past: "since the first pages of this book were written, the phenomenon it signals, as you and I are aware, has become more and more evident."[55] The collaborative nature of the enterprise, albeit under Scudder's ultimate authorship, is made plain in the reference to the book's expression of "our common thought,"[56] perhaps rooted in the European tour, which began in England.

Curiously, in her autobiography, Scudder precedes her account of the tour with a description of an earlier dream to which she attached special significance.[57] In this dream, she is a Northern Germanic "monk, or recluse" in the early days of Christianity who, by means of a boat with "neither sail nor oar," is borne to a far land in which she must carve the face of Christ on a cliff for the solace of travelers. On the completion of this task, fraught with anxieties concerning the existence of "the Lover" and human inability to represent His face, she turns from her work to behold Christ Himself. This journey is certainly rooted in narratives of early British Christianity, such as the "three Scots [who] came to King Alfred in a boat without any oars," recorded in the *Anglo-Saxon Chronicle* for the year 891.[58] Yet, we are perhaps reminded too of the Sending Boat that carries Birdalone to her unplanned destinations in Morris's *The Water of the Wondrous Isles* (1887). More than this, Scudder's dream recalls Morris's *The Story of the Unknown Church* (1856), both in its sculptor protagonist and in its enigmatic conclusion as the artwork is completed. Scudder's dream remained an "enduring support": "I have had such dreams sometimes; one can always distinguish them from the usual type." In terms of its subsequent relevance to her life, it may indeed be considered "a vision rather than a dream."

Theresa Corcoran's study of Scudder concentrates on the Italian stage of the journey, which focused her fascination with Italian spirituality, in particular with St. Francis of Assisi and St. Catherine of Siena.[59] Scudder's own account makes clear the "joy" her party experienced in England.[60] Although this experience does not overtly inform Scudder's subsequent work, she acknowledges the importance of the visit for Converse:

> After all, West Malvern, whither we went at once, meant more to her just then than Sicily would have done; for she was writing her novel, "Long Will," all about Langland and the Vision of the Plowman which came to him in those Malvern mists.

Langland, as I have discussed elsewhere, was a major influence on Morris's *A Dream of John Ball* and *News from Nowhere*.[61] In *Long Will*, Converse returns to the age of John Ball in the same way as Morris, depicting the survival of a protosocialist ideal beyond the defeat of the Peasants' Revolt.[62] By placing her focus on Langland rather than Ball, however, Converse emphasizes an explicitly Christian social vision that, in Scudder's phrase, "stretches out in phase after phase through the passing generations." Converse's novel, then, succeeds in marrying Morris's socialist Medievalism to a Christian message that counteracts his "irreligious communism" and articulates an integrated ideology encompassing previously conflicting impulses in Scudder's criticism.

"Forsooth, brothers, fellowship is heaven and lack of fellowship is hell: fellowship is life, and lack of fellowship is death."[63] So says John Ball in Morris's *Dream*, and it is a message that permeates *Long Will*. Converse's dedication "To ____" remains blank, but it is surely to the tutor who introduced her to Langland's *Piers Plowman* and Morris's *Dream of John Ball*, and who accompanied her on her visit to Malvern: Vida Scudder.[64] Converse's lines quoted at the start of this essay convey not only the "felawschipe" between author and dedicatee, but also the broader ideal of fellowship expressed in Morris's work and informing Converse's own novel.

The personal fellowship is acknowledged on Scudder's part by the "Comrade and Companion" dedication of *Socialism and Character*, while the broader social and political meanings of the term are intrinsic to her vision of the growth of socialism within the process of history:

> Only occasionally, under stress of some sharp immediate oppression, has a brief sense of fellowship sprung into transient flame, soon sinking into ashes. To-day that healthful fire is creeping steadily and stealthily on, spreading from land to land, from speech to speech.[65]

Indeed, at the time of writing, this "fire" must have appeared unstoppable. Socialism had become a major force, with the socialist press rapidly expanding and the charismatic labor leader Eugene V. Debs polling nearly a million votes in 1912 as candidate for the Socialist Party of America (founded in 1901).[66]

In extolling the virtue of fellowship and looking forward to mutual reciprocity in artistic, intellectual, and industrial spheres, Scudder turns again to Morris's *Dream of John Ball*:

> "Forsooth, brothers, fellowship is heaven and lack of fellowship is hell," said William Morris. From that hell, only socialism can set us free, for only under socialism can the meek effectively inherit the earth which shall nourish them unstintedly from the resources which it will be their privilege, in the serious and instinctive joy of fellowship, to maintain and to increase.[67]

Scudder makes no mention of the quotation's source, divorcing it from the fictional sermon of John Ball and attributing it directly to Morris. With Scudder's move from literary criticism informed by Christian socialist beliefs toward Christian socialism informed by literary scholarship, formal considerations no longer obscure an appreciation of Morris as they once did. Writing almost a decade after *Socialism and Character*, she acknowledges Morris's "charm,"[68] but without the caveats of old. For the more mature Scudder, Morris becomes no longer a Pre-Raphaelite but a socialist whose medievalist fiction—like that of her companion Florence Converse— embodies forward-looking political truth, no longer a mere "dreamer of dreams," but a visionary sharing her own "mood of prophecy."

By looking at him from this different perspective, Scudder at last sees Morris as a whole, rather than the conflicting writer-artist and socialist. He is an exemplar whom Scudder calls on at the close of *Socialism and Character*, her most politically significant work:

> And with relentless constancy, in season and out of season, the religiously minded socialist will seek to share his faith. "Education toward social- ism," that formula beloved by William Morris, will be his motto, whether he be engaged in political action, in journalism, in business life, in con- versation, or in saying his prayers.[69]

Not only is Morris perceived as a fully integrated writer, artist, business- man, and socialist, but also a model for that integration in others. He is perhaps a model for Scudder herself. In 1897, considering the suggestion that her social activism endangered her literary career, she replied,

> I must live if I am to interpret life. I cannot shut myself away and study me- dieval legends of the Holy Grail while men are perishing for the Bread of Life. No! I will work for my own generation; I will help the immediate need; I will abandon dreams of work that shall endure.[70]

In her career following her European journey with Converse, Scudder gained the resolve and conviction to do both. Alongside her later works of practical and literary socialism, she also wrote *Le Morte Darthur of Sir Thomas Malory and Its Sources* (1921), and without the "stabbing pain" of guilt concerning her privileged position, for even in the Medieval ro- mance of Arthur she perceives a "valid social document" of relevance to the modern reader.[71]

In terms of her dream, the period of drifting with "neither sail nor oar" came to a close in 1903, after which she was ready to embark on her self-ordained task of providing solace for travelers through this life. But this commitment and vision were obtained at the expense of her literary criticism, and though she would write of Morris again, it would always be about his political content rather than his literary form. For, like Morris, Scudder transcended the "dilettante Pre-Raphaelitism" of New England society, investing her love of the past with contemporary relevance and hope for the future.

Six years after retiring from Wellesley, Scudder returned in the spring of 1934 to fill a vacant teaching position. In recording this in *On Journey*, she makes her last mention of Morris, where he is one of her "old friends, the Victorians," and she recalls teaching *News from Nowhere*.[72] In contrast to discussions of the work early in her career, she offers no criticism, instead using the book to explore her students' visions of utopian futures. Her unified view of Morris allows her to see *News from Nowhere* as a mirror in which are projected our own ideals. She takes this view as an integrated and contented scholar, critic, educator, and Christian socialist, recognizing her "felawschipe" across time and continental divisions with her "old friend" William Morris.

NOTES

1. Florence Converse, *Long Will* (Boston: Ginn, 1903).

2. Fiona MacCarthy, *William Morris: A Life for our Time* (London: Faber and Faber, 1994), 604.

3. Norman Kelvin, ed., *The Collected Letters of William Morris*, 4 vols. (Princeton, NJ: Princeton University Press, 1984–96), 3:155–56.

4. Lindsay Leard-Coolidge, "William Morris and Nineteenth-Century Boston," in *William Morris: Centenary Essays*, eds. Peter Faulkner and Peter Preston (Exeter: University of Exeter Press, 1999), 156–64.

5. For an account of the growth of the Arts and Crafts movement, see Wendy Kaplan, *"The Art that is Life": The Arts and Crafts Movement in America, 1875-1920* (Boston: Little, Brown, 1987).

6. The primary source on Scudder's life is her autobiography, *On Journey* (New York: Dutton, 1937). Theresa Corcoran, *Vida Dutton Scudder* (Boston: Twayne, 1982) provides a critical biography focusing on the development of Scudder's Christian social thought.

7. Scudder, *On Journey*, 19.

8. Ibid., 28–30.

9. Linda Parry, "Introduction," in *William Morris*, Victoria and Albert Museum centenary exhibition catalogue, ed. Linda Parry (London: Harry N. Abrams, 1996), 13.

10. Scudder, *On Journey*, 78.

11. Reprinted ibid., 81. In 1890, Scudder would go on to edit *An Introduction to the Writings of John Ruskin*.

12. "How I Became a Socialist," in *The Collected Works of William Morris*, ed. May Morris, 24 vols. (London: Longmans, Green, 1910–15), 23:279.

13. The relationship between the two men is discussed in Peter Faulkner, "Ruskin and Morris," *The Journal of the William Morris Society* 14.1 (Autumn 2000), 6–17.

14. The letter to the *Pall Mall Gazette* is reprinted in Kelvin, *Collected Letters*, 2:514–18. May Morris refers to her father's admiration for *Unto This Last* in Morris, *Collected Works*, 16:xvii, while Scudder refers to it as marking "a turning point in [her] mental, and later in [her] outward life" in *On Journey*, 82–83.

15. Ibid., 84.

16. See Corcoran, *Vida Dutton Scudder*, 6–7.

17. Vida Scudder, *The Life of the Spirit in the Modern English Poets* (Boston: Houghton Mifflin, 1895), 89–90.

18. Quoted in *Collected Works of William Morris*, 22:xxxii.

19. J. Bruce Glasier, *William Morris and the Early Days of the Socialist Movement* (London: Longmans, Green, 1921), 171.

20. The lack of faith in Morris's work is a common topic for critical comment. See, for example, Sidney Lanier's "Paul H. Hayne's Poetry" in the *Southern Magazine* (January 1875), which, in questioning the common comparisons between Morris and Chaucer, highlights the gulf between "the faith that shines in Chaucer and the doubt that darkens in Morris." Extracts are reprinted in *William Morris: The Critical Heritage*, ed. Peter Faulkner (London: Routledge, 1973), 226–29.

21. Scudder, *Life of the Spirit*, 94.

22. Ibid., 276.

23. Ibid., 278.

24. Ruth Kinna, *William Morris: The Art of Socialism* (Cardiff: University of Wales Press, 2000), 4.

25. Scudder, *The Life of the Spirit*, 244.

26. J. W. Mackail, *The Life of William Morris*, 2 vols. (London: Oxford University Press 1899).

27. MacCarthy, x. This bias in Mackail's account is unsurprising in the light of Shaw's claim that from Mackail's point of view, "Morris took to Socialism as Poe took to drink": quoted in E. P. Thompson, *William Morris: Romantic to Revolutionary*, revised edition (London: Merlin Press, 1977), 742.

28. Scudder, *Life of the Spirit*, 147–8.

29. Ibid., 279.

30. From *The Earthly Paradise*, in *Collected Works of William Morris*, 3:1.

31. Vida Scudder, *Social Ideals in English Letters* (Boston: Houghton Mifflin, 1898), 61.

32. Ibid.

33. Scudder, *The Life of the Spirit*, 279.

34. Morris, *News from Nowhere*, in *Collected Works*, 16:134.

35. Ibid., 16:211.

36. Scudder, *Social Ideals*, 269.

37. This is not an uncommon reading. See, for example, John Goode, "William Morris and the Dream of Revolution," *Literature and Politics in the Nineteenth Century* (London: Methuen, 1971), 276–77.

38. Scudder, *Social Ideals*, 289–90.

39. Ibid., 291. *A Dream of John Ball* ends, of course, with a wry acknowledgment of the influence of Ruskin.

40. Kelvin, *Collected Letters*, 2:594.

41. MacCarthy, *William Morris*, 49.

42. Scudder, *Social Ideals*, 291. The complexity of possible responses to *A Dream of John Ball* has recently been discussed in Nicholas Salmon, "A Reassessment of *A Dream of John Ball*," *The Journal of the William Morris Society* 14.2 (Spring 2001): 29–38.

43. Vida Scudder, *Socialism and Character* (Boston: Houghton Mifflin, 1912), 60.

44. Ibid., 285–6.

45. Scudder expresses concern that "a satisfying and passionate love of 'the very skin and surface of this fair earth on which we dwell,' as William Morris puts it" may "replace all longing for a better country": ibid., 321.

46. Corcoran, *Vida Dutton Scudder*, 18.

47. Scudder, *Life of the Spirit*, 269–80.

48. Scudder, *Socialism and Character*, 286.

49. Scudder, *On Journey*, 191.

50. Ibid., 181.

51. Ibid., 183. The controversy is discussed in Scudder, *On Journey*, 180–84 and Corcoran, *Vida Dutton Scudder*, 25–27. It also provides much of the substance of Scudder's novel, *A Listener in Babel* (Boston: Houghton Mifflin, 1901).

52. Scudder, *On Journey*, 191.

53. Ibid., 220.

54. Nan Bauer Maglin, "Vida to Florence: 'Comrade and Companion,'" *Frontiers* 4.3 (1979): 13–20. See also Kate McCullough, *Regions of Identity: The Construction of America in Women's Fiction, 1885–1914* (Stanford, CA: Stanford University Press, 1999), 58–92, for a discussion that focuses on women's friendships in Converse's first novel, *Diana Victrix* (Boston: Houghton Mifflin, 1897).

55. Scudder, *Socialism and Character*, v.

56. Ibid., vii.

57. Scudder, *On Journey*, 236–7.

58. Dorothy Whitelock, ed. and trans., *The Anglo-Saxon Chronicle* (New Brunswick, NJ: Rutgers University Press, 1961), 53. Scudder's interest in the early English Church is evinced in her edition of Bede's *Ecclesiastical History of the English Nation* for Everyman's Library (London, 1910). It is interesting to note that, even in writing her introduction to this eighth-century work, she invokes Ruskin, noting that "in the midst of sterile turmoil, Order and Kindness, those two forces signalled by Ruskin as central impulses in a just society, ruled in the monastery and there alone" (xiv).

59. Corcoran, *Vida Dutton Scudder*, 32–38. See also Scudder, *On Journey*, 239–50.

60. Scudder, *On Journey*, 237–39.

61. Paul Hardwick, "'Biddeth Peres Ploughman go to his Werk': Appropriations of *Piers Plowman* in the Nineteenth and Twentieth Centuries," *Studies in Medievalism* 12 (2002): 171–95.

62. While Converse's *Long Will* is clearly descended from *Piers Plowman* and *A Dream of John Ball*, it is possible that *The Water of the Wondrous Isles*, with its female protagonist and "archaic" language, may also have been an influence. On the language of *The Water of the Wondrous Isles*, see Norman Talbot,

" 'Whilom, as tells the tale': the Language of the Prose Romances," *The Journal of the William Morris Society* 8.2 (Spring 1989): 16–26.

63. William Morris, *A Dream of John Ball*, in *Collected Works*, 16:230.

64. Scudder's book, *Social Ideals in English Letters*, had been based on a successful course that she taught at Wellesley, which had been attended by Converse. On the necessary silences the relationship of the two women in their writings, see Maglin, "Vida to Florence."

65. Scudder, *Socialism and Character*, 164.

66. Jacob H. Dorn, "Introduction," in *Socialism and Christianity in Early Twentieth Century America*, ed. Jacob H. Dorn (Westport, CT: Greenwood, 1998), 7. On the Socialist Party of America, see Albert Fried, *Socialism in America: From the Shakers to the Third International* (New York: Columbia University Press, 1993), 377–445. While a member of Boston Christian socialist societies since the late 1890s, Scudder became a member of the Socialist Party in 1911.

67. Scudder, *Socialism and Character*, 246.

68. Vida Scudder, Le Morte Darthur *of Sir Thomas Malory and its Sources* (New York: Dutton, 1921), 152.

69. Scudder, *Socialism and Character*, 430–31.

70. Quoted in Corcoran, *Vida Dutton Scudder*, 1.

71. Scudder, *Le Morte Darthur*, 8.

72. Scudder, *On Journey*, 213.

Chapter 12

"Count us but clay for them to fashion": Pre-Raphaelite Refashionings in Canada

David Latham

y title is from Francis Sherman's poem "A Word from Canada," which Sherman referred to as his "Jubilee verses."[1] It was published in the August 1897 issue of the *Canadian Magazine*, but it is not the kind of ode the colonists would expect to read for Queen Victoria's jubilee. As a message from Canadians addressed to the wind for delivery to the Queen, it begins conventionally enough with the exotic imagery of the remote colony: where the gray bergs drift down from Labrador, where the Pacific waves break against the pines, each Canadian labors throughout this land with loyal allegiance to the Queen, yielding rich tribute to the imperial center, listening for further inspiration. The response, however, is that of an aloof god:

> But unto thee are all unknown
> These things by which the worth is shown
> Of our deep love; and, near thy throne,
> The glory thou hast made thine own
>   Hath made men blind
> To all that lies not to their hand. . . .
> For what reck they of *Empire*,—they,
> Whose will two hemispheres obey?
> Why shouldst thou not count us but clay
> For them to fashion as they may
>   In London-town?[2]

Sherman concludes that the notion of the colonists extending the Empire
as a labor of love is an ideal that must be nurtured in imperial London as
well as colonial Canada. The extent to which Sherman describes the love
as both strong and sweet suggests that he was drawing on Matthew
Arnold's terms from *Culture and Anarchy* concerning the balancing of the
Hebraic principles of fire and strength with the Hellenic principles of
sweetness and light. Sherman thereby impresses on his Canadian readers
just how high the stakes are; through cooperative work, this new British
empire has the potential to become the ideal civilization.

It may have been this kind of idealism that led Rudyard Kipling to
confess his envy in a letter to Sherman: "It must be a gorgeous thing to be
one of the band of new singers. You don't know how much Canada lies in
your hands—and Canada does not either."[3] Ryerson Press editor Lorne
Pierce cynically qualified Kipling's comment: "Sherman no doubt felt
that it was a splendid thing to be a poet, but he suffered no delusions as
to moulding Canadian life and thought."[4]

I pursue the implications of these two poles—Kipling's romantic/
heroic construction of the poet as the maker/shaper/fashioner of national
identity and destiny on the one hand, and Sherman's deconstruction of
the poet as a follower of fashion, a mimic of others' fashionings. To do so
I focus on two Canadians who exemplify two different directions of Pre-
Raphaelitism, one concerning transatlantic exchanges, the other transborder exchanges. Francis Sherman is among the first set; his works
illustrate the issues of British cultural importation. Phillips Thompson is
among the second set; his political prose and poetry illustrate the issues
of appropriation and refashioning of Canadian Pre-Raphaelitism for the
American market. That the directions both Sherman and Thompson pursued so problematically could arise from the Pre-Raphaelite movement is
especially ironic, considering the origins of the movement.

As an English nationalist movement, Pre-Raphaelitism was a rebellion against not only academicism but against classicism, wherein the
historic and literary models that the English studied were Greek and Roman. Classical sophistication was now replaced by a primitivist interest
in the Medieval heritage of English mythology. Hence, during the greatest expansion of the Empire, the Victorians in Britain were rediscovering
their own pre-colonial springs: the Arthurian mythology that, when introduced by Tennyson, was at first criticized by a reviewer as "a forgotten cycle of fables which never attained the dignity or substance of a popular
mythology."[5] A few years earlier, in 1833, Samuel Taylor Coleridge was
more insistent: "As to Arthur, you could not by any means make a poem

on him national to Englishmen. What have we to do with him?"[6] It was Tennyson and the Pre-Raphaelites who so thoroughly foregrounded the Arthur legend that had been marginalized since Spenser, that it became Britain's own national mythology.

How does a colony respond to the colonizer's interest in cultural nationalism? *The Death of Elaine* (1877), the preeminent painting by Homer Watson, whom Oscar Wilde called the Canadian John Constable, is one example. Watson's powerful rendering of the Arthurian scene is most Pre-Raphaelite in subject matter. Beneath the moonlit towers of Camelot, the body of Elaine is laid out on a flower-covered barge, steered by the hoary-bearded figure from Tennyson's *Idylls of the King*: "Then rose the dumb old servitor, and the dead,/Oared by the dumb, went upward with the flood."[7] But its chiaroscuro veneer is more consistent with that employed by such Pre-Raphaelite precursors as Daniel Maclise, and it lacks the microscopic attention to detail and the technique of painting on a white-primed canvas, adding the brightest colors on a still-wet white base. Instead, *The Death of Elaine* exemplifies Franz Fanon's first phase of colonial literatures, wherein

> the native intellectual gives proof that he has assimilated the culture of the occupying power. . . . His inspiration is European and we can easily link up these works with definite trends in the literature of the mother country. This is the period of unqualified assimilation [when the] native intellectual has thrown himself greedily upon European culture to make it his own.[8]

Watson has imported the Pre-Raphaelite subject matter but not the technique. In contrast, a book design[9] by J. E. H. MacDonald, *A Word to Us All* (1900, Figure 12.1) demonstrates a refashioning of both subject and technique. It looks like pages from a Kelmscott Press book set in Morris's Troy typeface with pear-block engraved borders and initials. The vignette of the jackpines looks like a Canadian Group of Seven[10] Georgian Bay scene rather than a Burne-Jones engraving, but otherwise this production may leave us wondering how MacDonald in Toronto had got hold of Morris's Troy type from under the guard of Sydney Cockerell for a private press book pirated from the Kelmscott Press. But a quick glance leaves our eyes deceived. There is no lead type, and there is no woodcut engraving here. It is all done with pen in hand; this whole work is MacDonald's calligraphy. As recorded in the subtitle, this is a poem "written & illumined by James MacDonald" in 1900, years before founding the Group of Seven painters. What is more, it is an antiwar poem, a plea to Canadians to stay

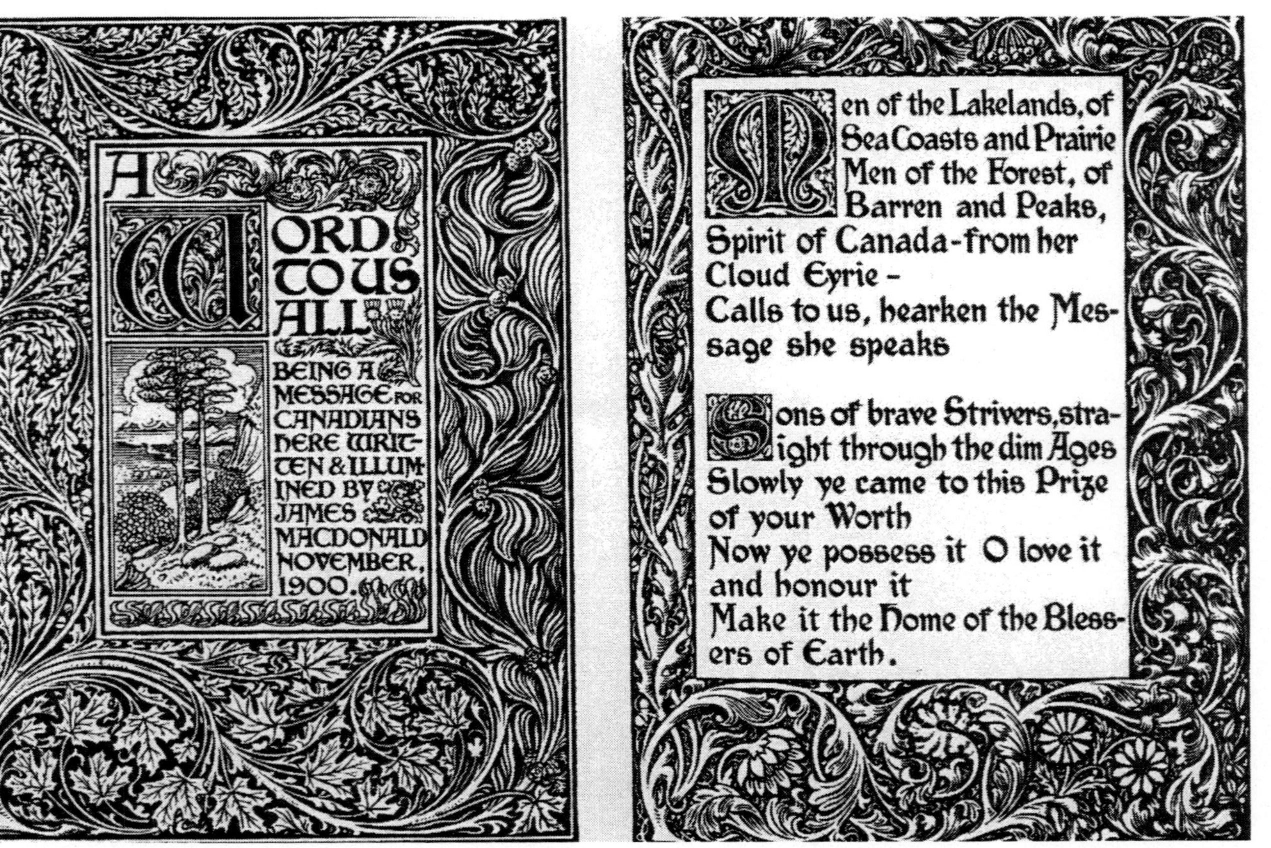

Figure 12.1. J. E. H. MacDonald, *A Word to Us All* (1900, leaf 1, pen-and-ink and watercolor). Collection of the author.

out of the Boer War. MacDonald adapts the medium of the fine-press work of the anti-imperialist Morris as the means to present his own unpopular anti-imperialist message: "A Word to Us All" in the guise of a Kelmscott poem.

MacDonald's brilliant treatment of image and text exemplifies a halfway stage that Fanon would identify as still within the second phase of the colonized consciousness, when the native intellectual shuns the imperial culture as a swamp that threatens to "suck him down."[11] But, because he now feels alien to his colonial community, "he is content to recall their life only." This is the phase of nostalgic consciousness, when old customs, traditions, and "legends will be interpreted in the light of [the] borrowed aestheticism"[12] of European culture.

Ironically, it was the art and poetry of the anti-imperialist Morris that served as the model for Canadian artists to present their work within the "borrowed aestheticism" of the imperial power. If MacDonald was attracted to Morris's 1890s productions for the Kelmscott Press, Francis Sherman was attracted to Morris's early poetry. Morris's *Defence of Guenevere* (1858) is the first and most exemplary collection of Pre-Raphaelite poetry. No poet imitated these poems more closely than Sherman. How Sherman came to write beyond the borders of Britain the most recognizably Pre-Raphaelite poetry of the nineteenth century is difficult to answer. It is true that a gifted school teacher, George Parkin, inspired his students during the 1870s with a love of Pre-Raphaelite poetry to the extent that Bliss Carman, Charles G. D. Roberts, and Francis Sherman emerged from Parkin's classes in the quiet town of Fredericton, New Brunswick, to become three of the country's leading poets.[13] But a more particular question to consider concerns Sherman's attraction in the 1890s to *The Defence of Guenevere* poems about the autumnal decay of Medieval wars and an English Camelot lost. What was the attraction, what was the relevance of Morris's poems to this new singer who objected to being counted as clay to be fashioned "as they may / In London-town"?[14]

An answer lies in the agenda behind Morris's poetry, a subtext that Sherman appears to recognize as indicated in the introductory and concluding poems that frame his *Matins* collection (1896). Morris's poetry and prose is almost always concerned with the subject of art. Obsessed as he was with his fears for the present and his hopes for the future of art,[15] Morris turned to the past to study the decay of heroic social orders, when the consequential loss of art was still a desperate threat to life rather than a factual condition that all must endure. This is the subject of *The Defence of Guenevere*, his first apologia, a defense of poetry waged against its initial demise during the late Medieval age. Framed with singers and storytellers, with old men's memories and young women's dreams, lives can be turned into legends and visions turned into chronicles.

The narrative frameworks of prologues, dream visions, choral refrains, inset songs, italicized stanzas, and parenthetical voices that characterize Morris's Pre-Raphaelite poetry are metafictional devices that foreground the construction of the text and complement the framed enclosures of towers, of diurnal and seasonal cycles, of actions arrested to reveal the mutable moment. This concern with the mutable moment is another characteristic of Pre-Raphaelite poetry, since it arises, in Walter Pater's words, from "the desire of beauty quickened by the sense of death,"[16] and leads to a pervading sense of degeneration from an idealized past. Set within the decayed orders of walled gardens in autumn and lands lost in war, the poems depict physical and psychological imprisonment. Art provides the only release.

Morris's last collection of poetry, the 1891 *Poems by the Way*, focuses on the transition from love to art, as Morris encourages the reader to share through the tale-telling, to embrace others not for consummation through love during one's own life but to inspire faith in a community spirit. The first poem "From the Upland to the Sea" acts as an introduction, inviting us to an awakening within this literary house of life. The premise of this first poem is one of pure love, an erotic devotion to the physical love of two people, the microcosm of heavenly paradise. Such purity, however, leaves nothing else to redeem its eventual decline or loss. As we read through the sequence of these poems, "by the way" we find the solution lies not with the urgency of personal renewal through love, but with the resolve for social renewal through revolution.

Sherman provides a similar framework for his *Matins* collection. As the title of his book suggests, Sherman is offering these poems as a replacement for the ritual recitation of the traditional morning prayers. The opening and closing pairs of poems that frame the collection outline the limitations of what Northrop Frye called the "garrison mentality,"[17] wherein the European settlers prefer to preserve their old world ideologies rather that explore new experiences. "At the Gate" envisions the gate through "the brazen bars" not as a passage from the brazen world of life to a golden world of art, nor to a paradise lost of a mythical Pre-Raphaelite Camelot. Rather, the newborn poet invites us to scorn with him the discourse of the Old Testament land of "death and sin" and dare instead to enter a New Testament land of life and love:

> Swing open wide, O Gate,
> That I may enter in
> And see what lies in wait
> For me who have been born!
> Her word I only scorn
> Who spake of death and sin.
>
> I know what is behind
> Your brazen bars;
> I heard it of the wind
> Where I dwelt yesterday:
> The wind that blows alway
> Among the ancient stars.
>
> Life is the chiefest thing
> The wind brought knowledge of,
> As it passed, murmuring:
> Life, with its infinite strength,
> And undiminished length
> Of years fulfilled with love.
>
> The wind spake not of sin
> That blows among the stars;
> And so I enter in
> (Swing open wide, O Gate!)
> Fearless of what may wait
> Behind your heavy bars.[18]

Sequentially, the poems that immediately follow from the gateway are songs of that new world of Canada that Kipling envied. In saying that "Canada neither knew nor cared"[19] about a singer moulding its life and thought, Lorne Pierce may have been correct about Sherman's reality, but he was wrong about Sherman's intentions to shape the land:

> Let us rise up and live! Behold, each thing
> Is ready for the moulding of our hand.
> Long have they all awaited our command;
> None other will they ever own for king.
> Until we come no bird dare try to sing.[20]

These rousing lines begin the first of four sonnets that gradually undermine the blindness of the colonizer who took the new world in summer for granted—as a place to rule over and exploit until the winter arrives to expose the folly that "no other ones have sinned as we":

> The Spring was with us and we praised not Thee;
> We gave no thanks for summer's strangest flowers.
> We built us many ships, and mighty towers,
> And held awhile the whole broad world in fee:
> Yea, and it sometime writhed at our decree.[21]

Here the role of the poet is limited to humbling the colonizer into kneeling in prayer to the god that should be shaping the process of colonization.

If these polemical framing poems encourage the young colony to resist the arrogance that led to the demise of past empires, what is the agenda at the heart of the collection—the Pre-Raphaelite ballads of warring knights and worried damsels? Starting with "Summer Dying," each of the next ten poems—"A November Vigil," "Between the Battles," "The Kingfisher," "The Quiet Valley," "The Conqueror," "The King's Hostel," "Between the Winter and the Spring," "The Window of Dreams," and "The Relief of Wet Willows"—could be a draft for another *Defence of Guenevere* collection of autumnal tales of the season of death.

"A November Vigil" and "The Kingfisher" typify the narrative framing devices of the Pre-Raphaelite ballad. Both of Sherman's ballads exploit the double narrative perspectives of an omniscient narrator and a first-person persona. "A November Vigil" uses this narrative framing device to objectify the maiden's projection of her inner nature upon the outer nature of the lunar night and the solar solstice. "The Kingfisher" uses the device to subjectify the balladic narration by a bird perched above a riverbank. Observing a fair maiden fall by the riverside where she mourns for her knight lost in war, the kingfisher empathizes with the maiden to the extent that it fails to recognize that she is the very same maiden seen some days ago there by the river with her beloved knight.

"A November Vigil" is more complex. This ballad begins with the voice of a jilted maiden confessing "aloud" her despair in nineteen quatrains. Interspersed with her voice are fifteen quatrains of a parallel narrative recounting the moon's reaction, a moon personified as if it too were lovesick for the absent sun. However, as the two narratives verge, the diurnal and seasonal cycles merge to serve as the archetype for the maiden's withered spirit. The romantic moonlight that first had risen red and then glowed "like her yellow hair," was now waning thin and gray: "It looked as if its soul were dead." As the moon dies with the approach of morn, the sun is killed by the snow, destroyed by the cold, wintry absence of love. Romantic moonlight and summer sunlight: the whole world feels dark and cold since her beloved—who once "said he had great joy of me"—turned to tell her "all of love's strange things:/ The paths love trod, love's eyes of flame,/ Its silent hours, its rapid wings."[22]

Never again to consummate her desire within her beloved's embrace, she is consumed now by her need to prepare her body for the hands of the undertakers, as she envisions her entombment with the vivid details that typify Pre-Raphaelite poetry:

> It were far better I should die,
> And have rough strangers come to bear
> My body far away, where I
>
> Shall know the quiet of the tomb;
> That they should leave me, with no tears,
> To think and think within the gloom
> For many years, for many years.
>
> The thought of that strange, narrow place
> Is hard for me to bear, indeed;
> I do not fear cold Death's embrace,
> And where black worms draw nigh to feed
>
> On my white body, then, I know
> That I shall make no mournful cry:
> But that I should be hidden so
> Where I no more may see the sky.[23]

Sherman has mastered the literary grotesque, the "definiteness of sensible imagery"[24] that Walter Pater identifies as a defining quality of Pre-Raphaelite poetry: the jarring juxtaposition of vivid details that produce the grotesque transgressions of decorum through an indeterminate focus-shifting between the spiritual and the sensual.

Besides exploiting the literary grotesque, these poems also typify the Pre-Raphaelite sense of degeneration from an idealized past, as in "The Quiet Valley" wherein the whole landscape has become a graveyard. Sherman's protagonists are not the victors of war but the defeated and the dying. "The Conqueror" is a dramatic monologue of a knight who insists on keeping his vow to return home at sunset to his beloved Lady after the long day's battle, and thus prove that Love's "prayers were not in vain." However, as the evening sky darkens, he is too weak to move, though still denying that her prayers will go unanswered:

> Yea, I must go.—What? Am I tired yet?
> Let me lie here and rest my aching side.
> The thought of her hath made me quite forget
> How sharp his sword was just before he died.[25]

"The King's Hostel" presents a similar situation from the perspective of the women who await the return of their warriors. Knowing that the king loves bright gaiety, the women prepare a room to welcome him back from battle: "Let us make it fit for him!"[26] The task seems difficult because the room is too dark and damp and narrow for such a transformation. But when the few survivors carry the king in to rest, the women understand that the tomb-like room suits the funereal occasion.

Sherman remains as steadfast as Morris in his focus on the decayed order wherein the season is autumn and the landscape is a graveyard. Yet a difference we find in Sherman's poems is that the natural cycle of the seasons is so much more foregrounded that nature in this new land emerges as the real subject. In "Between the Battles," a warrior is slain with the fall of the last red leaf of the maple. In "Summer Dying," the summer is personified as a weary warrior, much like Morris's Sir Peter Harpdon who "like[d] the straining game / Of striving well to hold up things that fall."[27] But Sherman's subject is clearly the summer season speaking its last words before winter carries out its death sentence. As summer clings to life, it recalls the sun rising at the morning's prime, the maples budding, the roses blooming, the robins crying, and again, like Morris's Sir Peter, summer yearns for romantic reunion:

> That I might know one night in June
> Two found most fair,
> And see again the great half-moon
> Shine through her hair.[28]

But the weary song of "hopeless war" returns to intrude one line at a time: "*Thy reign is o'er! . . . Thou must die! . . . Let winter be!*"[29] The poem recalls Swinburne's first chorus in *Atalanta in Calydon*, "When the hounds of spring are on winter's tresses," wherein the unconventional spring hounds down the fawns of winter, and it also recalls Isabella Crawford's similar diurnal version of the stag and doe of night hunted down by the warrior sun of day.[30]

Sherman has refashioned the golden world of Camelot lost by transfiguring it into the brazen world of seasonal dynamics that dramatize the struggles of each day of modern life in the new Dominion. By refashioning the Pre-Raphaelite tales within a seasonal archetype, he encourages the colonists to see their new land in the romantic terms of narrative. He does so first by adapting the popular Arthurian mythology of the Empire to the more dramatic seasons of the scarlet autumn and glacial winter of his Atlantic Canadian homeland, and then in his later poems, such as "An Acadian Easter," by mythologizing his own Acadian history, where the five-year feudal war fought from 1641 to 1645 between Charles Charnisay and Charles La Tour from their opposite sides of the Bay of Fundy[31] is narrated in the manner again of Morris's "Sir Peter Harpdon's End." If we remember the history of how Lady La Tour accepted Charnisay's terms for a truce, but which Charnisay then ignored by hanging La Tour's garrison one man at a time while Lady La Tour was forced to watch with a noose around her own neck, we should not be surprised that Sherman focuses on April as the cruelest month: "One may not remember in April how autumn was kind, long ago!"[32]

As the penultimate frame of the collection, "The Builder" should be read in relation with the other poems. It is Sherman's clever deconstruction of not only the general role of the poet as the "maker" and "fashioner" of culture, but of the particular role of Sherman himself as the author of *Matins*. The subtle polemic of "The Builder" is clarified by the blatant polemic of an earlier poem in the volume, "The Foreigner." As the Canadian and the foreign visitor walk together through the snow in the dark woods of hemlock, pine, and cedar, the Canadian discovers that his companion fails to understand the meaning beneath the "even and uneven lines" of surface detail that lay before them. Only the Canadian can perceive beyond the apparently constant "gray, gray" of the surface landscape to recognize the signifiers of spring. The bored foreigner will remain blind, while the Canadian attuned to the new world anticipates a spiritual rebirth. The foreigner is thus defined here as a stagnant state of mind.

"The Builder," however, reveals that Sherman is aware of the foreign trappings that colonize his own state of mind. It reads as an ironic commentary of his own homage to Morris, especially as it follows immediately after "The Relief of Wet Willows" and "The Window of Dreams"—the two ballads that are most allusive to Morris's *Defence*. Referring to the same vain "succours" that Morris's Lady Alice speaks of in "Sir Peter Harpdon's End,"[33] Sherman's narrator in "The Relief of Wet Willows" tells of the "seven men" returning home from their rescue mission as corpses mockingly strapped upright on their horses. Like Morris's Lady Alice, who sits "Looking out of a window into the street"[34] and imagines hearing songs of her bold knight, Sherman's Lady Alice in "The Window of Dreams" remains at the window, imagining the distant battles and the return of a ship with her beloved knight. But the relics that fill the interior of her room— her tapestries of long-haired ladies and men in combat woven in silk long since grown gray, the potted firs now dead, the vellum book unread, the trumpet now mute, the lute with rusted strings, the silver pennies tarnished black—suggest the futility of her vigil.

In "The Builder," the poet has fashioned a house full of relics similar to those found in Lady Alice's tower: dulcimers, brass candlesticks, illuminated calligraphy, "red gold" flagons, burnished armor. Though rich with Pre-Raphaelite imagery, the intent is parodic:

> Come, and share these things with me,
> Men have died to leave to us!
> We shall find life glorious
> In this splendid house of love;
> Come, and claim thy part thereof,—
> I have fashioned it for thee![35]

The poet's book of Pre-Raphaelite poetry is less a "house of love" than a display of Medieval artifacts, all that remain of the dead: the armor of the knights "dead, I deem, long wars ago"; the "dulcimers, whose tightened strings, /Once, dead women loved to touch/(Deeming they could mimic much/Of the music of the wind!)." Such a palace of art filled with exotica, with "Strange, delightful, far-brought things," stands as a mockery of the colony's interest in developing its own cultural heritage. The poet thus becomes an agent for stagnation through the affectation of the colonized consciousness, building palaces with imported artefacts rather than building a house into a home, a garrison colony into a national culture. The "dead . . . mimic much": Sherman reveals here in "The Builder" that he may have understood better than Kipling the delusions and the duties that challenge "new singers" in their attempt to mould the country in their hands.

The transatlantic exchanges between imperial Britain and colonial Canada became more complex when transborder exchanges with the growing imperial power south of the Canadian border shifted the site of contention from cultural importation to U.S. assimilation. With such pressures from two fronts, it is understandable how the emergence of what Fanon identifies as the third stage of the colonized consciousness, "the fighting phase," could be derailed. After having tried to lose himself in the people and with the people, the native intellectual will now try to "shake the people," turning himself into their awakener, becoming the "mouthpiece of a new reality in action." The writer produces "a fighting literature, a revolutionary literature, and a national literature." Phillips Thompson was the natural candidate to fulfill this revolutionary role in Canada. As Sherman epitomized Morris's poetry, Thompson, more than any other Canadian, epitomized Morris's politics.

Like Morris, Thompson resisted imitation; only within the genre of political poetry did he clearly imitate Morris. His *Labor Reform Songster* (Figure 12.2) is written in the same spirit as Morris's *Chants for Socialists* and includes one of Morris's labour hymns along with twenty of Thompson's own. His major book, *The Politics of Labor* (1887; developed from his 1883–86 columns for *The Palladium of Labor*), not only anticipates the issues of Morris's and Belfort Bax's *Socialism: Its Growth & Outcome* (1893; developed from their 1886–88 columns for *Commonweal*), but, moreover, exemplifies the evolving role of the dissident intellectual in colonial Canada.

The Politics of Labor emerged from what Hector Charlesworth recollected in 1925 as "the Canadian literary and journalistic Bohemia" of Victorian Toronto.[36] That the liveliness of this literary Bohemia has been largely forgotten is typically colonial: though each generation of young writers routinely disregards the previous generation, only colonials agreeably enforce such immature neglect. The Bohemian literati in Victorian Toronto played an important role similar to that of the intellectual in late-nineteenth-century Paris: Paul Bénichou and Tzvetan Todorov have identified the intellectual as a new "social category" that emerged after the decline of the church in the eighteenth century.[37] In Victorian Toronto the Oxonian Professor Goldwin Smith was the successor of Anglican Bishop John Strachan in presiding over the Toronto establishment; but what enlivened the city was the dynamic relationship between the entrenched establishment and the persistent presence of what Julia Kristeva would call for a hundred years later: the intellectual as an oppositional dissident.[38] Such was Phillips Thompson, the most readily reliable dissident. When Matthew Arnold lectured in Toronto, Thompson responded with a critique of the "flaws of the lecturer's reasoning." Arnold was not only "unscientific

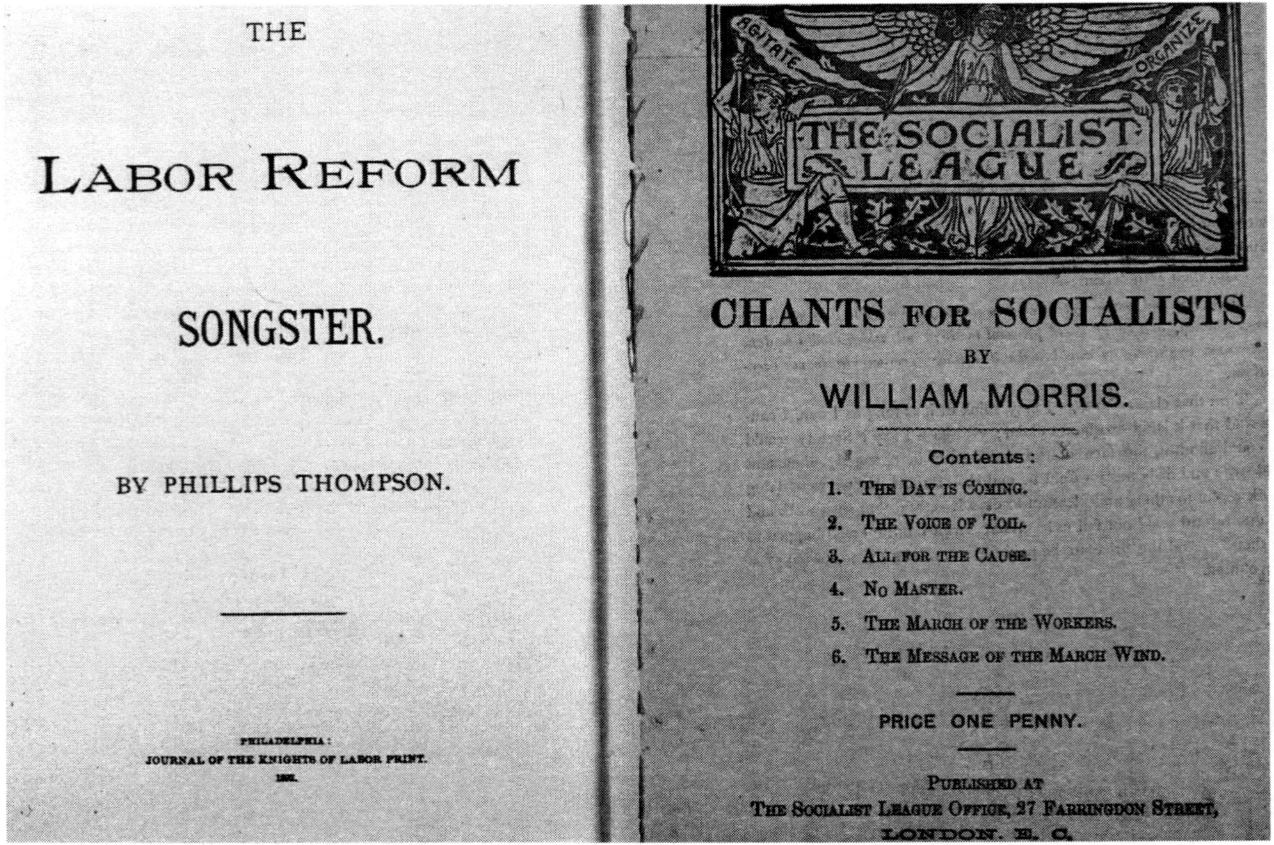

Figure 12.2. Phillips Thompson, *Labor Reform Songster*, title page (Philadelphia: Journal of the Knights of Labor, 1892), and William Morris, *Chants for Socialists*, title page (London: Socialist League Office, 1885); both collection of the author.

and unphilosophical," but guilty of breaching "fairness and justice" for dividing the social order into the "bad" masses and the "cultivated" aristocracy. Thompson counters,

> there is an immense reserve fund of latent courage, endurance, and heroism in the masses of the people which is only to be called out by the stress and strain of extraordinary crisis. We hold that the good sense and natural instincts of the masses are a safer guide than the learning and the reason of the cultivated few.[39]

Thompson thus stood firmly against the Arnoldian elitist program for conservative reform intended to preserve the good structures of the established social order; he argued instead for something much closer to the Morrisian democratic program for revolution. His commitment to radical politics went far beyond the metaphorical wave of large thinking described by John Morley in 1883 as characterizing Victorian Britain:

> Those who were capable of a large earnestness about public things . . . turned henceforth from the letter of institutions to their spirit. . . . A great wave of humanity, of benevolence, of desire for improvement—a great wave of social sentiment, in short,—poured itself among all who had the faculty of large and disinterested thinking.[40]

What might have developed into a discourse of dissent was subsumed by this wave of charitable concern. And yet, refusing to be engulfed, Thompson found hope in what he preferred to recognize as these "already existing streams of tendency [that] can be taken advantage of to further our ends."[41]

With *The Politics of Labor*, Thompson gathered the ideas he had been developing over the years in his newspaper columns and shaped them into a remarkable book that demonstrates some of the vision of Ruskin and the clarity of Morris. At times, he could sound as if he was articulating Morris's motto—"education towards revolution"; here, Thompson talks of revolutionizing the system through the education of desire:

> We have to create a revolution in public opinion before we can hope to revolutionize the system. We have to change not only men's formally expressed beliefs, but their aspirations and desires—to eradicate the deep-rooted selfishness begotten of competition, and to instill in its place a love for humanity and a strong sense of justice. It is an education of the heart as much as of the head that is needed.[42]

He stops short of Morris only in his reversal of Morris's fear of evolution and faith in revolution. Though Thompson and Morris were both pacifists by nature, Morris recognized with heartwrenching reluctance that a violent revolution is not only inevitable but that "the best we can hope to see is that struggle [to end class strife] getting sharper and bitterer day by day, until it breaks out openly at last into the slaughter of men by actual warfare instead of by the slower and crueler methods of 'peaceful' commerce."[43] Morris sought to inspire the vast majority to support the revolution in order to limit the number of resisters who would die. The alternative was to let the capitalist system continue to destroy the lives of multitudes. Thompson, though acknowledging this argument in his *Labor Reform Songster*— "They have murdered you by inches upon thirty cents a day,"[44] prefers instead to "educate and ripen public sentiment" for the organic change of social evolution, an "inch by inch" struggle for concessions as "points of departure" to establish "vantage ground" and "stepping stones" for "a new social order."[45]

In its carefully constructed framework, *The Politics of Labor* anticipates the dream-vision framework of the introduction and conclusion to Morris's *News from Nowhere*. Thompson begins his book with an epigraph from the favorite American poet of the Pre-Raphaelites, Walt Whitman: "I dreamed in a dream. . . ." The frame within a frame of this doubly removed distancing from reality is similarly employed by Morris in the opening chapter of *News from Nowhere*, with its self-reflexive intrusions—"says our friend who tells the story"—qualifying the narrative eight times in three pages. As Morris's narrator tells us of a friend who "tells the story" of a comrade who had a dream, and thereby leaves us longing to turn hearsay into substance, Thompson quotes a poet's dream of a dream, wherein a "new City of Friends, . . . of robust love" is "invincible to the attacks of the rest of the earth."[46] And as Morris concludes *News from Nowhere* with the resolve to share the dream of "mastery . . . changed into fellowship" so that "if others can see it as I have seen it, then it may be called a vision rather than a dream,"[47] Thompson concludes *The Politics of Labor* by returning to the "firmer faith" of Whitman for the solution to the despair that can defeat reform movements. Despite the "endless trains of the faithless, . . . of eyes that crave the light," each reader will aspire to contribute to the dream, each "will contribute a verse."[48]

Like Morris, Thompson recognizes that the horror we endure is not only the condition of the lives we live but, moreover, of the dreams we desire. "The world is not ripe for a social revolution,"[49] cautions Thompson, because training is needed to unlearn the prejudices taught in schools and perpetuated in the press. With our desires diseased and dreams corrupted, Thompson argued for the need "to counteract the false education which sets up the millionaire as a man to be admired and envied."[50] Such longing to be privileged loafers is not going to change the capitalist system.

Thompson raises the disturbing paradox concerning our respect for those who practice subversive resistance in history and in fiction, though we loathe and condemn such practices in our present lives. The Boston mobs who rebelled against the trifling tax on tea are "regarded by every American" as noble patriots who resisted tyranny. Those who praise the heroism of the mythical William Tell for "sending an arrow through the oppressor's heart and restoring his country's liberties . . . will in the next breath condemn the people's war on monopoly as the act of wretches who ought to be sent to the gallows."[51] All of us who cheer from our seats in the movie theater the hero who defies institutional powers should then recognize our own faces in the crowd that condemns such defiance in our daily lives.

Revolutionizing our minds and hearts is the prerequisite preparation for an evolution and elevation of humanity toward the new social order. As with Morris's conviction that decadent civilization must end if art is to survive, Thompson believes that "oratory and poetry and art" cannot be regenerated by a society that values cynicism and snobbery: "the influence which shall breathe the breath of life into the dry bones of literature and scholarship must come from below."[52] Only labor reform can resurrect life from the sterility of decadent values.

Such decadence has enfeebled Thompson's own "literary and so-called 'cultured' class," which valorized wealth and privilege at the expense of labor: "The culture of the college and of literary coteries . . . tends to prune and polish away whatever of native vigor exists." With no "lofty purpose" or "noble cause" inspiring their work, modern writers such as Henry James have degenerated into mere "book-makers" whose interest in "elegant trifling," "drawing-room manners," and "social etiquette" offer little more than the distracting "cynical polish" of a "nerveless, marrowless, soulless literature."[53] Thompson's own verse for his *Labor Reform Songster* was never intended to exemplify a living, soulful literature; rather, as with Morris's *Chants for Socialists*, it was written to rally the workers as a prerequisite step to reverse the decline of this enervated world: "Labor, in working out its own emancipation, will regenerate the world."[54] To those who wish to escape their social responsibility by looking nostalgically to the past for inspiration, Thompson insists that "here and now is the heroic age" in the "eternal battle of right against might."[55]

Thompson's songs of the Pennsylvania miner who struck a Pinkerton villain down, of U.S. patriots overthrowing "Briton's sway," of Jay Gould and "Wall Street's robber den,"[56] raise a question that has been inadequately answered. How did Thompson, the former member of the Canada First movement and an anti-imperialist, come to focus his major book (as well as his *Labor Reform Songster*) as a critique of the U.S. capitalist system? Thompson provides relevant comments in his *Palladium of Labor* columns, which he later revised into the extended argument of *The Politics of Labor*, but some of these comments are misleading. In an 1884 column, he explained that he employed "the term 'American' in its broad continental sense as including Canadians."[57] This apology is neither true in the literal sense that Thompson seems to suggest, nor in the ideological sense. Thompson is not writing of the working class as a new internationalist concept; he is not writing about the U.S. as the North American experience. Rather, he is writing of the distinctly American experience of the United States. This limitation is made clear by his deletion of all Canadian references from the *Palladium* columns he adapted for his *Politics of Labor* book: Ottawa, Toronto, and Hamilton are replaced by Washington, New York, and Pittsburgh.

And yet, though Thompson writes about the U.S., he does not write as a provincial American. That is to say, he writes with none of the American tone that would be comparable to the English tone of Morris, who writes with one eye on the present hellish condition of England and the other eye on a revolutionary society inhabiting a lovingly regenerated English countryside. Thompson writes instead as a Canadian outsider observing U.S. capitalism within an international context. Note, for example, the detached perspective of his discussion of U.S. enterprise as an anachronistic concept:

> "Enterprise" has long been regarded by Americans as a cardinal virtue, sufficient to atone for many defects of character. . . . Enterprise that flung caution to the winds, and risked everything on a single chance,—enterprise that took its life in its hand and braved all dangers, that encountered seeming impossibilities, and set at defiance all precedents and rules, has been the darling and cherished characteristic of those concerned in the development of the American continent.[58]

The ironic tone and the examples he cites reveal the outsider perspective of this dissident critic: the Union Pacific railroad, the gold-diggers inscribing "Pike's Peak or Bust" on their wagons; the maxim of Davy Crockett,

"Be sure you are right, then go ahead" being abbreviated to the popular "go ahead anyhow."[59] Thompson's description of the settlement of the U.S. frontier stands in sharp contrast to the government-moderated settlement of Canada, with the Canadian Pacific railway, the Klondike gold rush, and the mounted policeman Sam Steele reversing the paradigm of U.S. mythology. When Andrew Jackson stops Davy Crockett from crossing a bridge to pursue his foe, Davy pushes Jackson aside with the explanation that a man has to do what a man knows is right. In Canadian mythology, when Sam Steele stops the crowd of greedy gold-rushers on the Klondike trail with the explanation that they will have to wait their turn because there are not enough supplies and services to accommodate them all, the crowd turns back in a spirit of cooperation. The Canadian faith in the cooperative act of self-sacrifice for the good of the community runs counter to U.S. pride in the self-assertion of the individual.

Regrettably, the Crockett myth and the Horatio Alger myth of "the penniless Yankee boy, pacing the streets of New York or Chicago with the determination to make his fortune"[60] are promulgated through the popular press and thereby spread into Canada the myths of individualism and enterprise, myths wherein "one brilliant success casts into obscurity a thousand failures."[61] In noting that the concept of enterprise is no longer relevant now that "the rich men of the United States are notoriously hostile to democratic institutions," Thompson warns that "we in Canada have a vital interest in the coming struggle [between democracy and monopoly] as socially and industrially we are already a part of the American system."[62] Capitalist monopolists already govern Canada. No law "passed at Ottawa or Toronto has such vital, all-absorbing interest for Labor as the unwritten arbitrary law" determined by our real governors—the businessmen and landlords for whom Canadians could not vote. The formal pageantry of the governor-general in full dress and pompous speech has none of the impact of the secret decisions of "the financier and the representative of huge corporate interests."[63]

To counteract the furtive financiers and the popular mythology promoted in the press, Thompson aims his attack at the source of capitalism, at the American dream. His aim is to persuade Americans themselves to recognize the "virus of Mammon" inherent in the American dream. Canadians can no more escape the economic power of the American industrialists than they can resist the popular allure of the American dream, as Thompson's single reference to Canada in *The Politics of Labor* suggests— a reference to "French-Canadians" migrating to New England textile factories and North-West logging camps.[64]

Even when he quotes from Marx that "labor is of no country," Thompson speaks as a dissident outsider, deconstructing Marx's maxim for its positive and negative connotations. "Labor is of no country" serves as Thompson's epigraph for chapter 8 on "The Solidarity of Labor." As "we are entering upon an era of industrial internationalism," we must recognize our common interest in order for labor reform to succeed. But the corollary of the principle that "labor is of no country" is that "capitalism is cosmopolitan. It has no patriotism . . . it will levy its tribute from black or white, European or American, Protestant or Catholic with indiscriminating impartiality."[65] Whereas Marx's maxim was meant to celebrate the common interest of the working class, Thompson concludes that it now describes the unrestricted spread of exploitation: "The barriers of race and language and distance, which formerly restricted competition, are breaking down on all sides." Ironically, "the solidarity of labor as a force at the disposal of capitalism is an established condition which cannot be gainsaid."[66]

In 1887, the reviewers showed no concern with Thompson's American focus. Indeed, their indifference to national distinctions is consistent with the ideological context within which they set Thompson's book. Considering the "terrible riddle of social inequality" as universal and eternal (stated in a review in the Toronto *Mail*)[67] permits a complacent resignation to endure an unsolvable problem. Thus, the Toronto *Globe* could warn that a wishful remedy like Thompson's may harm the very "wage receivers" it is meant to help. Nevertheless, the reviewers generally respected Thompson's effort to resolve the inequities of the capitalist system. The *Mail* recognized Thompson as "an earnest thinker" whose "theories for the eradication of admitted evils are advanced temperately." The *Globe* distinguished him as having "a deep and true sympathy with laborers" that enables him to view the "social problems of industry with their eyes, whereas most economists gaze on the masses through middle class or bourgeois spectacles."[68]

After publishing *The Politics of Labor* and *The Labor Reform Songster*, Thompson returned from his ambitious dream of revolutionizing the world to his more modest campaign for palliatives for the local community. In such pamphlets as *Leasehold Arbitrations: How the System of Renewal Awards Results in Practical Confiscation* (1896), he campaigned for city legislation that would thwart the unjust arbitrators who awarded property owners exorbitant rental increases with no regard for tenants. Whether arguing for international or local issues, he resisted the conventional model of the Victorian critic as an Arnoldian insider, developing instead the Bohemian role of the critic as an oppositional dissident.

Considered in 1887 as an earnest and temperate intellectual campaigning for social welfare through cooperation, by 1894, Thompson was feared as a communist infidel too dangerous to speak on labor issues to the students' union at the University of Toronto; this suppression led to the first campus riot in Canada. The times had changed. After the Haymarket riots in Chicago and the Bloody Sunday violence in Trafalgar Square, his socialist agenda for labor reform had grown in prominence from a theoretical proposal in the 1880s to a political threat in the 1890s. But Thompson himself had not changed. His dissidence was still motivated by his liberal faith in the general goodness of humanity, still driven by his desire to regenerate our social order with "the grander, nobler ideal of a social condition in which 'all men's good should be each man's rule.' "[69] It is easy when we look back to the 1890s to recognize the unjust distrust of the dissident critic. That the heroic age for the eternal struggle is ever present suggests that it should be equally clear for us to anticipate today how future generations will recognize what we are failing to do now in the effort to contribute to a cooperative social order since Thompson marked for us its cornerstone more than a century ago.

Moving from J. E. H. MacDonald in 1900 to Francis Sherman in the late 1890s to Phillips Thompson in the late 1880s, I have reversed their chronological order to avoid suggesting a smooth progression from colony to nation, because I believe instead that Canadians have undergone a pendular swing from one empire to another. The effort to direct the development of a national culture remained as confused in the twentieth century, as it had been for Sherman and Thompson in the nineteenth. By the 1930s, such exponents of Modernism as A. J. M. Smith were oversimplifying the problem as a Native/Cosmopolitan debate.[70] The fashion-following that Sherman had found so problematic became the "cosmopolitan" ideal embraced by the Modernists who disliked the provincialism of a "native" or national culture. In their contention that good literature should not be recognizably Canadian, and that "following in the path of the more significant poets in England and the United States [would lead] to the creation of what . . . [they would] call 'pure poetry,' "[71] Smith and his fellow Modernists were epitomizing the cosmopolitan affectation identified by Frye as the garrison mentality and by Fanon as the colonized consciousness, "the unqualified assimilation" of native intellectuals who make European culture their own.[72] Forgetting the axiom that art achieves its universality only when rooted in a particular region, the Modernists pursued the same cosmopolitan assimilation that Thompson had warned against in the 1880s: "The culture of the college and of literary coteries . . . tends to prune and polish away whatever of native vigor exists."[73] Fashion-following, cosmopolitan assimilation, garrison mentality, colonized consciousness: each generation approaches the suppression of "native vigor" from its own perspective. The subversive efforts inspired by the Pre-Raphaelites in the 1880s and 1890s to establish a national cultural community no longer dependent on a foreign center were suppressed by the Modernists until the 1960s and 1970s and then replaced by the international postmodern concerns of the 1980s and 1990s. Today, Canadian political writers like Naomi Klein may be following a trend in our present "oh-oh" decade toward a return to the Native/Cosmopolitan debate, as we question whether Canada is now a more politicized postcolonial community or merely another assimilated segment of the Coca-Colonized global village.

NOTES

1. Francis Sherman. Letter to Fred H. Day (27 Oct. 1897). Qtd. in *The Complete Poems of Francis Sherman*, ed. Lorne Pierce (Toronto: Ryerson, 1935), 170.

2. "A Word from Canada," *The Complete Poems of Francis Sherman*, ed. Lorne Pierce (Toronto: Ryerson, 1935), 144. All subsequent citations of Sherman's poetry are from this edition.

3. Rudyard Kipling, qtd. in *The Complete Poems of Francis Sherman*, 14.

4. Pierce, *The Complete Poems of Francis Sherman*, 14–15.

5. John Sterling, Rev. of *Poems* (1842), *Quarterly Review* 70 (Sept. 1842): 400.

6. Samuel Taylor Coleridge. *The Collected Works of Samuel Taylor Coleridge* (Princeton, NJ: Princeton University Press, 1990), 14:441.

7. Alfred Tennyson, "Lancelot and Elaine," ll. 1146–47.

8. Franz Fanon, "On National Culture," *The Wretched of the Earth*, trans. Constance Farrington (London: MacGibbon and Kee, 1965), 176.

9. James MacDonald, *A Word to Us All* (1900; repr., Ottawa: Archives of Canadian Art / Carleton University Press, 1996).

10. MacDonald was a founding member of the Group of Seven painters in Toronto in 1913.

11. MacDonald, 176.

12. Ibid., 179.

13. For more on the influence of George Parkin, see Sir John Willison, *Sir George Parkin: A Biography* (London: Macmillan, 1929); D. M. R. Bentley, "William Morris and the Poets of the Confederation," *Scarlet Hunters: Pre-Raphaelitism in Canada* (Toronto: Archives of Canadian Art, 1998), 31–44.

14. Sherman, "A Word from Canada," 144.

15. *Hopes and Fears for Art* (1882) was the first collection of Morris's political lectures on the need for making art an integral part of everyone's life.

16. Walter Pater, "Poems by William Morris." *Westminster Review* 90 (Oct. 1868): 304.

17. Northrop Frye, "Conclusion," in *Literary History of Canada*, Carl Frederick Klinck, ed. (Toronto: University of Toronto Press, 1965), 830.

18. Sherman, "At the Gate," 31.

19. Qtd. in *The Complete Poems of Francis Sherman*, 15.

20. Sherman, "A Life," 1:1–5.

21. Ibid., 4:3–7.

22. Sherman, "A November Vigil," 59.

23. Ibid., 59–60.

24. Walter Pater, *Appreciations with an Essay on Style* (London: Macmillan, 1915), 207.

25. Sherman, "The Conqueror," 68.

26. Ibid., 69.

27. William Morris, "Sir Peter Harpdon's End," 218–19.

28. Sherman, "Summer Dying," 55.

29. Ibid., 54, 55, 57.

30. See "The Dark Stag" in *The Collected Poems of Isabella Valancy Crawford*, ed. John Garvin (Toronto: William Briggs, 1905).

31. Charnisay's feudal post was in present-day Annapolis Royal, Nova Scotia, while La Tour's post was across the Bay of Fundy in present-day Saint John, New Brunswick.

32. Sherman, "An Acadian Easter," 140. I would not claim that Sherman inspired "The Waste Land," but Morris's "Let us Go, You and I" from "Sir Peter Harpdon's End" (l. 668) is certainly the source for "Prufrock."

33. Morris, l. 514; Sherman, 78.

34. Morris, l. 498.

35. Sherman, "The Builder," 81.

36. Hector Charlesworth. *Candid Chronicles: Leaves from the Notebook of a Canadian Journalist* (Toronto: Macmillan, 1925), 72–73.

37. Tzvetan Todorov, "The Genealogy of the Intellectual since the French Enlightenment." *PMLA* 112 (Oct. 1997): 1122.

38. Julia Kristeva, "A New Type of Intellectual: The Dissident" [1977], trans. Seán Hand, in *The Kristeva Reader*, ed. Toril Moi (New York: Columbia University Press, 1986), 293–94.

39. Thomas Phillips Thompson, *The Politics of Labor* (New York: Belford, Clarke, 1887): 139.

40. John Morley, *The Life of Richard Cobden* (London: Chapman and Hall, 1883), 59.

41. Thompson, *The Politics of Labor,* 140.

42. Thompson, *Politics of Labor*, 83.

43. William Morris, "Useful Work versus Useless Toil," in *Hopes and Fears for Art & Signs of Change* (1885; repr., Bristol: Thoemmes, 1994), 108.

44. Thomas Phillips Thompson, "Thirty Cents a Day," in *Labor Reform Songster* (Philadelphia: Journal of the Knights of Labor, 1892), 15–16.

45. Thompson, *Politics of Labor*, 202.

46. Ibid., 4.

47. William Morris, *News from Nowhere* (London: Reeves & Turner, 1891), 237–38.

48. Thompson, *Politics of Labor*, 212.

49. Ibid., 81.

50. Ibid., 83.

51. Ibid., 78–79.

52. Ibid., 207–8, 210.

53. Ibid., 169.

54. Ibid., 193.

55. Ibid., 210–11.

56. Thompson, *Labor Reform Songster*, 8, 19, and 30–31, respectively.

57. Thomas Phillips Thompson, *Palladium* (30 Aug. 1884).

58. Thompson, *Politics of Labor*, 65.

59. Ibid.

60. Ibid., 66.

61. Ibid.

62. Ibid., 217.

63. Ibid., 220.

64. Ibid., 175.

65. Ibid., 175–76.

66. Ibid., 175.

67. Review of *The Politics of Labor. The Mail* [Toronto] (2 Nov. 1887), 8.

68. Review of *The Politics of Labor. The Globe* [Toronto] (29 Oct.1887), 13.

69. Thompson, *Politics of Labor*, 198.

70. The native side of the debate was represented by poets like E. J. Pratt who focused on Canadian subjects; the cosmopolitan side was represented by poets like A. J. M. Smith who advocated Eliot and Auden as models of Modernism. See David Latham, *Oxford Companion to Canadian Literature* (Toronto: Oxford University Press, 1997), 38, 42.

71. A. J. M. Smith, "A Rejected Preface," in *New Provinces: Poems by Several Authors* (1936; repr., Toronto: University of Toronto Press), xxix.

72. Fanon, 176.

73. Thompson, *Politics of Labor*, 169.

Chapter 13

KEATS'S POETRY AS A COMMON THREAD IN ENGLISH AND AMERICAN PRE-RAPHAELITISM

Sarah Wootton

uch recent scholarship has sought to reexamine and reclaim the American artists who consciously styled themselves after the English Pre-Raphaelite Brotherhood.[1] The American Pre-Raphaelites were a group of artists who concentrated on detailed landscapes and still-life subjects. However, American interest in Pre-Raphaelitism was not limited solely to these subjects; and, in contrast to the current critical position in this area, American Pre-Raphaelitism survived past its initial group of eager devotees. Although direct Pre-Raphaelite influence is not always clearly identifiable in works that come after the original practitioners, generations of American artists were indebted to the aesthetic principles of their forebears. This essay focuses on John White Alexander (1856–1915), an artist who was not a member of the U.S. Brotherhood, yet his work shows evidence of his interest in Pre-Raphaelitism. His painting, *Isabella and the Pot of Basil* (1897), explores the Pre-Raphaelite movement's diverse forms and international relationships with subsequent art movements. In addition, Alexander's Pre-Raphaelite tendencies correspond to the fortunes of the movement and its practitioners in England between 1870 and 1900.

One parallel between Alexander and the English Pre-Raphaelites is immediately apparent: the subject of *Isabella and the Pot of Basil* comes from Keats.[2] The poems of this Romantic poet inspired the original members of the Pre-Raphaelite Brotherhood (P. R. B.) and their successors in England, and a similar pattern of inspiration may be traced in the works of the American Pre-Raphaelites. George H. Ford even suggests that this Keatsian kinship provided the catalyst for the formation of the original

P. R. B., "a group in which an admiration for Keats was almost a badge of membership,"[3] and William Holman Hunt himself claimed that "our common enthusiasm for Keats brought us together."[4] The artists of the P. R. B. produced provocative paintings, such as William Holman Hunt's *The Eve of St. Agnes* and John Everett Millais's *Isabella and Lorenzo*, which interact with the Keatsian subtexts of politics and sexuality: visual representations of Keats's poetry by American artists are equally suggestive.[5]

In 1990, Susan Casteras bemoaned the "utter vacuum of information" on the P. R. B.'s influence in America.[6] In conjunction with *The New Path: Ruskin and the American Pre-Raphaelites*, for which Casteras also contributed an essay on the 1857–58 exhibition of English Art in America, *English Pre-Raphaelitism and Its Reception in America in the Nineteenth Century* remedied this gap in the literature of Pre-Raphaelitism.[7] Both books focused on the Association for the Advancement of Truth in Art, a society inspired by the English P. R. B. and the two American journals, *The Crayon* and *The New Path*, which expounded the Pre-Raphaelite cause.[8] Founded in 1862 by eight individuals, including the artists Thomas C. Farrer and Charles Herbert Moore, the association was attracted by the defiant attitude of the original Brotherhood, and, as an extension of his forthright views on English Pre-Raphaelitism, they shared the support of John Ruskin. Published in New York in 1847, *Modern Painters* had a profound influence on American artists and critics. A writer for *The New Path* proclaimed: "By the mercy of God, Ruskin has been sent to open our eyes and loose the seals of darkness. He has shown us the truth and we thank him and give God the glory; and the truth once clearly shown becomes ours if we receive it,"[9] while the editors of *The Crayon* maintained that "it will scarcely be possible that any Art should arise here [in America] of which Ruskin and his ideas should not be a large component."[10] Such hero worship is perhaps unsurprising: each volume of *The New Path* began with a letter of support from the esteemed art critic himself. Ruskin acknowledged the positive reception of his work across the Atlantic, thanking America for a "heartier appreciation and a better understanding of what I am and mean, than I have ever met in England."[11] Presumably, Ruskin's professed gratitude for the recognition of his work partly derived from the promise of devoted disciples: as Kathleen A. Foster comments, "Americans were likely to adhere to the letter of Ruskin's Pre-Raphaelite law."[12]

The association's esteem was not limited to Ruskin. The artists of the original Brotherhood, who appropriated the ideals propounded in *Modern Painters* and conceived a revised aesthetic, also merited praise. A writer for the *Andover Review* described how Americans "had regarded its [Pre-Raphaelite] shibboleths with a secret awe" and, referring specifically to John Everett Millais, described the viewing public "as much delighted as if a god had stepped down from the home of the Immortals to entertain them with a picture-book."[13] Certain works by Millais, such as *A Huguenot, Eve of St. Bartholomew's Day 1572* (1857), greatly appealed to an American audience. Similarly, William Holman Hunt's *The Light of the World* and *The Awakening Conscience* were singled out as being "well worth any passionate art-pilgrim's while to come across the Atlantic to see."[14] Not everyone was equally effusive about the English Brotherhood or its impression across the Atlantic. Critics for both *Frank Leslie's Illustrated Newspaper* in 1867 and the *Nation* in 1865 asserted that "American art has not yet been influenced by the famous school,"[15] and, more recently, William H. Gerdts stated that American Pre-Raphaelitism was "practised by a rather obscure company of talented men and women."[16] Contrary to this position, numerous artists, including Thomas C. Farrer, Charles Herbert Moore, and William James Stillman, adhered to Ruskinian tenets or displayed Pre-Raphaelite traits in their paintings. Casteras also supports this view, albeit tentatively and with reservations: "English art had some perceptible effects . . . for a fairly short but *intense* span of time."[17]

Noticeably, Casteras stresses the shortlived nature of American Pre-Raphaelitism, confining the movement to "roughly 1855–67, basically the same period when the individual members of the Brotherhood benefited from considerable attention from the American public and press."[18] However, what begins as the "fairly short" span of twelve years is revised elsewhere; according to Casteras, "changes became evident by the mid-1860s . . . partly because Ruskin's ideas had lessened but also because of the demise of *The Crayon* in 1861 and of *The New Path* six years later," and prior to this assertion she speculates: "by about 1860 American 'brethren' were similarly less likely to be favorably singled out for their Pre-Raphaelite tendencies."[19] It is interesting to note the number of exceptions to these proposed dates. According to Gerdts, "after 1867, Pre-Raphaelitism was no longer in the mainstream of American art," yet a substantial section of his essay is devoted to those artists, such as the painters Fidelia Bridges and Margaret J. McDonald, who persevered with Pre-Raphaelite precepts beyond this date.[20] In addition, Gerdts highlights three artists—Henry Newman, John W. Hill, and his son John Henry—who "carried the Pre-Raphaelite commitment through the end of the nineteenth century and even into the twentieth."[21] Casteras similarly notes a host of artists who remained faithful to the cause; to give one example, "the Pre-Raphaelite influence . . . stayed with [Elihu] Vedder throughout his career," and Vedder's *St. Cecilia* of 1897, painted in the same year as Alexander's *Isabella*, is highly reminiscent of the second-generation Pre-Raphaelite painters Edward Burne-Jones and Simeon Solomon.[22] Furthermore, while Casteras gives the dwindling popularity of *Modern Painters* as a reason for American Pre-Raphaelitism's sharp decline, Kathleen A. Foster states, "in the realm of art and ethics, where his opinion held special authority, Ruskin made himself the mentor or nemesis of almost every American artist active between 1845 and 1875; as late as 1900, he held even greater sway over an enormous popular American audience."[23]

We can account for this contradictory presentation of American Pre-Raphaelitism post-1860 by reconsidering the modern-day studies on the movement. Linda S. Ferber concludes her essay on the realism of American Pre-Raphaelitism with the following assertion:

> It is also apparent from this survey that, while their heyday was short and their numbers small, a distinctive body of work was created by the American Pre-Raphaelites—a body of work which was both a part of and apart from the mainstream, which attracted equally articulate and passionate champions and critics, and whose significance and influence must now figure in reappraisals of mid-nineteenth-century American painting.[24]

Alongside Casteras's study, *The New Path: Ruskin and the American Pre-Raphaelite* has "reopen[ed] a largely forgotten chapter."[25] That chapter almost exclusively focuses on landscape painting, the most self-evident and homogenous group of paintings influenced by Pre-Raphaelite and Ruskinian principles. These two studies estimably rectified the "peculiar lacuna" that existed in Pre-Raphaelite scholarship and the history of American art.[26] However, a small lacuna yet exists in the study of American Pre-Raphaelite nonlandscape subjects.

In the final chapter of her study, Casteras raises the issue of genre and highlights a few artists, namely Farrer, "the only member of the Association's circle to paint figural scenes," who deviated from the landscape norm. However, she maintains, "in spite of the existence of such figural experiments in and permutations of Pre-Raphaelitism, the American form of this style was preeminently a landscape phenomenon."[27] This conclusion is informed by much contemporary criticism; for example, W. J. Stillman's comment to William Michael Rossetti on the exhibition of English art: "Then you have too much neglected landscape, which to us is far more interesting than your history painting."[28] And James Jackson Jarves wrote in 1863,

> Figure painting . . . has not yet won a position. The rare and isolated instances of bold effect in this direction only prove the general truth, although leaving us hopeful for the future. Indeed, the public have no sympathy for it, owing in part to lack of artistic culture, and in part of the inability of our artists to express themselves sufficiently well as to command attention.[29]

Thus, when the laborious working method overcame the idealism of "truth to nature," the American trend for Pre-Raphaelite landscapes, and by inference the movement as a whole, diminished. Yet, as Casteras is aware, "in America, as in England, this halt did not totally preclude an impact from the 'intervention' of Pre-Raphaelitism."[30] Even with the original movement in England, the factors that distinguish a true Pre-Raphaelite painting are contentious. Neither Millais, Hunt, nor Rossetti were fastidious in their application of the movement's principles (and, certainly, from the beginning each artist developed an idiosyncratic approach to the Pre-Raphaelite aesthetic). As a result of stylistic differences and a marked individualism among the original Brotherhood, the historical, literary, and religious works that began the movement may possibly be discredited in favor of the "truly" Pre-Raphaelite landscapes of Brett, Inchbold, and Dyce. The eclecticism evident in English Pre-Raphaelitism from its very beginnings does not seem to be tolerated in Casteras's rather purist approach to, and study of, American Pre-Raphaelitism. Certainly, the minute detail and vivid veracity of the Pre-Raphaelite landscape appealed to American artists and constituted its main area of influence during the years 1855–1867, but the wider appeal and more diffuse manifestations of the movement are apparent in countless paintings after this final date, including John White Alexander's *Isabella and the Pot of Basil*.

Alexander's *Isabella* is evidence of the "lasting influence" of Pre-Raphaelitism on American art.[31] This painting is just one example of the progression and diversification of American Pre-Raphaelitism after the 1860s. In 1916, a contemporary critic of the artist proclaimed: "John White Alexander's record of achievement is one of the brilliant pages in the history of American art,"[32] and Sandra Leff echoes such effusive praise: "In the early 1900s John White Alexander was considered one of the four preeminent American painters of his day, the peer of Whistler, Sargent, and E. A. Abbey."[33] Yet, as Leff bemoans, the intervening decades have rather neglected the prominent turn-of-the-century painter: "Alexander's sudden fall from favor coincided with the profound shift in taste around the time of World War I, which affected an entire generation of painters."[34] A similar neglect of the "post-Pre-Raphaelites" and the so-called Last Romantics, often overlooked as belated Victorians, occurred in English art. And as Leff records how Alexander has been "reexamined and discovered to be of enduring interest,"[35] so certain English artists and groups of painters have been recently rediscovered.[36]

Alexander represents "an exemplar of his epoch," subject not only to the fickle misappreciations of the viewing public, but to the intense changes and discord of the period in which he worked: "the artistic traditions of the nineteenth century were already in dispute: an artist was bound to sense that an era was ending and another beginning to replace it."[37] As Sandra Leff states, "his biography sounds uncannily like a fiction of the period: epitomizing the American dream of being self-made and successful,"[38] yet even in his conformity there remains an element of idiosyncrasy. There is something "intensely modern" in the story of an orphaned boy who taught himself to draw by copying the illustrations in *Harper's Weekly*, then moved to New York to secure a position in the art department of the same publication, and subsequently saved three hundred dollars in three years to visit Europe.[39] In 1877, Alexander traveled to Paris and moved quickly on to Munich, a place that strongly influenced his early style. Although it may not seem radical in retrospect, "the atmosphere in Munich encouraged experimentation, and at a certain point, the concern with technique became an anti-realist, expressionistic current."[40] Firstly, Munich Realism encouraged Alexander to concentrate on a single form against a contrasting background (presumably leading to his interest in portraiture). Secondly, and perhaps more importantly given the previous discussion of American Pre-Raphaelitism and genre, Alexander chose to specialize in figure paintings rather than landscapes. Influenced by the European emphasis on painting from a model, Alexander undoubtedly contributed to the "emergence of figure painting thematically the most significant development in late-19th-century American art."[41]

When Alexander returned to New York in 1881, however, his work represented "a bold style in advance of American tastes." As Leff states, "He was disappointed at his work's reception, but instead of retrenching, he became more experimental."[42] Alexander did not question his unorthodox aesthetic, including a working practice that controversially bypassed the developmental stage of studies and sketches, but surged forward. As Leff comments,

> What ensued was Alexander's shift from an essentially realist style to an
> idealist, subjective one that was moreover thoroughly in tune with the most
> advanced ideas of the fin de siècle. However, it was a style that fulfilled, in
> practice, the sympathetic, advanced theories about painting he learned in
> Munich as well as his own burning desire to develop a personal style.[43]

Leaving the less sophisticated art climate that New York then represented
and moving back to Paris facilitated the progression of Alexander's art.
The artistic climate in Europe during the final decade of the nineteenth
century not only accommodated but also fostered the painter's propensity
for experimentation.

In contrast to the neglect Alexander received from his native public, artists abroad welcomed him with open arms. In 1893, the painter ex-
claimed to his surprise, "I find they know all that I have been doing for
years,"[44] and continued in his praise by stating, "then there is the intimate companionship of the first artists of the world—which money cannot
buy."[45] Recognition began in the same year, 1893, with the exhibition of
three portraits displayed together in a panel at the Société Nationale des
Beaux-Arts; Alexander was subsequently elected an associate of the society, and a year later became a full member:

> This distinguished honor by the French society placed Mr. Alexander at
> once in the front rank of the younger painters. His ability was recognized
> and his success as a painter was assured. Recognition in other cities fol-
> lowed closely upon the Paris success. He was invited to contribute to the
> exhibitions of Europe and of the United States.[46]

Alexander's success in Paris greatly increased the painter's popularity at
home. In 1897, the year *Isabella* was exhibited, the Pennsylvania Academy of the Fine Arts in Philadelphia awarded him the Temple Gold
Medal, and, in 1909, Alexander was the recipient of the highest distinction American artists could confer on a fellow painter, the presidency of
the National Academy of Design.

His years in Europe not only established Alexander's international
reputation, but also signaled the development from his formative to his
more mature style. Moving to Paris "initiated a period of intense, sure
activity that Alexander's stunning output of paintings in the 1890s represents," and Leff hails *Isabella and the Pot of Basil* as "one of his masterpieces."[47] Painted at the height of his Parisian career, *Isabella* exemplifies
many of Alexander's characteristic traits; he retains the prominent single

woman, but modifies, to striking effect, the presentation of the figure. At this time Alexander moved to "a linear as opposed to painterly handling of form."[48] resulting in, as Trevor J. Fairbrother comments, "voluminous dresses [which] are arranged in broad decorative sweeps."[49] However, the sweeping, fluid lines of the dresses—best illustrated in *Repose* and *Alethea* (both painted in 1895)—are not merely ornamental. *Isabella*, for example, is particularly striking due to its asymmetrical composition: "the curvilinear lines used to define the billowy gown contrast with the rectangle of the canvas."[50]

In terms of design, *Isabella* is a typical work from this phase of Alexander's career: yet, conversely, Alexander's interaction with Keats's poetry produces a painting that does not reside easily in the artist's oeuvre. Significantly, Alexander's *Isabella* continues a tradition of Keats-based paintings that oscillate between convention and radicalism. In England, a number of late Victorian artists capitalized on the popularity of Keats' poetry, producing paintings that were distinctly uncharacteristic when compared with the rest of their work. For example, the English painter Frank Dicksee was best known for paintings such as *Chivalry* (ca. 1885), in which traditional gender stereotypes are reinforced: masculinity is triumphant, conquering the combatant and claiming the sexuality proffered as reward by a rather fearful femininity. Yet Dicksee's visualization of Keats's ballad, "La Belle Dame sans Merci" represents a rather subversive divergence from the norm. In short, Dicksee invokes a Keatsian narrative in order to reform traditional gender spheres and to relocate the dominant spirit within the woman. Similarly, Russell Flint was famous during his lifetime for his "delicate romanticism" and classical nudes in Mediterranean locations, but through Keats's "La Belle Dame sans Merci" he responds to the contemporary position of women's rights as it arose out of the crumbling infrastructure of the Victorian male hierarchy.[51] Keats's poetry entices artists out of their comfortable—and highly marketable—niches.

One of the chief characteristics of Keats's verse is the exploration of semantic fault lines in which new ideals struggle to separate themselves from the inheritance of the old. Before the legacy of the past can be circumvented or erased, old and new are forced into a strained cohabitation. Keats probes these potentially volatile social junctures in his narrative poems; for example, "The Eve of St. Agnes" juxtaposes the conventions of prearranged marriages with the impulsiveness of romantic love. Julie F. Codell reads this poem as the dramatic "collision of dying feudalism with emerging capitalism,"[52] an interpretative model that can also be applied to Keats's "Isabella." The poet's ambiguities and ambivalences, cocooned within a Medieval and therefore removed past, prompted even the most conservative painters to explore the "slippery blisses" of the Keatsian subtext and to produce their own startlingly reevaluative interpretations.

In contrast to that of Dicksee and Flint, Alexander's approach to art was suited to the ambiguous and thematically experimental nature of Keats's poetry. While Keats's poetry appealed to the "sensuous suggestion" of Alexander's use of line and color, and while the potential to depict an otherworldly heroine proved tempting to countless artists with Pre-Raphaelite tendencies, it is the use of light, shapes, and surface within the composition of the painting that evokes the poem, "Isabella; or, the Pot of Basil" (1818).[53] For Fairbrother, Alexander captures "the essential mood of Keats' poem . . . the emotional pitch."[54] This is partly achieved by what Howard Russell Butler identifies as "the most interesting feature" of Alexander's style, "the quality of his large areas of shadow."[55] Indeed, the painting is dimly lit, reflecting the "deadly dark" of Keats's macabre tale: the murder of a lover by the heroine's brothers, the terrible visitation by his ghost, the decapitation of the corpse, and Isabella's "heavy sorrow" and brooding grief. The strange lighting of the painting, including the curious luminosity of Isabella's white gown, conveys an eerie, supernatural quality that also suggests the unnatural incarceration of the heroine. Like so many Pre-Raphaelite icons, Isabella seems trapped or contained within the frame of the painting. Exacerbating this general tendency is Alexander's personal style; emphasis is placed on the arrangement of shapes on the surface of the canvas, and strong lines of contrasting colors, such as the black and white stripes of Isabella's gown, highlight the patterns of color on the surface. Consequently, there is little depth but much studied density in Alexander's composition, visually encapsulating a scene "all close" and "shut from view."[56]

Similarly, William Holman Hunt's earlier version on this theme generates an unhealthy claustrophobia with gloomy recesses and dark furniture contrasting against the heroine's white diaphanous dress. *Isabella and the Pot of Basil* (1867) was one of the few paintings by Hunt to be shown in America. Loaned to the Metropolitan Museum, New York in 1876, Casteras describes how the painting drew huge crowds, but few specific judgments were offered by critics on this work: "it can only be surmised how this painting . . . affected American viewers or artists."[57] Casteras does speculate on how "Americans knew and admired John Keats' poem of the same title, and works such as William J. Hennessy's *Mon Brave* of 1870 seem to allude to the poem and perhaps also to Hunt's composition," but Alexander's *Isabella* remains outside the compass of Casteras's Pre-Raphaelitism.[58] The influence of Hunt's version in England is unmistakable; the painting was so widely disseminated in the form of Blanchard's engraving (published in 1871) that the *London Times* declared it to be "a picture which has long since become the classic rendering in art of this last episode of Keats' poem."[59]

Alexander's debt to Hunt is clear in both the choice of the scene and the arrangement. Like Hunt, and the numerous artists who pictured Isabella after 1867, Alexander focuses on the denouement of Keats's poem in which the distracted heroine tends her pot of basil. In addition, a direct influence is evident in the relationship between the presentation of the heroine and the relative position of the audience. In Hunt's version, the viewer is invited to penetrate the recesses of private bereavement; similarly, we are forced into the position of transgressing voyeur in Alexander's work. The darkness of the paintings and the averted gaze of both heroines admit the viewer's intrusion: they are observed, and therefore subject to scrutiny, whereas we remain under cover. This relation is not effected solely through the visual medium. In Keats's poem, a hierarchy of surveillance is established: the brothers, like the viewer, attain ascendancy by spying—they "invade/[Lorenzo's] Calm speculation."[60] By contrast, Isabella's eyes are described as being either "pale" through weeping or "dead" (presumably as a result of her introspective monomania).[61] Lorenzo, however, occupies an ambiguous position; while he is blinkered by his love, rendering him vulnerable to the penetrative glare of the enemy, Lorenzo does comprehend the power of observation: "I would not grieve/thy hand by unwelcome pressing, would not fear/thine eyes by gazing."[62] Yet, he also watches Isabella closely and equates viewing with possession:

> He knew whose gentle hand was at the latch
> Before the door had given her to his eyes;
> And from her chamber-window he would catch
> Her beauty farther than the falcon spies.[63]

Therefore, parallels are evident between Alexander's and Hunt's respective versions and the source of inspiration. The female figure is the principle subject of both paintings and the poem, yet as is evident in Isabella's position in the early stages of Keats's narrative, even Alexander's and Hunt's prominent, columnar figures are objectified by the current purveyor. Exacerbated by the visual medium, these women are presented for the delectation of the viewer: Hunt described his Isabella as a "delicious subject." Alexander and Hunt share the common Pre-Raphaelite trait of surreptitious specularity, yet significant differences are apparent in their respective renderings of "Isabella." Hunt's heroine does not seem to be unduly perturbed by the loss of Lorenzo. Like the basil plant she enfolds, Isabella is thriving whereas Alexander's heroine more closely resembles Millais's earlier incarnation of Isabella—pale and sickly, reflecting the "gradual decay"[64] of her beauty in Keats's poem. Alexander's portrait represents a visual testament to Isabella's undiagnosed wasting disease. By contrast, Hunt's heroine circumvents this disturbing aspect of Keats's poem; his heroine is languid but not diseased. Lorenzo's death generates an invigorating eroticism that "fleshes out" Hunt's "stunner."

Hunt's *Isabella* does, however, retain a disturbing power: the viewer is directed to the necrophilic union between the heroine and her beloved corpse. Codell suggests, "even in this gruesome scene the sensuality of fine cloth, perfumes, and oils are ritually acknowledged" for example, the scattering of roses and passionflowers on the exquisitely crafted altar-cloth contribute to the feeling of a profane sexual communion.[65] The theme of forbidden desire is also present in Keats's poem. After the early inhibitions of the lovers are dissolved by Lorenzo's death, thus releasing them from social conventions, Isabella nurtures her sexual supplement, that is, Lorenzo's head; the sensual description of the silken scarf to enfold Lorenzo's member in "odorous ooze," suggests a sexual interchange of bodily fluids.[66] Describing Hunt's painting, Codell suggests: "Isabella's physicality may also represent her sexual awakening and her capacity for physical love."[67] The patterned rug that has slipped from Isabella's waist provocatively reveals a transparent dress through which we can discern both her dark pubic hair and the radiance of her skin's texture. Similarly, Alexander's painting captures the "amorous dark"[68] of Keats's poem, with the heroine secretly caressing her pot. As Fairbrother suggests, "the subject's shoulders are wantonly bared, and a slightly erotic mood prevails."[69]

In Hunt's painting, however, female sexuality is not only equated with death, but material riches. Primarily, Hunt emphasizes the luxuriance of Lorenzo's decomposition in the rich ornamentation of the painting and the thriving bush that has germinated out of his murder. His severed head is indeed a "prize" precious to the heroine, just as the painting itself accrued rewards for the artist.[70] Ernest Gambart purchased Hunt's full-length portrait of Isabella on completion for £2,500, a figure as significant to our reading of the painting as the heroine herself. Unlike Hunt's earlier sketch based on Keats's "Isabella," *Lorenzo at his Desk in the Warehouse* (1848–50), concerned with issues of hierarchy, injustice, and personal ambition, this second scene exchanges social commentary for the personal politics of wealth. For example, the majolica pot that occupies the center of the work is an elaborate vase designed and painted by the artist himself. In Alexander's version a rustic earthenware pot rests on a plinth, and, in Millais's *Isabella and Lorenzo*, a similarly commonplace pot is discernible on the balcony to the right of the heroine, ominously prefiguring the end of Isabella's alliance with Lorenzo. By contrast, in Hunt's *Isabella*, the beautiful furnishings reflect the artist's investment in the work; the accumulation of details—inlaid wood, marble floors, columns, and gleaming silver—create an impression of his own self-worth. Hunt had been paid a staggering five and a half thousand pounds (the highest price paid to date to a living artist) for *The Finding of the Saviour in the Temple*, and was investing in *objéts d'ârt*, particularly majolica, for its appreciable value.[71] The glare of riches, which Hunt employed as a critique of the middle classes in *The Awakening Conscience* (1853–54), defines the artist's identity as *nouveau riche*. Ironically, Hunt embraces a characteristic that he subsequently professes a desire to see eradicated from English art: decadence.[72]

Significantly, a number of critics note a similar tendency in Alexander's painting. The summary of *Isabella* for the online catalogue of the Museum of Fine Arts in Boston reads: "Painted in Paris at the very end of the nineteenth century, this picture's theatricality and macabre theme reflect the decadent tastes of the period known as the fin de siècle,"[73] and Fairbrother comments on the "decadent, fin-de-siècle taste" exemplified in the painting. Yet, elsewhere, Fairbrother contrasts the two paintings:

> Hunt's historicist and anecdotal concerns engendered a wide-eyed, entranced Isabella in a rich, colorful scenario with marble floors, exotic furnishings, and a large basil plant. In contrast, Alexander chose a spare setting and a Whistlerian, almost monochrome palette to make a visual metaphor for his bizarre subject—a slow, wasting death brought on by remorse.[74]

Indeed, having dispensed with his loaded brushwork of the 1880s, Alexander's *Isabella* is subdued or, as Howard Butler suggests, "restrained. . . . His art was clean, pure, and healthy."[75] Firstly, as Leff identifies, "he now uses a coarse, absorbent canvas and prepares the paint so that it saturates and virtually dyes the canvas. . . . It reflects light diffusely

[and] makes the broad areas of color 'vibrate,' . . . rather than sparkle."[76] Secondly, and perhaps most importantly, Alexander restricted himself to muted, tonally related colors (a basic palette of blacks and whites is elaborated with green hues and a touch of lavender in *Isabella*).

A number of American artists at this time display a spiritual affinity with Whistler's Aestheticism, and Alexander's *Isabella* is, as Leff points out, "really analogous to Whistler's titles employing the terms 'symphony' or 'arrangement' along with the predominant color."[77] After meeting the painter in Venice during his early European travels and maintaining a close friendship with the Aesthete, Whistler began to exert a strong influence on Alexander's work.[78] Alexander's *Isabella* undoubtedly owes as much to Whistler as to Hunt. Yet the style of neither artist completely dictates this composition. Alexander's art displays traits of individual artists, for example, Velásquez and Rodin (of whom he drew a portrait), and a number of art movements, including Symbolism and Art Nouveau. The "purposefully ambiguous nature of Alexander's paintings, which are suggestive rather than explicit" exemplifies the Symbolists' rejection of definition and explanation, and, like Symbolist painters, Alexander's art predominantly appeals to the senses.[79] In addition, the development of Alexander's "characteristic style and the style of Art Nouveau were coincident—occurring in the same place, and just about the same time."[80] One of the basic tenets of Art Nouveau ideology was the improvement of people's lives through beauty, an objective that Alexander shared. William Gerdts sees *Isabella* as "undoubtedly . . . the American masterwork of Art Nouveau painting."[81]

However, Leff identifies a noticeable tendency regarding the manifestation of influence in the artist's work: "Alexander's Symbolism was characteristically American in its avoidance of some of the darker, more decadent manifestations seen in paintings by European Symbolists."[82] She argues that Alexander's work "holds its own" with his European counterparts, yet remains distinct: "A further element in the appeal of Alexander's paintings, no less palpable today than in their own time, is their seeming ability to embody both American innocence and European experience."[83] Casteras is similarly eager to emphasize the separateness of American Pre-Raphaelitism, even though the movement took its lead from England. With their interest in naturalistic landscapes, "American artists had absorbed and transformed the English version" of Pre-Raphaelitism,[84] and even the adherence to Pre-Raphaelite principles was a particular "American Ruskinianism."[85] As Casteras states, "the American transformation of Ruskinianism and Pre-Raphaelitism resulted in a kind of hybrid pictorial realism that was both derivative and unique."[86]

This combination of influence and individualism clearly extends to Alexander. A contemporary critic described Alexander as a "unique figure," yet Alexander's work is also, to an extent, derivative.[87] English Pre-Raphaelitism obviously influenced Alexander, and, in particular, the style of Edward Burne-Jones is discernible in *Isabella*. Yet this influence may not necessarily be direct. Whistler, to whom Alexander owes an obvious artistic debt, developed his own style with reference to Burne-Jones and Albert Moore. Alexander draws inspiration from a number of contemporary sources to give the viewer a multifaceted *Isabella*: she is simultaneously a Pre-Raphaelite "stunner," an Art Nouveau *belle époque*, an enigmatic and ethereal Symbolist icon, and one of Whistler's monotone studies of women. Leff is equally keen to stress the "high degree of interrelationship among these influences," but also emphasizes: "Despite the relative ease of listing a number of artists and styles which clearly played a part in the development of John White Alexander's mature style, finally the style is an unmistakably personal one."[88]

The 1995 *Symbolist Europe* exhibition catalogue referred to Alexander's *Isabella* as a "reinterpretation, after Holman Hunt."[89] Although the American artist drew inspiration from the English Pre-Raphaelites, his 1897 version of *Isabella and the Pot of Basil* was certainly not an imitation. Alexander's *Isabella* significantly deviates from Hunt's, unlike many of the English paintings that attempted to capitalize on the popularity of the latter's decadent and highly marketable version. One English critic described *Isabella* as "a design which every black and white artist is doomed to attempt sooner or later." Indeed, Jessie Marion King was just one established name who illustrated an edition of "Isabella," while artists such as Eleanor Fortescue Brickdale and Henrietta Rae produced full-scale oil paintings on this theme.[90] Christine Torney writes, "a dreamy Isabella embracing a pot of basil becomes a stock property. . . . The poem loses, through these artists, the power to disturb."[91] Hunt's painting is, therefore, the standard by which all subsequent visual interpretations of Isabella are judged. Representation replaces the source, and Keats is "written out" of the creative relation. The exclusion of the "original," however, has profound implications for interpreters who interact not with Keats's poem but Hunt's visual rendering. Arthur Hughes's *The Eve of St. Agnes* (1856), for example, is an interesting painting that permits a "reading" of the triptych sequence, yet it bypasses Keats's text by using Hunt's 1848 *Eve of St. Agnes* as a model; the third section of

Hughes's piece is virtually identical to Hunt's in terms of composition and color. Borrowing Hunt's images rather than disseminating Keats results in regurgitation.

Half a century after Hughes was working from Hunt, John William Waterhouse's 1907 version of *Isabella* shows a clear debt to Hunt's painting (and, as Anthony Hobson suggests, to Arthur T. Newell's *Isabella and the Pot of Basil,* which was exhibited at the Royal Academy in 1904).[92] Waterhouse's Isabella is not facing the viewer and does not stand but kneels before the pot, yet the encircling position of her arms, denoting possession of the vigorous plant, mirrors the posture of Hunt's heroine. The symbolic details are also direct borrowings; for example, the skull head that appears on Hunt's majolica pot decorates the stone plinth on which Waterhouse's urn stands, and even the design of the watering can is noticeably similar. The position of the viewer as figurative trespasser forms another point of comparison. In Waterhouse's version, the viewer does not approach by the steps in the background but is positioned on the opposite side of the vulnerably oblivious woman. In addition, Waterhouse's painting also resembles George Scharf's illustration to "Isabella" in the 1854 Moxon edition of Keats's poems.[93] However, as in Alexander's painting, the influence is not necessarily direct; Hunt appropriated aspects of the drawing, including the large urn with its mass of basil and the healthy portrait of the heroine with black tresses. As Keats's poem is a reinterpretation of Boccaccio, which translated oral tales into a written form, Hunt's *Isabella* is not an "original" or the primary source of his artistic contemporaries and successors. Hunt's work represents a single, albeit highly influential, stage in the creative continuum. During the High Victorian period, this process became congested. From the brief analysis above, Waterhouse's *Isabella* comprises five key influences: Keats's poem and Boccaccio, with whom the artist was familiar (see his painting *A Tale from The Decameron*), but the other three derive from a fifty-year period in the nineteenth century. Waterhouse's painting can almost be seen as a collaboration, a rearrangement of old and, more significantly, new interpretations.

While there are similarities between Waterhouse's version of *Isabella* and Alexander's—notably the intrusive perspective of the viewer—the latter painting deviates in two key aspects. In contrast to Waterhouse's, and by implication Hunt's painting, Alexander has suppressed almost all extraneous detail. His version does contain a few symbolic features, for example, the white blooms that adorn the base of the pot and the single bud that has fallen to the floor beneath the heroine's skirt, but there a noticeable lack of clutter. The viewer's attention is fixed on the central figure, not diffused over the whole area of the canvas. Alexander's *Isabella* is streamlined rather than ponderous, stark rather than excessive.

The other important departure signaled by Alexander is a fidelity to the literary source. Writing in an exhibition catalogue in 1917, Leslie J. Skelton states that it is well-known how Alexander drew inspiration for *Isabella* directly from Keats's poem. Fairbrother reinforces this view by stating that Alexander's painting coincides with the "quintessentially Romantic concern of Keats' poem."[94] Significantly, Alexander shares with Keats an aesthetic grounded in "discreet voluptuousness."[95] Unlike Hunt's heroine, who is engaged in a sexual display, Alexander's *Isabella* is in the first flowering, and simultaneous falling, of awakening sexuality. Alexander, like Keats, captures the liminal state between innocence and experience: the poet's attempt to sustain this tension against the flow of the narrative necessitates the death of the hero, the heroine's fixation, her subsequent disease and death, whereas the painter can capture the single moment of fruition. To appropriate the title of one of Leff's articles on Alexander, both poet and painter can be described as "Master[s] of Sensuous Line" and a subtle yet pregnant ambiguity is equally evident in Alexander's art and Keats' verse.

The complex, dualistic, and indeterminate qualities of Alexander's art are all traits shared with his poetic predecessor. Yet not all American Pre-Raphaelites proved to be such kindred pioneers. The English movement negatively influenced a number of the American Pre-Raphaelites. Casteras identifies one example in William Hennessy's 1870 painting *Mon Brave*: "While Holman Hunt's 1867 *Isabella and the Pot of Basil* is one obvious parallel to *Mon Brave*, so too is *Mariana*, whose altar of love and curtained bed are recurring elements in Hennessy's picture, along with the shared reliance upon a 'secret' floral language."[96] As in the English tradition of Pre-Raphaelitism, especially among second and third generations, the practice of artistic interbreeding is apparent in America. This is nowhere more evident than in the tributes, or what Casteras terms "visual footnote[s]"[97] to English Pre-Raphaelitism. Following the immense popularity of Millais's *A Huguenot, Eve of St. Bartholomew's Day, 1572*, paintings, such as *Gone! Gone!* (1860) by Thomas C. Farrer and Aaron D. Shattuck's *Shattuck Family with Grandmother, Mother, and Baby William* (1865), incorporate engravings of Millais's work. Furthermore, as well as the overt references to a single work by Millais, a more pervasive and unaccredited debt to the Pre-Raphaelites is discernible in Farrer's painting. In addition to *A Huguenot*, Casteras also identifies

Autumn Leaves and Ford Madox Brown's *The Last of England* as primary sources. Like Waterhouse's *Isabella*, Farrer's Pre-Raphaelite heroine is an amalgam of preexisting paintings, highlighting the originality of Alexander's painting. Alexander's recourse to the English Pre-Raphaelites, mirroring his attitude to artistic influence, is characteristically discerning. Alexander's interest in other artists and movements was, as Leff states, "selective."[98] As a contemporary critic of Alexander's wrote: "he is modern to the finger-tips; his work is racy of the modern feeling and independence."[99] To appropriate Casteras's term, Alexander "flirted" with Hunt, among other artists, and his style is essentially eclectic: yet, as Leslie J. Skelton states, "You can never mistake a canvas by Alexander for that of any other artist."

However, even though Alexander is determinedly singular, retaining an integrity that few English or American Pre-Raphaelites seemed capable of, his work has wider implications. *Isabella* is a particular, and rather striking, painting, an amalgamation of borrowings and modification, adherence, and transformation, yet it is also illustrative. Alexander's painting accentuates a trait identified among American artists—a customized Pre-Raphaelitism. The American movement highlights both the desire for credibility and shared identity and, in its short-lived battle for authenticity, the need for National and stylistic autonomy. This early conformity, followed by generations of difference and deviation, benefited American Pre-Raphaelitism. Painters, such as Alexander, circumvented the incestuous glut of Pre-Raphaelite paintings based on Keats's poems in England. Alexander's *Isabella* may have been described as a "reinterpretation, after Hunt," but where the latter heralds the degeneracy, decadence, and marketable dilution of English Pre-Raphaelitism, the former confirms the progressive potential of American Pre-Raphaelitism. Scholars have largely limited the reign of American Pre-Raphaelitism to little longer than a decade in the mid-nineteenth century, yet the analysis of just one painting, some fifty years later, offers an insight into a later, and equally fascinating, reincarnation of this enduring movement.

NOTES

1. I would like to thank the British Academy for the generous research grant that enabled me to view and study Alexander's paintings.

2. The edition of Keats's poems referred to throughout this essay is *John Keats: The Complete Poems*, 3rd. ed., ed. John Barnard (London: Penguin, 1988).

3. George H. Ford, *Keats and the Victorians: A Study of His Influence and Rise to Fame 1821–1895* (London: Archon Books, 1962), 107–8.

4. Hunt's formative relationship with Keats's work is recorded by the artist in his autobiography, *Pre-Raphaelitism and the Pre-Raphaelite Brotherhood*, 2 vols. (New York: AMS Press, 1967), 1:105–7.

5. The relative neglect of Keats for about a quarter of a century after his death in 1821 has been well documented. Even though his friends and relatives had been expecting some record of his life, internal wrangling, and a lack of public interest in England dissuaded many candidates from the undertaking. In 1835, John Taylor lamented: "I should like to print a complete Edition of Keats' Poems, with several of his Letters, but the world cares nothing for him—I fear that even 250 copies would not sell" (*Keats: The Critical Heritage*, ed. G. M. Matthews [London: Routledge and Kegan Paul, 1971], 9). Yet, as Hyder Rollins suggests,

> Meanwhile the poems of Keats had "taken" a number of times in America. His reputation was increasing every day among "aristocratic" college students, critics, and ordinary readers on the Eastern seaboard. [Joseph] Severn's impressionistic judgment, "in America he [Keats] has always had a solid fame, independent of the old English prejudices," is not far from the truth. (Hyder Edward Rollins, *Keats' Reputation in America to 1848* [Cambridge, MA: Harvard University Press, 1946], 26)

During the years directly after Keats's death, Byron was all the rage in both America and England, and "poor Keats" was better known for his tragic life than for his verse. The apogee of American acclaim for Keats coincided with the centenary of 1895; in 1894, just three years before Alexander painted *Isabella and the Pot of Basil*, American admirers presented the first bust of Keats in England to the Hampstead Parish Church.

6. Susan P. Casteras, *English Pre-Raphaelitism and Its Reception in America in the Nineteenth Century* (London and Toronto: Associated University Press, 1990), 13.

7. Susan Casteras, "The 1857–58 Exhibition of English Art in America: Critical Responses to Pre-Raphaelitism," in *The New Path: Ruskin and the American Pre-Raphaelites*, eds. Linda S. Ferber and William H. Gerdts (New York: Schocken; Brooklyn Museum, 1985), 109–33.

8. In contrast to the journal of the English Brotherhood, *The Germ*, which was published only between January and April 1850, twenty-four issues of *The New Path* were published in two volumes over a period of two and a half years (from May 1863 to Dec. 1865).

9. Charles Herbert Moore, "Fallacies of the Present School," *The New Path* 1 (Oct. 1863): 61–64.

10. "Sketchings," *The Crayon* (2 May 1855): 283.

11. Qtd. in ibid.

12. Kathleen A. Foster, "The Pre-Raphaelite Medium: Ruskin, Turner, and American Watercolor," in Ferber and Gerdts, 78–107.

13. Helen Bigelow Merriman, "The English Pre-Raphaelite and Poetical School of Painters," *The Andover Review* 1 (Jun. 1884): 604.

14. "London Art News," *Photographic and Fine Arts Journal* 7 (Jul. 1854): 216.

15. Qtd. in William H. Gerdts, "Through a Glass Brightly: The American Pre-Raphaelites and Their Still-Lifes and Nature Studies," in Ferber and Gerdts, 72.

16. Ibid., 39.

17. Casteras, *English Pre-Raphaelitism*, 149, my italics.

18. Ibid., 148–49.

19. Ibid., 149, 24.

20. Ferber and Gerdts, 68.

21. Ibid., 73.

22. Casteras, *English Pre-Raphaelitism*, 181.

23. Kathleen A. Foster, 82.

24. Linda S. Ferber, "'Determined Realists': The American Pre-Raphaelites and The Association for The Advancement of Truth In Art," in Ferber and Gerdts, 35.

25. Ibid., 9.

26. Ibid.

27. Casteras, *English Pre-Raphaelitism*, 183.

28. William J. Stillman, letter to W. M. Rossetti (15 Nov. 1857), qtd. in W. M. Rossetti, ed., *Ruskin: Rossetti: Pre-Raphaelitism, Papers* (London: George Allen, 1899), 187–88.

29. James Jackson Jarves, "Art in America, Its Conditions and Prospects," *Fine Arts Quarterly Review* 1 (Oct. 1863): 393.

30. Casteras, *English Pre-Raphaelitism*: 189–90.

31. Ferber, "Determined Realists," *The New Path: Ruskin and the American Pre-Raphaelites*, 35. I would like to thank Courtney Rae Peterson, Department Assistant for Art of the Americas, Museum of Fine Arts, Boston, for the helpful information and secondary sources she supplied.

32. *Catalogue of Paintings: John White Alexander's Memorial Exhibition* (Pittsburgh: Carnegie Museum, 1916): 8.

33. Sandra Leff, "Master of the Sensuous Line," *American Heritage* 36 (1985): 83. E. A. Abbey (1852–1911) was working for Harper and Brothers when Alexander arrived in 1875 as an office boy before being promoted to full-time illustrator. They shared an interest in English art, and, in particular, the P. R. B. Abbey's debt to the Pre-Raphaelites is evident in his attempt to visualise Keats's "The Eve of St Agnes." The illustrations, published in *Harper's New Monthly Magazine*, are hardly noteworthy apart from those that evoke an atmosphere of cold and piety (reflecting the opening of Keats's poem). The illustrations that accompany the key scenes, however, borrow heavily from the paintings of Hunt, Hughes, and Millais. See *Harper's New Monthly Magazine* 60 (Jan. 1880).

34. Ibid.

35. Ibid., 84.

36. See *The Last Romantics: The Romantic Tradition in British Art*, ed. John Christian (London: Lund Humphries, 1989).

37. Sandra Leff, *John White Alexander, 1856–1915: Fin-de-Siècle American* (New York: Graham Gallery, 1980), 7, 10.

38. Ibid., 7.

39. Gabriel Mourey, qtd. in *Memorial Exhibition of Paintings by John White Alexander*, introd. Leslie J. Skelton (Colorado Springs: Colorado Springs Art Society, 1917).

40. Leff, *John White Alexander*, 11.

41. Ibid., 10.

42. Leff, "Master of the Sensuous Line," 87.

43. Leff, *John White Alexander*, 12.

44. Qtd. in Leff, "Master of the Sensuous Line," 87.

45. Qtd. in Leff, *John White Alexander*, 9.

46. *Catalogue of Paintings*, 21–22.

47. Leff, *John White Alexander*, 12, 15.

48. Ibid., 12.

49. Trevor J. Fairbrother, "John White Alexander," in *A New World: Masterpieces of American Painting 1760–1910*, eds. Theodore E. Stebbins Jr., Carol Troyen, and Trevor J. Fairbrother (Boston: Museum of Fine Arts, 1983), 304.

50. Leff, *John White Alexander,* 13.

51. A[lfred] L[ys] Baldry, "A Romanticist Painter: W. Russell Flint," *Studio* 60 (1914): 254.

52. Julie F. Codell, "Painting Keats: Pre-Raphaelite Artists Between Social Transgressions and Painterly Conventions," *Victorian Poetry* 33 (1995): 350.

53. Charles H. Caffin, "John White Alexander: The Painter of Idealized Sentiment Through Portraits of Women in Poses," *World's Work* 9 (Jan. 1905): 568.

54. Fairbrother, "John White Alexander," 304.

55. Howard Russell Butler, "The Field of Art: John White Alexander: The Man and his Work," *Scribner's Magazine* 58 (1915): 387.

56. "Isabella," ll. 81, 430.

57. Casteras, *English Pre-Raphaelitism*, 118.

58. Ibid.

59. *The Times* [London] (15 Mar. 1886): 12.

60. "Isabella," ll. 182–83.

61. Ibid., ll. 258, 453.

62. Ibid., ll. 61–63.

63. Ibid., ll. 17–20.

64. Ibid., l. 256.

65. Codell, "Painting Keats," 360.

66. "Isabella," l. 411.

67. Codell, "Painting Keats," 361.

68. "Isabella," l. 206.

69. Fairbrother, "John White Alexander," 304.

70. "Isabella," l. 402.

71. See Anne Clark Amor, *William Holman Hunt: The True Pre-Raphaelite* (London: Constable, 1989), 193–94.

72. See Julie F. Codell, "The Artist Colonized: Holman Hunt's 'Bio-History,' Masculinity, Nationalism and the English School," in *Re-framing the*

Pre-Raphaelites: Historical and Theoretical Essays, ed. Ellen Harding (Bournemouth: Scolar Press, 1996), 226.

73. See "A Guide to the Collection—Object Detail: Art of the Americas": http://www.mfa.org/handbook/portrait.asp?id=337&s =1.

74. Fairbrother, "John White Alexander," 304.

75. Butler, "The Field of Art," 388.

76. Leff, *John White Alexander,* 12–13.

77. Ibid., 13.

78. Toward the end of his first stay in Europe, Alexander settled in Venice where he met Whistler while making a series of etchings by the canals. An incident recalled by Alexander reveals the respect Whistler had for his friend. While Alexander was employed on a portrait of Whistler, the sitter began to "correct" the sketch. Enraged, Alexander threw the canvas across the room and started again. A contrite Whistler sat patiently and approved the second likeness by scribbling his signature onto the work. See *World's Work* 9 (Mar. 1905): 5993–94.

79. Leff, *John White Alexander,* 15.

80. Ibid., 16.

81. Quoted in Ibid., 16.

82. Ibid., 15.

83. Ibid., 16.

84. Casteras, *English Pre-Raphaelitism,* 191.

85. Casteras, "The 1857–58 Exhibition of English Art in America," 114.

86. Casteras, *English Pre-Raphaelitism,* 27.

87. Butler, "The Field of Art," 385.

88. Leff, *John White Alexander,* 14.

89. *Lost Paradise: Symbolist Europe* (Montreal: Montreal Museum of Fine Arts, 1995).

90. See Jan Marsh and Pamela Gerrish Nunn, *Women Artists and the Pre-Raphaelite Movement* (Somerset: Virago, 1989), 144.

91. Qtd. in Lynne Pearce, *Woman/Image/Text: Readings in Pre-Raphaelite Art and Literature* (London: Harvester Wheatsheaf, 1991), 98.

92. See Anthony Hobson, *The Art and Life of J. W. Waterhouse, R. A., 1849–1917* (London: Studio Vista and Christie's, 1980).

93. *The Poetical Works of John Keats*, illus. George Scharf (London: Edward Moxon, 1854), 209.

94. Fairbrother, "John White Alexander," 303.

95. Caffin, 5694.

96. Casteras, *English Pre-Raphaelitism*, 78–9.

97. Ibid., 81.

98. Leff, *John White Alexander*, 14.

99. Caffin, 5682.

CONTRIBUTORS

FRANCESCA VANKE ALTMAN is Curator of Decorative Arts at the Norwich Castle Museum and Art Gallery. Her research interests focus on Orientalism in nineteenth-century fine and decorative arts and the history of Islamic ceramic collecting and historiography in Britain. Her publications include "Arabesques: North Africa, Arabia and Europe" in *Art Nouveau 1890–1914* (V&A, 2000) and chapters on Orientalism in forthcoming books on William Morris (University of Toronto Press) and the Great Exhibition of 1851 (Ashgate).

FLORENCE S. BOOS is a professor of English at the University of Iowa and vice-president of the William Morris Society in the United States. She has published a number of editions and edited collections, written critical studies of the poetry of Dante Gabriel Rossetti and William Morris, and most recently prepared a two-volume scholarly edition of Morris's *The Earthly Paradise* (Routledge, 2001). She is currently at work on an anthology of poetry by working-class Victorian women for Broadview Press.

SUSAN P. CASTERAS, former curator of paintings at the Yale Center for British Art, now serves as Professor of Art History at the University of Washington. The author of scores of books, articles, and essays on Victorian visual culture, she is currently working on a book on Victorian religious painting. Recent projects include articles on a wide range of topics, including Victorian fairy painting, Henry James and the Pre-Raphaelites, and representations of childhood; forthcoming essays cover such subjects as sempstresses, women travelers, and the iconology of emigration.

LINDA A. GROEN is an independent scholar who works at the Royal Netherlands Academy of Arts and Sciences in Amsterdam. She studied art history at the University of Amsterdam, where she specialized in Symbolist and Pre-Raphaelite iconography.

PAUL HARDWICK is Lecturer in English at Trinity and All Saints, University of Leeds. He has published articles on Medievalism in the nineteenth and twentieth centuries, as well as on topics in late Medieval literature and history. He is former editor of *The Review of the Pre-Raphaelite Society*, to which he continues to contribute reviews.

TATJANA JUKIĆ is Assistant Professor of English at the University of Zagreb. She is the author of *Zazor, Nadzor, Sviđanje: Dodiri Književnog i Vizualnog u Britanskom Devetnaestom Stoljeću* [Like, Dislike, Supervision: Literature and the Visual in Victorian Britain] (Zagreb, 2002) and a number of articles in English and Croatian.

CHRISTOPHER M. KEIRSTEAD is Assistant Professor of English at Auburn University, where he specializes in Victorian poetry and travel writing. He has published articles on Arthur Hugh Clough, Elizabeth Barrett Browning, and Charles Dickens. He is currently at work on a book manuscript titled *Victorian Poetry and the Encounter with Europe*.

DAVID LATHAM teaches English at York University, Toronto, and is editor of *The Journal of Pre-Raphaelite Studies*. His recent books include *An Annotated Critical Bibliography of William Morris*, with Sheila Latham (Harvester, 1991); an edition of William Morris's *Poems by the Way* (Thoemmes Press, 1994); *Magic Lies: The Art of W. O . Mitchell*, edited with Sheila Latham (University of Toronto Press, 1997); *Scarlet Hunters: Pre-Raphaelitism in Canada* (Archives of Canadian Art, 1998); and *Haunted Texts: Studies in Pre-Raphaelitism in Honour of William E. Fredeman* (University of Toronto Press, 2003).

BÉATRICE LAURENT is Maître de Conférences at the Université des Antilles et de la Guyane in Martinique, where she teaches the history of British art. Her essay on Dante Gabriel Rossetti recently appeared in *Flight from Certainty: The Dilemma of Identity and Exile* (Rodopi, 2001), and she has published articles on William Holman Hunt in *The Journal of Pre-Raphaelite Studies* (Fall 2000) and *Loi et Transgression* (Université de Strasbourg, 2002). Her next book is *La Peinture Anglais*, forthcoming from Editions du Temps.

JULIETTE PEERS works in the Frances Burke Textile Resource Centre, RMIT University, Melbourne and lectures in the School of Fashion and Textile Design, RMIT University, Melbourne. She has published internationally on nineteenth-century Australian art—especially sculpture, women's art, Symbolism, and Pre-Raphaelite influences in Australia. Among her major publications are essays on Thomas Woolner and Bernhard Smith in *Pre-Raphaelite Sculpture* (Lund Humphries, 1991), the latter essay providing the first academic art historical analysis of the career of Bernhard Smith.

ÉVA PÉTERI received a dual M. A. degree in English and Hungarian and a Ph.D. in literature from Eötvös Loránd University, Budapest, where she is now a lecturer in the department of English Studies. She teaches courses in nineteenth-century English and American literature and culture. Her field of research includes the literary aspects of Pre-Raphaelite art and the Pre-Raphaelites' influence in Hungary.

MARGARET D. STETZ is the Mae and Robert Carter Professor of Women's Studies at the University of Delaware. Her major publications include *British Women's Comic Fiction, 1890–1990* (Ashgate, 2001); *Legacies of the Comfort Women of World War II*, coedited with Bonnie B. C. Oh (M. E. Sharpe, 2001); and three books coauthored with Mark Samuels Lasner: *The Yellow Book* (Houghton Library, 1994); *England in the 1890s* (Georgetown University Press, 1990); and *England in the 1880s* (University Press of Virginia, 1989). She is a founding editor of the journal *Turn-of-the-Century Women* (1984–90), and has contributed essays to volumes such as *Nineteenth-Century Lives* (Cambridge University Press, 1989), *Transforming Genres* (St. Martin's, 1994), and *Women and British Aestheticism* (University Press of Virginia, 1999). Her articles have appeared in numerous journals, including *The Journal of Pre-Raphaelite Studies, Victorian Studies, Nineteenth-Century Literature*, and *Nineteenth-Century Studies*.

THOMAS J. TOBIN holds a master's degree in English literature from Indiana State University, a Ph.D. in English literature from Duquesne University, and a second master's degree in library science from Clarion University. He is the Instructional Development Librarian at Southern Illinois University, and his publications include *Pre-Raphaelitism in the Nineteenth-Century Press: A Bibliography* (English Literary Studies, 2002) and articles in such publications as *The Journal of Pre-Raphaelite Studies*, *The Review of the Pre-Raphaelite Society*, *Victorian Periodicals Review*, and *Parenthesis: The Journal of the Fine Press Bookbinding Society*. He has contributed entries to the *Biographical Dictionary of Literary Influences: The Nineteenth Century, 1800–1914*, and his web site, *The Pre-Raphaelite Critic*, is an award-winning resource for scholars of the movement.

SARAH WOOTTON is a lecturer at the University of Durham. Her book *Consuming Keats: Nineteenth-Century Re-Presentations in Art and Literature* is forthcoming with Palgrave. She has written widely on Victorian art and poetry, including essays in the *Tennyson Research Bulletin* and the *Thomas Hardy Journal*. Her essay on "Keats and Early Pre-Raphaelite Art" won the Keats-Shelley Memorial Prize and has been re-published in the *Keats-Shelley Review* and *Folio*. Professor Wootton is the reviewer of the Romantic poets section for *The Year's Work in English Studies*.